To Dr. David Brady

w/ Respect & Gratitude,

John W. Del Vecck

Dr. Jeff's

The Life of Men

Love, Sex, Myth, Medicine and…
Political Correctness

By Dr. Jeffrey Rabuffo

Founder: New England Men's Health Initiative

"*Every woman who loves a man, cares about men, is interested in learning about men, must read this book.*"

Regina Catalano

Dr. Jeffrey Rabuffo

Comments:

I believe every woman who loves a man, cares about men, is interested in learning about men, **must read this book.** How much better would relationships between men and women be if more women learned how little we know about the internal lives of men and the issues they as a population are up against as regards their health, physical and psychological? From a human perspective, it's sad and concerning to know that so many men are living lives in which they feel they cannot speak of those things that burden them. The women who love men, and I am one of them, stand to benefit tremendously from Jeff's perspective as a physician who has touched the lives of so many men over the span of his extraordinarily accomplished career.

Regina Catalano

Dr. Jeffrey Rabuffo

Dr. Jeff's

The Life of Men

Love, Sex, Myth, Medicine and...
Political Correctness

Dr. Jeffrey Rabuffo, M.D.
Founder: New England Men's Health Initiative

A
Dr. Jeff Says
Book
2015

Dr. Jeffrey Rabuffo

The Life of Men
Love, Sex, Myth, Medicine... and Political Correctness

A **Dr. Jeff Says** Book

PRINTING HISTORY
Dr. Jeff Says edition November 2015

FIRST EDITION

Dr. Jeff Says, LLC
PO Box 2575
Middletown, CT 06457

ISBN: 9780692532010

Library of Congress Control Number: TXu 1-958-572

PRINTED IN THE UNITED STATES OF AMERICA
10 9 8 7 6 5 4 3 2 1

SIXTEEN TONS
Words and Music by MERLE TRAVIS
© 1947 (Renewed) MERLE'S GIRLS MUSIC
All Rights Administered by WARNER-TAMERLANE PUBLISHING CORP.
All Rights Reserved
Used by Permission of ALFRED MUSIC

Dr. Jeff's: The Life of Men

Love, Sex, Myth, Medicine… and Political Correctness

A Note from Dr. Jeff

A half of a century is a long time. If you spend it in one profession hopefully you develop some insight, judgment, experience and wisdom. I think it was so with me. If you include medical school, internship, residency, military service, and private practice, I've been taking care of men for that long. In that time I've seen many changes in our society; and from my point of view, although my focus has been on the care of men, the most significant change has been the rise of the feminist movement. The onset of feminism was a terrific time for women. During the early period they developed a stronger gender identity, became organized as a social movement, fought for equal pay, dramatically expanded their career opportunities, and essentially changed the delivery of healthcare to their gender.

The advent of birth control gave women the freedom of opportunity to enter more than *just* nurturing roles: mother, teacher, or nurse. One opportunity of which they took advantage was to markedly increase healthcare's focus on breast cancer. Women created an industry called by some in the media *The Big Pink*, a multimillion dollar industry designed to promote care and treatment for breast cancer patients, and to expand research into the causes and cure of the disease.

A number of years ago I heard a talk by then head of the National Institutes of Health (NIH), Bernadine Healy, to a national meeting of urologists. She commented on the research dollars going to breast cancer versus the research dollars going to prostate cancer. I remember her asking, "Where are you guys?" Those of us in the audience looked at each other in bewilderment. As practicing doctors we did not really pay attention to the politics of healthcare financing. We, probably naïvely, thought that some wise people, or committee, made intelligent decisions about these things. Most of us did not know what a lobbyist was. The disparity between breast cancer financing and prostate cancer financing was enormous—at that time something like 10 to 1.

That was my wake-up call about my profession and my gender. I began to pay closer attention to non-medical healthcare issues and to their spillover into society. I both admired and applauded the Women's Movement, and I was amazed by its effectiveness. Good for them. As that new philosophy spread throughout society major changes occurred. The role of women was redefined, and by default so too was the role of men. Women became more prominent in all aspects of our society; men became less so. Women created organizations, joined them, and formed sisterhoods to support their agenda. Men did not.

Fast-forward to the current decade. The role of men in society has been diminished. We now see books titled *Do We Really Need Men*, or *The Forgotten Parent*. The media frequently portray us as beer drinking incompetents; and who hasn't seen a commercial or a scene in a movie where a man gets kicked in the testicles to the hilarious roar of the audience. Then there are the ubiquitous shows on television, albeit mostly comedies, where the male character is just plain dumb.

During my practice years I often talked to my male patients about these trends; and often I noted a quiet, resentful acceptance of the phenomenon. Many men were worried about the impact this new environment would have on their sons. The men I know are intelligent, resourceful, caring members of society, but that is seldom acknowledged and seems almost to be a secret. Men have the same work and family issues, and money worries, as women. We rarely have time to attend Little League or soccer games. For some reason these are not issues for society, but they are for men. Having treated perhaps 100,000 men over 40-years has given me the experience, insight and, hopefully, the judgment and wisdom to tell their story.

Dr. Jeff's
The Life of Men

Dr. Jeffrey Rabuffo

TABLE OF CONTENT

Dr. Jeffrey Rabuffo

Dr. Jeff's: The Life of Men

Love, Sex Myth, Medicine… and Political Correctness

A seed. An egg. Conception. A cell. Division. Two. Mitosis, cytokinesis, karyokinesis. Most of us have seen the graphics in school—or at least at the beginning of The Big Bang Theory TV show. Cells: 2, 4… 16… 256… millions… by the ninth week of the chain reaction the male fetus is being bathed in testosterone and Müllerian Inhibiting Substance (MIS). The male brain differentiates, the male body defeminizes. This is a human, biological gender-binary process 180 million years old. Male brain structures and circuits organize for exploratory behavior, spatial-relationship processing, problem solving, muscular activity, aggression, defense and sex. Every cell of every structure contains an X and a Y chromosome. Every cell is male. Men are men because we are wired that way. We are wired that way because of the Y-plan construction schematic, and because of the hormonal bathes.

Biology is basic. To deny it is to deny the humanity of men.

Dr. Jeffrey Rabuffo

Introduction

After more than four decades as a urologist and State Police physician I have a story to tell, and the story is about men, about who we are and why we are the way we are. It is about all the stuff we do, all the stuff that happens to us, all the ways we cope, the hardships we endure, and how we support our families and our nation. It is about the three Ps of the male biological imperative—provide, protect and procreate; and what happens when the three Ps are disrupted.

These topics and issues are a vast and ever-changing sea, yet they are dependent upon certain basics, certain constants. Men are composites of all their genetics, their chemistry, their upbringing, and their experiences. They are generally good, wholesome people to be respected. There are trends and movements afoot which are subtly or overtly treating masculinity as pathology, which are denying the very humanity of being male. Why? Where will this take us?

The superficiality of behavior can be modified; upbringings can be manipulated. Men can be taught more manners, to be more polite, more civil, more passive; but you can't change who we are. You can't change our genetics, our chemistry, our physiology. Biology shapes us, shapes how we see the world, how we act and react. What needs to be changed is the movement that is trying to change us.

A quick word about me, about my experiences, and about what I bring to this exploration: I graduated from Georgetown Medical School; served as a General Medical Officer in the United States Air Force; practiced in central Connecticut for four decades, administering to nearly 100,000 patients; developed a medical park complex and surgery center; initiated legislation to advance men's health; opened the first hospital-based hospice in Connecticut; ran clinics in South America for the indigent; fought insurance company over-intrusiveness in men's healthcare; and established the New England

Men's Health Initiative. I am a husband, a father, a grandfather. I grew up in an Irish/Italian-American family where touch—hugs, caresses, pinches on the cheek—were the norm. As a man, as a doctor, I'm concerned about various current medical, social, political, financial, and cultural trends that are detrimentally affecting American males—from young boys to teens to adults to sages (that's us old guys). Oh, and I also love to race sailboats.

In this book we will review and explore new revelations about the basics, about how they are manifest, and how they are being manipulated. We'll look on with a bit of amusement at recent news articles based upon scientific studies using the most advanced brain mapping and scanning techniques; articles with splashy title like The Economist's *Vive la difference!* that declare "men and women do not think in the same way." For scientists using diffusion tensor imaging (DTI) and positron emission tomography (PET) these discoveries may be *A Ha!* moments—and the science *is* fascinating and important—but the reaction from most men has been, "Huh? Didn't you know that?!"

These revelations have given us greater detail and a better understanding of the 'mechanics' of how men perceive and interpret the world, but the basics haven't changed. Do not interpret that statement rigidly. The basics support a vast, fantastic and exciting array of life and behavior. Still, a denial of the basics contributes to inner and social conflict, destroys complimentary relationships, and may lead to abuse.

What I want to do with this book is present what I think is the real side of men. I want to relate what I have been hearing from men in my urology practice over the past forty years. I have had many conversations with these gentlemen, and have consistently been impressed but the fact that what they are thinking and feeling is very unlike what society is thinking and feeling about them.

Society (however that may be defined) needs to know that its projected ambient view of men does not reflect reality; that justifications for skewing reality are essentially justifications for lying; and that behaviors and plans built upon distortions seldom produce desired results. Indeed, like medicinal side-effects, unintended consequences may derail the best intentions.

Over my long years in this profession one of the things I saw was that men are perceived as gorillas; as if all they think about is sex, beer and football; as if they never do housework; as if they don't care about their kids. That seems to be both a typical, and a media, view of men.

If you watch TV commercials you'll see that men are always the stupid ones. There's an ad for vegetable juice where a guy in great shape is doing sit-ups. His trainer, a hot-looking honey, is next to him. She has her hand on his knee, and asks, "Are you working hard?" He grunts out a yes. She asks, "Are you eating all your vegetables?" He mutters, "I try to." And she whacks him in the head and says, "Coulda… Shoulda… had a…"

Maybe I'm overly sensitive to it. Guys don't know how to eat! They don't know how to clean a toilet! They don't take care of themselves. They're irresponsible, totally incompetent, sex-driven creatures! And it's funny to watch them get hurt. Guy on TV gets kneed in the groin, cries out, "Oh! My ba…!" Men cross their legs and groan, women titter. Somehow that's okay.

But those are not the guys I know. I have been treating men for more than forty years, and men, down deep, are not like that at all. Men are warm, caring people. They are protectors and providers. They have human needs for intimacy and touch. The women who are involved with these men seem to agree with the general perception that guys are apes, "…but not my guy! My guy is warm, fuzzy, and caring." There are psychological and physiological reasons behind this disconnect which we'll get to later.

Genetically men are the hunters, the wild and strong ones within family units, the ones that protect that unit. They are self-sacrificing; likely because, unlike women, men are biologically expendable. Lots more on this later, too, because that's a concept some may have difficulty grasping. Men tend not to stand up for themselves because their brains are built to focus upon standing up for those for whom they are responsible. When responsibility is removed—by new cultural norms or government policies—misfortunes ensue. We'll discuss the role of traditional male characteristics on culture; and the long-term effects on both men and culture of ignoring, denying, regulating or outlawing these traits and values.

Men should not expect women to think like men; and women should not expect men to think like women. We are different—complimentary but different. Think Yin and Yang. Think Jerry McGuire saying, "You complete me." Expectations to the contrary lead to frustration, disappointment, resentment and anger—often without justification.

In this book we will go through a progression of topics beginning with what makes men men, and the new data about basic male brain biology. We'll talk about how this affects our thoughts and feelings, actions and drives. Upon this foundation we'll build our exploration of how the male interacts with his environment—from conception to legacy; from biological imperatives to health, to healthcare, to the expendability of men; from little boys to sages. We'll investigate the male need for intimacy, and the state of male relationships—within ourselves, with the women in our lives, with other men, and with society.

As complex physical creatures our health, healthcare, and health maintenance are important. We'll talk about testosterone and prostates, PSAs and prostate cancer, about ED, Low-T and TRT. We'll talk about aging, retirement, and legacies; and we'll challenge the notion that *normal* aging inevitably means becoming a crotchety old man. Sages have a lot to offer. With proper care the 'symptoms' of aging can be delayed for decades—life should be vibrant.

Abuse is a benign word. We will touch on the emotional murder caused by male-child sexual molestation. This is a very deep and disturbing topic, and is the subject of the follow-up book to *The Life of Men*.

We'll also be talking about boys in crisis and the crisis in our schools, about warping natural behaviors; about men in crisis in marriages, families and careers; and about how all of this also negatively impacts women.

In the section *The Doctor Is Out* we'll analyze how medicine became 'managed,' how this affects our lives and the quality and delivery of medical care. Physicians tend to be caretakers and rule-followers. This has had major ramifications on the business of medicine. We'll examine what 'managed' actually means—including the differences between healthcare and health insurance, and the struggle between patient-centric care and data- or matrix-centric management.

In this environment we'll look at what is driving medicine: science, insurance, lawsuits, profits, politics and bureaucracy. The Business of Medicine has produced a medical-industrial complex, Big Pharma, big corporations, and an American apparatchik bureaucracy which is being augmented by new governmental overlays. Is this the best we can do? It seems to me that the shortsightedness of policymakers, pundits and the press creates a public ambiance absent of projected, long-term ramifications. Trouble is brewing.

Our approach is holistic. How do all these elements and relationships interact over time? What's working? Where? And what and where are parts not working at all?

As a nation we are in need of enlightened leadership. Men, as providers and protectors, tend to be self-sacrificing [in medicine and in life].They tend to focus on goals to the point of dismissing emotions and self. Dismissing emotions to accomplish a mission does not imply cruelty or not caring. It often means the exact opposite. What will be the ramifications of denying, discouraging, or damaging these traditional male virtues? Where will enlightened leaders come from if these virtues are destroyed?

Some advocates, academics and politicians perceive an on-going War on Women. From financial and cultural perspectives we'll show that there is an undeclared war on virtually all people—male and female—and we'll examine how those wielding power—male and female—use divide and conquer techniques to enhance themselves.

Sixty years ago my father complained about the country "going to hell in a hand basket!" I don't think it did, but now I think he was on to something. Perhaps it is a perception driven by age, by a deficiency of hope caused by one's future being foreshortened. Youth tends to feel invincible and perceive life as unending. Properly so! That equates with hope. I have great trust in our future generations to straighten out some of the current hand basket mess. Let make sure we don't destroy the tools they'll need to do so.

What will be the future of Men? Of masculinity? What will be the role of men in American society? Our goal is to explore the realities and complexities of the life of men. We have a lot to investigate.

Qualifiers

In this day and age, confronting the subject of human characteristics may be seen by some as controversial, inflammatory or offensive. Words are easily misinterpreted, quoted out of context, or purposefully misrepresented. I wish the reader to keep the following paragraphs in mind while perusing *The Life of Men*.

This book is not an attack on women or on the women's movement. Nor is it a denial of The War on Women. Women have—and this has varied greatly by time and culture—long been subjugated to the strength and will of men. Social, cultural and biological roles and influences come into play when interpreting history. Seeing events or trends from a single angle produces biased conclusions. Personally, I celebrate the rights women have gained over the past century.

The *war* today might be better described as a war on people. It includes a denial of chemical and physical realities of humanity, and a supplanting or manipulation of reality with skewed or conjured images for the gain of those with special-interests. Within this *war* there is a battle raging—an assault on boys and men, on masculinity, on male virtues and male values. Both misogyny and misandry are to be condemned. They are enemies of humanity.

On characteristics, degrees and numbers: When we talk about human characteristics we are describing general attributes which should be seen as *degrees of* on continuum scales. That is, when we talk about men being providers and protectors, we do not mean that all men manifest these characteristics equally, nor do we mean that women cannot or do not also provide and protect. These characteristics are a matter of degree within the primacy of our genetic make-up.

Providing and protecting, emphasis on strength, self-sufficiency or valor: these generally have a different priority within the brains of men versus women, but as with all human characteristics there is a significant overlap between the sexes. Some women are physically stronger than some men. Some are faster. Some are taller. Imagine overlapping bell curves with means, averages and standard deviations—with the tails of some characteristics barely touching, yet with the means axis of other characteristics being nearly identical.

The foci of our general statements are populations not individuals. We will not be concerned with political correctness, but we will attempt to clarify statements which might be misconstrued.

On sexuality and the sexual orientation of men: Thinking of men's sexuality as either heterosexual or homosexual is as inaccurate as thinking of humanity as being split into five distinct races—black, brown, red, yellow or white. Human characteristics, controlled by multiple genes manifesting in complex patterns, present along spectrums of possibilities as continuums not as points or absolutes.

The amount of testosterone a man produces is a characteristic which falls along a continuum from little to overflowing. If the extreme points of male sexuality are the heavily-bearded Neanderthal to the most effeminate guy in town, there are men genetically occupying every point between. Testosterone and other hormones—which vary in strength between individuals, and vary over each individual's lifespan—affect the degree of manifestation of male characteristics. By statistical definition the bulk of men fall within a

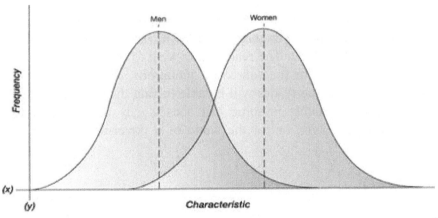

Note:
This very basic diagram would indicate that the characteristic occurs with identical frequencies *within* the categories: Men and Women; but that the magnitude measure of the characteristic between the two groups is different. Where the curves overlap, some men and some women are identical in this characteristic. When plotting specific characteristics the curves are not necessarily identical in shape, and the distance between the means (dashed vertical lines) may be miniscule or vast.

single standard deviation from the norm. Being further from the norm does not mean a man is not a man. Culture and social expectations, or political correctness, may push individuals to declare or to choose alternate expressions of sexuality, either more moderate or more excessive than that to which they are chemically fated. There are those who oppress others due to specific characteristics they dislike in those 'others.' This is not something I condone. However, the gender-binary in and of itself is no more oppressive than the lumen-binary of day and night.

Case studies and examples: At times I refer to 'my patient,' to 'a guy at the gym,' to 'a friend.' The incidents are based upon conversations, interviews and observations, but the examples given may be a composite of numerous individuals. Names, unless documented, are fictitious. Anecdotes are meant to be illustrative. No one should assume or conclude that any anecdote herein is based upon a specific person.

Sources

Dr. Jeff's The Life of Men is not a textbook and has not been formally footnoted, however many sources have been quoted in the production of this volume. The reader may wish to refer to Sources at the back of the book for the source of quotations, statistical data, et cetera. In most cases the reader will be able to find the original source simply by author's name; in some instances it may be necessary to scan for the study name or for the name of a government office or agency.

PART I: Biology is Basic

*"Of all the gin joints in all the towns in all the world,
she walks into mine."*

Humphrey Bogart as Rick in *Casablanca*

Let's look into Rick's brain. Ilsa walks in. Rick sees her. The *medial preoptic area* (MPOA) of his **hypothalamus** lights up. This brain structure is 2.5 times larger in a man's brain than in a woman's. Instantaneously it triggers a determination of potential female fertility.

Imagine looking into a man's brain while he is playing hoops, designing and building intricate objects, protecting his loved ones, or planning his legacy. Imagine seeing which structures *light up*, which circuitry is *live*, which hubs or loci are collaborating to produce the next thought, the next behavior.

Image this man a million years ago. Perhaps he is on the open plains of Africa or in the midst of the central Asian tundra. He is part of a 'family' unit; part of a complimentary gender binary seemingly designed to ensured species survival. He is the risk taker, the protector, the provider. His counterpart is the analyzer. Both are essential. He is quick, aggressive, defensive and decisive. She is slower. She remembers faces, recalls utterances, and retells the past. He provides the seed for the next generation—a quick act; she is the incubation chamber—her role will last twenty thousand times longer than his ending with the birth of a child. Childbirth marks the beginning of new roles for both. She nurtures and guides the youth—the next generation. Life continues. He is self-sacrificing, willing to die to protect the others. She is self-sacrificing, but must live to sustain the young.

Morph the image to a modern city anywhere on the planet: the need of the species still require the complimentary gender differences developed over millions of years and embedded in human physiology, in brain structures and in hormonal chemistry. There is no way around this. Biology is basic.

Man is a life form, an animal, a mammal. Biology Is Basic. It is a phrase we will frequently repeat. The most basic motivation of any species—plant or animal, grass or gnats, gnus or humans—is to pass on its DNA and ensure the continuation of its specie. At a genetic level life wants to keep living. For humans, underlying everything else is this one drive. It is the foundation of every thought, every action, every behavior. It includes not just voluntary behaviors and conscious and subconscious thoughts, but physical growth and all involuntary chemical actions. It even includes death, as death is a part of the life cycle and rejuvenation of the species.

At the biological level the individual is subordinate to the species. What are the implications of that statement?! Might we project that this is the root of selfless behavior, charity, and/or valor?

In the human species the biological roles of the male and female are different. These roles are built into our bodies and into our brains. Rick's brain is hard-wired differently than Ilsa's. This creates and accommodates his gender-specific functionality. Basic biology does not limit or restrict these differences to acts of procreation but displays them in virtually all behavior. It starts in utero.

From conception to approximately eight weeks all human fetuses are functionally female, and functionally identical. As embryos develop, those with Y chromosomes call forth testosterone. This hormone continuously circulates throughout the developing body, bathing every cell. Those cells with androgen receptors absorb the chemical messengers, incorporate their data or act upon their commands, then manifest specific male characteristics. If there were no testosterone, or no androgen receptors, we would all be female. One might claim man was made from the rib of a woman! *(1)

In conjunction with testosterone (T), Müllerian Inhibiting Substance (MIS) forces anatomical changes: T turns on the blueprints for building maleness; MIS deconstructs and destroys the vestiges of

*1: This is an over-simplification. At least thirty genes contribute to the manifestation of sexual differences.

femaleness. Female anatomy transforms into male anatomy. The clitoris becomes the penis; the vulva, the two labia, become the scrotum; and the ovaries that remain in the abdomen of the female descend through the inguinal canal and drop into the scrotum becoming the testes.

The anatomical alteration coincides with brain transformations which lead to male personality traits. These traits, within the complimentary gender binary, optimize the most basic motivations of every species—as stated, to ensure species continuation.

So how does the male brain differ from that of the female brain? Scientists using modern, high-tech tools—Positron Emission Tomography (PET) scans, Diffusion Tensor Imaging (DTI) and functional Magnetic Resonance Imaging (fMRI)—have only recently delineated and defined many of the fundamental physical structures and interconnected circuitry of the male mind. Let's review the "mechanics." (Later, in *How Men Perceive and Interpret The World*, we'll look at the role of men in society, at how boys are shaped, and where nature is being warped, against the backdrop of these basics.)

The following structures are larger and more active in the brains of men than in the brains of women. What does this mean? Think of these loci as telephone exchanges, or as computer chips—greater size means more intra- and inter-hub capacity, more connections, more volume, more megabytes of data being transferred, more codes being shared. In other words, more attention, more thought, and more command and control over movements.

The ***medial preoptic area of the hypothalamus*** (MPOA) is 2.5 times larger in the male brain than in the female. Men are visual creatures! When Rick sees Ilsa this area of his brain spontaneously lights up. It alerts other structures to stage for potential pursuit. But it is much more complex than that. Ilsa's image, or even just Rick's conjuring of her image, is enough to fire up his MPOA. Advertisers use this. They flash a partial image of a beautiful woman in the third or fourth second of a commercial; the image being partial is important because the male mind needs to complete the image; and advertisers know men will watch the next twenty seven seconds with the expectation of seeing her, hopefully completed, again. The MPOA is nearly instantaneous. You're in a restaurant with your wife; a gorgeous woman walks in; your eyes catch her curves; though you try to hide it your MPOA sizzles like sparklers on the 4th of July and subconsciously you make a determination if she's fertile and a potential mate. You're mature enough to avoid the thought, "She wants me," but you are not fast enough to disguise your intrigue or to avoid your wife's foot kicking your shin.

In the *dorsal premammillary nucleus* (DPN) of the male hypothalamus the circuits are configured to detect threats and to defend. When we talk about men being wired to protect, it is the DPN that is police headquarters. The intelligence section providing warnings and sounding alarms is located in the **amygdala**, but it is the DPN that cocks one's fist and focuses one attention on the source of danger. Faster and larger in men, the DPN makes us sentries or hotheads. Hormones throw fuel on the flames. Learned disciplines and training allow other brain areas to exert control.

One of these controllers is the *rostral cingulate zone* (RCZ) which gives the dorsal premammillary nucleus and the amygdala a whack upside the head when they become stupid paranoid or anti-social. The RCZ reminds them it's nice to be nice, sweets attract sweeties, candy is dandy (even if liquor is quicker).

The *temporal parietal junction* (TPJ) is the guy fix-it zone. This structure works more quickly in men than in women. It likely developed to find solutions to problems of immediate peril, but may now be the reason why guys shop, decide and buy in 1/13th (0.069) the time that women spend. [Okay, I just made that figure up! It's from my experience with my wife.]

Another area that more actively rocks and rolls in men's brains than in women's is the dopamine-manufacturing center known as the *ventral tegmental area* (VTA). Think motion, action, impulse and pleasure. Think fun. Think adrenalin rush and dopamine reward. Dopamine is more powerful than cocaine. This is the Guys-will-be-guys area; The Oops! Oh Geez, what-the-hell-have-I-done-now?!-area; the risk taker and thrill seeker area. Male connectivity here tends to run laterally versus the front to back connectivity in this region of the female brain. (We should note that this is the opposite of the prefrontal cortex where in women signals move laterally, and in men axially.)

A college friend reminded me of an old drinking song about masturbation. There's an undeniable truth in the words, or perhaps I should say an undeniable sentiment. With hormones raging and dopamine coursing college boys would sing:

Last night I stayed up late to masturbate,
It felt so good; I knew it would,
Last night I stayed up late to practice vice,
It was so nice; I did it twice,
> *Pull it, palm it, beat it against the floor,*
> *Rub it, scrub it, slam it in the door,*
> *It'll come up for moooore…!*

Wait a minute! *Slam it in the door*?! Men are built to seek pleasure. When hormones are raging and dopamine is coursing pain may be ignored. This is the job of the ***periaqueductal gray*** (PAG) which balances physical pain against the pursuit of pleasure, particularly sexual pleasure.

Imagine a caveman making love while his knees are smashing and bloody against a rocky floor, or perhaps a modern guy trying to get it on in a sports car. The PAG likely also actives while playing sports— think of a grinning toothless fighter winning a title belt. Now think seriously. Think of a soldier in an impossible combat situation, or Daniel Boone at the Alamo, knowing he will not make it out alive but determined to go down with gusto.

On the female side of things, and no surprises here, ***the mirror-neuron system*** (MNS) is larger and more active. This is an emotional-empathy feedback loop… you know, "Let's talk about our relationship." As if that weren't enough, the ***anterior cingulate cortex*** (ACC) in women is also larger than that structure in men; and it is more often turned up to high. This is the pondering options and assessing contradictions center. It is highly self-conscious… the seat of the area that causes wives to ask, "Do these pants make my bum look big?"

Men think via their TPJ like fighter-bombers streaking toward a target; women approach similar problems via their ACC like cruise ships docking. Both approaches get you there: one quickly with no baggage and you won't have seen the sites; the other will have stopped at every shop in every isle in the Caribbean and have a permanent photo album to prove it.

Finally there is the ***prefrontal cortex*** (PFC). It is not a private first class; it is the commander-in-chief. The PFC exerts command and control over all those impulsive areas that get us into trouble. No gender-biased glass ceiling here... the female PFC rises to take command (usually referred to as maturing) one to two years more quickly than its male counterpart, which likely is still basking in some dopamine thrill or trying to memorize the lyrics to *Masturbation*.

As if structures and connectivity weren't enough, our chemical/hormonal makeup is different, and the concentration and locations of our cellular hormone receptors are different. Women produce testosterone and men produce estrogen. These are subordinate yet important hormones in the *opposite* genders. We'll note that significance shortly. Chemically testosterone and estrogen are related. It is but a matter of moving a few molecules around. Functionally they are very different, and they are only part of the story.

Our blood circulates throughout our bodies approximately once each and every minute of our lives—1400+ times per day, a half million times per year. It circulates more quickly if you're running, playing soccer or having sex. [An aside: varying rates and pressures of fluid assists in keeping pipes and blood vessels clean ... so frequent sex helps circulation!]

Along with other functions, our blood distributes hormones to our cells. These hormones—complex multi-protein chain molecules— wash over cell walls in interstitial (between cells) space. If a cell surface has a receptor for the specific molecule, the hormone molecule *sticks* to the cell wall until it is allowed passage into the interior where its data is transferred to the cell nucleus for processing. The lymphatic system also transports hormones. This *open* or unpressurized system is much slower, less important in surge hormone responses, but certainly significant in longer-term growth and immune functions.

Dr. Louann Brizendine notes in her book, *The Male Brain*, that "Hormones can determine what the brain is interested in doing. Their purpose is to help guide social, sexual, mating, parenting, protective, and aggressive behaviors." Conversely, physical activity or sensation (visual, auditory, tactile, olfactory and taste) can trigger the release of hormones. Seeing a plunging neckline, an auto coming at you in your lane, or some other guy checking out your honey activates the instant release of hormones. There is a constant stimulus-action-reaction-feedback interchange between the organism (man) and his environment. Intensity of stimulation affects the intensity of sensation, setting off more or less (or no) reaction. Hormones may determine what receives our attention, but what grabs our attention also stimulates our hormone production and release.

In men TVO is dominant—and makes us want to control the remote. Actually it should be TVOC—testosterone, vasopressin, oxytocin and cortisol. We've noted that from the moment the male gonads differentiate and become testes in the eighth or ninth week after conception, testicular hormonal secretions masculinize the developing embryo.

From the birth of a boy to approximately his first birthday testosterone continues to induce male brain and body characteristics. At one, testosterone ebbs, falls asleep and hides. It won't play a significant role in emotions or growth again for a dozen years. This does not mean boys won't be boys. The young mind has already been masculinized and MIS secures these changes. When T awakens in puberty muscle mass increases, the penis and testicles enlarge, body hair emerges, the voice drops. The boy changes into a creature that walks like a man, talks like a man, smells like a man, and focuses on sex like a man. Proper nurture—education, training and discipline—are essential keys to civilizing this wild beast, the teenage boy. Later we'll explore various sensible, and a few imbecilic, manners which have been or are being attempted to accomplished the task, but for the moment let's look at enhancing and controlling hormones.

V is for valor and *vasopressin*. This peptide hormone is synthesized in the hypothalamus, and stored in vesicles at the posterior pituitary. It is one of the foundations of the male biological imperative--to protect. When released, along with controlling the body's retention of water and therefore blood pressure, vasopressin acts like a U.S. Marine. There are V-receptors along the *reward circuitry* of the ventral forebrain that are stimulated during positive social behaviors. This creates motivation to experience repetitions of those positive behaviors, particularly in highly charged sexual situations such as pursuing and picking a mate, and pair-bonding. So strong is the desire for repeated experience, some call V the hormone of monogamy. But vasopressin can have a dark side. When other males are present it enhances aggressive defense of mate, family and/or turf. It is one of the hormones of valor and protection.

Chemistry gives us a clue to the emotional binary of love-hate. Into the hormonal mix stir oxytocin, a five hundred million year old nine-molecule neurotransmitter and peripheral hormone related to vasopressin. The ensuing cocktail has been called the Love hormone, but it would be equally correct to call it the Patriot hormone as it reinforces pro-social behavior *after* bonds have been established, or the xenophobic hormone as it increases defensive responses to the unexpected.

Oxytocin is important in establishing *in-group* trust. Without trust there can be no empathy. Nor can there be romantic love. Without empathetic ability there is no social bonding—not even between fathers and sons. Those with the lowest levels of O might be sociopaths. But O in balance with V promotes not just feelings of safety and security, but also behaviors which lead to those qualities.

Rounding out the big four is *Cortisol*, often maligned as the Stress Hormone because it increases blood sugar and suppresses the immune system. Released in response to eminent danger, C does increase glucose (blood sugar) allowing the brain to go into hyper-drive when most needed, while also providing energy reserves to skeletal muscles. In preforming these functions C diverts fuel from low-priority systems (immune system response to xyz virus while being chased by a saber-toothed tiger or street-mugger is low priority), and inhibits the body's inflammatory response.

Cortisol mixed with testosterone, oxytocin and epinephrine (adrenalin) is explosive. There are moments when men must be so charged—think of soldiers in combat. But there are costs: short-term bursts may create unresolved snapshot memories of emotional or traumatic events which replay in a mind searching for resolution (PTSD); and long-term, stress- induced cortisol production is destructive to bone formation and immune functions.

The supporting cast: Throughout the life of men *Müllerian Inhibiting Substance* suppresses female traits. This hormone is definitely not a politician. It reinforces traits of the strong silent type.

Prolactin: Once a man's mate is pregnant this chemical kicks in telling him to treat his woman more gently.

Androstenedione: A T precursor released by the skin as a pheromone, it attracts and seduces women. Most men have limited sensor ability to detect this pheromone.

Estrogen: Recall that we all started out functionally as females. Estrogen is the *works* hormone, the motor oil that allows our Ferrari-brain machinery to operate on high-octane T without burning out a bearing or snapping a cam.

Dopamine: This neurotransmitter also affects body functions. It is our go-go juice, important in rewarding and reinforcing physical and mental activities. It is the chemical of pure joy during sex.

There is a fourth dimension to consider along with structure, connectivity and hormones: Time! Not simple time, not clock time, but individual biologic time. One might call it aging, but it is not necessarily tied to birthdays. Maturation is closer, but that generally is used to describe the period of puberty to early manhood, and time changes are continuous throughout the life of men. Time is important. In the young male different structures develop at different ages, with the most dramatic developments being triggered by adolescent-DNA messengers telling the body "It's time." When procreation becomes possible, sex-dependent adaptive circuitry emerges optimizing the continuation of the species.

Men and women think differently. It is nearly impossible for us to not. Basic biology does not limit or restrict differences to only a few components or compartments. It expresses—sometimes subtly, sometimes outrageously—across virtually the entire vast array of our thoughts, acts, actions and behaviors. The fact that the brains and thought processes of men and women are different is directly related to structure, connectivity and chemistry. Why is that a surprise? It's news, but it shouldn't be. It's like someone announcing, "Women have breasts." Yes, they do! That we think differently is big news because people have forgotten that we are different. The movement to make everyone the same—as if you can't be equal unless you are identical—has denied these differences. So this *news* that we think differently is really an example of how far down the skewed roadway of political correctness we've travelled.

There is a purity, a perfection, in mankind as first conceived. One does not necessarily need to believe in creation stories to see this, as it demonstrates itself nearly 300,000 times each day around the globe in the birth of every child. Whether mankind was created by a loving god, by nature, or purely by the accidents of chemistry, the sight of a child, the innocence, the lack of malice, makes strangers smile and old men beam. It inspires the artist. It is evoked by the finger of Michelangelo's Sistine Chapel God giving life to man and creating the perfect being. That perfection is biological. It is incredibly complex, but it is basic.

PART II: How Men Perceive, Interpret and React to the World

My father was a writer. His buddies described him as "a man's man." He never went to college, but he was the first public relations guy for the Columbia Broadcasting System back before it became known as CBS. He started out as a sports writer. He used to tell this story. He really didn't understand baseball. When he would be watching a game with one of his colleagues and the crowd would erupt, he would drop his pencil. He'd bend down, come back up and say, "I didn't see that. What happened?" And the guy would explain. That's how he learned the game of baseball.

Eventually he became the editor of The Ice Cream Trade Journal, was given an honorary degree by Cornell University, and even wrote the entry about ice cream for the Encyclopedia Britannica.

As a man's man he would go out and play cards, or go drinking with his buddies. They'd go to conventions, and he would be with the president of Borden's or the president of Schrafft's or some other executives from dairy companies. They'd stay up most of the night drinking. One night they were in Chicago, and they heard all these sirens. They were playing gin rummy. One of the guys said, "What the hell's going on?" My father got up, opened the window and looked out. He came back to the table and said, "The building's on fire." The other guy said, "Sit down. Let's finish the game." And they did.

That's how guys were in those days. They were hard ass. They were guys. They were doing what guys did. They all smoked. They all wore their hats on the backs of their heads. There was this bonding. They were men and they weren't ashamed of it.

Were these basic male traits, or were they learned behaviors of the culture at that time?

A friend of mine who was a young boy in the 1950s tells this story:

My mother had a saying, "Forty scars makes the man." Crash your bike and end up with road rash from shin to hip and wrist to elbow, while daubing it with Mercurochrome she'd say, "Forty scars..." Burn your hand in a campfire, "Forty scars..." Have the stick-ball bat break and stab you, "Forty scars..." The saying calmed us. Scars were inevitable. Perhaps it enabled us, maybe even encouraged us, to take risks. Forty scars was a common adage in our neighborhood. By the time I was ten I was counting my scars. Twenty six! At this rate, I thought then, "I'll be a man in two years."

Do mom's still comfort their sons with those words? Or has risk aversion in all its many forms stifled male adventure? Or perhaps worse: has risk suppression created an atmosphere in which the risky behavior of boys is done behind closed doors, in the woods, or in back alleys?

American attitudes have changed significantly over the past fifty or sixty or seventy years; as has the proclivity to initiate a lawsuit. Some of the changes have been for the better; some, I believe, for the worse. We know biology hasn't changed—the basics are still the basics.

Not long ago I was with another friend and his sixteen-month old grandson. Recall, the brain of the male toddler is fully a male brain. This was so very apparent as we watched him. His mother and grandmother remained inside the restaurant as we took the antsy little guy out. As soon as we got to a short set of stairs and a ramp behind the building, and let the lad go, he attacked the stairs as if he were on a mission. He climbed. The stairs were pretty difficult—equivalent to two- or two and a half-foot (2 ½ foot) steps for an adult. He climbed up, then down, up, then down. Perhaps twenty times until he had mastered the task. Then up, out across the landing and down the ramp, up, across and down the stairs gripping handholds to the side he'd discovered himself. Then up again, over again, and again, and again. Boys like to be in motion. If you observe closely you'll notice that it is not random movement but meaningful action.

I'd seen him demonstrate similar behavior in the restaurant with a lidded cup of water and a straw. What may have appeared to some to be play or making a mess was actually very purposeful *experimentation and discovery* of spatial and physical properties—without, of course, the verbiage. What happens to a boy's confidence and learning if these behaviors are continuously and overly reined in?

Perhaps you've seen a toddler throw a fit when someone tries to control his behavior. Frustrated, it is as if the boy is saying, "I'd rather do it myself." Think of the *Terrible Twos*. How much of this *bad* behavior is a result of exasperation from wanting to do something—being on a mission to learn, to achieve, to conquer a task—but either being physically unable to complete the task, or being restricted from it, and being unable to verbally communicate needs and wishes? Add to that frustration hormone withdrawal. Remember that the testosterone baths from the eighth or ninth week in utero ebb to almost the vanishing point between a guy's first and second birthday. That might throw me into a snit, too!

Can cultural changes actually change the natural characteristics of men and boys? Is the changing role of masculinity in American society superficial or profound, beneficial or detrimental? What are the ramifications if toddlers are restrained and do not learn that they can, to some extent, control and be responsible for themselves and the physical world about them? If unrealistic restraints continue through elementary school and into puberty are the ramifications exacerbated? Does the lack of strong male role models intensify problems for boys? At a very basic level, what cultural and biological roles do risk-behaviors and other typical male traits serve?

There are no short, accurate, answers. Fundamental ideas play an essential role in the forming of any theory so we need to look at the biological basics to extrapolate to generalizations, but the speculative leap from structures and chemistry to cultural behavior is, at present, hypothetical—as in hypothesis, not as in imaginary. The need to make these complex connections is deserving of deeper exploration and intense research.

Pain: If It Hurts, Smile!

Years ago when I was head of a Boy Scout troop one of the kids was hurt on a camping trip, having whacked his thumb with the back of a hatchet. The other leaders were telling him, "Be Tough. Don't cry. Be a man." You know, you are not allowed to cry if you are a man. If you cry you're a sissy.

I saw this again just a couple of weeks ago when my grandson was playing ball, got hit, doubled over, grabbed his crotch and gave out a mighty groan. While the moms were tittering, "Oh my God, he got it in the..." the coach was saying, "Tough it up. Take a deep breath. Breathe through it."

Some academics and pundits say we taught previous generations o boys these attitudes and behaviors, and that this was a mistake. Maybe that's true, but it begs the questions, "Why was it taught? Why have boys been told not to cry, to be strong, to hide their pain?"

Men do cry; even 'real' men. They might not cry in public; it isn't, o at least it wasn't, acceptable public behavior. But they would do it in the confidence of my office. I saw many men, particularly prostate cancer and kidney stone patients, where the pain was severe and emotions were on the surface. Sometimes I would get a phone call where the patient said, "I'm having a lot of pain." I'd ask, "Have you taken the pain pills?" He'd say "No." I'd say, "It is okay for you to take the pills." Then he'd ask, "Are you sure? I don't want to get addicted." It was almost as if he were saying, " have pain. I'm really in a lot of pain, but I'm not supposed to acknowledge my pain. I'm supposed to be able to handle it. I'm not supposed to seek relief." If you are a man and you have pain you're supposed to tough it out because if you don't you're not manly. Guys beat themselves up for giving in.

Cross-cultural stories from classical literature going back millennia tell of men and boys braving their way through pain. The concept o embracing pain or of turning pain into power is not new. Challenging oneself in the face of pain to do better, to do more, to reach a higher level, to be more intense is typically male. So are the feelings that you've got more important things to do than to "…deal with this crap." It is not a matter o men simply *telling* boys not to cry. Men set that example for boys and for other men. I was discussing this with a patient who told me this story:

> The most amazing instance of pain control I ever saw was when I was sitting next to our top sergeant, Ray M. This was in Vietnam in 1970. I was with Alpha of the 2d or the 502d Infantry. Usually Tops stayed back at basecamp running the company orderly room, but our Top had come out to the field to spend some time with the unit. We were sitting on a log out in the jungle in the mountains south of the DMZ. The company was resting, and we were in the middle of the DDP (day defensive position) with the CP (command post). I think we were out there with one platoon and the CP and the other two platoons were in the patrol area but not with us. We had with us a tracker dog team which was a black lab, a dog handler, and a tracker; and we were investigating an area where we had found

enemy land lines strung between bunker complexes. We're sitting on this log, and the dog handler had rested his M-16 rifle up against his ruck. He had left the selector on semi-automatic. The dog moved, the rifle fell, the trigger caught on something, and the rifle went off and shot Top in the back. The bullet may have nicked the frame of the ruck so it may have been slowed, but Top still got shot in the back. Of course the second the shot went off everybody was down searching, "Where did it come from?!" Top is still sitting on the log, and very calmly he turns and says in an even voice, "Men. I think I've been shot."

That wasn't totally uncommon, but when other guys got shot you generally saw a lot of pain on their faces, even if they were silent. One thing ingrained into us was, *Don't Make Any Noise.* Noise meant the enemy could locate you and attack. I remember guys getting pretty seriously wounded, obviously in a lot of pain, and not making a peep. I've read stories about guys screaming, about wounded guys calling for their mothers. I never witnessed that. I don't recall anyone screaming or crying if we were in a bad area. Guys were pretty hard; hard on themselves and on each other. But there was a reason for it.

Do these behaviors serve a cultural and/or biological purpose? Are there valid reasons why fathers teach their sons not to cry? Are there valid reasons to deny pain? Pain and the perception of pain are two different things; so how we deal with pain, and why we deal with it in the manner we do, are not straight lines. The context of the pain is a factor. Plus pain comes in many forms, some certainly more serious, more immediate or more chronic, than others. The "Be a man" lesson also comes in many forms—some appropriate, some not.

When I was a medical student the standard drug to give to patients for pain was Demerol. We'd go in to see a post-op patient and ask, "How are you feeling?" He'd say, "I'm having a lot of pain." You'd go back to the nurse and you'd say, "He says he's having a lot of pain." She'd say, "I just checked on him and he was sleeping." So you'd nod and say, "Oh, okay. He's not really having pain." It turned out that Demerol didn't work for pain. We don't use it anymore. What it did was sedate the patient. We weren't treating the pain; we were putting him to sleep. We'll talk more about medical responses to pain in later sections, here let's explore a bit deeper our cultural response and the reasons for varying attitudes.

With women, when they have pain, it is common for people rush to their aid and offer comfort and understanding. It is not that women succumb to their pain; not that they feel it any less or any more than men. But their reaction to being in pain, or to others in pain, tends to be different. Women are more nurturing. They express pain differently than men, and it has different meaning to them. For them there's a built-in support system. "We're a sisterhood, and we love you. We know you're going through the misfortune of breast cancer. We know you lost your hair, but you're as beautiful as always." You can see the compassion. It's palpable.

You don't get this with guys, particularly young guys. With guys their problem-solving brain kicks in. They are more likely to say, "Have you tried XYZ?" Or, "What are you going to do about it?" Or it becomes a competition, "Man, you think you hurt! I ripped a muscle in my shoulder, and..." Or they may even quip, "Crawl off into your cave and lick your wounds, man. Come back when you're useful."

One of the outgrowths of this is the perception that men don't take care of themselves, and don't care about taking care of themselves. Tens of thousands of my patients cared deeply about taking care of themselves, but often they hid it; and many, many times they put the concerns for their families ahead of concerns about themselves. They could stand the pain until they could no longer stand the pain. Unlike women, for them there was no cultural vehicle to express the agony they were enduring.

There are, of course, all sorts of variations. Guys with less testosterone tend to be softer; guys with more tend to be more aggressive, harder, and harder on themselves. They also seem more likely to address pain—theirs and others—with humor. Below we'll look at the roles humor, teasing, and bullying play in the life of men.

So why are we this way? Why has this been a male pattern for millennia? Perhaps as hunters and protectors—if you think of those activities much of the communication was silent, tacit, and nonverbal—success required men to be quiet. And stoic. Not crying, not making a sound, signaled to everyone that you were manly, that you were strong, that you were one of the alpha males strong enough to be a leader. Because you could endure pain you wouldn't be distracted by it, you wouldn't be diverted from the goal, whatever that goal might have been. And you would reap the rewards of being the alpha—you know, like getting the girl!

We are still protectors and providers, if not necessarily hunters. Strength in all its manifestations still matters. To those seeking to soften boys, to make them less aggressive and more sensitive, to feminize the culture and change the role of males, shouldn't we ask, "How valid is your argument that changing male characteristics will result in something positive?"

Risk: He Flies Through The Air With The Greatest Of Ease...

Little boys are physical. Later on in their lives this will have implications for intimacy and touch, but at one, three, five or seven, it's all about motion. They scurry around crashing into things, falling over, knocking things and each other down. They climb to disturbing heights without thought of being able to descend. Quite simply, they get into all kinds of trouble. It's amazing any of them survive to puberty. Then things get worse. Ask an insurance underwriter about boys and cars. And if they make it to thirty they repel down mountain cliffs or bet on the stock market! What is all this risk-taking about?

Can it really be biological; really be about getting the girl, protecting the turf, and providing for the family—or at least about preparing for those exploits?

We know, starting in utero, boys more than girls are wired and programmed for motion—watching it, causing it, doing it. "...critical movement circuits [have been] laid down from the blueprint of their genes and sex hormones... For a boy, the genes that turn on will trigger the urge to track and chase moving objects, hit targets, test his own strength, and play at fighting off enemies... [they] weren't taught to be action oriented; they were following their biological impulses." (Brizendine)

During the juvenile pause (approximately one to ten or eleven years of age) when testosterone ebbs, the hormone MIS continues to inundate a boy's brain. Structures and circuits for exploration and action continue to be enhanced. Play is practice for adult actions. Think of other mammals—cute little kitties or bouncing bear cubs— and how aggressively they play-fight. Boys are mammals, too. It makes little difference if you give a boy a cap gun or a mauve magic pony (which in his mind becomes a laser phaser blaster capable of destroying alien vessels at light-year distances), circuitry and structure will lead him to play-fighting, to competing, and to testing his speed and strength in preparation for the adult activities of protecting and defending.

Boys tend to play with boys; girls with girls. As good friend Graham Seekamp, who has taught fifth grade for 16 years, explains, "On the whole you'll see that with kids in an unstructured situation like recess, a large majority of the boys tend to do stuff with other boys, like play football in the field or kickball on the diamond. The majority of the girls will be jumping rope or playing four-square. There is a tendency for kids to hang out with their own gender, but it is not rigid. You do have a group of girls who like to play kickball with the boys; and a small group where both boys and girls will be using the basketball hoop. Still, without anyone saying anything, there is a flow. Some kids are very sports oriented. You can tell that it is the sport that intrigues them, not whether the other players are boys or girls."

Many teachers in many schools have told me that kids are no longer allowed to play dodge ball. They are not allowed to play tag. They're taught that they might get hurt. *Might get hurt!!!* Can anyone live life without getting hurt?! Other rationalizations drive these school policies—from avoidance of lawsuits to the theory that if anyone loses at anything it hurts their self-esteem. Getting hurt *is* part of growing up, part of the human experience. According to a British study the average person can expect to be hurt 9,672 in their life time (Fung). Other data shows the average American will break between two and three bones before they're *done*.

Nurture is extremely influential in whether a boy becomes a risk-taker or a risk-avoider. Think of the classic example of the seven-year old walking on the top of a fence: dad views it with pride, says nothing; mom comes out and screams, "Get down! You're going to kill yourself." Several things may happen here. The boy gets down, internalizes the warning, never goes back up, and learns to believe that he cannot do such physical feats. Or while he is on the fence the warning scares him, his confidence collapses, he falls, gets hurt, never goes back up, never again risks death and destruction, goes inside and watches TV—by the time he's forty he weighs 270 pounds and his cardiologist is warning him if he doesn't start exercising he won't make it to fifty. Or maybe he makes it to the end of the fence, jumps down, grins at his mom, runs off to his next adventure, and at twenty six wins an Olympic bronze in freestyle skiing.

Children can be taught to avoid some or nearly all risks. They can be taught to be afraid. They can even be taught to succumb to minimal pain. Some of these teachings, for the most idealistic reasons, are being institutionalized by social forces attempting to create a gentler society, as if these changes in characteristics will be benign. A boy, a group of boys, a nation of boys can be taught to be cautious, but there is a biological basis for rough and tumble play. Still, boys can be coached out of it. A boy, or a man, can be taught to deny his instincts. He can be taught to be soft and sweet in a feminine—not a masculine—way. He can be taught that his natural inclination to run, to jump, to challenge himself physically is potentially so dangerous it must be avoided.

I'm afraid the country is developing too many *soft* males; too many kids who don't know how to stand up for themselves. It is not just that they've been formed to be soft, to avoid rough actions and risks, but they've also grown up with the notion that they are entitled to things from society. They are not used to being self-sufficient. They are used to having things done for them. There is a confluence of interest in these effort—by schools, legislators, insurers and others who wish to control risk-taking, or who just wish to control others (much more on this in later sections).

Other factors which lead to pain or risk avoidance: these are from the horrid and malicious end of the spectrum. There are abusers who thrive on striking fear in the brains of children; and bullies who set no age restrictions for their victims. They too seek control over individuals, and their abusive acts destroy self-confidence and diminish normal risk-taking behavior. We are going to set this class of conduct aside for the moment. This is aberrant behavior, criminal behavior. I do not want the reader to confuse what we have said above with the felonious and wicked acts which result in emotional murder.

But back to risk-taking and getting the girl!!

Until puberty it is all practice. As testosterone again begins to flow, practice becomes preparation. It may be sub-conscious, but it *is* about getting the girl; or in biological terms about procreation and the continuation of the strongest gene pool. In cultural terms "getting the girl" has millions of different variations, but they are all still about getting the girl; about the strongest, most able guy walking off with the prettiest maiden. *The Man On The Flying Trapeze,* first published in 1837 (original verses below), tells the story. There are a dozen verses interspersed with the chorus, the final being a comeuppance— of the girl not the guy.

> Once I was happy, but now I'm forlorn,
> Like an old coat that is tattered and torn;
> Left in this wide world to weep and to mourn,
> Betrayed by a maid in her teens.
>
> Now this girl that I loved, she was handsome,
> And I tried all I knew, her to please,
> But I never could please her one quarter so well
> As the man on the flying trapeze.
>
> Oh, he floats through the air with the greatest of ease,
> This daring young man on the flying trapeze;
> His actions are graceful, all girls he does please,
> My love he has purloined away.

Of course, at least in this case, the exciting acrobat, the guy with testes big enough to risk swinging by wires strung from the roof of the Big Top, steals the handsome gal away from the wimpy poet. A hundred and fifty years later the story hadn't really changed, although the trapeze was replaced with an F-14 Tomcat. Still the risk-taker, Top Gun Maverick (Tom Cruise) got (to nail) the handsome gal, Charlie (Kelly McGillis). Three thousand years earlier it was Paris winning (or abducting) Helen from her husband Menelaus.

Is risk taking really that simple? Earlier we saw that the ventral tegmental area of the brain of both men and boys instigates physical actions, and that it is the dopamine-producing rewards center and the risk taker. Once testosterone begins to flow again after the juvenile pause, it drives risk-taking behaviors. The earlier cumulative push and pull of nature and nurture has formatted a boy's personality to accept or reject the chemical stimulation. He may be set to give into, to control, or overly control his urges.

Oh, by the way, in the conclusion of *The Man On The Flying Trapeze*, our aerial artist has taught the young girl gymnastics, dressed her up as a boy, and has her doing his act for him while he relaxes.

Oh, she floats through the air with the greatest of ease,
You'd think her a man on the flying trapeze,
She does all the work while he takes his ease,
And that's what's become of my love.

Trust: On the Eighth Day God Created Beer

My father and his friends played cards and drank. That was a pretty common male behavior in the 1940s and 1950s. The card playing seems to have waned, but social drinking—despite growing public health notices, increased DUI law enforcement with lower blood-alcohol limits, and by some segments of society a stigmatization of it as crude—has not.

Like other behaviors, alcohol consumption has been around for some time—at least, according to archeologists who have found jugs designed for the intentional fermentation of beverage—back to the Stone Age. That's 12,000 years or more of beer, brats and barroom brawls... well, maybe not the barroom. And the brats are optional. Still, consumption of fermented beverages dates back to prehistory, to the beginning of civilization. No one knows when the first human got a bit tipsy. What we do know is how alcoholic beverages have been used, the affect they have on the male brain and male behavior, and the cultural meaning or interpretation associated with those behaviors.

Early libations were not just for nutrition, although this aspect should not be ignored. First and foremost, in the long history proceeding the icebox and refrigeration, alcohol preserved liquids. The ability to store food released mankind from the continual need to hunt or scavenge allowing our ancestors to create stable social groupings. You've probably seen internet jokes or cartoons about beer creating civilization; they have more basis in fact than I suspect most of us ever realized.

Early alcoholic beverages were probably more like soups than today's filtered pilsners, but by 6000 years ago the arts of wine and beer making were pretty refined. The uses, abuses and adulations of alcohol are fairly well documented. Beer and wine came to be considered Gifts of the Gods. They were used in religious rites, and for medicinal, antiseptic and analgesic purposes; and "to enhance the enjoyment and quality of life." (Hanson) Even back then, although the benefits to the majority were recognized, there were warnings of misuse and abuse.

Dad was not an alcoholic. Nor were most of his friends. To them, even if not stated, alcohol was a social lubricant. On the face of it that statement may seem shallow, but alcohol plays a significant role in the traits and behaviors of trust, humor, bonding, teasing and bullying.

For each characteristic or behavior, particularly for those under attack, we should be asking the same question: what biological or cultural purpose has this serve?

In some cultures—in Korea, with the Montagnards in Vietnam, and here in America even if it is not usually recognized—if you are come into a group of men, you are not likely to be trusted if you will not drink with the group. This is important amongst Korean businessmen. They want you to get drunk with them because that lets your guard down. When everybody lets their guard down the feeling is, "Now I see the real you. I can trust you because we let our guard down in front of each other." That's part of a social ritual. In Vietnam, Montagnard tribal people stored rice wine in large jars. The number of jars a man had was a symbol of his status and wealth, (much like oil in the potlatch ceremonies of American Indians of Pacific Northwest.) When Special Forces teams would go to live in these villages, the elders would throw elaborate ceremonies at which the soldiers would eat and drink with the village leaders. Those Americans that would drink with the elders, and get drunk with them, became part of that community.

Is this much different than the ritual of American teenagers--high school friends—going out together and get drunk for the first time. I think most college campuses in the U.S. today are dry (which has done little but to drive the drinking either off campus or behind closed doors), but a friend recalls when he was in school in the mid-60s. "We did a lot of drinking. Actually, they had stopped just a year or so earlier, faculty-sponsored beer-ball games on the quad. It would be the faculty team against a fraternity team. In these softball games, after you got a hit you had to stop at each base and chug a beer before you could advance to the next base."

The camaraderie built on those games no longer exists on campuses. Today, perhaps small groups of friends go out and get drunk or stoned together, but it is not officially condoned. Still, it represents that same dropping of personal defenses and being open to others that these rituals if foreign cultures create. If you can do that, and if they will be that open to you, you are friends for life. In essence drinking with your buddies is a test of each other's ability to trust. If you go out with someone who doesn't drink there is almost an apology attached.

This is not a commercial for breweries, wineries or distilleries. Let's separate this kind of drinking with the coupling of drinking and driving, which we recognize as so dangerous to self and others that we strongly oppose it. We are talking about drinking in social circumstances in which vehicles or machinery or weapons are not present. We are also talking about occasion drinking, not continuous drinking, and not the addictive drinking which defines alcoholism. [Approximately ten percent of the population is genetically predisposed to alcohol withdrawal symptoms which create overpowering urges similar to opioid withdrawal.] As noted, warnings of misuse span the millennia. This is a serious issue dealt with elsewhere; here we wish to explore the influences on biology, behavior and society as part of our investigation into how men perceive, interpret and react to the world.

Alcohol easily crosses the blood-brain barrier. It affects virtually all structures including the ventral tegmental area (VTA)—our dopamine-manufacturing, impulse and pleasure center, the dorsal premammillary nucleus (DNP) configured to detect threats and defend, and our prefrontal cortex (PFC) which with enough alcohol goes AWOL.

Alcohol in moderation—the first couple of drinks of the evening—also releases oxytocin, the Love hormone, the hormone responsible for feelings of security, in-group trust, and empathy. Recall that oxytocin reinforces pro-social behaviors after bonds have been established, but also increases defensive responses to the unexpected. It might equally be tagged the Trust Hormone. We've seen this expressed in the examples from Asian tribal peoples to American high school boys. As noted by the British Social Issues Research Center, "…it is unreasonable to suppose that such practices could have survived in such a dominant, pan-historical and pan-cultural manner if they were wholly maladaptive."

Trust is a paramount prerequisite of civilized society. Without trust no social associations work—not with a mate, not within groups, communities or nations, not even within oneself. (More on the breakdown of public trust in other sections).

Civilization: Created by Beer; Held Together by Laughter

Let's jump to bonding, teasing, humor and bullying before we jump to any conclusions. We've been talking about when men get together and drink. Why do they do that? What's the meaning behind it? We noted, when men drink alcohol they let their guard down. Not just their physical guard, but their emotional as well. You learn, or I learn, what the other guy is really thinking. It establishes a trust within our relationship. Within that crowd you develop a sense of security, a sense of camaraderie. I can be myself; I can show myself; I can trust myself to my friends. You have a few beers or glasses of wine and you start to tell people what you really think. Likely they'll agree with you. If they don't, if you're with the right crowd, they'll guide you in the right direction. It creates a mini-society. There is a common perception: Oh, the boys are out drinking again; they're out pounding it down to get drunk because they don't want to deal with the world; they don't want to deal with their responsibilities; or just because guys are guys. It may sit well with some, but it is shallow thinking. Social behavior lubricated by alcohol is a ritual. A corollary feeling might be, "If you are not willing to let your guard down, how can you be my friend."

Other behaviors have similar meanings and consequences when viewed from a social perspective. Recall the rough-housing little boys: seldom does that lead to intentional harm, yet often it leads to lasting friendships. The "Nah, nah, you're it!" and the later humorous quips, benign digs, and out and out ragging on each other ("Your mother wears combat boots.") all have meaning beyond the words spoken.

I think jokes are first of a reflection of what's going on in society at the time. I had this Jewish family practitioner that I knew. He would call me once a week and tell me the latest Jewish joke. He was not good at telling Catholic jokes. He just didn't have it. I would tell him Italian jokes. "A wop, a kike, and a parrot walked into a bar…" There's a camaraderie in this that says, "I matter enough to this person that he would think to tell me a joke." If it's off-color, or not main stream (not pc), it meant he trusted me enough to tell it to me; and also that he likes me enough to share a happy experience with me.

In the OR, the people who told the raunchiest jokes were the nurses. Joke telling is not strictly gender limited (think of. overlapping bell curves!) If they had a joke, they'd come up to me and say, "Did you hear Dr. Johnson's latest joke about the woman with one boob?" If I said, "No," they'd proceed to tell me. In my mind it reflected the feeling that we're part of one society, one group, one herd, whatever you wanted to call us. Joke telling was an affirmation of that. It established that we are part of this mini-society; and it tells the individual that he or she belongs. We never went and told these jokes to the chief of nurses or anybody outside of the group.

This group of guys I hang out with, laugh with, eat and drink with… I was complaining about the price of heating oil. One of the guys owns a trucking company, and he says, "Why don't you call Jimmy Vee. He gives me a good deal." So I call Jimmy Vee. It turns out that Jimmy's father, who is 102 years old, was a patient of mine. He's still alive. They mentioned my name to him and he tells them, "You better take good care of him cause he's a good doctor. He took good care of me." It's embarrassing sometimes; but we become part of a group, and a group takes care of its parts. I called them and the receptionist said, "I don't know. All our people are out on calls," yet within an hour they sent someone out to my house. It's part of belonging, and that is a human need.

We were talking about laughter. I always felt good, or like I mattered, if someone sought me out to tell me a joke. They were usually funny. If it wasn't funny, out of respect for the guy you'd laugh anyway. [Or groan. Give him a little dig back.] But it is an acknowledgement of this very important interaction. Plus it makes you feel good.

In the family, when nephews go out with the older guys, they learn how to act and what to do. The older guys imply that they're going to protect the younger people. One of the things I said to one of my nephews: "I'm the guy that you can tell anything. If you ever get your ass into a jam and you don't want to tell your father, tell me. I'll help you." I'm not the disciplinarian, I'm the godfather. That's my role. I'll be there.

It's important. It's more than just having fun. It is about establishing your identity; establishing your place in the family, your place in the group, your place in society. It solidifies your view of the world. It gives you a place to belong, which is necessary for your humanity. You know, No Man Is An Island. That's how we establish our identity. I'm a Rabuffo. There has always been a certain amount of pride in that. "Look at me: I'm one of them."

Laughter bonds people together, but it's more. I used to crack jokes with my patients. We had these things called The Cancer Talk, where a guy would find out that he had prostate cancer. We'd sit down in the office at the end of the day so we could take two-hours if we needed to. And I'd go through what he had, what it meant, what I thought we should do—second opinions, other tests. I'd lay it all out. Usually his wife was there to hear it. And usually what would happen is one of the two would confess, understandably, that they were really worried.

I came up with this to say. "You're going to be fine. This is just one of those things that happen in life. You're going to be okay." I wouldn't be lying; I really believe that. Then I'd say, "If you really want to worry about something, worry about the Red Sox." They always laughed. But the point is I had addressed their fears and concerns, and now what they were hearing me say was that this really was not something to worry about. And now they're thinking, "I'm not going to die. This is not going to kill me." To me it was a very effective way to get the point across. Much better than saying, "You're all right." It also told him I was on his side; and that I thought enough of him to tell him this joke.

One of my partners heard me say that once. He was one of the younger guys, and he said, "That doesn't come across well. You shouldn't be joking with someone who has cancer." I said, "Why not? What do you want me to tell him?" I'm not lying. My goal was to put it in perspective for him. Yes, you have cancer. This is not lung cancer. It is not pancreatic cancer. You are not going to die from this providing we take care of it.

Laughter is an important part of society; and it is an important part of the way men deal with intense situations, and with each other. I don't know if women go up to other women during a crisis, and say, "Did you hear the one about the guy with three balls...?" Humor and telling jokes is one way of establishing your masculinity. It implies more than just that you have a sense of humor; it implies a sense of knowledge of the culture. If you don't have that intelligence and the background to understand the subject, you're not going to get the joke. I took care of a lot of Indian guys from Aetna—all the computer guys. I would never say anything like that to them. They had no clue about the nuances of the Red Sox. And I didn't know any cricket jokes.

For most of the guys it was a great stress reliever. I guess I was lucky in that way. When I would get stressed my sense of humor would take over. Some people would think I was being disrespectful, but I was just dealing with the stress of the situation.

Joking, joshing, ribbing, ragging on each other are all types of teasing. With guys these behaviors may be verbal, but often they have a physical component. Sometimes it's elaborate; sometimes it's a punch to the shoulder, a "Ha! Gotcha!" punctuation to a quip or pun; sometimes it's a slap on the back or a grasping of one's shoulder with a, "You'll get it sooner or later, Turkey!"

Teasing may, depending upon ones perception, be seen as bullying. Let's distinguish between the two. Bullying is a malicious and on-going form of teasing. Teasing plays a role in the socialization of the individual. It makes you, or at least encourages you, to conform to the group, and that makes you part of the group. If you can take it, if your behavior changes without fundamentally changing who you are, you open yourself up to being friends with additional people.

Severe, malicious and on-going teasing is a different category. It is motivated by the desire to breakdown the other, to fundamentally change him or them into someone he or they are not and do not wish to be; or even can't be. That's bullying.

Light social teasing by peers often increases an individual's self-esteem. As one is accepted into the group the biological and chemical functions of the brain activate. His concept of self-worth increases. He is accepted for his sameness AND his differentness. Social teasing can be a test of your manhood, to see if you can deal with it. It can be seen or felt from the perspective, "The guys like me enough to rag on me. They know I can 'man-up' to it." If I'm teasing you and you tease me back... it's a ritual to see if you are capable of being one of us.

Bullying is different. Context is pertinent. Think of the rituals of military basic training. For most recruits there is a tremendous amount to learn, a tremendous adjustment in how one lives, and that is coupled with the need to re-socialize to a new and alien culture. This is accomplished with severe physical tests, harsh discipline, and at least in the old days, screaming, cussing and debasement—"You maggots!" The more a man accepts that socialization, the more deeply he assimilates into the group. Were the behaviors of most old-line drill sergeants used today in civilian life they'd likely be locked up. There is no denying that the method was effective and efficient. Does it fit our definition of bullying?

Not long ago I read a story about a young artilleryman who had been deployed to Vietnam. His unit was in a relatively remote area. Although enemy action was infrequent his platoon sergeant rode all the men of his battery to perform all the tedious tasks of building and maintaining their defensive position. The sergeant was inhuman, nasty, hard-ass. He demanded perfection. He forced the unit to drill not only for fire missions but also for ground attacks; forced repetitive drills until reactions were rote. The young artilleryman hated him... until the night when, proceeded by a mortar bombardment of their position, a ground attack was launched by an overwhelming enemy force. The attacking troops breeched the perimeter. The ensuing battle caused many wounded, and in the darkness the identity of men scurrying within the perimeter was masked—friend or foe could not be ascertained. To make matters worse, men in the OP (observation post outside the perimeter set up to provide early warning) had been severely wounded. The platoon sergeant, after organizing inner defenses, repeatedly crawled out to the OP, put soldiers upon his back, and crawled back to the base where they could be treated by a medic. The perimeter defenses held, the long night ended, but the platoon sergeant was killed on his last attempt to save one of his men. They young artilleryman wrote that it was not until the battle was over that he realized that the sergeant's demands were not malicious, not bullying, but were acts of love. "You gotta love somebody a whole lot to pick on 'im and teach 'im things." (Sammy Davis, MOH recipient; My Sergeant.)

We do not take bullying lightly. There are circumstances where meanness and rejection drive individuals to suicide. It cannot be downplayed, and where and when teasing crosses the line, authority must step in. That line, as seen with our military examples, is moveable. Little boys compete with each other from as young as two—perhaps even younger. By kindergarten the alpha males are already dominating their group. Where the line between bullying and teasing is established affects personality development.

In my mind, if you are being bullied, or think you are being bullied, and authority steps in and halts the actions of the bully, it teaches you that society is there to protect you. That's good. But if it is light teasing that's stopped that may teach the individual that he doesn't have to defend himself. He can ask the teacher, the mother, the father to defend him. In these cases the kid doesn't learn how to deal with conflict. That challenges his self-esteem. If you get bullied and you don't respond your sense of self-worth is lessened because you are "letting it happen." The child may also feel that others do not think enough of him, do not respect him enough, to not bully him. Think of all the stories and motion pictures that have been developed around the little guy who takes it, then can take it no longer and bloodies the bully's nose. The karate kid is a hero; at the end of the story his self-esteem is off the charts. Where the line should be drawn, where authority must step in, is not an exact formula. Right now, political correctness says that if you walk into a room and someone is wearing bright orange pants with a green and pink polka dot tie and a red sports coat, and you say, "That's an ugly combination," PC says that hurts their self-esteem. People get censured for those kinds of remarks, even if in the long run those kinds of remarks would bring the garish dresser into the fold. In the push-pull of changing regulations as to how and where to set the threshold, one wonders if the social role of teasing is even considered.

Bullying, of course, is not restricted to boys. Perhaps because the anterior cingulate cortex is larger in females than males, and one female biological role is to recall social history, girls seem less able to let go of grudges. Our favorite 5th grade teacher, Graham Seekamp, notes, "Girls in the fifth grade sometimes develop these click-y relationships where they'll accept certain girls into their circle but they'll shun others. There's this very mean kind of behavior which we try to squelch, but it will show itself during unstructured times like recess. Some years are worse than others. If you watch them at recess, you'll see girls trying to hang out with other girls that they see as popular; but the popular girls will purposely do mean things to make other girls feel left out. Make them cry."

Asked if the school can halt those behaviors, Seekamp says, "We try. It's not easy. You have to catch them doing something that's blatant, and a lot of times the behavior is subtle and covert. They'll try to stay within the rules, but you can tell that they are purposely making life hard on someone."

Another friend, David H. Larson, Ph. D. (superintendent, president of superintendent association), a staunch defender of public schools tells us that although some inner-city schools are failing, most schools in America successfully turn out well-educated, well-socialized kids. His perception on who bullies most: "One of the toughest groups I had to deal with was Hispanic females. They'd get into fisticuffs with one another, and it was like a vendetta for life. The African-American kids would become friends again, but the Hispanic girls, you think you have your problem solved, and a month later they're at it anew. They couldn't give it up. I don't know if it's a cultural thing, but they were more difficult to deal with than others." [More on schools, regulations and the legality behind bullying in later sections.]

How much teasing is too much? What is the social cost of not being able to joke with co-workers, or of not being able to party on campus with friends? What is the cost when concerns about bullying, down to the lower elementary grades, stops kids from teasing each other? There is a cost paid for these social restrictions; and, of course, a cost if there are no restrictions at all.

If anti-bullying stops teasing which plays a role in bonding and socialization, the bonds that are established are weak and socialization is incomplete. When this happens we must ask, what ramifications are there to individuals and to the social order? At some point authority has to intervene, but the issue is where society places that point. Fifty years ago it may have been too far in one direction. Now…? Think of the six-year old who is accused of sexual harassment for kissing a classmate on the cheek… is this really an incident of bullying? We need to be sure the point has not shifted too far in the direction of over-protection, or that it is not used as an excuse for expedient purposes with *zero tolerance*. Too much authority, or too rigid authority, is tyranny. Tyranny is official bullying.

We've jumped the gun here on ramifications and consequences which are covered in much greater detail in later sections, but I wanted to show that basic traits and characteristics overlap. We're breaking them down, but recognize that any breakdown is simplistic. To some extent, all elements are in play at all times. The breaking down merely allows us to more easily analyze who we are.

Competence: He Aint The Sharpest Knife In The Drawer

He's a few slices short of a loaf. That jackrabbit couldn't find his way out of a one-corridor maze. Benign jabs. They get much harsher. Jabs and digs, even within a bonded group, are indicators of competition. Men compete; women cooperate. Men compete with each other. If no one is around, a man will compete with himself. Compete means to do better, to go further, to reach higher, to accomplish more. Competence is a qualitative comparison. It measures ones capabilities and achievements matched against those of others. Competence implies comparison which in turn implies competition. The male quest for competence is seeded in the biological imperative to procreate and the compulsion to compete for a mate, but it reaches into every aspect of our lives.

Men don't like incompetence. They don't like stupidity, inefficiency or dependence. They don't like these things in others, and find them frustrating in themselves. Tolerance for incompetence can be taught. Society can raise incompetence to the level of a virtue, or teach boys that it is inevitable, but that is not our natural state.

A few months ago I was at a local radio station to talk to the program director, a very self-assured young woman, about doing a program on men's health. On the way out I spoke with her assistant, a young man whose title was something like studio gofer. He was interested in the topic, particularly when I explained it would be about more than our health, that I was also concerned about the changing role of men in American society. He asked, "How so?" and I briefly delineated various trends set off by social movements and institutionalized by the laws and regulations of the past few decades. He said, "Yeah. I can see that. Boy, men are really stupid." The way he said it made me return his question, "How so?" He answered,

"Women are organized. They can do anything. But us men, we don't know anything." Me: "Really?" He went on about how men can't live by themselves, how they aren't self-sufficient. "We're bumbling idiots compared to girls."

What shocked me was that he believed everything he was saying. He had grown up in a segment of this new American culture, and was a product of the denials of traditional male virtues. I didn't challenge him. At that moment it wasn't a conversation I wished to have. But later I mentioned it to a guy who works for Pro-Health, a statewide organization of family doctors. I had been talking to him about doing something about men's health. He said, "We're doing global health care now. We do populations. We manage diabetic populations; we manage chronic pain populations; we manage women's health." I asked, "If you're managing women's health, why don't you manage men's health? If you're doing one, how can you not do the other?" We got into a discussion about where men fit. He said, "Yeah. We don't seem to have any heroes any more. We went from Marcus Welby, MD to Peter Griffin (the dad on the TV adult cartoon Family Guy). I'm concerned for my kids. That's who their role model is. That's not right." I said, "Oh boy! Tell me. I worry a portion of our young American men are being left behind." I did not say to him, but I thought, perhaps your kids are watching too much TV. Perhaps they should be witnessing heroes in other areas of life.

At that time I hadn't yet thought about the young men who never develop the attributes we see as being part of being a man, or the situations in which this development is stilted. But why should we (or I) be surprised when we meet the resultant of a trend that has been gathering steam for half a century. The behaviors and beliefs of some men have changed—socially and personally—but their circuitry and chemistry have not. There's the contradiction. Young men are being shortchanged, and many are shortchanging themselves.

Unlike the typical TV commercial caricature of American men, American men are not bumbling idiots. They don't like incompetence, ignorance, inefficiency or dependence. As noted, there are basic reasons for this. Men are wired to compete with each other. The quest for competence, and the respect for the ability to accomplish and to act, is tied to the need to compete. Competition is an innate factor in the search for a mate, in the urge to continue, to provide for and to protect life. The alpha male (recall this behavior begins by two years of age or even earlier) is always pushing to do better, to go further, faster, higher, longer. The scholar-athlete is an alpha characteristic. From a biological perspective the best, strongest, smartest, most agile wins. He passes on his DNA to the next generation.

To be competent, or to strive for competence, permeates all other behaviors. In the modern world we might use the term professionalism, as professionalism connotes competence, but there are many components—in both our professional and our personal lives. Competence is a factor in leadership, in socialization, in bonding. From competence and self-sufficiency comes respect which is a necessity in the ability to bond with others and to make others want to bond with you. Recall that trust is also necessary for bonding and for leadership. Characteristics form overlapping circle.

Competence may mean winning. The joy of victory is tied to the release of oxytocin and vasopressin, as are the pleasures of other accomplishments—big and small. The more one accomplishes the better one feels, up to the point where one might be bursting with pride. It is almost impossible to overstate the male need to achieve. There are also the vicarious thrills of watching the accomplishments of those to whom we've bonded—our mates, our children, our siblings, our classmates, our teams, our national images.

What happens to a man, to his psyche (or mental state if you prefer) and to his behavior, when he no longer strives to accomplish, or if he is blocked from being able to accomplish? Or when he does accomplish something, when he builds something, and someone denies that he built that? What an insult that is!

An element of competence is self-sufficiency. The more one depends upon on others, particularly if that dependence is without need, the less one respects oneself, and the less respect one is paid by others. The more one is competent, the more he is self-sufficient; the more he is self-sufficient, the more he is capable of taking care of others. Said another way, the more competent the man, the more he is capable of fulfilling his biological roles of provider and protector.

Being competent, being a protector and being self-sacrificing are elements of leadership. A key characteristic of the very good leader is his attention to the goal or mission, and his ability to dismiss the emotional affects that the goal might have on others. For the moment we will disregard the value, worth and morality of the goal—great leaders, unfortunately, can be good or evil. Where the nice guy is calm and caring, the competent leader might seem cold and callous. His focus is on the future, on where he is leading his followers, not on the here and now, not on their current feelings.

Competence means accepting responsibilities or at least having the capacity to accept them. Being given a responsibility—this could be a five-year-old's chore of feeding the dog or taking out the garbage—is a confirmation of self-worth. It says to the receiver, "I trust you. You are trustworthy." Removing responsibility—as sometimes happens to sages in assisted-care facilities, or fathers from families via the side effects of social programs—removes meaning from life.

Recognize the interplay between competence, responsibility, trust and truth. Competence begets trust. The more you trust someone, the more responsibility you give them. The more responsibility someone is entrusted with, the more he is likely to rise to the level of accepting that responsibility—thereby becoming more responsible and more competent. A corollary to developing trust and responsibility is the necessity for honesty and truth from both the giver of responsibility and the one entrusted with it. Dishonesty, lies and corruption break trust; trust broken destroys relationships and destroys the process that develops responsibility.

Maliciousness is not necessary. The less you trust someone the less responsibility you give him. If there is no level to which he may rise, he will remain at a lower level of responsibility and competence.

This is true in the relationship between parents and children. The self-image a child internalizes regarding his own level of responsibility and competence may establish those characteristics in him for life. It is also true for communities and for a peoples' relationship to their government. This is the problem with the "nanny" state. It implies that people are incapable of choosing for themselves or of taking care of themselves—they are not competent enough, or not responsible enough, to manage their health or finances so the state must step in and do so for them. At some point they accept being less responsible. That equates with ceding freedoms.

Ceding or the forceful removal of responsibility reduces the meaning of life. There are personal and cultural ramifications to that reduction in meaning which we will analyze in detail in later sections. In short, on the street life becomes cheaper, violence is less restrained. In homes and facilities crankiness overtakes the celebration of having lived well.

The quest for competence can be educated out of boys, as in the example of the radio station gofer. Boys can be convinced they cannot become capable, productive members of society, that they are disorganized bumblers, or that they are not as capable as women and they shouldn't strive to be. If they are raised that way, that may become their reality. But their biology will be telling them something else. That contradiction leads to trouble.

Love: Sex, Drug & Rock'n'Roll
Or Touch, Visual Stimulation and the Need for Intimacy

Before we get into trouble let's look at elements and expressions of love; after all we men are the romantic gender. Are you surprised? Truly we are. Despite all the images in the popular culture; despite the projections of men as the stumbling klutzes in relationships; and despite all the advice columns, romance novels, and chick flicks aimed at female audiences, it is us guys who are the real romantics. We have to be. If we weren't we wouldn't bond, and procreation would fall off. Our circuitry and hormonal make up, once we've selected a mate, lock in our bonding decision; we're more apt to bond for life than women, more apt to become a one-woman man. But popular culture, particularly popular female culture, is illiterate and can't read us. [This is why no woman should be allowed to read this book. Why should we give away the Rosetta stone?] We, men and women, boys and girls, may or may not be from different planets, but there is little doubt we speak different languages. So, fellow Martians, follow along.

We express our passions differently than women; and we relate to each other and to the physical world in a way women do not. It starts young. Boys are physical beings. They express themselves physically. They grow up, become men, yet still remain physical beings. We may learn other ways to express ourselves; we may learn to control our physicality, but in basic ways we are still the little boy expressing and interpreting love and intimacy, emotions and data through touch and physical acts.

Men like to touch. Women do too, but in a different way. Boys touch things. It's part of being physical. Little boys more than little girls seems unable to control the urge to touch (or taste) everything in their vicinity. Men like to touch others. It's the way we express friendship with each other—handshakes, fist bumps, slaps on the back, chest bumps, even ritualistic daps; and intimacy with the fairer sex—hugs, caresses, massages, a soft hand following a soft curve. We'll get into the bio-neuro-chemical mechanics in a moment (and into the legal troubles in a later section), but first: Yes! We also like to touch ourselves.

Little boys play with their penises. So too do preadolescent and adolescent boys, and young and middle-aged men, and old guys. A man is obsessed with his penis—seemingly from birth, perhaps from in utero—for his entire life. It never ends. It's universal across age groups and cultures. Moms, if you have little boys, get used to it. It's not evil or dirty or perverted. It is difficult for us guys to understand why the women in our lives are not equally obsessed with it. What is all this about feminine equality if you can't be equally obsessed with our members?

Our penis brings us joy and pleasure. It is connected to all our brain structures, to our pleasure centers and dopamine-production facilities. It is our tool for the biological imperative—to procreate. Yes, we do think with it. We express our emotions through it. We talk to it, to him, to the little man, to my johnson, to Willie, to Mr. Happy. [Send us an email with the name you call yours: drjeffsays.com. Maybe we'll start a list on our blog and send a copy of this book to those with the most unique moniker.] Privately it is our identity. If it has a problem, we have a problem. (More on this in the section, The Doctor Is In.) If it's standing tall and strong and saluting, so are we. When we talk about emotional intimacy, our penis is our consultant".

Okay, we've gotten that out of the way. It's a given, but it was necessary to lay it on the line.

Men have a need for emotional intimacy, just as do women, but men tend to express their emotions more physically than women. That is, we perceive and express emotional intimacy through touch and sex. Men are also more visual. We want the lights on. We want to see those wonderful curves. Women are more auditory. They want to hear you say, "...leave the lights on. I want to see you beautiful body..." To men physical touch is an emotional expression. And not being touched means rejection.

Being physical is more than sexual. Men think physically. We think via touch and manipulation of objects. If the object is only an image in our minds, or merely a description, our intracranial actions (thoughts) are similar to if we were actually holding a solid.

Have you ever watched a little boy fidget while solving a problem? Dr. Brizendine explains, "Boys react more physically to their environment than girls do..." by embodying the movements they make. "Their muscles are practically twitching in response to everything they see going on around them. ...boys use their muscles and nervous systems more than girls to think and express themselves..."

She gives the example of a boy's reaction, as if seen via fMRI technology, to the word *slug*. The "...sensation area in the brain for slimy and squishy is activated. Then the movement area... for slow and slithery is engaged, and even the emotional area... for disgust... These brain areas are needed for him to completely embody, learn, and remember the meaning of *slug*. Scientists refer to this process as embodied cognition, because the muscles and body parts he uses to learn a word will stay connected to the meaning of the word."

Boys, when learning, mentally rotate objects, automatically "...using both sides of their brain's spatial-movement area in the parietal lobe." Interestingly, girls only use one side of their brain for this function, and it is not automatic. When solving spatial relationship problems, the visual cortex of boys connects directly to the parietal spatial-movement areas. Neurons fire, muscles twinge, the body twists as if the objects were real, and a "visceral sense" of three-dimensionality is produced. Boys reach the answer to these kinds of problems more quickly than girls, but when asked to explain how, they tend to twist and turn and gesture. "The boy's body movements were their explanations."

Men squirm less. We haven't outgrown it. We've simply learned to control the outward manifestations of our thoughts. We're more physical and visual creatures than women, and we still relate to the world in these modes. And sometimes we still squirm.

A college-educated friend tells of being in military service with less educated individuals. One of his jobs required that he interview other soldiers. "I never met a dumb soldier," he said. It was in response to a politician denigratingly saying that if boys couldn't get into college they could always go in the military. "I met some soldiers who others thought were dumb, but once you talked to them in depth you found that it was not a matter of being stupid or of being incapable, but only a matter of having fewer language skills. They were intelligent in other ways. Some were very mechanical. These guys were looked upon as being dumb because they didn't speak well, but once you got to know them you found this wasn't at all true. Many had an innate understanding of materials and of physical motion. It was more than just soldiering and needing to know the space-time-velocity of projectiles. These guys were brilliant in this way. They would make great engineers, but if they worked for a company that required employees to write prose reports, they'd never become more than maintenance men."

I found the same thing among the many patients I had who were machinists at Pratt & Whitney or at one of the other manufacturing centers in the area. I had many conversations with these guys. I would say, "How did you learn to do that?" They would usually say, "My father taught me," or "I got a job when I was sixteen at this place, and they taught me." These are the guys who build aircraft engines. That is an amazing skill. I so admire that they can take a block of steel and turn it into these amazingly complex machine parts.

I said to a few of them, "How come I get paid what I get paid, and you get paid what you get paid? I don't really see the difference. I don't know how that evolved. Maybe it evolved because we used to be witch doctors and we threatened people!"

In reality it evolved because modern occupations with verbal components tend to be tied more closely to financial structures where a verbal component is also prized. Traditionally, and by nature, men related to the world physically—whether they were hunters or gatherers or sod-busters. As physical creatures, strength, speed, stamina and an understanding of objects were assets. These physical and tactile traits were intensified by natural selection. Yet in today's world of unending (if shallow) communications, the need for non-verbal thoughts and expressions so necessary to production (provide) and security (protect) is more easily dismissed.

Over eons we developed to express our emotional needs through physical contact. These traits carry over to our relationship with women. Modern man still expresses his emotional side via physical contact; and his emotional needs, within a relationship, are for, and are expressed by, physical contact.

Sex and Intimacy

Contact for a man *is* intimacy. Touch means something to us. With our mate or significant other that intimacy may mean sex, but it may at times mean holding each other, hugging, holding hands, or patting one's wife on the ass. Intimacy does not always mean intercourse, but that, of course, is for most men the ultimate intimacy.

The touch of intimacy is, as we've seen, connected to all parts of our brains and in turn to all parts of our bodies. When little boys embody the word *slug*, that's trivial compared to the embodied cognition that happens when a man is in a physical-emotional relationship with a woman. His muscles and body parts connect to the meaning centers (PFC), and just about all other centers, of his brain. As Dr. Brizendine says, "Once a man's love and lust circuits are in sync, he falls just as head over heels in love as a woman—perhaps even more so." I'd echo the even more so.

In the section on relationships we'll discuss the intricacies of, and impediments to, intimacy. Here we are only concerned with the basics. People ignore fundamental biological differences in a rush to be equal or chic or politically correct. At times men ignore, and women deny, our sexuality. But that's a veneer on reality. It is the source of frustration and conflict, and tends to lead to sexless relationships.

Men need intimacy. They need touch. They need to connect. After his second marriage imploded a young friend said to me, "That's it. I'm never going to date again. I don't want to see anybody." He bought a motorcycle. He cruised the New England countryside. He had a wonderful time. He told me, "I've got more money than I've ever had before because I'm not spending it on somebody else." He described how great he felt, how wonderful it was to be single and unencumbered.

Then he got invited to a Christmas party. One of his buddy's wives said, "What are you doing Christmas eve? We're having a party. Do you want to come?" He said, "Yeah, okay." And he met a girl.

He's a runner. She's a runner. She's the same age he is. She's got two boys like he does, and they're the same ages. They talk. The next thing he knows she invites him over to the house. He gets along with her boys; they do stretches together, go for a jog. So he and this gal hit it off. They make a date for New Year's Eve. This has all happened in four or five days.

Another friend is hosting a party. "Do you want to go?" "Sure." She sends him a picture. He had asked her to do this, but she send him a picture of her butt because she works out and she takes a picture of her butt every week to make sure, according to her, that it is looking okay and it is not fat or jiggle-y or beginning to sag. He shows me the photo and all she has on is this red thong. He's giggling. He can't control it. Then New Year's Eve comes and they go to the party. Of course, on the 30th she's sent him a frontal picture sans clothes, so he's primed; and of course they spend all night in bed. I hear the gory, or maybe glory, details. He's hooked.

The next morning one of the guys at the gym is talking to him, and he tells the guy the story. This guy is tittering like a teeny-bopper [vicarious enjoyment mixed with envy]. The whole thing about, "I don't like women; I don't want anything to do with them," simply evaporated into thin air.

There is a genetic need, a biological urge, to do this. He is now getting into the protective mode. He's going to buy her some clothes so they can run together. He's showing her exercises to do to give her better arms. He was going to her house tonight because she was cooking him dinner. You can see where this is going. The point is there is an underlying need to do all this. There is obviously a need for sex, but it is more than that. There is a need to connect. We'll meet them again in the chapter on relationships.

The flip side: I would hear this from patients, and I hear it in the gym, "Hey Doc, is there something I can do to get my wife to have sex with me? She's always too tired or too busy or too this or too that." Yes, there is. We'll get to it, but here simply understand that this plaint is not only symptomatic of a breakdown within a relationship, but it is revealing about our male need to touch, to connect, to love and to be loved.

Men are passionate even if popular culture does not recognize it, or portrays men's passions as lust. Indeed, that's a problem right there.

How can a man show his passionate side if there's a chance he'll be labeled a pervert? So men hide their feelings, mask their romantic side. That way, we don't get squished.

Romance is all the good feelings we have that come with bonding and protecting and caring for. It includes physical caressing and holding and love-making. It is not just that men can be romantic. By nature we must be romantic. We are wired to be givers which is part of providing and protecting. Our drives, along with our competition for a mate, are part of romance. Pleasing a woman is a core element. If we are to be successful we must please the one for whom we compete— that is, of course, unless you're a caveman and clunk her over the head with your club. Our strivings are most apt to be successful if we believe—to the very embodied-muscle core of our being—that we are in love. What could be more romantic?!

The psychologist B.F. Skinner defined love as mutual positive reinforcement. In chemical/hormonal terms we might talk about the potent, male dopamine-oxytocin-vasopressin rush produced by *being in love*. Yet men are oft times portrayed as duds in the romance department as if only the female perspective is relevant!

No wonder so many men turn to casual sex, drugs and rock'n'roll. Or worse. Or much, much worse.

Boys Behaving Badly: Corruption, Greed, Coercion, Rape, Murder

We've been talking about mostly the positive attributes of male values and traits; and our perspective has been from the angles of biological imperatives, brain connectivity and hormones. We've been light-hearted with many of our examples, and we've poked fun at rogue behavior, rules and trends. I fully recognize that this is only part of the story. Not all male behavior is positive. Things go bad; boys behave badly. Wrath, greed, sloth, pride, lust, envy and gluttony—the seven deadly sins—seem ubiquitous. We need to talk about the bad... the really evil stuff men do. We need to recognize the basics and the basis of these many and varied forms of abuse. And we need to answer the question: are crimes of greed and gluttony aberrant modes of the biological imperative *to provide*; are rape, lust, incest and adultery warped forms of *to procreate*; and are assault, battery and murder sick outgrowths of *to protect*?

If yes, then why? How? What's behind these aberrations? Indeed, are they aberrations or are these behaviors innate, inevitable, perhaps normal extensions of the who and the what... of the animals... that some say men are? Or is bad behavior an indication that something has gone wrong with an individual's genes, or a culture's socialization process?

We know too many men who have behave badly: not, "BAAAAAD," as in "Yo! Dude, you Bad!" but bad in the traditional interpretations of wrong, malicious, evil or destructive. I'm tempted to copy the headlines from today's paper, but why? You already know the content: assault, robbery, rape, rioting, looting, stabbing, cheating, bilking, influence peddling, arson, rip-off scams of every ilk, lying, swindling, extortion, kidnapping, slave-trading... Good Grief! We can be a nasty species—nasty to others, nasty to other species, nasty to the environment, nasty to ourselves... beheadings, terrorism, pogroms, war, genocide. The list goes on. (I'm going to stop. My congressional rep might read this, and I don't want to give her any more ideas.)

Civilization developed to control our behaviors, to rein in our excesses. From the very first batch of beer men have warned others of immoderation. Discipline, knowledge and codes of conduct are social necessities. Traditionally they did not deny basic instincts but they did control them, corralled them, limited them to acceptable manifestations. At least that was the aim. This is not a book on theology, but we would be remiss not to point out that the canons of most of the great religions of mankind enhanced traditional traits and values, and denounced behaviors which suppressed the ability to meet those imperatives. The seven deadly sins are the classification of vices in the Christian ethic. They have been used for nearly two thousand years to enlighten mankind, and to guide men away from treacherous behavior—behaviors the church saw as having a primary focus aimed inward, upon one's self and for one's own glorification, instead of a primary focus aimed outwards toward others, toward the universe, and toward God.

If one deeply ponders the traditional role of religion (and one needs here to ignore the corruptions of these human institutions), he see that the precepts, properly and honestly followed, establish limitations and guidelines that enhanced the basic imperatives of provide, protect and procreate—cross-culturally from Native

Americans to kosher laws regarding the preparation and handling of food in the time before refrigeration and chemical preservatives.

Traditional laws were there to protect, but they only worked if they were in harmony with our biological basics; if they recognized that they could not change those basics but could only guide and direct men to act in positive ways.

We still haven't answered the question: What's behind bad behavior?

Is it genetic? Are some individuals or some groups predisposed to viciousness? "The tainted history of using biology to explain criminal behavior," writes Patricia Cohen in the article *Genetic Basis for Crime: A New Look*, "has pushed criminologists to reject or ignore genetics and concentrate on social causes: miserable poverty, corrosive addictions, guns. Now that the human genome has been sequenced, and scientists are studying the genetics of areas as varied as alcoholism and party affiliation, criminologists are cautiously returning to the subject."

Ms. Cohen lays out the state of thought on the subject by quoting numerous studies and experts. Most of them focus on violent crime; few words are spent on white-collar crime. She cites Harvard psychologist Steven Pinker on understanding the genetics of violence: "It is not a claim about how John and Bill differ, but about how every male is the same." Pinker further says this understanding can, "tell you what aspect of the environment you should look at."

That sounds good. Expert after expert talks about aggression and violence, some about how predisposition is not destiny, others about how marriage redirects males from competing to investing in their families. More good-sounding thoughts, but it seems apparent that many social scientists developed their theories from their political ideologies, not from broad-based, unbiased observation. First off, one gets the feeling that they do not understand violence or aggression, that few have ever been part of the warrior class. There is no crime in that, but when pundits and papers hype their findings, and advocacy groups develop and demand action, legislators respond by proposing laws to correct the *inequity*. If the bias or banality is questioned, advocates tend to righteously entrench and attack the questioners. It is as if advocates become as deeply addicted to their fantasies as hardcore heroin users to their drugs. Pundits and special interests join the fight and become aggressive and vicious if the fantasy is shown to be fallacious.

That seems to be the current state of political discourse in America. It is a tragedy.

Of the above example one needs to ask, "Why do all, or nearly all, researchers start with the assumption that violence is bad? Is all violence bad behavior? What about using violence to protect self and loved ones? What about defensive wars? If you were Yadizi (a Kurdish, non-Muslim ethnoreligious group) and you and your family were being assaulted by ISIS, would violent defense of self and community be acceptable? Considered okay? Labelled good? Can violence be good?! Does violence ever serve a biological purpose— like helping to sustain lives? Is that okay? If yes, how does one learn to exercise *good* violence? How does one learn to control the aggressive behaviors in violent acts so that they are directed only to stop, subdue or destroy the one(s) who are attacking? How can violent defense be marshaled against violent offense if there is no preparation? Or should one learn to always turn the other cheek? Might xenophobia sometimes be a positive attribute? The questions researchers are not asking are as important as the ones they address.

When I read these articles and the studies they cite I find I'm often gritting my teeth. One can pick a point of study—this is not only a valid course but is a necessity to penetrate deeply into any subject— but one must always place that point in perspective and understand that if one's findings have internal validity within one's study, that does not necessarily mean they have external validity in the greater context. To assume so is arrogance.

A note on race, genetics and crime: we've alluded to this earlier. I do not believe race exists in any sort of pure form. Race, as defined by the amount of melanin in one's skin, is an erroneous mental construct. The quality, *color,* in humans is a genetic continuum from very light to very dark with nearly an infinite number of tones in between. That does not mean I do not recognize how color has been used for millennia to segregate or to oppress populations.

This is not the same with maleness. The male biological imperatives cross all races, all cultures, all generations. These imperatives are a much more important factor in behavior than is skin color. Focusing on skin color continues the abuses of the past. There are cultural and colorful overlays of all the groups about the globe, but wherever, whenever and whoever the men are, the basic biology of maleness remains the same. The cultural brush may camouflage it, but it does not change it.

Ferguson

As I have been writing this section, riots have again broken out in Ferguson, Missouri. The television pundits have regurgitated the standard boilerplate stories about socio-economic deprivation causing violence. I haven't heard one say, "...the programs and funds that have already been expended to elevate people haven't worked." What seems to be ubiquitous is more of a simplistic apology, kind of a paraphrase of the lyrics from Westside Stories' *Gee Officer Krupke*, ...These children are depraved on account that they're deprived.

Ladies and Gentlemen, the programs haven't worked! At least not in the way they were sold. The War On Poverty has had severe side effects. Some housing programs resulted in the still-birth of economically stagnant communities. Affirmative Action, for all its positive contributions, essentially condemned the majority of the people it was designed to help to the waste heap of society. Still, what I hear pundits and legislators say is, "Let's have more programs that do more of the same, just more intensely." Hey! Listen up! The programs haven't worked! They haven't worked in socio-economic terms. They haven't solved the problems of poverty, crime or violence. When socio-economic programs remove from men the responsibility to provide for and to protect their children and their families, those programs devalue men and decrease the meaningfulness of their lives. Some social programs certainly offer much needed short-term relief, but it is the long-term ramifications, the negative side effects, of these programs which have made them failures. Not only have they not supported the basic biology of men, but many of the programs destroy the very goals and needs generated by the biological imperatives. They interrupt the very most basic patterns of masculine identity. They destroy men being men. Responsibilities, as Dr. Pinker alluded, focus a man's energies on his family; without responsibilities men become the children of *Lord Of The Flies*.

This, of course, does not explain all bad behavior. Still, denying or denouncing the practice of educating or indoctrinating men in traditional values--a la the church and the 7 deadly sins, or the Boy Scout Promise, or any of the other codes of ethics or conduct that societies have produce--enables men to do almost any evil. Civilization does need laws, codes of conduct and ethics; but those laws, codes and ethics, to be effective, need to be in harmony with our biological imperatives.

Greed and gluttony are the antithesis of *to provide*; rape and incest are antagonistic to the imperative *to procreate*; and murder has little to do with *protection*.

Identity: Raising The Sick Puppy--Story, Self-Image and Behavior

We are what we eat... mentally. Trash in, trash out. No different than our physical diet. Enough of the wrong foods and your willie lays flaccid in your drawers (more on that in the section The Doctor Is In). Enough mental trash in—thoughts, pictures, words, attitudes—and you end up with ED: emotional dysfunction; or, if you prefer, existential dysfunction. Your man-brain lays limp in your cranial cavity. In your diet desserts are okay; but if sweets or artificial sweeteners, or hot peppers or dirt, comprise the bulk of your intake, you are going to be one sick puppy.

What goes into our minds becomes the fodder our biological computers transform into our thoughts, attitudes, actions, and identities. This is nurture exerting its sway upon nature. Over time that fodder, morphed and massaged, becomes our personal story and world view. Our story, the story we tell ourselves of ourselves, establishes the framework of our behavior. Each of us has had innumerable entries impacting the way we see ourselves; and these, in turn, impact the way we behave and the way we interact with others. Said another way, the story we tell ourselves of ourselves creates our self-image, and behavior tends to be consistent with self-image. As a man thinketh, so he shall become—his story controls his behavior. So too does ambient cultural story control cultural behavior. As story changes, individually or culturally behavior changes.

Try this. Complete the following sentence. I am a _____. Fill in the blank with how you describe yourself. It can be one word. I am a doctor. I am an: athlete, baker, cabinet maker, eccentric, foodie, good guy, hotdog, ideologue, joker, klutz, lawyer…sailor, skier, skydiver… Add an adjective. I am a retired doctor. I am a weekend athlete. If you filled in *an athlete*, isn't that your self-image, or at least one important element of it? Do you not behave in athletic ways—play sports, climb mountains, bike, hit the gym? If you identified yourself as a baker—professional or just for fun—you bake, don't you? From your oven comes pies, cakes, cookies, casseroles (I'm afraid I'm not a baker. What else does a baker bake?). I am a doctor. I practice medicine.

Our stories are, of course, much more complex; and cultural story is exponentially more complicated. The one word answer is only to get the ball rolling. I'm a father—I take care of my children. I'm a grandfather. (We'll talk about relationships in the next section, and about sages when we get to retirement and legacies.) I'm a husband, a friend, a writer, a speaker. Our personal identities are built on or influenced by familial and cultural stimuli, by academic teachings, by media projections and governmental rules and definitions, plus, plus, plus… We are the story of ourselves, a composite of a million inputs. As our 'diet' changes, our story changes; as our story changes our self-image changes; as our self-image changes so too does the resultant effects—that is, our behavior changes. The story we tell ourselves of ourselves has ramifications. Trash in, trash out. Skewed data in, inappropriate behavior out. Positive, productive, accurate, vital honest input… you get the idea.

What happens if the culture in which we live spews forth stories and images of traditional men being incompetent bumblers, or being apes, or being perverts? What if the images continue for generations? You might be thinking, "That's ridiculous! This is too complex a situation for it to have any effect." But isn't this parallel to what the women's movement fought so hard against—the whole idea of the June Cleaver supportive wife and stay-at-home mom? Didn't they fight for the concept that women can do anything that men can do? Didn't they—and quite successfully—convince generations of girls and young women that they were as capable, or more capable, than boys? Then why would anyone think that "putting boys in their place," or building "more sensitive (feminine) males," would not have an impact on male development? We'll look at the specifics of this in the section Men In Crisis. Here I want to establish the framework for that and other discussions.

We are in a time of change in the cultural definition of masculinity, a period in which maleness is being projected as no longer acceptable. When men or boys were projected as strong, independent, and responsible citizens their behavior tended to emulate those characteristics. If men are now shown as powerless, foolish, careless clods those characteristics too will be copied, won't they? Of course there are many factors influencing each individual, yet the more we portray men as bumblers and incompetents, the more bumbling and incompetence we should expect to see. If men internalize these skewed and altered images of themselves, their self-image changes; consequently their behavior reflects the change. They become the studio gofer.

An example: You undoubtedly have heard the old saw, "Big boys don't cry." We've mentioned this earlier when talking about scouts and hatchets and bonding; we've talked about it sometimes being inappropriate—particularly with very young boys. And I've mentioned that in my practice many men have been reduced to tears by pain or by the anguish of projecting the impact a particular diagnosis will have on them and their families. But let's look at this in the light of biological identity—of maleness.

Dr. Will Courtney, PhD, author of *Dying To Be Men*, [described as a powerful, effective voice about... the changing roles of fathers, boys and men] states that "There is a very powerful cultural myth in our society that men simply don't get depressed. What that tells men is that they *shouldn't get* depressed—or at least, not express it. And so they don't. They're more likely than women to try to hide their depression or talk themselves out of it—which only worsens it." I would not dispute much of Dr. Courtney's words, but I would challenge the blanket clause, "which only makes it worse."

Depression may be damaging to some men in some circumstances; and clinical depression may be severe and can lead to suicide. That cannot and should not be dismissed. But where does the concept that men are exempt from depression come from in the first place. If this is a cultural myth, how did it come about? Certainly it is at least as old as Sparta, as the Roman Legions. Certainly it is trans-generational and transcultural. Of course big boys cry! Of course men get depressed. But there may be valid reasons why their crying or whimpering has been restrained; why their depression often goes unexpressed. [We will not get into the over-usage of anti-depressant drugs in our culture, or the studies showing spontaneous improvement over time as a factor equal to or more effective than drug therapy. I do however encourage the reader to research those factors.]

Fettering open displays of tears or melancholy serves cultural purposes—foisting upon men the greater responsibility of meeting their biological imperatives as providers and protectors. What meaning does that have? What effects ensue? Is responsibility, as we've previously stated, a confirmation of self-worth? What happens to male emotions and male behavior when a man's self-image tells him he is worthless? [Or powerless, the fertile fields from which gangs recruit by offering potency through violence and organized numbers?] I would postulate that being responsible, that having one's self-worth confirmed, and thus feeling worthwhile, contributes greatly to reducing depression. Further, teaching young boys that big boys don't cry protects them from the devastating effects of meaninglessness, and helps them build stronger senses of self-worth based upon their growing abilities to meet their biological instincts.

Herbert Hendon and Ann Pollinger Haas in *Wounds of War: The Psychological Aftermath of Combat in Vietnam* explain how positive cultural images both insulate veterans from the symptoms of Post-Traumatic Stress Disorder (PTSD), and, more importantly, prepares or predisposes soldiers *before* combat for proper action during battle which essentially creates circumstances in which PTSD is less likely to develop. Telling a kid to "Suck it up," or a guy to "Drive on!" may be the kindest comment you ever make.

Let's get back to *story* for a moment—to personal self-image or identity, and to ambient cultural story. There many factors influencing how one sees oneself or one's group, one's community, one's nation, the world. Modern, effective, and seemingly pervasive factors include the new media—internet, cell phones, cable channels and all the digital variations—along with the computerization and fractionalizing of marketing. Recently I was discussing gender identity with a close friend, Psychologist Dr. Robert F. Reynolds, Ph. D, Clinical Director of The Reynolds Clinic. I mentioned that I'd read of California's list on state forms of something like forty seven gender-identity options, and of how technology has played a role in the growing strength of once marginalized segments of society. Dr. Reynolds pointed out that "the rise of the internet has given validation to people who thought they were the only ones who thought or acted in a certain way. It has emboldened and empowered groups from which we never before would have heard, but they are now coalescing. For better or for worse they get validation. It helps give them confidence. And they get some attention for that. Before too long you have something like a movement."

Dr. Reynolds continued, "I was watching TV the other day. There now is a whole TV show on a hospital that specializes in sex change operations. It's a cable show. Very well done. It tracks the lives of people who have decided to do this, and gives you an insight into why they've made the decision. Very powerful. This wouldn't have happened ten or fifteen years ago. But it's happened now because of the expansion of the internet, and the expansion of cable TV. There are now more places for people who have had no voice to find a voice."

Yes there are. Dr. Reynolds is absolutely correct. But it raised in me questions about validity and voice. I thought about Einstein's remark about possibilities being limited by reality. The fact that on-line communities give validation to splinter groups—be they gender identity, religious, political fringe movements, or terrorists—does not mean the beliefs of those groups are rational, justifiable or legitimate. If everyone in a group comes to believe that up is down, that does not mean up is down, it means the group is standing on its collective head. Consensus is not validation of reality; it is merely a display of group-think. It is the story a group convinces itself is reality, and that story helps establish the identity of the group and the self-image of the group's members. Forty seven gender-identities, of course, are not the same as forty seven genders.

Still, recall that behavior tends to be consistent with self-image. Validation of gender-identity number forty-seven means someone's behavior will reflect that fantasy.

Much worse is when validation of identity is the product of a group that systematically and consistently denounces outside groups. Think bad behavior. Think the KKK, ACORN, or ISIS. Individuals who identify with these groups believe their worldview is correct; that their behavior is justified. What has to change for their behavior to change is their worldview and self-image.

Niche marketing reinforces individual and group self-image. There is tremendous power in the computing ability which identifies individuals with specific characteristics, and marketers of all kinds take full advantage of this technical attribute. It makes no difference if the *product* being marketed is a book about gardening or a political or social agenda, marketers want to reach *like-minded* people who will buy, or buy into, their product. Go to a progressive or conservative website, or a transgender or gun rights website; sign up for their newsletter. Within a week see how many other like-minded sites pop up on your display screen. The Cookie Monster cannot eat the cookies quickly enough for you to avoid this. It is a very effective marketing technique; one which most of us voluntarily and gladly accept. Why target foodies with mountain climbing gear, Republicans with progressive social programs, or Socialists with want ads? But there are consequences, side effects if you will, of niche marketing. It abets the fragmentation of society; it reinforces the division of the country into specific, separate segments with disparate world views. Niche marketing is a matter of preaching to the choir, of fortifying existing beliefs and identities. But it also destroys the universal touch points a society needs to be cohesive. The more one identifies with a point of view, the more one is apt to seek out confirmation of that view—the audiences for Chris Mathews or Rush Limbaugh don't much overlap. Without universal elements culture becomes fractionalizes, Balkanized. When this happens, alienation of one group from the next follows, and closely behind alienation are anger, aggression and xenophobia. We see it in Ferguson.

Conclusions

We have been painting this picture of manhood as it was, and manhood as it is becoming; and the consequences of what's happening because of that shift. As masculine values have been attacked, denounced and devalued we are left with this new society with new and ever-deepening problems.

Our earlier words on risk aversion, teasing, drinking, self-sufficiency, independence and competence were not idle chatter.

We've talked about how men behave, how they react to the world, how they misbehave, and how their role in society has been changing. That role, at any point in time and in any culture is a product of cultural story working on and within the biological mechanism. Boys and men can be taught to believe almost anything, can be lead to be almost anything--good or evil, or can be taught and lead to be almost nothing. When it comes to boys and young men, they are templates that evolve into their biologic role best if coached wisely.

The *story* paradigm can be used to forecast the behavior of not just individuals but also of groups and cultures. Behavior, individually or culturally, is consistent with self-image. Self-image is built on all the inputs and experiences that we, individually or culturally, internalize. New behaviors reflect new input. If cultural images of men and masculinity change, and if men internalize these new, skewed and altered images, their self-image changes. If their self-image changes, their behaviors change. Said another way, this explains why and how the skewing of reality for political correctness, political ploy, profit, or power destroys honest social interaction and results in the kind of messes we see around us today.

We mentioned stick-ball bats and other *risky* behaviors. Maybe boys don't play stick-ball anymore because they might get hurt or hurt someone else. When my friend mentioned his stick-ball bat breaking, I chuckled. I actually had that happen to me. I didn't stab myself. I went around and whacked the kid next to me. But nobody said, "Don't play stick ball." The other kid's folks probably never heard about it; and nobody thought about suing the broom handle company. The culture has changed. I do not believe these changes are good, at least not for the development of boys into men.

It goes back to self-reliance and accountability, or at least it should, shouldn't it? But that seems to be disappearing. Removing responsibility removes meaning from life. Removing from men the need or the ability to provide and protect, or separating those imperatives from to procreate, produces a shallowness, a void, which in turn invites irresponsible behavior. Life becomes free to become frivolous or evil. The old adage, *idle hands are the devil's workshop*, seems appropriate.

We evolved as a civilization based upon our hormonal roles, and those roles evolved genetically and biologically. We can be coached into any role that seems era-appropriate. Current American social influencers should be aware of that, and of the fact they might get exactly what they are wishing for. We seem to be developing a group of boys who are merely developing into older boys. If boys don't become men (or girls don't become women) then they are always counting on the adult or the authority figure to take care of them. Ultimately government becomes the supreme authority figure, the adult nanny that establishes regulations and metes our punishments.

Traditional values were built upon our biological make-up; upon the biological imperatives to provide and to protect. Denying those imperatives denies the humanity of men. The ramifications of that denial are the creation of a mishmash of new values which leaves today's young males with a confused definition of what it means to be a man.

That's why I think the world, if not going to hell in a hand basket, is at least in serious trouble. Much of the younger generation has not been raised to do traditional male things. One of those things is being the protector. As we get older we depend upon our sons or other young men to protect us. If they don't know what that entails, what's going to happen?

Dr. Jeffrey Rabuffo

PART III: Relationships

I grew up in New York City. I remember sitting with my father while Mayor Fiorello LaGuardia read the comic over the radio during the newspaper strike. But mostly I remember being outside, away from the house, away from authority figures. If group-think influenced us, the group was small, our closest friends; and physically there, not there by digital representation. That's how it used to be. Of course we had the bases and biases of our families and our schools, but outside we learned to relate to others in an almost freelance fashion.

When we came home from school we'd walk three blocks down to the diamond and we'd play baseball, or we go out in the street with a broom handle and a pink Spaulding ball and play stickball. Or maybe we would play Stoopball where you would take that same pink Spaulding ball and bounce it off the steps. How many bounces you got before someone caught it determined if it was a single, a double, a triple, et cetera. I once tried out for a basketball team. I missed a jump shot and it was, "That's it, Kid. Beat it."

Much later, when I was a young dad we relocated to a Connecticut suburb, and there was T-ball. I had no clue. My wife said, "They're having sign-ups for T-ball." I said, "What's that?" She had to explain it to me. I asked, "Why would anyone want to do that?" The whole idea of structured sports was foreign to me. I was a great baseball fan. I loved the Brooklyn Dodgers. But for children, I didn't get it. I remember some of the other fathers saying, "You gotta go down and watch the tryouts." "Tryouts?!" I was baffled. It took me a while to understand this was a whole different world. Pretty soon there were constant games or meets or some other functions. Recently I discussed this with some friends. One tells a similar story, but he grew up in a Connecticut suburb, so it wasn't so much the place as it was the time. Times had changed. Freelance relationships seemed a thing of the past. Here's what he told me:

When I came home from school I went out and delivered newspapers. It was really my brother's route. He was older than me, but I started delivering part of the route the summer I turned eight. As soon as we'd finish delivering we'd go up to the school grounds. I didn't play much baseball, but we played football all the time. And other things—kickball, red rover, tag. Sometimes we just wrestled on the grass. What was new to me with my kids was the degree of organization of sports and all the other activities. My kids got into soccer, two stayed with it through high school. One didn't. He kind of revolted against the system; got into hiking, climbing, biking and kayaking with a few like-minded friends. But the level of organization of sports for the other two changed our family dynamic. There is no doubt that they learned perseverance and self-discipline, sportsmanship and teamwork. I don't second guess the value of those lessons. But it seemed like the sport-of-the-day and the team-of-the-moment became more important than the family. Still, we were lucky because the area was wooded and when they weren't at practice or at a game they were outside. They had that free time to do things, to explore, to imagine, to find their limits.

In earlier sections we spoke about how society has changed, and how the role of men has been altered. Those changes have led to changes in life-style, in self-image, in relationships and in meaningfulness. Some of the changes have been for the better, some for the worse; some have led to more and better sex, some to sexless marriages; some to closer families, some to a complete breakdown in the family structure. Society has fragmented; parts work for some, other parts are a total mess. So, how do men relate to others: to other men, to women, to elders, to kids? What's basic? What's changed? What's better? What's worse? What's veneer? What's real? What do men consider important? How have relationships changed over the past half century? Where to start: perhaps with fathers and families, then on to wives, lovers, or significant others?

We are our father's sons; and we are our sons' fathers. What could be simpler? Our fathers are our first heroes. Boys want to emulate their dads. First of all, dad is huge. When you weigh twenty or thirty pounds and are just learning to crawl, walk and run, dad can do anything. He can climb stairs. He can open doors and go outside. And he's so strong. He can lift us up and toss us about and catch us… scaring the shit out of us yet making us giggle like he's a one-man amusement park. We not only want to emulate him, we have a need to emulate him. If he's angry, that really scares the shit out of us.

In some traditional cultures kids are seldom disciplined. There is an old Khmer precept that says if you want your children to behave in a certain manner, act that way and they will follow you. I have friends that practiced this; who seldom or never used any sort of Puritanical discipline, but who worked hard on how they behaved. Their kids grew up to be disciplined adults. With my kids I was the disciplinarian. At times I was pretty strict because I thought it was the right thing to do. We had some spankings, just like my dad would do if I got out of hand. My kids also grew up to be disciplined adults, but when I would see my sons discipline their sons, I would cringe. I didn't like that. I *really* didn't like that. I'm still not certain what's the best approach; but note, in both cases, a loving dad is there.

If he's not there, there is a hole in our existence. Over my lifetime there has been a lot of talk about the sins of the father being visited upon the son. There has been much less said or written about the attributes of the father and the forefathers being inherited by the sons.

I think some elements of the relationships between fathers and sons have changed for the better. One patient told me, "When my kids were small, I was too serious. My brother, more of a card than me, would come over, sit on the floor with the kids, dump the laundry basket on his head, and have all of them laughing. He was Uncle Fun. But I couldn't do that with my kids. I do it now with my grandson."

But going back to when I was growing up, my father was the protector and the guardian. And he was the disciplinarian. Mom deferred consequences to dad: "Wait until your father gets home. Then you're going to get it!" I think this was the norm for those times, and because of it boys learned not to share their thoughts or feelings with the old man. If they shared them with anyone, they shared them with their mothers. Still, generally, boys of my generation were not raised to share their emotions with anyone. It was kind of a John Wayne or Daniel Boone or stoic Indian chief thing.

That's changed. I think the relationships that many fathers and sons have today are a lot better. The disciplinary tyrant has been replaced by the mentor. Boys are more apt to share their hopes and fears; and as they get older sons are more likely to listen to advice from dear old dad. That didn't exist decades ago to the extent it exists today. Dads respect sons; sons, in turn, respect dads. This, of course, assumes that there is a father in the household. We'll get to that shortly.

It also assumes the best case scenarios. Like characteristics, relationships span a broad spectrum—in this case from the worst despot to the most guileless pushover. I've had patients where dad was "too close" or "too much in the son's head" and that set off competition and resentment. Dad built a multi-million dollar business, gave it to his adult son, wanted to stay on as a consultant and wanted to continue telling the son not only what to do but also how he should think about what he was doing. The son didn't want any part of it. Instead of saying, "Gee, here's a guy who created this company from scratch, he has a lot to say," the son wanted to take over, run the business as he saw best, maybe modernize the structure and traditions of the venture. Or he wanted out. To dad, maintaining what he had built was more important than recognizing his son as a responsible man. To the son, dad was still the guy tossing him around, scaring the shit out of him; but he wasn't giggling anymore.

Mentor or disciplinarian, raising kids is a conundrum, and the style we use affects our relationships. There is a natural rivalry between fathers and sons; just as there is the potential for a natural alliance. Now that it is more socially acceptable for men to reveal their emotions, the competitions may be diminishing and the alliances strengthening. "More socially acceptable… to reveal their emotions" is not the same as saying "Big boys should cry." We are not talking about whimpering. We are talking about revealing hopes, aspirations and fears, and making sound decisions using both the younger man's enthusiasm and the older man's experiences. Dad & Sons become a team. Let mom be the disciplinarian!

Back to schools and sports teams and organizational time: I remember those days when I was in private practice. There were just two of us, so I was on call every other night and every other weekend; but I was beginning to recognize the importance of the games to the kids. As doctors we didn't yet have beepers or cell phones, so if I went to the school my only access was via the public telephone in the school. We had a phone exchange. I'd call up and say, "I'm going to such-and-such school, and I'll check in every half hour." One time I went to check-in and the school was locked. I panicked. I was very anal about being available. So I left and went home. A lot of my inability to attend the kid's games was because there was no communication. When we got beepers you still had to get to a phone. Eventually we got cell phones, but that came long after that stage of my family life. I feel bad that I wasn't able to do more of it, to be at more games, to cheer the kids on. It was the job. That guilt, for me and for many guys like me, is one of the elements enabling recent changes in social dynamics, as it keeps us from objecting to changes we, if we consider them at all, might challenge.

When the kids were in high school I tried to keep family time sacred. We used to ski. On Friday nights we would pack up and go… except the kids had a basketball game. So we'd have to wait until 9:00 o'clock before we could go. Once I said to the coach, "Why don't you have the games on Thursday, because this really screws up the family weekend." He said, "We don't want to have them on a school night." I said, "Bullshit! You have them on Tuesdays." That got me nowhere. It was an interesting time.

Now my middle boy coaches my grandson's basketball team; my oldest boy coaches track. They had been on those teams in high school. I'm still of two minds. There is the discipline that kids learn from playing organized sports, and I think that that's excellent. Yet if it is overdone… well, I keep coming back to when I was young. Being out all the time, on your own all the time—unstructured time, you develop a different attitude towards people, different trusts and fears, different ego-boundaries. I think one becomes more of a free thinker. Outside of school and church there was very little that was regimented while we were growing up. Even when we went to the school grounds, as kids we picked our teams ourselves. We made up any new rules we wanted; changed the game to be whatever we wanted.

I think of a friend's grandson who at three months old was already in daycare. So from that age, like many children today, he was in an institution. It might be a loving, very competent and nice facility, but it is still an institution. For those of us in our generation, it started later. None of us started school until five years old. Our family values were pretty well established if not completely firm. Now kids start in daycare, then go to pre-school or Head Start, then they're in school. And school goes until they're seventeen, or maybe with college until they're twenty one or twenty two. To the point that they become young adults they have known nothing but institutional oversight. I'm not sure how well that's working. If you think about it, the number of kids that drop out of high school before they graduate is 8.1%. The figure is higher for boys (9.1%) than girls (7.0%), and higher amongst minorities of both genders. The most concerning figures, however, are: the large city dropout rate is 41%; 75% of street crime in the U.S. is committed by dropouts; and 60% of black males who drop out of high school spend time in prison. We are failing these children, these boys, and we are failing ourselves; but the answer is not to increase the institutionalization (more programs) of society. That will only further disrupt the relationship between generations, between fathers and sons, between Uncle Fun and his nephews; and likely will make matters worse. Institutions sort people by age. Clustered same-age groups which do not learn the wisdom of yore establish their own social hierarchies based upon the strongest alpha male—call it Lord Of The Flies-syndrome, if you'd like.

Obviously I think the kids today are subjected to too much organization; too much institutionalization. So I ask, what have been the effects of the reduction of family time caused by organized school functions, by the elevation of the importance of school and other organizations over the importance of family? What effect does that have on boys; on their relationships with their fathers, with other men, with the women who come into their lives?

Sometimes kids are foisted into before- and after-school programs because both parents are working long hours just to pay taxes and make ends meet, or because it is considered safer than allowing them to be on the streets or home alone. I understand the enigmas of feeling one must choose for their children highly structured lives, particularly in the inner city. The attitude is not unknown in the suburbs. I had that same conversation with my son. I wanted to come down to see the grandchildren, but it was, "Well, we've got soccer... or dance... or the activity du jour." I said to him, "Why are they in all this stuff?" He said, "To keep them safe. To keep them out of trouble. It keeps them away from bad people."

In the late 1940s in Brooklyn I used to walk five blocks to school; back home at lunchtime, back to school. That's just how it was. In the name of security, our kids and grandkids are all in highly-structured environments. Highly-structured lives does not equal highly-structured thinking or disciplined behavior. The codes of conduct that youth used to learn—perhaps religious, perhaps academic, perhaps the Boy Scout Promise—seem generally to have fallen into disfavor.

In the name of security we are all under surveillance. What does that do to our self-image, to our feelings of trust in each other, and to our confidence? What are we losing because of structure? I think independence; maybe self-reliance. You don't have to rely upon yourself because someone else is responsible for you; for your actions. Maybe innovation, too, is being lost because you don't have to come up with anything on your own. It used to be parents would say "Go out and play," and kids went out and figured out something to do. I think that freedom to discover oneself is being lost in our society; lost on today's kids. They're not coddled, but they are either continuously directed on what to do, or they're given something to entertain them and consume their time.

Children become imprinted with certain modes of behavior. A young boy's eyes are always watching, his ears always listening. His brain is like a sponge soaking up the water of whatever river he is in. The behaviors he sees, hears, and senses become his norm. The norms young boys are seeing today are not the norms young boys saw twenty years ago, or forty years ago. Society is working from new norms. Perhaps today, while we are seeing more and more government intervention—it's not necessarily malicious intervention, it's what people have come to expect—but perhaps that's the base of what's happening in our culture. People and politician—maybe they do the things they do because that's what they've come to expect from each other and from themselves.

I think my generation was the last one that, on whole, took care of itself. Today you don't hear any politicians saying, "Take care of yourself," or "Ask not what your country can do for you..." That extends to health care. We'll get to that in later sections. For now just one point—many people don't feel responsible for taking care of themselves. They might take care of themselves, they might eat right, but they don't say, "My health is *my* responsibility." It is more as if they are saying, "There is a whole system out there—hospitals and emergency rooms and insurance companies—and that's where the responsibility for my health care lies."

I don't know if this is rooted in kindergarten play, but the more control our institutions exert upon our children, the more our children are open to, or accepting of, institutional or governmental oversight in their lives. The more people accept or relate to institutions, the less need they have to relate to individuals. Keeping your doctor isn't as important as having an omnipresent, soulless medical complex. Raising your child isn't as important as is letting a village raise that same child. To me, these are unacceptable tradeoff.

A kid goes to breakfast at school, goes through school, has an organized after-school program, has another organized activity, then he goes home. Parents are thinking I have to do this because this is the only way to keep him safe. But if you think about long term, unintended ramifications… of course you don't want them to become gang bangers, but kids revolt against a "nanny" existences if they're controlled from the time they rise to the time they go back to sleep. Or they become numb. Remember: 41% of students in large cities drop out of high school. School has been devalued because the individual has been in school almost continuously since birth. [In the section Boys In Crisis we'll look at what has changed in the schools over the past half century that has negatively impacted boys.] School is not seen as a privilege, not as a right, not even as something mommy and daddy work hard to provide. It is felt as a given. With too many of the kids that have always been cared for, one of two things happens: either they're seeing school as irrelevant in their lives and they dropout because they're rebelling, or they leave school because it does not occur to them that they will not be taken care of. Being cared for is an expectation. This *need* may make kids *more* susceptible to the lure of gangs. And not having mom and dad around, for whatever reason, doesn't help deepen family relationships, does it?

My friend with the paper route was the fourth of four children in his family. He likes to say that because of the others, he was raised on a principle that gave him a wonderful advantage in life—he calls it *benign neglect.* "Benign neglect," he says, "is under-utilized. It allows people to be more creative, more innovative. It lets them find out who they are." I love the concept... kind of a *Catcher In The Rye* concept where the protectors or guardians remain in the treeline surrounding the field and only interfere (come in to save the day) if absolutely necessary.

M. Scott Peck, in *The Road Less Traveled*, spoke of a similar concept. In a section titled *Self-Sacrifice* he writes of a father, a minister, who could not understand why, after giving his wife and two sons "everything," she was suffering from chronic depression and his boys had dropped out of college and were living at home receiving psychiatric attention. "I do everything in my power to take care of them and their problems," he's quoted as saying. In his consternation he then asks, "...what else am I to do? I love them and have too much compassion not to take care of them." Peck discusses the notion that real love includes "...that not giving at the right time is more compassionate than giving at the wrong time, and that fostering independence is more loving than taking care of people who could otherwise take care of themselves." He goes on to say that, in his desire to 'love' them, the minister's "injudicious giving and destructive nurturing" essentially had infantilized his family.

In my own neighborhood I saw the detrimental effects of raising children in such a way that they never had to worry about making decisions or suffering consequences of their own actions. Most of those kids became misfits and are now unable to take care of themselves. I raise my children quite differently, made them accountable for their actions and encouraged them to try and figure things out for themselves.

Whether it is an institution or a family gone awry independence and self-sufficiency suffer. Where growing up in a super-structured environment promotes *groupthink* and flimsy ego boundaries (eventually leading to feelings of worthlessness and depression, and possibly to suicide and a host of other tragedies), benign neglect—I prefer the term *constructive neglect*— promotes the exact opposite. With super-structure, compared to the person who has gone out and found out all these things on his or her own, children don't find out who they are or what limits they have—or more importantly, what limits they don't have. And meaningfulness is lost.

So, what effect has the new structured environment had on the men who were raised in this environment? How has it affected their marriages or other relationships with the women in their lives? What are the long term social ramifications—that means relationships—on everyone living from birth to death within the rigid structure of the Borg Collective?

Attraction: Sex, Love, Marriage, Hope, and the Need for Permanency

Paraphrasing Leo Tolstoy's opening line in *Anna Karenina*: All happy marriages are like one another; each unhappy marriage is unhappy in its own way. More than one hundred and thirty five years since the Russian master penned that line, the essence of his words still resonate. Tolstoy used the words families/family where I've inserted marriages/marriage. In the wake of our changing culture, perhaps the word marriage should be replaced with relationship, but that term is too broad for this section, so understand that in this section when we say marriage we are including all the various types of permanent and semi-permanent, religiously-sanctioned and civil, co-habitations.

"Hey Doc, how come I can't get my wife to have sex with me?" As mentioned earlier, because the guys know I'm a urologist, I heard this in the gym all the time. "Hey Doc, is there anything I can do to get my wife… She's always too tired or too this or too that." I would also hear this in my practice. This is a very common problem in marriage; maybe the most common problem. The sexy doll we married just doesn't seem to be interested. That's disturbing for guys. Most guys really love their wives. They feel rejected. They love their families. They feel lost. They're not screw offs or screw ups. We know that everybody has a need for emotional intimacy. That's a psychological given. Everybody needs that. It's as basic as food. If you're not eating at home, you still need food.

What attracts men? What reels us in? There are a lot of fish in the sea, but is there one special person, one soul mate, out there for you? It seems that there is a biological element to whom we choose as a mate. Some psychologists tell us it's all based on our mothers—that the imprinting of newborns is so powerful we "marry our mothers." That may have some validity. What we can say with more surety is that the perfect person for any individual is based upon childhood experiences. A boy goes from an attachment to his mother to an attachment to *a girl*. Who you're attracted to, according to various studies, is based upon experiences when you were an infant and a kid. So the attractions we feel, the attractions that drive us, have their roots in imprinted experiences from infancy; and those experiences, on whole, have been changing.

In a conversation with a friend, he said to me, "As you were talking about who catches our eye, I was thinking about how I react. Who am I attracted to? Or what physical characteristics make me zoom in on a chick? And I know, with me, it's virtually invariable. To me, the most attractive women have a very distinct face-shape. Yeah, I like tits and legs and ass, but somehow the face-shape is more important than those features. If she's a blue-eyed brunette with that face-shape, the attraction is higher; but a blue-eyed brunette with a different face-shape I'm probably not finding her attractive at all. I mean this as in, 'Do I want to get to know her on a deeper-level?' basis. I find African and Asian women with that face-shape more attractive than blue-eyed brunettes with different features. If I'm looking through a magazine that woman catches my eye. It's immediate. I've been trying to figure it out. It's not even the whole face. I think it's the curve of the cheek down to the jaw. Someone said to me, 'When you're an infant that's the part of your Mom's face that you see when she's holding you.' Maybe that's it. There is nothing conscious about it. And to make it even more weird, I immediately bestow all sorts of positive attributes on her. I know I do it. I've caught myself doing it. But I can't help it."

Guys are always talking about what attracts them to women. "Man, look at the rack on that one!" or "Oooo! Great legs!" But that's a different level of attraction. That's immediate sexual attraction without thought of long-term mate attraction. A smooth complexion may subconsciously indicate health, a thin waist may indicate availability; but the sexiest thing on a woman, and I think this is more universal than most guys will admit, is her smile. If a woman smiles at you it is a totally different experience than if that same woman is not smiling. I read somewhere that one of the better aphrodisiacs for a guy is a woman who wants to make love to him. If some woman that you find attractive smiles at you, the message is, 'She wants me,' or at least 'She's willing to check me out.' How disappointed we are when we find out that she's only being polite, or only wants to be friends, or—horrors—only wants us to buy something she's selling! How thrilled we are when it leads to a first kiss.

That Kiss! That Kiss! Upper Persuasion for Lower Invasion...

Oh, to report this seems, at first, disappointing, almost cruel. Kissing didn't start out as upper persuasion for lower invasion, but as a way to share germs and build immunity. Yes, swapping spit has a biological function. It likely originated with moms and maybe dads feeding infants pre-chewed food [don't gag—visualize birds feeding their brood in the nest]. This food was not only soft and more easily swallowed, but it contained probiotics and other good germs from mom or dad which aided in the maturation of baby's digestive system. Someplace along the line mouth-to-mouth contact took on additional meaning, and the act became tied up with bonding hormones and circuitry.

On his website, Dr. Joseph M. Mercola tells us that kissing relieves stress, releases epinephrine (which lowers LDL cholesterol and dilates blood vessels thus lowering blood pressure), alleviates pain, washes away teeth plaque thus preventing cavities, burns calories, increases self-esteem, tones facial muscles, and releases serotonin, dopamine and oxytocin strengthening the bonding circuitry in one's brain. "...sex, kissing, or even hugging, these forms of affection have primal, biological roots that impact our bodies, typically in a beneficial way."

And kissing feels good. With the right person it tastes good. The taste of a kiss has amazing ramifications on short-term and long-term attraction. When the bioactive testosterone in a man's saliva is absorbed through the mucous membranes in a woman's mouth, it activates the sexual-arousal centers in her brain. Now we're getting someplace—hopefully beyond second base.

"Saliva contains molecules from all the glands and organs in the body," Dr. Louann Brizendine points out. "So a French kiss serves up our signature flavor... [passing on] information about each other's health and genes..." These amazing machines that our human bodies are have built-in intelligence far beyond what most of us realize. "If [a woman's] genes [are] too similar to [a man's] and the kiss taste[s] sour, it could [be] a sexual deal-breaker."

Dang! The body knows more than what the brain recognizes. Maybe Tic Tacs or Altoids to the rescue! Aaahh… unfortunately, no. However, if a woman is on daily oral birth-control pills her sensitivity to acrid breath, and thus her selectivity, is reduced. There might be a deal in here after all! In all seriousness this has profound ramifications which we will explore in the section on the women's movement and the sexual revolution.

The Elderly Couple

Allow me to jump to the other end of life, to successful long-term marriages, because there are patterns and lessons here which we should keep in mind. We'll come back to today's struggling relationships and the changing role of men in a moment.

One of the most admirable characteristics of patients I cared for was the long marriages of the most elderly. I loved seeing these people. When they married there was no question it was for life. They each had a role to fulfill. In my office the woman was often referred to as "Mother." She had provided food and cooking and clothes and all the other household support functions so the guy could go out and work and earn a salary to financially support that same household. For decades he came home with filthy clothes. For decades she told him to take them off and she'd wash them. These couples would sit next to each other in my office; they frequently would hold hands; and they would answer questions for each other. She'd say, "Oh, Dad does this," or he'd say, "Mother takes that medicine." Usually one of them would bring their little package of medications, accompanied by a list of these medications written in a very shaky hand. They always acted like they had always been together, like they were married. I never once heard one say, "I'm working harder than you," or "I worked more than you." I think they each knew their roles, and they lived them without resentment.

I was also always struck with the admiration and care they showed toward each other. They would help each other get undressed and dressed, and one of them always took notes for the benefit of the other so they would remember what I said. They gave each other allowance for their infirmities. Their patience with each other was godlike. It was always a pleasure to see the concern and happiness expressed between them.

Every once in a while one would show up at the office without the other. He or she would tearfully tell me that his or her spouse had died. Most of the time the survivor was terribly upset, and very depressed. If an adult child came to the office, he would express concern about the health of the remaining parent. More often than not the second half of the couple would pass away a short time after the first had died. When the patient came in after the death of the spouse I always tried to point out how lucky they were to have had a spouse that they were together with for 50 or 60 years. I would also point out that I didn't see such long relationships anymore. I think that part made me the saddest.

I once asked an elderly couple who had been married 68 years what was their secret. The wife, her long white hair tied up in the bun, was sitting in a chair in the office with her hands resting on a cane. She was rocking back-and-forth just to help her pass the time. When I asked her that question she stopped, shrugged, looked up at me and said, "Just stick around, I guess." This wasn't fatalism. It wasn't resignation. These people long ago had made a commitment to each other. They had assisted each other throughout their lives, and apparently agreed to different complimentary roles in their marriage. I never saw them bicker or insult each other. That just didn't seem to happen. They were polite, concerned and loving towards each other. For me they were iconic.

I think their expectations were perhaps more realistic than those of young couples today. Society changed. Women feel—true or not—more empowered, or more entitled to a greater say. In my experience the change in society occurred with the invention of the birth control pill. Women were no longer relegated to being "just" mothers, or nurses or school teachers. There was, as we will see, a whole new world that opened up to them.

Today: Built on Yesterday's Smiles and Yesterday's Scars

I have been married—twice. I've learned a few lessons along the way. I've absorbed others, almost as if by osmosis—from my patients, from guys in the gym, and from countless talks with friends. Every individual brings to a marriage the best and the worst of his or her family, his or her upbringing. The cumulative weight of past smiles and scars, triumphs and terrors heavily influences intimacy, or the lack thereof. No matter the outcome of a relationship, when it has ceased, we are biologically programmed to rejuvenate romance. Men need intimacy. Sex is the way we express our emotions. Yet there are a whole lot of other factors that play a role in the intimate relationship between a man and a woman which have everything and almost nothing to do with sex. Unless you're both put together in a way that allows you to be mentally and emotionally close to others, you're going to have problems in relationships.

Family upbringing can imprint individuals with either the sense that touch and closeness are desirable, or are unpleasant. In some families, and in many institutional settings, closeness is barely in their social vocabulary. When one is raised thusly, that's how one acts, that's how one thinks, that's what he or she brings to their marriage. That was foreign to me—having grown up in an Italian-American family where touch, hugs, caresses, and pinches of the cheek were the norm. It wasn't just the Italians in the neighborhood; that seemed to be the norm too of all the different ethnicities. To come across coolness, aloofness, or the habit of individual family members isolating themselves within a home, was an oddity we generally dismissed.

In practice I was exposed to a plethora of *other* scenarios and situations. I had a patient whose wife had grown up in a military/CIA family. Prior to her marriage she had lived all over the world—from Japan to Formosa (Taiwan) to Europe to Washington. Think of her folks as a reserved Mr. & Mrs. Smith but without the smiles of Angelina or Brad. I heard the story about how she grew up, about how she was never allowed to bring friends into the house. In her youth she evidently never established a long-lasting relationship with anybody. It affected their marriage, and it was affecting my patient.

I think these are issues that few people talk about before marriage. When everyone is smiling and the pheromones are wafting, young men generally don't sit down and analyze: Is she capable of being close? Does she establish good intimate relationships? The questions instead might be: Is she going to work when we're married? Are we going to have kids? Whose house are we going to go to the first Christmas, her family's or mine? Is she ready to get married, ready to settle down, because she's partied enough? We don't even ask if the sex is going to go on forever. Maybe get steamier? We just assume.

That, at least, seems to be the extent of most guys thinking. From talking to friends, guys in the gym, patients, I'm not sure any young guy has ever been very thoughtful about these issues until after he's found himself in the midst of them. Of course, by then he's no longer a young guy. If some psychologist had said to these guys, "We're here for the pre-marriage conference; is your fiancé capable of being close?" most likely they'd have said, "Huh?" If you grow up in a culture like the one many of us in my generation grew up in, being close and being around a lot of people was a given.

With many of the wives, apparently it's not.

One patient's wife was an alcoholic. In those days alcoholic connoted skid row bum, so people hid their addiction. She was not a bum. It turned out that both her parents were alcoholics, so she was kind of doomed from the beginning. As I read more and more trying to understand this situation, I found that one of the things with this personality type is they have a problem with intimacy. They can't get close, and alcohol is a way of dealing with it. Seldom does anyone raised in such a family ask, "How come we don't hug? How come we don't touch?" It's habitual. It's like being right-handed. If you grow up with no closeness, with no touch, it seems normal. That is then carried forward into future relationships.

At the time I had a friend who was going through similar difficulties in his marriage. I would call him and ask, "What is it? What is it that's driving the wedge between you two?" He finally came up with, "She's just not close to me. She wants her privacy. She'll barely stay in a room if I'm in it." It got so he'd go out to a party, pick someone up. That was how he fulfilled his need for emotional intimacy. That need is very real, and often it's not recognized or acknowledged as a human need. Guys, husbands, are demonized, picked on. It seems almost as if all women know this. You hear on the news, "General Jones had an affair," but you seldom hear, "Where was the wife in all of this? What was she like? What was her role?" The implication is, "There goes the testosterone again. That pig!" I think this is important.

In the '60s or '70s or even the early '80s we seldom used the term emotional intimacy, and less often held the concept that some people are not capable of it. I certainly did not think of it as a characteristic to be viewed on a broad spectrum continuum, and even though I was a physical guy, I was not thinking it was in the natural of men to express love and emotional intimacy via sex. But the more men I talked to and the more patients that complained about lack of intimacy, the more I realized the importance of the issue. The ability to be emotionally intimate varies greatly.

Many men have stories about dating after divorce. After being married twenty seven years, then divorcing, I began thinking, 'What kind of girl do I want?' I started dating, but I didn't like the feeling some women gave me—kind of like they wanted to 'latch on.' I was going out with this one girl and we're on our third date—we're having dinner—she goes, "So! Where is this relationship going?" I blurted out, "I was hoping to make it through dessert."

I finally decided I wanted someone who was good-looking, someone who had a good job, all the physical and mental stuff I thought was important. I met a hospital administrator who fit the criteria. She was well-bred, she was good-looking, she was pleasant, and she was a successful, competent professional. But there was something not quite right. I still don't know what it was. We spent quite a long time together, and even though I was becoming more and more uncomfortable, I was too stupid to say "No." I didn't know how to break it off.

She had a chip on her shoulder, an attitude she usually concealed, but that screamed, "I'm a woman, and I'm as good as any man." And she was. No one disputed that, especially not me. I loved the fact that she was a highly-competent and high-achieving woman. But if I talk about 'the girls' in the office, she'd say, 'The Women.' I'd say, "Why is it 'the women'?" She'd answer, "Because that's what you should say." I'd come back with, "That's not what they say. They refer to themselves as 'the girls in the office,' and refer to the doctors as 'the guys.' That's just the way we talk. It's not derogatory, not disrespectful, not anything negative." It got to the point where I'd say, "You know the UCONN women's basketball team? They call them the Lady Huskies. Why don't they call them the Women Huskies?" I would try to point out how inane were all these semantic gymnastics. This is before the term politically correct became commonplace. When we went out, I was the guy so I paid for all meals, and for everything else until finally I said, "Hey, wait a minute. If we're equal, then you're going to pay for half the meals, and you're going to pay for the gas to go on trips, and when we're sailing you're going to buy your own foul weather gear. We *are* equal, aren't we?" She didn't like that. Toward the end, when I went to kiss her I was never sure which side of the face to go to. It was clumsy. Perhaps I no longer tasted right. Eventually she told me she hated sailing. She had never said that before. Our relationship just petered out.

I was not feeling, "Thank God. Someone up there is looking out for me." I was feeling, "I'm done. I'm finished. I'm outta here." I was about to move to Boston when I met That Someone who knocked my socks off. It was like, DOINK! Blond. Blue-eyed. Warm. Fun. Our first date we stayed out all night. I don't know what that's all about. Likely my medial preoptic area flaring like a Roman candle.

As earlier mentioned, no matter how many bad marriages one has, people seem to still want a permanent relationship. Recall my young friend, the runner, who had met a wonderful woman, also a runner, at a Christmas party. Recall their encounter came after two failed marriages, and after he'd sworn off women forever. He is a microcosm of how this thing works. He was never going to see another woman again; wasn't even going to look; was going to ride his motorcycle off into the sunset. When he met her it took him about one minute… as he also had that DOINK! moment. Another friend, a real estate agent at the time, tells the story of holding an open house when the owner's sister came by, or as he described it, "The most beautiful women in the world walked into the living room and said, 'Hi.'" Within a week he told her (didn't ask) that he was going to marry her. She answered, "I know."

Mistakes: There Is No Errors and Omissions Insurance

We've been talking about the effects of family, the effects of upbringing, and the withdrawal of the female within the home; and we've attempted to connect the dots between upbringing and the lack of emotional intimacy. We've noted that emotional intimacy is the basis for the relationship between a man and a woman; and that all the rest are just add-ons. I think we've established that men need emotional intimacy and that touch and sex are the way men express their emotions. So what gets in the way? What causes her to withdraw her love; or what we interpret as her love? How can we turn her back on? Yup! We're back to: "Hey Doc, how come I can't get my wife to have sex with me?" Maybe it's antidepressants, maybe the Seven-Year Itch, maybe it's doing the dishes.

About 20 percent of all American women are on antidepressants. Antidepressants kill sex drive. There is a thriving industry selling mood stabilizers and happy pills, and another sizable industry attempting to counter the sex-killing side effects of those drugs. In the New York Times, Roni Caryn Rabin reported that "Over the past two decades, the use of antidepressants has skyrocketed. One in 10 Americans now takes an antidepressant medication; among women in their 40s and 50s, the figure is one in four." One in four! Twenty five percent! Are you sh*tting me?!

John M. Grohol, Psy. D., notes in an article in World Of Psychology, "In 2012, [antidepressants] accounted for more than half of the most-commonly prescribe psychiatric medications in the U.S.— 13 out of the top 25 medications were antidepressants. Sadly, one of the more common side effects with SSRI [*Selective serotonin re-uptake inhibitors*] antidepressants is sexual. A lack of sexual desire, no interest in sex, and uncomfortable sex are all connected with taking an antidepressant." Dr. Grohol recounts a study on exercise, antidepressants, scheduling sex, and sex drive. "Exercise immediately prior to sexual activity significantly improved sexual desire..." he noted; and, "Scheduling regular sexual activity significantly improved orgasm function [in women]..." But it wasn't quite that simple. Exercise in and of itself wasn't found to warm her up. The above underline is mine. Timing is everything!

Another recent article reports that many middle-aged, white, solidly middle-class women use wine to overcome the sexual lethargy induced by drugs. One should raise a flag of potential substance-abuse or drug-interaction caution; but most guys are willing to just go with, "Hey, whatever works." One might speculate that women, too, are missing and seeking the intimacy that men require; so there are more reasons for the disconnect than just SSRIs.

We should not mix up emotional intimacy with emotional maturity. When you look at the evolution of sexuality, or theories of sexuality, in the United States over the past fifty or sixty years—going back to when I was in medical school--psychiatrists were saying if a woman could have only clitoral orgasms it was a sign that she had not matured emotionally, and that she had not developed completely as a woman. In other words, these women were considered to still be infantile; and this clitoral orgasm business was just a matter of penis envy. To me, even at that time, this was bizarre. But that's what many doctors and psychiatrists believed, and that's what we were taught. Then came the studies by Masters and Johnson. They found that some women had vaginal orgasms, and they were not reducing women who could only have clitoral orgasms to some sort of infantile status. They found—and since the invention of the MRI it has been confirmed—that the clitoris is not just a small protuberance above the vagina, but an anatomical structure that mimics the erectile tissue in the male. It comes down around the vaginal orifice, so, during sex some women can have vaginal orgasms and some women can have clitoral orgasms. It's anatomical. It has nothing to do with emotional maturity.

A half century ago, the concept of emotional immaturity and the lack of orgasms was accepted by medicine, and by mothers. Everybody was kind of dealt a raw deal. Women thought they weren't mature. Guys thought they weren't doing the right thing, or thought maybe they married a woman who wasn't mature. These things got in the way of sexual satisfaction and emotional intimacy. Then all that was exposed as fallacy. For a while it seemed as if men and women might be on the same page. But that never fully came to fruition. What to do?

A recent article in the New York Times Magazine talked about a drug that a particular pharmaceutical company was trying to create that would boost a woman's sex drive. They had done numerous studies to find out if low female libido was hormonal, fatigue, or 'the kids.' Their goal was to produce a moneymaker like Viagra. [Viagra, or course, does nothing for male libido; it simply preps one physically, i.e. promotes one's fluid- dynamics, for sex.] What the company's studies found was there is nothing wrong with the sex drive of most women! The researchers then studied the relationships these women had with their husbands, boyfriends or live-ins. They found the women had lost virtually all desire for their men, *but* if they showed the same women pictures of some other guy they considered attractive, the women had significant, healthy (physical) sexual responses. Many women seem to be wired in such a way that after about five to seven years the person to whom they are married, or with whom they are involved, no longer turns them on. Just as with the kiss, there's this whole physiology behind how men and women relate, of which we, or they, are often unaware. What we've imposed upon physiology is a set of Judeo-Christian or other religious behaviors, or a secular set of ethics or a moral code, that society tries to make fit our physiology. If those codes are out of line with biology they become a source of conflict. Thinking about this strictly from a preservation-of-the-species perspective, one might speculate that biologically a new mixing of genes, meaning a different partner, is preferential. Hollywood called it *The Seven Year Itch*. They blamed it on the man. But it may well be that a woman's desire for her mate is biologically pre-programmed to expire, and that this expiration of love is the initial motivation behind the man's roaming behavior.

In discussing this with a friend he asked, "You've got the physiology and you've got Judeo-Christian concepts imposed upon physical relationships, what about other religions? What about Hinduism or Islam?" I am not in any way, shape or form an expert on religion, but I did treat a lot of Indian consultants that come to Aetna's world headquarters in Middletown. I took care of a lot of their employees, and a lot of Indian guys were having problems having sex. As near as I could tell it was a cultural thing. They didn't seem to feel that sex was okay. It was as if they thought there was something abnormal about it, but they needed to do it anyway. As far as Islam goes, I'm not sure what the whole basis is of the head scarf and keeping the women under stringent control (or of the more extreme sects' practice of female genital mutilation). Why would anyone want to keep half of the population under such control? What's the basis for that? Is it an outgrowth, devised for a harsh desert environment, of provide and protect? Or is it because women are viewed as some kind of threat? Is it: if I look at you I'm going to get excited and want to have sex, and sex is wrong? That would be kind of a briar-patch phenomenon. However one looks at it, we should all recognize that every culture establishes norms and taboos which deviate from the strictly physiological, from the biological imperatives.

Let's get back the itch. Recently there was an article in the Wall Street Journal by Elizabeth Bernstein which asked what to do (or how should a couple deal with it) *When he wants more and she says no*? Lots of good points: he feels rejected even if she doesn't want him to feel that way (remember we express ourselves physically, so we tend to take physical rejection as a rejection of *who* we are). "Increasingly," the article stated, "experts believe sex is a more emotional experience for men than for women... Men, much more than women... desire to please..." (like I've said, we are the romantic gender) "...for some men, sex may be their primary way of communicating... [they] may rely on their partner not just for sex, but for most of their nonsexual touch as well..."

The sexual narrative of too many relationships runs something like this: Hot and heavy slowly tapering to sporadic and disappointing before becoming non-existent. After five to seven years she is no longer interested in the physical interplay, which seems to have a physiological basis. For both, the emotional bond remains. He still needs touch and sex for emotional intimacy. He interprets her lack of interest in sex not simply as rejection of sex with him but as a rejection of him; that is, "She thinks *I'm* garbage." This gets very personal. "I must be a lousy husband. I can't support her in the lifestyle she deserves." And it can get weird. What happens in a man's mind when intimacy is lost or denied spans the scope and breath of negative thoughts—from anger and aggression to depression and self-recrimination. "I'm not good enough for her." "She should have married a wealthy guy." I've heard many variations. "She'd only be happy with a muscleman with ten million bucks in the bank and a ten-inch dick." There is a sensed, non-verbal, genetic component to these thoughts: she will not have sex with me because I'm unlovable; because I'm unlovable we will not procreate (even if one already has children); if we do not procreate I cannot fulfill my biological imperative; if I cannot fulfill my biological imperative, I am worthless.

Some guys become resigned to it—usually after trying chocolates and flowers, wining and dining, or any of a gazillion other "romantic" solutions. And practical solutions, too. Remember, most of these guys still love their wives. And they love their kids. And they are programmed to provide.

One patient told me about a conversation he had with his dad. He was in his mid-forties and his dad was in his mid-seventies. The older man was asking his son, as I think most dads do, "How is everything going? How's the wife? How's business?" My patient lamented to his father, "Dad, twenty years ago, way before I got married, you said to me that as the husband and the father 'The shit's going to come down on your shoulders. That's just the way it is.' Well, it has." My patient went on, "Shit happens. I'm juggling wife, kids, the house, the job. It all comes down on me, and I gotta handle it. My wife and daughter are only capable of certain things. The blood-stone metaphor comes to mind. I guess I've learned to accept it. It's just a shit deal. It's not the best deal. But it is what it is, and it ain't gonna change."

Certainly some of this may be generational. My daughters are more capable than most women I know from my generation (that's the most positive results of the Women's Movement which we'll get into this in later sections) but, at least from my patients, many younger women still rely on the guy to take care of all the physical assets—house, cars, etc.

But, handling it all doesn't turn her on. Nor does splitting tasks equally. That may, indeed, even turn her off more quickly. According to the New York Times Magazine article *The Sexless Marriage* by Lori Gottlieb, husbands who cook, vacuum, do the laundry and generally handle the shit deal (what social scientists refer to this as "an egalitarian marriage, meaning that both spouses work and take care of the house and that the relationship is built on equal power, shared interests and friendship…") don't get laid.

Pardon me for being crude. Let me restate this. Equal power, shared interests and friendship are the elements of a good business partnership, not the elements upon which emotional intimacy, touch and sex are built. As Gottlieb puts it, "No matter how much sink-scrubbing and grocery-shopping the husband does, no matter how well husband and wife communicate with each other, no matter how sensitive they are to each other's emotions and work schedules, the wife does not find her husband more sexually exciting, even if she feels both closer to and happier with him."

From a woman's perspective Gottlieb quotes couples therapist Esther Perel, "Egalitarian marriage takes the values of a good social system—consensus-building and consent —and assumes you can bring these rules into the bedroom. But the values that make for good social relationships are not necessarily the same ones that drive lust… …most of us get turned on at night by the very things that we'll demonstrate against during the day."

Good grief! No wonder so many guys feel it's a no win situation. We bend over backwards to provide and to please, and we end up realizing that she fantasizes some other guy's ten-inch dick, and maybe some handcuffs, might please her more! No one tells us, or them, that there is a female-borne physiological basis for this emotional/physical disengagement.

We, us guys, at this point we're still committed. We're all in. We defer to our mates and to most other women. Deference and chivalry are not dead: they are part of our make-up, elements of provide and protect. This deference to women can be altered the by social norms of the time and the place—each era and culture having their own nuances. It can be pushed to extremes never anticipated by biology; and over the ages, backfire reactions to it might be a causative factor in individual, religious and/or cultural abuse of women. Amid changing gender roles in 21st Century America deference tends to be passive acquiescence.

Not long ago I was to deliver a lecture to a nursing class (all female) comparing prostate cancer to breast cancer. In my notes I had statistics showing that the incidents of death from the two diseases were nearly identical. My talk followed that of a breast cancer patient. This woman wore a baseball cap because she had lost her hair. She talked about the surgery she had, about the way the radiologist had talked to her, and the way she'd pumped herself up to deal with these horrible ordeals. As she was relating what she'd been through, it didn't sound as if there had been much compassion by her male physician and male radiologist. She said, "When the radiologist called me he said, 'There's a lot of stuff in there that doesn't look good.'" His report was technical, terse, and cold. Or that is the way she heard it; the way, in the shock of the moment, she interpreted it.

Watching her—she was like a champion for these young female nurses—I thought if I make this prostate cancer comparison, it is going to seem as if I'm demeaning the significance of breast cancer; perhaps even as if I wished to belittle this woman who had struggled so hard. It occurred to me that this was not the place to show that there's a disparity in the perceptions of male and female health. It might almost sound as if I were saying, "Don't pay so much attention to her; guys are just as vulnerable!" Of course that's not what I meant, but that is the way I feared it would be perceived.

So here I am—a proponent of men's health initiatives, an advocate for men getting the attention they deserve, for men's diseases being equally recognized, and for the acknowledgment that men have increased disease rates because of the stress created by social attacks—here I am with an opportunity to point out this situation to a group of health professionals, and out of compassion for this woman I change the tone of my remarks.

If I think of how men deal with women, it is often a matter of giving them preferential treatment. At least in today's America. One of the reasons men don't stand up for themselves is because they are standing up for their mates, their sisters, their mothers. That's a male characteristic that's built into us. There is another element: the fear of being criticized for being politically incorrect if you take the opposite tact; if you say, "What about me as a guy? What about my prostate health? What about my need for emotional intimacy? What about my sex life?" No guy wants to be thought of as anti-women, mainly because we're all afraid we'll never get laid again. So we are afraid to ask these questions, and to stand up for ourselves. We often don't recognize our own complex psycho-physiological needs. Henceforth, we will no longer be concerned with political correctness. We will ask. We will be aware of our needs. We will, however, always still be concerned with providing for and protecting our loved ones.

The Seven Year Itch

With all these things going on, the relationship scenario may take bizarre twists. Hot and passionate went to sexless while we took care of the house and cars and kids. Now our eyes wander. Our mind convolutes. Fantasy and masturbation can only relieve just so much. The seven-year itch becomes a compulsion—affair or professional!

A few years ago there was an article in Scientific American titled, *Why Do Men Buy Sex?* The authors dissected the behavior of men with prostitutes. One interesting finding: 45% of all men had been with a prostitute. That was a cross-cultural average with American men being on the low end of the scale (17%), Spaniards being closer to the norm (40%), and Germans topping the list (70%). These numbers take the behavior out of the realm of mental aberration or illness; as the author notes, "…the behavior is prevalent enough that psychologists cannot easily write it off as pathological." Still there has been this idea, this element of the ambient cultural story, that if a man patronizes a prostitute there is something wrong with him; that he hates women, or perhaps he had problems with his mother. What the study found was men, beyond enjoying the sex act, were fulfilling a need for emotional intimacy; the same need women say they have—but for men emotional intimacy is expressed through sex. [Seems we've heard that before.] They also reported that men are more visual than women; and that intimacy for women seems to be more auditory based (put that arrow in your quiver). The conclusion was visiting a prostitute was normal behavior; that men went to prostitutes because they weren't getting their *emotional* needs met.

The study did not go into the ramifications these behaviors have upon relationships, however in France, Italy or Germany they seemed to be more accepted. Here in America, if you're caught, you are a pig, a pervert, at best sick, and likely a sexual predator deserving of incarceration and the loss of all your property. A man having a tryst, affair, or clandestine rendezvous with a mistress or lover is viewed and labeled in similar fashion: hashtag #pig, #swine, #gross&disgusting.

Not long ago there was an article in the Hartford Courant about a private detective whose business was tracking down guys who cheat. He explained that before he takes a job he always interviews the woman to determine the state of the relationship—because he didn't want to spend a lot of time taking pictures of people doing nothing wrong. If he was convinced there was no sex at home, he would guarantee his client that he would catch the guy with his pants down "...cause if he wasn't getting it at home, he was getting it someplace else."

Think of Eisenhower with his driver (Katherine), or Petraeus and his biographer Paula... In the gym one guy said, "Hey, did you hear Petraeus was caught having an extramarital affair?" (or more likely he said, "...was caught screwing around?") Another guy answered, "Yeah, but did you see his wife?" The guys automatically understood that the wife was part of the equation, possibly was not taking care of herself, was not trying to be attractive to him, and they assumed the marriage was sexless. The media was #casanova, or whatever negative terms they could apply and imply; but reporters never asked about her role in what is much more complex than just two individual sneaking off in the night

This may not apply to every guy, but from what I would see in my practice, or what I hear in the gym, most guys are home-bodies. They love their wives. They love their families. They love their homes. This is basic—coming from the impulse to provide and protect. But guys get lonely. I heard it all the time. "I was on a trip... "I was in Detroit... "I was gone for three weeks... "I met this girl in a bar, and, you know, we went upstairs... "I want to make sure I don't have some kind of disease." I never heard a guy say, "I was in a bar and I was really horny." They always used the term "lonely." I think social scientists should explore that term in detail. It is seldom talked about. "I'm lonely," a friend confessed to me long before I began this study. "There's no emotional intimacy," were his exact words. "It's not a matter of sex. She's withdrawn... withdrawn from me. I love her to bits but she's not there. She's there for three or four minutes, then she goes off to the other room to read. I've talked to her over and over about it, but it's not going to change. There is nothing holding us together." Patients and friends have described many variations of withdrawal. Some wives "go out with the girls," others watch unending TV; yet others, and this is a more modern version, are addicted to Facebook, Instagram, Twitter and a myriad of other digital distractions.

As I ponder this phenomena and the social perception of it, I think guys are getting a raw deal. A guy gets lonely, he has emotional needs, he wanders. What should society expect? Perhaps our society is more tolerant today, but the air of tolerance barely wafts to a cheating husband. He is automatically deemed wrong—a pervert, a single-minded and simple-minded sex-crazed sleaze. He is ostracized. He also may beat himself up over his "weakness." Headlines tell us that 50% of all men cheat, but they seldom add many of these men are cheating with women who are also cheating. And the legal system was designed (by men long before feminists became powerful) to protect women. The private detective shows the judge the photos and he's out of his house. Take that you cad!

Earlier we talked about guys crying or not crying, and I said I've had thousands of guys cry in my office. Often it was about the *loss* of their kids. Guys talk about their kids. Guys care about their kids. Divorced guys always talked about how much they missed their children, yet the woman always got custody of the kids. If a woman has a problem with a man, she can get him removed from the kid's lives. She goes to court. She says, "He's threatening... he's this, he's that." I spoke with a judge about this not long ago. He said to me, "The court always acts on behalf of the safety of the child. We shoot first and ask questions later. If we think the child is in danger, and the man is usually the one that's named, then we remove the man."

If you think about the number of times you've heard of guys no longer having custody, you realize that removing the guy is essentially automatic within the system. The specifics of the case are overridden by the politically correct assumption that the guy is going to be aggressive; that he presents a physical danger to the ex and likely to the kids. The truth is many of these guys miss their kids terribly. They are shaken to the core by a system they see as biased; a system that just clumps them all together with the few who are actually violent. Think of the film, *Mrs. Doubtfire* with Robin Williams. He goes to these extraordinary lengths to see his kids. But in reality if guys go to get the child or children... well, I recently heard a story about a guy who got his kids and took them to his house for Christmas, and the wife had him arrested for kidnapping. How absurd is that? The whole legal system is pre-set to pounce on the male in any family dispute situation.

Young guys see this—see all the biases set against males—but they are told it is proper, it is for everyone's safety, it is natural, the new, corrected cultural. No wonder they're confused, afraid of commitment and marriage, and rebelling.

Young Guys Are Confused

In the last years of my practice I saw numerous young men who were in the twenty- to forty-year-old age group, who were confused regarding their relationship with women. I'm not talking about the mechanics of sex or the issue of gender-identity. I'm talking about the male pre-set wiring to provide and protect that has been interrupted by changing cultural norms; and that seemingly was being interpreted by these guys as *be subservient*. These guys stood behind their wives or girlfriends or significant others and provided support for their wishes, demands, or careers. Not necessarily a bad thing. Women have done this for men for eons. But it is a bad thing when it is done at the expense of men developing their own abilities to provide by achieving in their own name or self. As I think about it now, this is the exact same bitch that women had half a century ago. If a man does not, or cannot, develop his abilities, he cannot achieve; if he cannot achieve, he cannot provide; if he cannot provide, he cannot fully give to or share within his complimentary unit—the couple or family.

It is not that these guys were inept or complete failures. But they had been taught that their achievements—career or personal—were far less important in their lives than *happiness,* or some other metaphysical quality; and that by some ethereal reasoning their achievements and those qualities were mutually exclusive. They are not. Achievement, competence—all the male virtues we've spoken of earlier, enhance happiness.

Some of these guys might have described themselves, or might have been described by others, as metrosexuals. When I first hear that term I thought it meant gay, but that obviously was not the case with most of these guys. They were highly masculine; participated in many traditional "male" activities from watching sports to drinking, from climbing mountains to other tests and feats of speed, strength and agility. Many had active, heterosexual sex lives with varying, if transient, partners; but in business and social interactions within the new, gender co-equal workforce, many took the back seat or the less aggressive stance. They also tended to dress in ways that five decades ago would have been thought effeminate—colorful, stylish, eschewing the grays and browns of yore. Truth is, they looked very nice, but I think this was and is symptomatic of the confusion caused by the changing role of men in American society that is in conflict with their biological imperative. At thirty they were rebelling against the concepts of marriage and fatherhood, some laughing it off as "confirmed bachelorhood." Yet it had a very different feel from the confirmed bachelorhood of the past. Dr. Helen Smith notes in her book, *Men On Strike* that "…men aren't dropping out because they are stuck in arrested development. They are instead acting *rationally* in response to the lack of incentives society offers them to be responsible fathers, husbands and providers." By the time those men were in their forties, at least those who had gotten married and were my patients, they were asking were, "Doc, what can I do to get my wife to have sex with me? She's just no longer interested."

Frankly, My Dear...

This state, for many men, cannot last forever. We are not infinitely patient. Many of us follow the Rhett Butler path. In *Gone With The Wind* do you recall how deeply in love Rhett was with Scarlett? She married him but she could not or would not express her love for him. Intimacy—emotional and physical—was limited by pride, jealousy, manipulation, and her love for another man. Trust was destroyed. Even though, late in the story, Scarlett's desires reverse and she attempts to repair the relationship, he has been so hurt by her years of rejection he can no longer forgive her. Love has died. She has poisoned the well. Biologically the toxic relationship has altered the chemically-established bonds in his brain. The story is classic not because of the Civil War history but because so many couples endure parallel (if less dramatic) relationships. How many men have walked out, climbed on their Harleys or into their Subarus (one's political persuasion is irrelevant) and muttered as they rode off into the sunset, "Frankly, my dear, I don't give a damn?"

But there are caveats, off-sets. One might use the vernacular, "This sucks." That's one of the reasons we attempt to avoid this happening. It's a last resort. Divorce, especially in the short run, is bad for brains and bank accounts.

A growing number of books and articles suggest that we, as a society, need to rethink marriage, need to look beyond the concept of long-term relationships. Some of these writers have advocated redefining marriage in terms of friendship, finance, real estate, and/or partnership. That's well and good, I suppose, but these proposals leave me scratching my head. To me there is a shallowness in this kind of thinking. Recall the iconic elderly couples mentioned earlier. When I compare their commitment to each other to these proposals for the new-marriage, or the open-marriage, I feel that what is left out of the latter concepts are the qualities of meaningfulness and hope—and all those two words imply.

Meaningfulness and Permanency

Men seek meaningfulness. Does my life count? Do I matter? It can be religious or secular. Has my life had any meaning? It can be celestial or specific, a look forward or a look back. Think of the old man in the cemetery at the end of the film *Saving Private Ryan*;

turning to his wife he asks if he has led his life if a way worthy of the sacrifices others made to make his life possible?

In our lives we have relationships—physical or metaphysical—with people, things and concepts outside of ourselves. For life to have meaning what we do, what we work for, what we concentrate on, needs to be something bigger, something more significant, something more essential than ourselves. It is a natural male trait to believe and behave in this manner—protect and provide does not imply the self, but implies selflessness. Perhaps the object of our focus is magnificent. Perhaps it is limited to our close environs. But that focus being outside of ourselves, and being greater than ourselves, is the secret to meaningfulness. This is not really a secret at all. It is well-known, and has been seemingly for all human history, as it should be because it is tied up in our biology.

Bigger than implies otherness; *working for*, or *with*, otherness implies relationships. Every relationship—two or more people—is bigger than you. A relationship may be with a life partner, parents, kids, pets, friends, spiritual beings, even inanimate projects or objects which take on a life of their own. Recall that men relate to the physical world differently than women. This includes relating to everything from barbells to machine parts, from construction equipment to the objects we are constructing. These are relationships and they can be meaningful. I have seldom met a woman who understands this; and seldom met a man who doesn't.

A family is bigger than a couple. Some relationships involve our allegiance to group, community or nation. Some are trans-generational.

An essential element of meaningfulness is hope. This, perhaps, is where it becomes complicated. Hope is the most important of all feeling because hope implies not just the present but a time beyond the present, and it implies continuation and fulfillment. The realization that there is a future, that there is something more than today, more than the immediate, causes us to forecast permanence, or at least semi-permanence. Think of the word permanent. This may seem circular, but permanence conveys a projection into the future. Permanent relationships equate with hope. This is key—hope for oneself, for one's future and the future of one's relationships, and for the future of one's species.

What should we be hoping for? Security? Love? Sex? Intimacy? Immortality? Right now we are in a project; we are producing a book and launching a men's health initiative. Those projects require projections into the future. We anticipate positive outcomes. Personal relationships also mean projecting into the future. Our relationships are products of our behaviors and actions. We foresee continuity. Continuity implies permanence or at least semi-permanence. That implies hope. That is the exhilaration, the up-ness, of every new relationship. One is looking into the future, not stopping and concentrating on the present or mulling over the past.

The need for permanency is more than cultural. It is biological. It takes numerous forms, but each serves the same biological need. As we have shown, men have an innate need for intimate, permanent relationships with women. This is more than merely psychological if psychological is construed to mean independent of physiological. Thought patterns are heavily influenced by our chemistry and our wiring; and our wiring has been heavily influence by our chemistry beginning some seven months before birth. The average man's need for a relationship with a female is psycho-physical. One can't get around that. As we've said, Biology is Basic.

We can see that men have a need to permanently, or at least semi-permanently, connect with women. The need for these relationships is tied up in protect, provide and procreate, and in the continuation of the life of our species. For millennia this was identified as marriage, although that seems to have, or to be, changing. Even after people have had a bad marriage, they'll go do it again. And again. Even when they say they'll never do it again, they do it again. In spite of all the problems in male-female relationships, there is a biological drive for that relationship that goes beyond just sex.

In this section we've talked at length about the problems in relationships between men and women, but truly our emphasis should be on the glories, the splendor, the magnificence of relationships; on all that they can be, and all they can mean. The ultimate *product* of the relationship between a man and a woman, viewed from the biological perspective, is a child. When the child is produced purposefully this is the most intimate expression of love. Yes, kids are the manifestation of our biological imperatives; and those imperatives seem designed to produce the expression of hope in permanency, in a future beyond ourselves and our lives.

The Answer

I know, I never did answer the question, "Hey Doc, what can I do to get my wife to have sex with me? She's just no longer interested." The below suggestions assume she's still talking to you, that the relationship has not deteriorated beyond the point of no return, and that she is not clinically withdrawn. Try these:

Number 1: Be *The* Guy in the relationship, not the subservient wuss.

Number 2: Listen to her, but don't fix all her problems unless she asks you to fix them.

Number 3: If you are a sports couple remember sex is more likely right after the hike or the tennis match than after showers and dinner.

Number 4: Realize that foreplay is different for men and women. Sure, you're ready in thirty seconds. That's biological. For her foreplay starts some time earlier… usually at least a day. This requires planning and scheduling on your part.

Number 5: Long ago Ogden Nash told us, "Candy is dandy but liquor is quicker." It seems to be true, but be cautious with this one. We're talking a glass or two of wine not getting her smashed. This is only for those who are not addicted to alcohol.

Number 6: Don't be a jerk. This is not a contradiction with number one. Be gentle, be kind, learn how to please her and what drives her libido. Maybe she likes roses, maybe handcuffs. Likely she won't tell you, but make it your mission to find out. Understand that this is a loving, emotionally and physically intimate relationship, not a contest. You don't win by winning.

When the Answer Doesn't Work

And if none of that works… then what?!

Then it's decision time. These decisions will be very personal and very specific to each situation, to each relationship, to each guy. This section is not meant to be advice; it only delineates some of the options, and some of the reasoning behind those options.

No sex: accept it or don't accept it; make accommodations or make wave? Each choice—*and man up to this, these are choices, your choices*—has a host of sub-choices, a sea of nuances. If you accept the fact that she's never going to have sex with you again you can be furious or passive, celibate or have an affair, take yourself in hand or whither in self-denial and self-recrimination. You can remain aloof, keep it private, bitch about it to your friends, or fight about it in public as if your attempt to humiliate her is going to have a positive influence on the situation.

The decisions here are personal and may or may not be permanent... BUT your decisions should be conscious decisions, ones made after intensive thought and self- and situation-analysis, not ones blurted in the heat of arguments. Recognize that your decisions will have long-term life consequences not simply on you but on your wife, your kids, perhaps their kids, your friends, maybe even your community. These consequences will not necessarily be negative—don't read that into this thought.

As noted earlier, we guys tend to first blame ourselves. That's probably a good thing because it leads to the analysis which should take place before any decision is made. When it doesn't lead to analysis and decision, when it is allowed to fester unresolved, it can lead to depression or other self-destructive health consequences. Accommodation and acceptance may be a solution. They should not be interpreted to connote "unresolved."

Let's take a quick look at the elements of the relationship. In most marriage two people have entered into a formal or tacit agreement to meet the physical and emotional needs of the other. There are consequences for both in this relationship when sex is removed. It is easier for men to deal with this issue if the sex is absent because his wife is ill. It is problematic when the woman decides to eliminate sex from the relationship for no obvious reason.

Removal of sex is a relationship changing issue, and there are consequences for the women just as there are for the man. The point of asking the question "What happens now?" is more reflected on the woman. If she is the one that made the decision to not have sex, she should be the one that has to be very aware of the consequences. Unfortunately in our society the women's decision does not seem to get much attention, but the man's reaction to his wife's decision is often criticized.

We need to put more emphasis on the consequences of the wife's decision. This is the whole point. It's her decision to realize that the consequences may affect the family and the kids. In my clinical experience, when the wives were confronted with the consequences of their decisions, many of them changed their mind.

If, within your relationship, you don't or won't accommodate and accept, perhaps the alternative is divorce, yet there are still other options. Some couples tacitly or overtly amend their relationship and acknowledge that the other's need for touch and emotional/sexual intimacy will be fulfilled by another. This might include a traditional European-style mistress or lover; it may be private or public; and seemingly today it may be opposite or same gender.

The important point is to make a decision, but make certain it is a conscious decision made with all the elements and options on the table. If you don't make the decision, life has a way of making it for you. In that case, you'll likely come up with the short end of the stick.

NEXT UP

Next up: the numerous and varying dynamics behind the feeling that many men have that they are being rejected—personally by women, and on a much larger scale by the new American culture. It starts early… with the manipulation and destruction of boys.

PART IV: Destroying Boys
CULTURE WARS & THE ROOTS OF CRISIS

1960: Old Miss Vinegarbottle asks her classroom a question. Dick and Jane each raise a hand. Miss Vinegarbottle calls on Dick. Women protest the war being waged against them.

1980: Ms. Balsamic asks her classroom a question. Dick and Jane each raise a hand. Ballsy, as the kids call her, calls on Jane. Women protest the war being waged against them.

2000: Vine-of-the-Autumn Skye asks her classroom a question. Jane raises her hand. Earlier Dick was told to "go color," for the work was too difficult for him. He is off to the side quietly drawing a picture. Autumn calls on Jane. Spot barks approval. Women protest the war being waged against them. The state legislature passes a resolution creating a commission to study why Jane is in the minority in coloring.

2015: After screwing office boy Dick in the unisex bathroom, CEO Jane asks her best friend forever, Spot the Fourth, "How come I can't find a real man?"

Qualifier

It is easy to be misunderstood or misinterpreted. Each reader brings his or her own worldview to all the words he or she reads, all the news he or she watches, all conversations he or she enters. If the words are in agreement and the material reinforces one's perspective, that material is easy to accept as *true*. By contrast if one's current perspective is in disagreement with the material, that material is often dismissed as false. In either case additional qualities not in the material tend to be ascribed to the material.

As I launch into this topic I wish to make it clear that I believe one should draw a clear distinction between the Women's Movement that supports women's rights, that advocates for the betterment of women, and that fights against limiting women's contributions to society; and what I will label as radical or toxic feminism which denies the inherent traits and nature of men and attacks men's rights as a way of redefining woman. Gender scholars of this second wave clearly state that they are out to change the masculinity of boys. I strongly support the Women's Movement as it has fought for the rights that all humans should have. The radicalization of an element of that movement, as we shall see, has been abusive, and destructive to men, and most particularly damaging to boys.

Slugs and Snails

Let's return to 1960. Old Miss Vinegarbottle asks Dick, "What are little boys made of?" Dick answers, "Slugs and snails; And puppy-dog tails." Miss V smiles approvingly. Forty years later Vine-of-the-Autumn Skye asks Jane, "Of what, Jane, do you believe little girls are made?" Jane answers, "Sugar and spice; And everything nice." Ms. Skye turns red with rage that Jane's troglodyte parents have taught her this tripe. "No Jane," Skye glares at the little girl. "That's a sexist rhyme designed by old white men to keep you in your place. Little girls are made of grit and steel surrounding a magnificent brain, all capable of thought and action independent of the need for male approval."

Whoa! I'm thinking even as I write this that I'm going overboard. But am I?

Listen up, *boys and girls*, today's classroom, as we will see, is not like yesterday's classroom. The other day on the news there was a story about a six-year-old boy who kissed one of his classmates on the cheek. The poor kid was suspended, or maybe expelled, because they labeled the kiss sexual harassment. As I'm watching this story I'm going, "What?!" I remember being in grammar school. We would leave school and march in twos down the street to the corner, then the nuns would disperse us. There was this really cute girl I liked, and one day—I was probably seven years old—I gave her a great big smack on the cheek. She just kind of giggled. I don't remember planning it. Being an impulsive boy, I just did it. I guess the nun said something to my mother who said something to my father who said, "So I understand you kissed a girl." I said, shyly, "Yeah." He said, "Was she cute?" I nodded, and he said, "Good for you." It wasn't, "Son, I heard you got laid last night." It wasn't anything like that. It was very innocent. He was proud because I was being a boy. That's what boys do. Boys kiss girls. Girls accept the kiss and giggle.

The attraction between the sexes starts off when people are very young. It is already up and running by the time you're six. It is not sexual in the manner adults think of that word. It is not foreplay aimed at intercourse. It is normal, an early expression of emotions; and an essential experiment in social contact. This is the way *boys and girls* learn. The natural process is, and should be, gradual. When it is thwarted early on, that disruption manifests itself at puberty—a time when the bodies of tweens and teens are being flood with hormones— and children emerge into this phase of life without the learned socialization necessary for healthy relationships.

Suspending a six year old boy for kissing a classmate on the cheek is far more abusive to that child's psyche than the act for which he was suspended could ever be to the psyche of his 'victim'. The American Psychological Association, according to Christina Hoff Sommers, found that of young boys "being shamed and treated as deviants... [their] suspension maybe correlated with school disengagement, poor achievement and dropping out." This form of child abuse is now becoming, or has become, institutionalized protocol because warped minds have lobbied for, and legislated, it. That kiss is one of many incidents which cumulatively have significant consequences. School districts may fall back on, "We're following protocol," or "...following state law." Those excuses are indictments of superintendents, school boards and legislators. They are not valid justification for abuse.

Let me back-up to fifty or one hundred years ago. If the rhyme that girls are sugar and spice was designed to subjugate girls by convincing them that to be girls they needed to behave in a lady-like fashion, were the lines about boys an attempt to tell boys that to be boys they should be slimy and slow? If one accepts the motivation behind the first premise that it was designed to dominate girls, doesn't one need to accept the latter as a way of demeaning boys?

Put this way, the premises and arguments seem a bit inane, yet we encounter this mode of thought, and worse, over and over again. In today's classroom a teacher acknowledging *girls and boys* may be subject to discipline. **Nebraska School Tells Teachers To Avoid 'Gender Expressions,'** one headline reads. The article explains that training documents tell teachers not to use gender binary models or gender expressions. That is, instead of saying "boys and girls" a teacher might say "those born on even days and those born on odd." The document further instructs educators:

> When you find it necessary to reference gender, say 'Boy, girl, both or neither.' When asked why, use this as a teachable moment. Emphasize to students that your classroom recognizes and celebrates the gender diversity of all students... Be intolerant of openly hostile attitudes... Take the opportunity to push the individual on their statements about gender. Being punitive may stop the behavior, at least in your presence. Being instructive may stop it entirely.

Defending this position, Lincoln Public Schools superintendent Steve Joel declared "...our position... is inclusiveness... I'm happy, I'm pleased, because we have to create an awareness amongst ourselves, that we have kids coming to us from so many different backgrounds, and some of those are confusing to the students themselves, to other students, and to some of our staff."

The last paragraph of the article reads:

> The materials also contained a handout on "the Genderbread Person," put together by self-identified "social justice comedian" Sam Killermann, which explains that "gender is one of those things everyone thinks they understand, but most people don't. Like **Inception.** Gender isn't binary."

The mistake being made by Messrs. Joel and Killermann is to not distinguishing between gender-identity and gender. There are, biologically, two genders—this is the way it has been for 180 million years or more. Biologically, the gender binary is complimentary. On the other hand, gender-identity can be nearly infinite. Teaching, sans gender, is abusive, as it denies the biological nature of boys and girls. And it is confusing to boys and girls! May I suggest that if Mr. Joel and others truly wish to back their policies and protocol, and provide true teaching moments, they voluntarily undergo castration, not replace or rebuild parts by transgender operations, and become neithers. In this way he, or they, or *thithers* (to coin a non-gender pronoun), will be free to identify with, and champion, strawberries or ferns which reproduce by stolons, spores or rhizomes. The validation of personal sexual-preference identification, and the essential denial of not only the realities of masculinity, but of femininity as well, are not and should not be the roles of public education.

How did we get here? How did we get to the point where top education officials confuse biological gender with gender-identity; where a teacher's direction to her classroom, "Boys and girls, open your books," is considered exclusionary; where 'teaching moments' are used to subjugate, indoctrinate or bully students into the politics du jour? I read about a "transgender" case in California [based upon California law AB 1266] where five and six year old boys and girls are allowed to use either the boy's bathroom or the girl's bathroom (or shower or locker rooms) if he or she declares him or herself transgender. I'm thinking (excuse me for this), "What idiot came up with this regulation that tells a five or six year old that they know that they are transgender oriented?! Isn't that what adolescence is, or was, supposed to be all about? Isn't that when you discover what your sexuality really is? Yes, in adolescence and later in life one may find he or she has a different sexual orientation. That is natural and normal to a certain percentage of people, and it can't be changed back by fiat. But that knowledge doesn't set in at five or six—at least not without aberrant outside influences. There is no such thing as a transgender five year old."

And what are the repercussions?!

The culture war is on-going. It has many unidentified, clandestine and chaotic elements; and the unintended consequences or collateral damages are only now being exposed.

Again, let's return to 1960. Societies and cultures are always changing. We could pick an earlier date: perhaps 1920 when the Women's Suffrage Movement finally secured the vote for half the adult population; or we might choose 1840 when American women organized their first rights movement; or perhaps 1869 when Wyoming became the first state to approve voting rights of women. But these dates, as important as they are, did not have near the cultural impact as the 1960 invention and introduction of the first oral contraceptive pill.

In my experience that is the defining moment, the seminal event, leading to the cascade of cultural changes over the past sixty-five years. Women were no longer relegated to being "just" mothers, nurses, or school teachers; no longer restrained in career development by the interruption of childbirth and childcare; no longer limited, if they so choose, to any subservient status. A whole new world opened up to them. And this was good. The event also had multiple and mixed side-effects for the economy, for families and for children. Other inventions and initiatives multiplied and enhanced the cultural effects—indeed, the cultural tsunami—set off by the introduction of the pill. To speak of the issue from only one side, positive or negative, is to display ignorance of the interconnectivity of the many elements, actions, reactions, and unintended consequences of this most historic episode.

At the time of the rise of the feminist movement women did not have the same opportunities as men. At that time most of the jobs open to women were jobs suited to the average woman's physical attributes. Most women were not suited for the heavy labor—construction or manufacturing— jobs of the day. Physically [in the world of that time] they were more suited for teaching, nursing, secretarial work, and motherhood. Motherhood in the time before near universal personal transportation and the rise of telecommunication was a job that tended to tie women, especially those with young children, to the home in order to care for those children.

The development of more universal, individual transportation, and the increase in machinery, added to birth control, increased personal freedoms. The new discussion became whether a woman should be a career woman, a working mother, or 'just' a mother. Some people still insisted that women should primarily be mothers because that reflected their biology; and at some point being labeled a stay-at-home mom became a put-down, an accusation that a woman was not fulfilling her potential. The argument may have swayed back and forth, but the reality became women moved into the work force *en masse*.

In many industries robotic arms came to handled heavy lifting. Ditch diggers and grave diggers with shovels were replaced by backhoes that did not require massive biceps. The digital chip and miniaturization further lightened manufacturing and construction. The move from a manufacturing economy to a service economy increased female workplace *friendliness*. Women sat at computers or in a boardroom as easily, physically perhaps more easily, than men. [We'll address heavy labor, Marines, and women in the military in a later section.] For middle-class families two-incomes became the norm, and higher family income became an element in the inflation equation. As the economy exploded, contracted, exploded again and contracted again in what seems like normal economic cycles, two incomes became mandatory.

Working mothers now found an inherent conflict between time spent at work and time spent with the kids. [Although it has seldom been noted—except by guys like me who have heard it hundreds of times from patients in my office—Dads, too, felt that same conflict, yet virtually every guy who mentioned it to me believed he did not have a choice. Pro-Choice has never, to any significant degree, applied to men. Cultural bias, and biology, still tells men they must leave the house and go out to do battle. Perhaps it is more biology—we are the guys who always went out and slayed the dragons, moved the boulders and did the heavy work. But many guys still wished they had a choice.] The structure of labor changed, the structure of personal and familial finance changed; and a woman's need for a man was changing. Well get back to this in a moment. Some of the changes impacted kids. Some have been devastating to the social and psychological development of boys.

In The Classroom

Meanwhile the cultural tsunami had been playing out in the classroom. A confluence of interests hit our boys like an unstoppable wave.

I discussed this phenomenon at length with Dr. Robert Reynolds, who we met earlier. Dr. Reynolds is the Director of The Reynolds Clinic, a treatment center "dedicated to helping students, families, schools, and individuals cope with attention, learning and behavioral challenges." (www.reynoldsclinic.com). Our session started off with how family difficulties are exacerbated by having a child with special needs. Dr. Reynolds explained, "If you have a child with special needs, your challenges are significantly greater than a parent or couple who don't have such a child. As a result it oft times puts additional stresses on the marriage, driving parents against one another. Typically—and this sounds stereotypical but it is the case—men will take a more hardline approach to their kids with special needs than women. "Bob, you can do it. Be a man." That kind of attitude. The mother more frequently takes a more nurturing and supportive role. At some point the two of them start arguing about which is the best path to take. The father saying, "You're coddling the boy. You're making him into a namby-pamby. A marshmallow." And the mother is saying, "You're hurting his self-esteem. You're criticizing him all the time. You're down on him all the time." So the two of them are now going like this (brings fist together) all the time because they have a different perspective. The divorce rate is much higher for couples with special needs children than for couples with children who don't have special needs.

"Although we see those same tendencies in families with children without special needs, these differences come out much more strongly, and are much more problematic in families with a child with special needs. Let's not forget, it is more often a boy child who has these needs. If you look at statistics for kids diagnosed with ADHD, it is 4 to 1 boys. If you look at statistics of children who are learning disabled, or for children who have behavioral issues like *oppositional defiance disorder*, it's 4 or 5 or 6 to 1. So you now begin to see that the stresses in the family over how to parent this boy. The child is growing up with mixed messages, and it leaves him somewhat confused. The next generation of men are often being negatively impacted because of the confusion of what do we do for a child with special needs."

We discussed various family situations, and the possibility of getting the parents on the same page; even the potential benefits of the dual hardline/coddling approach if done by loving parents who show mutual respect for their differences. After all, children do not learn best if all their teachers and mentors have only one story and one attitude. Then our discussion settled in on boys, ADHD, causes, treatments, outside influences, and ramifications. "I didn't know that the gender differences were so great," I said. "Is there a reason for that?"

Dr. Reynolds responded, "There are all kinds of speculation. I just read an article about brain development… about the frontal cortex and pre-frontal cortex. These are the parts of the brain that regulate our ability to self-regulate. We find that by the age of five or six the female brain is much more prepared to engage in environments which require discipline, focus and concentration, than is the male brain. The pre-frontal cortex is more differentiated. At this point the capillary development and the neural pathways are more complex in the female child than in the male, so you put those brains in environments where one has to sit still and pay attention and focus. The female child's brain is much more equipped to do this than the male's. Boys at this age are easily a year or two behind in terms of this piece of physiological development."

This immediately brought to mind various points made by Dr. Louann Brizendine in *The Male Brain*, and various other references I'd read about gender-specific brain development and structural differences. And it brought to mind Christina Hoff Sommers' caution on grade disparity:

> Teachers as early as kindergarten factor good behavior into grades—and girls, as a rule, comport themselves far better and are more amenable to classroom routines than boys...." Girls develop non-cognitive skills earlier than boys to include "...self-control, attentiveness organization, and the ability to sit still for long periods of time.

What are the ramifications of normal boy behavior and teacher bias to the "more amenable classroom comportment?" With Reynolds I played devil's advocate. "We're talking about kindergarten, first and second grade," I said, "If the boys are allowed to rough'n'tumble during that time, and perhaps the girls don't particularly want to play that way... but boys want to do this because their brains are not developing for self-regulation but for experimentation and action... and you force boys to be more like girls, and to sit and concentrate, is that the reason more boys than girls are diagnosed with ADHD? And if so, are we denying the normal developmental pattern of boys versus girls?"

Reynolds' answer should have far-reaching repercussions. "Not only that," he said, "we also use that as an excuse to medicate these boys [at ages 5 & 6!!!!] because now they have an illness, when in fact I don't believe they have an illness."

I do not recall the name of the book I read about the No Child Left Behind laws, but the premise was: In order to get higher grades boys were being medicated to calm them down so they would study and not go off and roughhouse; better grades meant more accolades for the school system and in turn that meant more funding. There is, thusly, a political, financial, and bureaucratic motive to drug kids.

Reynolds confirmed this, saying, "When we look at the research that is done in this area, it is almost always supported by the pharmaceutical industry which has a vested interest in diagnosing and medicating, or having these children diagnosed and medicated, because that's a huge profit center for them."

Note the confluence of interests of lobbyists, bureaucrats and industry. And we are just looking at the tip of the iceberg. The day before my meeting with Reynolds I had listened to a program about what the host described as "a diagnosis in search of a population." The syndrome was to be called Sluggish or Lethargic Tempo Disorder.

Reynolds said, "You mean Concentration Deficit Disorder. That's the latest one." He was well aware that at least several companies were pursuing the inclusion of this new disorder in the Diagnostic and Statistical Manual (DSM) of the American Psychological Association. This is the bible of mental health diseases and disorders. If a condition is not included in the DSM, it doesn't exist; but if it is in there, doctors and therapists can diagnosis it and prescribe medication to effect it. "Hypo- tempo…" Reynolds began, then paused and said, "Kids who are basically lethargic. They are using that as another explanation or reason why we should medicate these children. It's the same kind of cluster of symptoms as ADHD, but it's distinct from ADHD. As a result we have another reason to diagnosis kids and medicate them."

What he said next shook me.

"Basically, if you think about it—*these are the kinds of things that keep me awake at night*—historically, many of the people in our society who have made great contributions to the evolution of our country probably would have been diagnosed with ADHD had they had that diagnosis back in the late 1700s or 1800s or 1900s.

"One of my heroes is Thomas Edison. If you know anything about Edison, you know he would have been diagnosed ADHD in a heartbeat. And learning-disabled, as well. What's to say there's not a Thomas Edison sitting in the fourth grade in Hartford or Waterbury or New Haven, who is running around, out of his seat, disrupting the class? What are we going to do with that kid? We're going to medicate him. If we medicate him, is he still going to be the next Thomas Edison? I have my doubts. We are getting a better behaved child, but what's the cost; not only to that child, but also to society? What are we losing?"

This raises the concern that programs, policies and definitions surrounding ADHD are the *cause* of the problem; and that for many 'ADHD' boys, perhaps for most, their pre-medicated behavior is normal. What *is* abnormal are the regulators who mandate treatments which coerce conformity to aberrant, docile male behaviors. As Christina Hoff Sommers puts it:

It became fashionable to pathologize the behavior of millions of healthy male children. We have turned against boys and forgotten a simple truth. The energy, competitiveness and corporal daring of normal males are responsible for much of what is right in the world. Being a boy is not a social disease.

More than a few of my patients have had these feelings about their sons, but few have read Sommers' *The War Against Boys*, or been able to express it as clearly as Dr. Reynolds. We'll talk more about this—particularly about the Biederman Scandal at Harvard University, the corruption of academic research, and the influence of Big Pharma—below; but for the moment consider that if direct or indirect compensation to a school system, or to a state from the federal government is tied to test scores, then money becomes a major motivating factor in schools trying to get kids to sit down, settle down, be quiet, and hopefully score higher on some sort of standardized examination. This is one of the problems—out of a cluster of symptoms leading to a societal disorder—that is derailing American education... and its focus, as we've see, is overwhelmingly on boys.

Fifth grade teacher Graham Seekamp, who we met earlier, never heard of Sluggish or Lethargic Cognitive Tempo, but chuckled at the description, "Don't we all have that, at least a bit, every day?" He immediately recognized the pattern as "...looking for a clientele so they can make more money..." then added, "It would mean kids would have to have personalities that fit between Sluggish and ADHD... kind of 'must be pasteurized and homogenized.'"

For some time Seekamp's school was run on principles and practices derived from the positive-self-esteem movement, with much emphasis aimed at "creating a positive school environment," the kind of place Sommers portrays when she states, "As our schools become more feelings-centered, risk averse, competition-free, and sedentary, they move further and further from the characteristic sensibilities of boys."

Seekamp's boots-on-the-ground perspective: "For a long time in education there has been the thought that you should never make a student feel bad. Our previous vice-principal was into making sure that everyone was always feeling good. You know, kids naturally, at times, want to be involved in competitive situations. We have what we call an *Olympic Day*. Under the previous guy there were no teams that were allowed to be winners and no teams that were allowed to be losers. Everybody had to go out and have a good time. We couldn't hand out ribbons. We had done that in earlier years, but now it was "Oh no! We can't do that anymore!" We couldn't do a tug-of-war because one team would feel bad if the other team won."

Seekamp's school was part of a nationwide trend. In Michigan one school included the following paragraph in its Field Day flier:

The purpose of the day is for our school to get together for an enjoyable two hours of activities and provide an opportunity for students, teachers and parents to interact cooperatively. Since we believe that all of our students are winners, the need for athletic ability and the competitive "urge to win" will be kept to a minimum. The real award... good feelings...

Of his school following that practice Seekamp said, "I thought it was ridiculous. And a lot of the other teachers, including the female teachers, thought it was ridiculous. They'd say, 'When these kids get older they're going to realize that there are winners in life and losers in life. Somebody is going to get the job. There's one job slot and two hundred applicants. There's going to be one winner and 199 losers.' So... in some ways this denial of competition and of winners and losers is harmful. It's not preparing kids for the real world."

One might ask, "Well, if all the teachers recognize the problem, why don't they do it differently?" Seekamp answers, "If our school administration adopts a philosophy, then we have to stand by it and support it. For those years that this guy was vice principal that was the way things got handled. Even disciplinary actions... you now, he didn't want to make anyone feel too bad. He didn't want them to feel the school was coming down on them. But then you, as a teacher, became powerless as far as discipline went."

TPNN contributor Jennifer Burke put it this way:

… [It is as if] there is no such thing as exceptionalism. Individual accomplishment is frowned upon and the collective is pushed and celebrated. No wonder we have a generation of self-absorbed individuals who believe that society owes them something.

This is not across the board. We do not have a generation of self-absorbed individuals. There are many locations which have resisted these policies, or even revolted against them. And there are things that individual teachers do which ameliorate official demands. In Seekamp's school things have changed. "The guy we have now is good. Now we do have winners and losers. Of course we do it in a tasteful way." Some problems persist; others emerge as policies are updated.

Let's visit Graham's classroom and review some of the problems he confronts: the ones he solves and the ones which remain beyond his control. My hope is that you will see why I chose him as my example of a great teacher.

Graham Seekamp has taught 5th grade in a central Connecticut suburban community for sixteen years. His town once could have served as the model for Thornton Wilder's *Our Town*. It is now a town with some blue-collar neighborhoods, but mostly it is middle-class. By blue-collar we don't mean to suggest residential areas for industrial- and trades-worker's families as it might have been in the 1950s, but that there are now lower socio-economic neighborhoods. Like many idyllic New England towns, it is not what it once was. Many people have moved in from the abutting city—a city with numerous problems. "If you reach a certain level and you can move across the town line," Graham says, "then you've kind of made it." [As an aside, note, for a number of years Graham's own children attended school in the city.]

Of the five 5th grade classes in his school Graham is the only male teacher. All the first- through-fourth grade teachers are female, but, as he notes, "We're very uncommon in that we have two male Kindergarten teachers." The gym teacher and one of the school administrators, a vice principal, are also male. "That's about it." In the town's other elementary schools there are a total of four male teachers. In the middle and high school the percentage of male teachers increases significantly.

First problem: Why Johnny doesn't read. Graham relates the following incident.

"When you go from 5th grade to the middle school, there is a required reading assignment that has to be done over the summer. Last year they told the teachers the kids had to read three books, one that was mandatory. They also elected to have the kids read other books which would be put on a checklist as part of the Governor's Readers Challenge. One of the books they picked out—this was the mandatory one, the one every kid going into the 6th grade had to read— was a book about an adolescent Indian girl who is going through various issues assimilating to American life. Show me any 5th grade boy who is going to want to read about a girl from India assimilating to American life! And I have to be the teacher and hand this book out to the kids and tell them to obey the rules. You can hear the boys, 'We gotta read this?!' I'm going, 'Yup. Yes, you have to read this,' but I'm thinking to myself, this wouldn't have turned me on when I was ten years old, that's for damn sure. I was one of those kids who, when I was ten years old, they couldn't make read a book. I needed to be interested in a certain subject matter, and then I'd read everything I could on it. I wouldn't have read that book.

"Of course when the summer reading list committee was having their meeting, the number of male teachers in the realm was far outnumbered by the female teachers. It was, 'Well, we're going to make the kids read this. We picked it, and this is the book that's going to get read. Does anybody have any questions?'

"I said, 'I don't think too many of the ten-year-old boys are going to be interested in this book.'

"They came back with, 'Well, we thought about that, and we looked at some other books we thought were possibilities, but we thought this would be the best one.' They didn't want to know what I was saying. They had already made up their minds. The head of the reading department is a woman. All these people had made up their minds."

This may seem like a minor incident, but what this action does is set up the boys for failure; exactly as would mandating a book on NFL quarterback stats set up girls for failure. The first impression the new 6th grade teachers are going to have of many of these boys is one of kids who do not finish their assignments.

As Graham says, " You try promoting reading, but you wouldn't have done anything but turn me off to reading if I were ten and I was told I had to read that book. Whether it's a good book or a bad book isn't the issue. It's the subject matter. You want to turn me off to reading tell me I *have* to read this book. Boys need to have some choice on what they read; they need to be allowed to follow their interests."

Next problem: Teaching to mandated, standardized tests and to Common Core curriculums limits teacher initiative, creates more sedentary classrooms, and promotes unhealthy lifestyles. As does pandering to irresponsibility. Great teachers are able to avoid only some of the pitfalls.

Boys need to be physical. Graham, who is also a personal trainer at a local gym, promotes movement. "You have boys that do well in elementary school," Graham explains, "but on the whole girls tend to do better because sitting in a chair at that age, doing what you're told, et cetera, seems for many girls just easier… it's just not a boy thing. I think more administrators are becoming aware of this. In our school we are strongly advised to have what we call a Morning Meeting where the whole class goes to the carpet, and we have some kind of a game or a greeting. Different people are allowed to share, or we'll have a game that promotes movement.

"I think this is good. Being a personal trainer, what I've done with my kids is I've actually taught them exercises. We do them at that time of day. Many times I'll take the kids outside and we'll do exercises outside. Some days I'll have the kids take a hike with me through part of the woods by the school. Or maybe we'll go out on the playground and I'll teach them how to do dips off the bike rack, or how to do some sort of quick obstacle course. We'll get out there for 15 minutes and then comeback.

"There's nothing from the Board of Education that says the kids should be exercising more, but being a personal trainer and seeing what's happening to our society, I see a bunch of kids who are nine and ten years old and we have a chance to teach them a little bit about fitness and regular fitness skills that they maybe will have with them for the rest of their lives. So I try to institute that. I tell them that. I say, "Hey guys. You know you can either learn some of this stuff now or you can come back to me later in life and pay me $60 an hour, and I'll teach you the same thing." They think that's funny.

"We'll get out and be doing these different activities. I'm the only class in the whole school that does it. The administrators don't say, 'Everybody go out there and do what Mr. Seekamp does.' Nobody says I can't do it. I do it. They see me out there in the parking lot doing relays with the kids or whatever we're doing at that point in time. They don't think twice about it. I've done it every year I've been a teacher.

"The gym teacher thinks it's good. He and I always chuckle, 'Here we are, every day being told to do x, y, and z to get these kids ready for these mandated tests. Mandated tests! All these mandated tests. Sit down, sit still, learn the answers to these specific questions. But nobody seems to care if these kids are healthy. What good are these tests… are having the kids prepped to pass these tests, if they're getting diabetes when they're ten years old, or they're getting heart disease when they're sixteen? What good are these scores if they can't live a healthy life?' So he and I get a chuckle out of the irony of this.

"He'll say something in his class. 'You guys have no energy. You're low on carbs.' But none of the kids know what a carb is! So in my class, in my health and nutrition unit I'll make sure we talk about carbs, proteins, and fats. I'll make sure they know how to read a food label. Then it starts to make sense. But nowhere in our curriculum does it say to do that. And most schools don't; most kids don't learn this stuff. It's not difficult for them, and the kids love to learn about it. But it's not on any standardized tests. I have parents come in and say, 'Suzie says were not eating a balanced diet at dinner. Now we have to spend $50 more on groceries every week because we have to eat the healthy food and not all the crap! But you know what, I'm happy you're doing it anyway.'"

I pointed out to Graham that he might tell these parents that, in the long run, they are likely saving a lot more on medical bills than $50 per week. I also point out that according the articles in Psychiatry Advisor, physically active kids tend to have better cognitive functions and brain activity, and that physical exercise may be an effective way of threating ADHD.

Graham acknowledged, then continued his story. "I still live in the same town I teach in, and being a personal trainer in town I see a lot of my kids when they are older. They went to middle school; they went to high school, they got drafted by colleges for sports... I see them in the gym when they're working out. They'll say, 'Hey, Mr. Seekamp...' That's all right, just call me Graham. These kids are now 18, 19, 20 years old. 'Mr. Seekamp... the best thing I remember about your class was the exercises. Do you still go on hikes with the kids?' 'Oh yeah, we still do them.' 'I remember you used to make us do pushups, or relay races, or sit-ups. You still do that?' 'Oh yeah. We still do all of that.' 'That's great!' That's what these kids still remember after being in my class 10, 12, 15 years ago. But it is something that we are not told by the administration to do, yet obviously it was important in some of these kid's lives. Out of all the things they learned that year and over the years, that's the one thing that pops out in their mind.

"What I've seen is that just getting them up and getting them moving, they become more engaged in whatever they'll be doing when they are in their seats—the writing, reading, math or whatever."

Another part of this story is how Graham handles health and nutrition. "I let the kids have a healthy snack every day. I like to make sure I'm eating a healthy snack, too. It's a good idea to promote eating throughout the day rather than only three big meals. So, at the beginning of the year we talk about what is a healthy snack. Somebody will say, 'Raisins.' Someone else, 'Fruit.' We come up with a list... granola bars, et cetera. Somebody will say, 'Potato chips,' and I'll go, 'Well... let's look at them. This, this, this... maybe not so healthy. Let's leave that off the list.' We end up with a long list of foods that are acceptable as a healthy snack. As the year goes by someone will try to test the waters. They'll have forgotten to bring in a snack, and they'll raid their lunchbox and have a 'Scooter Pie.' [*Scooter Pies are a version of* Moon Pies *named after NY Yankees shortstop Phil "Scooter" Rizzuto. They have two graham-like crackers sandwiching a layer of marshmallow covered with chocolate.*] So I say, 'Sam, is that really a healthy snack?! Why don't you save that for lunch?' And the kids will all chuckle."

This seems sensible enough, doesn't it? Nothing hard here. No controversy? But...

"This past year one mother got on my case. Her daughter brought in Oreos. I said, 'Suzy, that's not a healthy snack. Why don't you get something else? Fruit, or whatever.' The next morning her mom demanded to meet with me and the vice principal. She didn't even let me know what the problem was beforehand.

"So we had this meeting. The mother says, 'I don't think it is appropriate. She comes home talking about steroids, about how she can and can't eat certain foods.' I said, 'She is probably talking about steroids because I stress drug free athletic, and we were talking about things the kids had heard in the news about baseball players using steroids. I was talking about how that is not the way you want to do things. You want to eat right; you want to train hard. That's the way to attain certain goals.' The mother has now stated her position, 'My daughter is allergic to so many foods, if you tell her she can't eat certain foods she's going to end up not eating anything and she's going to waste away.' The assistant principal decided it. 'We can't tell her what she can or cannot eat at a certain time of day. If you're going to have a snack, you have to let her have whatever she wants.' I'm thinking, Oreos! Oreos! You want your daughter to eat Oreos? Go right ahead.

"In these battles, you try to be a role model to these kids. In 16 years I never had a problem with it. But that's what came up last year. The principal wasn't entirely supportive. It was either let her have whatever she wants, or don't have the snack at that time. So what am I supposed to say to the class, 'Kids, we're not going to have a healthy snack at ten o'clock in the morning anymore because Suzy's mom wants her to eat Oreos at that time.'? I'm thinking, All right! Fine! We'll just do it your way. She can eat Oreos. The rest of us will eat our healthy snack.

"The whole principle behind it burned me up. On top of this the mother was a teacher herself... either a middle school or high school science teacher!"

What comes to my mind is that parenting in that fashion is a form of child abuse. But it is not as abusive as the hysteria over guns.

One more problem: Hypersensitivity to the word "gun" or to violence in stories: To me this is a sad story, a near tragic story. It is along the line of stories Dr. Reynolds tells about ADHD boys, but in this case the attempted control is not because of hyper-activity, nor were drugs used to straightjacket the kid. We've all seen in the news stories about six- or seven-year olds being disciplined, suspended or expelled for ghastly infractions—like chewing pop tarts into the shape of pistols, or drawing a dagger during an art lesson. What would you do if your ten-year-old son was a protégé playwright?

Graham tells us: "For a long time, in our school, the rule was that if the kids were writing a story they could not write about shooting, they could not write about guns, they could not write about anything violent. For a long time I thought this too, because I had other teachers, women, saying, 'Oh, you can't let (a student) write about shooting a gun, or even having a gun in the story.' My approach to it was: My goal is to get this kid to write. If he's going to be motivated to write because he has a hero character with a machine gun, and he's on a battlefield, okay, let him write about it! Why not? The goal is to get the kid to write, not to tell him what he can and can't write; not tell him he can't write about guns or tanks or war. If you do that you just shut off about half of the 10-year old male writers because that's what they want to write about. They want to write about the blood dripping out of wounds. Don't automatically think *pathological*, instead maybe think, important American literature, think *The Red Badge of Courage* by Stephen Crane (1871); or think about heroes, think about Audie Murphy. Boys are going to write about guns. They want to give you details about what an AR-15 or an M-16 looks like. Let 'em. Let 'em do it. You're going to get them to write! Isn't that the goal to get the kid to write? Let 'em do it! If you tell 'em we're going to write but you can't write about this, this or this... you shut off their creativity. And the boys want to create.

"In the books adults read now-a-days, say Stephen King, you get all the gory details, and that's acceptable. Boys, if there's a car crash, they're going to want to describe somebody flying through the windshield with cuts all over their body. That appeals to the way boys are. The girls are all going to say, 'Oooooo, ooooooo, I hate that story.' But the boys are enthusiastic. They're asking, 'Then what happened? Did he get up and walk away? Was there blood dripping everywhere?'

"We are now (in my school) in an environment where that's okay. But there is still that rift. The woman that teaches next to me (another 5th grade) had a kid in her room last year who was probably one of the brightest kids, if not *the* brightest kid, in the school. He was a bit socially aloof, but he was extremely intelligent. He had a fascination with World War II, with Hitler and the Nazis, and with what they did. He had obviously read a lot… whatever he could before someone took it away. So at the beginning of the year he was writing a play. A ten-year old boy, on his own, writing a play! Nobody told him he had to do this. His play dealt with Nazism and the persecution of the Jewish people. My colleague found out about it and she was, 'I can't believe he's writing about this. This is awful.' She tried to put the brakes on the whole thing. 'You can't write this. You're going to go down and talk to the assistant principal.'

"I'm thinking, if he were my student, I'd say, 'Okay. Try to be tasteful with it. Try not to go too crazy with it.' But I'd let him keep writing. Well, she wasn't going to let him write it. He got sent down to the principal. She demanded the principal read it. I really couldn't say much because he wasn't in my class.

"The other side to this is that I have his class for social studies. We were teaching about Vikings. I got to know this kid. Others were saying, 'Oh. He's so quirky. He's violent…' Well, he wasn't any of those things in my class. He was extremely interested in everything we talked about. Okay, it was about Vikings and battleaxes and swords, so we had his interest, and he did great. He kind of sensed that I was on his side. He'd run things by me. He'd go out of his way to say hi to me, and I'd say hi to him because I felt sorry that he was trapped in a class where he wasn't able to express the enthusiasm he had for this subject. I would probably have just let him go with it."

At this point in the story I stopped Graham and asked, "How is he with other kids; with being touched by other kids?" I asked that question because I was thinking about Adam Lanza, the shooter in the Sandy Hook killings. Lanza was very smart, and quirky… maybe way beyond quirky.

Graham said, "He doesn't seem to mind being touched. He has friends he hangs out with. He's not one of the jocks, so he doesn't really do a whole lot with the kickball games and stuff. But because he is so intelligent he manufactures things to spend his time on… like the play he was writing. He doesn't seem to me to fit that crazy mold of a serial killer. Not even close. He's interested in some of the more violent types of things, but seems like a pretty normal kid. His language is more sophisticated than what you'd expect from the average 5th grader.

"Through this whole incident I'm thinking, *A 5th grade boy writing a play! Don't squash it. Celebrate it.* Our male vice principal—he had read Sommers' *The War Against Boys*—had a good handle on the situation. He said, 'Well, he's not doing any harm. And he's writing. He's writing about something he's interested in. You know what, unless it is blatantly pathological, let the kid write.' Had he not felt that way, the kid would have been stopped."

I thought long and hard about this. What would be the long term results if that boy had been condemned—because stopping him from writing would be a form of condemnation, wouldn't it? Would his attitude about school, and about writing, have changed? He might be the next Tom Clancy or Ernest Hemingway, but maybe he would never write another line. This notion that all violence, including even the mention of violence, must be avoided, as we've seen earlier, is nonsense. Exactly like castigating men for telling their sons, "Big boys don't cry," the images or citing of violence has meaning. Shouldn't we be asking: Does the teaching a boy constructive violence serve a cultural or biological purpose? Does avoiding proper images of violent actions create a void in a child's education which someone else, perhaps someone far less savory than a teacher, coach or scout master, may fill? Is this avoidance of our cultural duty, this reluctance and absence of teaching, an abuse of boys? Does this set them up for exploitation by gang leaders or others who do not have their best interest at heart?

Above I used the phrases, *constructive violence* and *proper images of violent actions*. Heroic stories—from the core of classical literature to Saturday morning cartoons—universally tell the story of the journey of the hero and his reluctant use of violence, physical or mental, to overcome evil. A young boy's superhero play or a ten-year old playwright's manuscript (like the one above about resisting Nazism), build a sense justice and morality in the child. Isn't that a cultural purpose?!

To me it was exhilarating to hear Graham's stories. Something I have long suspected: despite the continuous flow of criticism and warnings about our "failing schools," despite the bureaucratic nonsense and over regulation, and despite the attacks by various rabid elements, there are still good people and great teachers; there are still people making a difference in the lives of our youth; there are still professionals wanting to do the right thing. Their efforts breaks down when they are made powerless and feel they can no longer impact young lives. Those circumstances are not universal; nor are they undisputed. The battle continues.

Graham has given us some interesting insight. His experiences are mainly with a highly-rated, suburban elementary school. What's happening in lesser-rated schools, particularly those in economically-challenged neighborhoods? What's the national picture? A significant portion of our boys *are* being left behind; their futures sacrificed to social-engineered programs and political correctness. Let's look at some additional examples.

Recently there was a TV news exposé about elementary schools in New Haven. The report was about students attacking teachers— kicking, biting and scratching. These students were kindergarteners. Instead of giving the teacher the authority to grasp a kid by the shoulders and sternly say, "You can't do that. Sit down," the solution being sought was "We need more resources. We want to have another person in the classroom." But that person still was not going to have the authority to subdue an out of control child, no matter the degree of the assault. That person would be there mainly to document the event! As I watched I thought, *Is this the final breakdown of society where the mother, perhaps only 20, has never disciplined the child—perhaps because she was never disciplined, or worse because she was abusively disciplined?* Where, I asked myself, has sensibility gone? Is the Age of Reason, the Age of Enlightenment, completely dead?

The purpose of that 17th-century movement was to fundamentally transform society by promoting the scientific method— that is promoting the use of rational thought patterns (formal logic) that analyze problems using clearly stated principles and criteria (hypotheses) to investigate issues on the basis of evidence, to test that evidence, and to derive conclusions from the process which either validated or disproved the hypothesis. As a boy, as a student, as a doctor I thought I, we, all of us, lived in an enlightened age. Yet we seemingly have reverted to an age in which political sound bites have replaced intellectual conclusions derived from evidence.

To a five-year old, being enabled or allowed to be out of control, is frightening. It conveys an environment in chaos. It promotes insecurity. Please, someone, do those little kids a favor, swat them on the fanny—not hard, not with malicious anger, but as a loving mother might. I'm against abuse, including abuse of teachers being bitten and kicked by five-year olds; *and* the abuse of those same five-year olds put into a politically-correct, chaotic environment. Needed: a quick, firm spank and a firm voice telling them to sit down. Regain respect. Without it the kindergarten classroom becomes an abusive jungle for all.

The problem, of course, may be more complicated. I am assuming these children have not been brain-damaged from before birth. I add this here for the reader to pursue in depth elsewhere for we can only delve into so many corners. According to a number of nurses and colleagues I know from the area who specialize in labor and delivery, a significant percentage of the children born in central Connecticut are born addicted to various drugs—narcotics, prescriptions, over-the-counter drugs, or alcohol (10% to 11% nationally). Two thousand years ago the Romans made it illegal for a young couple to imbibe during their first two years of marriage because they understood, or suspected way back then what we would today call fetal alcohol syndrome. It seems they were more enlightened than we are now. Drug or substance abuse during pregnancy can have devastating effects. Drug abuse during pregnancy *is* child abuse. Moms *and dads* are responsible, and should be held accountable. Children are the treasure of our species. In classroom situations, some of the kids who are out of control are out of control because of prenatal abuse. This is a separate problem from the legislated enablement of chaos, and it requires distinct solutions.

David Larson's response to my call for a quick swat on the butt was, "The teacher would be arrested." We met Dr. Larson earlier. Now retired, he has been a teacher, coach, principal, superintendent, President of the Connecticut Association of School Superintendents, and an evaluator of International School Accreditation for the New England Association of Schools and Colleges. He continued, "But you're right, those behaviors, they don't start in school. That's the home. Teachers now… we have kids who are coming to school soiling their pants. They're five years old and have never been potty trained.

Teachers have to have extra pairs of pants for these students. And they'd have to go in and wipe the kids butt. That's parenting. Quite frankly, you have 15 and 16 year olds who [gave birth] but are not responsible. They don't know how to parent. They may not have been parented themselves. You don't find that stuff in the suburbs but you do find it in urban areas.

People say American schools are failing. Our schools are not failing. Could some be failing in Hartford and Bridgeport? Yes. But you get to suburbia, they're doing just fine. Richard Rothstein, a sociologist from the University of California, did a study and concluded that schools can only be responsible for up to 40% of students' success or failure; the other 60% include pre- and post-natal care, parenting, diet, parents with jobs, single or two-parent households, etc."

Dave Larson and I talked at length about various influences, from in utero to high school and college. One comment of his I cherished, "In my father's generation there was a feeling of patriotism—not so much flag-waving *but the desire to make our country work.* I always felt we also strove to make our country work. I was blessed... being in public education and being in positions of authority, I was able to sit on the front porch of democracy, and watch it, and help it, and nurture it. I don't know if people now in the positions of authority feel that. I felt it because it was inculcated from my father's generation to me. My generation didn't do as good a job with the younger people."

Didn't do as good a job... Didn't inculcate... Why? What changes, what influences, what special interests, what laws are behind my generation's not doing as good a job? Or behind us not having the will to make the country work?!

The Biederman Scandal

Before we talk about the radical end of the Women's Movement—I was about to call it the Estrogen Mafia—or the statistics comparing the changing educational levels of boys and girls over the past fifty years, or about the various uses and abuses of civil rights laws, let's look at an example of academia and the private sector teaming up illegally to the detriment of boys. The significance of this example goes far beyond the issue of ADHD, the corruption involved in research, and the resultant diagnostic parameters policies/regulations, because all these elements interact with and mutually reinforce current, debilitating cultural, political, and financial trends. This interaction has created, and continues to create, an ethos detrimental to male development. We briefly mentioned this confluence of interest earlier when discussing ADHD and Lethargic Cognitive Tempo with Dr. Reynolds.

The Biederman scandal exemplifies the corruption of academia by powerful political and economic forces. Allegedly "scientific" research from a major university had hidden predetermined conclusions designed to support the ultimate goal of pharmaceutical corporations—massive profit. Essentially, the researchers and the corporation were out to make a killing.

Dr. Reynolds explained that a vast majority of this research was funded by drug manufactures, and that this alone, *if properly disclosed*, is not an issue. "They study these children with the conscious or unconscious agenda of finding ways to help these kids. You know, 'Better Living Through Chemistry.'"

Let's look at what happened.

Joseph Biederman, a child psychiatrist at Harvard Medical School and Massachusetts General Hospital, along with two colleagues, Thomas Spencer and Timothy Wilens, who are considered "...responsible for trailblazing the use of antipsychotic drugs in children, are facing sanctions for their failure to declare their acceptance of millions of dollars from pharmaceutical companies between 2000 and 2007." (Owens) A U.S. Senate investigation begun in 2008 alleged there was a potential conflict of interest due to the large, undisclosed payments.

Reynolds noted that Biederman was probably the country's top researcher dealing with children with special needs. "Study after study, and result after result from his clinic and his lab was showing how kids basically needed medication because they have all these behavioral issues. Then it came to light about the millions and millions he was being given... enriching himself both personally and his operation."

Biederman is known for pioneering "the diagnosis of bipolar disorder in children and adolescents, a disorder previously thought to affect only adults." As one of the world's most influential psychiatrists, his "...work led to a 40-fold increase in the pediatric bipolar disorder diagnoses, and an accompanying expansion in the use of antipsychotic drugs..." (Owen) Although Harvard, Mass General and the National Institute of Health all have regulations limiting or forbidding the practice, "Biederman and his colleagues... failed to accurately disclose the large consultancy fees they were receiving from pharmaceutical companies that make antipsychotics..." The cumulative fees amounted to $4.2 million. In their defense the psychiatrists averred that their "misconduct was an honest mistake..." (Owen).

So what potential effect has this honest $4.2million oversight had on boys? "All of his work is being gradually discredited," Dr. Reynolds commented. "Unfortunately, it is the major body of research that we have, and that has guided our understanding and treatment of kids with special needs. The field is in a great deal of turmoil... [Biederman has] been the handmaiden of the pharmaceutical industry."

One in thirteen, or 7.7%, of America's 55 million schoolchildren take psychiatric medications. That's 4.25 million kids. Of those 4.25 million, 81% have been diagnosed with ADHD. That equals nearly 3.5 million, and at least 4 out of 5 are boys; so some 2.75 million current schoolboys are on ADHD meds! Seen in terms of just boys, that's 1 in 10, 10%! Via these boys alone, the overall revenue generated from the sale of ADHD drugs is an estimated $3.3 billion per year.

Of the non-ADHD psychiatrically medicated 19%, the diagnoses span the gamut from oppositional defiant disorder, anxiety, depression and bipolar disorder. Schizophrenia and other severe conditions make up a very small percentage of all diagnoses. Studies have shown that depressed children put on ADHD drug therapy are 1.5 times more likely to develop bipolar disorder than children without depression put on the same medications.

An interesting aside: the National Health Interview Survey concluded that "...significantly more children on Medicaid or Children's Health Insurance Program were on medication for emotional and behavioral problems... [than children] with private insurance [or] ...children without insurance." (Gordon) We'll get to the causes and ramifications of this later.

So what is the scandal here? According to Jacob Azerrad, PhD, a clinical psychologist and author of *From Difficult to Delightful in Just 30 Days*:

> The real scandal perpetrated by Biederman has nothing to do with his consulting fee shenanigans and everything to do with the real life (and death) consequences of the methods now used by pediatric psychiatry to tag normal childhood behaviors with diagnoses – like "childhood bipolar" – and the pediatric medical profession's complicit acquiescence to such malarkey. It has been nothing short of an epic assault on our children by those who prescribe antipsychotic medications as an antidote to normal childhood behavior...
>
> The result: a generation of parents looking for ... quick fixes for run-of-the-mill behavior... Drugs like Risperdal, Trileptal, and Clonidines... the long term effect of their use in toddlers is dangerously unknown. Their immediate side effects, however, are well documented and include drooling, ticks and excessive weight gain.
>
> ...It used to be that children once had discipline; now they have a diagnosis.

Dr. Reynolds explains that the diagnosis ADHD, and chemical therapy for it, began in 1980 when the disorder was first included in the Diagnostic and Statistical Manuel. "Once a disease gets into our psychiatric manual—that's sort of like our bible—then that's open territory for pharmaceutical companies to try to come up with some solutions." The ADHD population steadily increased from 1980 to current levels, and a huge bureaucracy built up behind it, surpassing any original expectations. "Kids who would never have been thought to be disabled now got additional funding from local, state and federal governments. But at what cost to the kids? There's been a long battle within the psychological/psychiatric community regarding the long-term effects of these medications. Some of us believe they retard social development, others believe they facilitate it."

In case you might be thinking one can buck the system, realize that *The System*—schools, state agencies, etc.—can and will enforce compliance with prescribed protocols, and if necessary will do so in the most coercive manner. For example, there is the case of the Detroit mom who was "...thrown in jail for exercising her parental judgment about her daughter's best interest." The crime: mom was weaning her daughter off Risperdal. It made no difference to the agents of Detroit Child Protection that the drug has "multiple, harmful severe adverse effects [including] an increase in prolactin level... abnormal breast development and milk secretion (in boys and girls), sexual dysfunction, and bone density loss." (Sharav)

The literature is chock full of such cases. And if that isn't bad enough, kids who are wards of the state (in foster homes) tend to be medicated at greater levels—as high as 52% in one state—not to help the children but to make them more docile and thus more easily controlled. One in three kids on Medicaid in the same state were "prescribed mind-altering psychotropic drugs" in 2010. I have harped on this before, but I will repeat it: This is child abuse.

If Lethargic Cognitive Tempo is a diagnosis in search of a population, what about the origins of Attention Deficit/Hyperactive Disorder? Behavioral neurologist Dr. Richard Saul claims there is no such thing as ADHD. Dr. Saul has practiced medicine for fifty years and has seen thousands of patients demonstrating the cluster of symptoms which define the disorder. He notes that Ritalin, the most commonly prescribed med for ADHD, stimulates the brain to reduce fidgeting but, for some, it not only increases fidgeting but "creates its own matrix of side effects including dangerous behavior." (Wilde) Dr. Saul calls its use "neglectful." And wrong. He is convinced that an array of attention disorder symptoms are caused by iron deficiency, and points to a French study showing 84% of ADHD subjects with low iron levels versus only 18% of the non-ADHD subjects. Dr. Saul's solution sound strangely to me like Graham Seekamp's teaching methods—eat better and exercise properly.

Think about it. There may be no such thing as ADHD yet we are medicating 2.5 million boys for it! And those medicated boys know they are being medicated, and they suffer the side effects of the chemicals. Boys, like Giovan Bazan below, know they don't feel quite right. The sensation of not feeling right is distressing and depressing. Distress, anxiety and depression are all avenues leading to additional medications; and medicating depressed boys with ADHD drugs seems to cause a rise in bipolar disorders. Also, Ritalin and Adderall are psychostimulants that negatively impact normal childhood development by artificially triggering the release of norepinephrine, a neural transmitter that facilitates memory formation but also stimulates the fear reaction. These meds sets up, particularly in children exposed to trauma, increased risk factors for PTSD; and possibly increased risk of suicide. With all this in mind, the Biederman scandal becomes even more disconcerting.

Giovan Bazan, whose mother died when he was very young, was a foster child. Now in his 20s, he describes being drugged since age six, and by his teens being on so many drugs the mixture caused seizures. At 18, and finally out on his own, Bazan went cold turkey from the psychotropic drug cocktail he'd been force to ingest for twelve years. He now believes that he would have been a better child had someone "just taken a look at what was going on in my life." (Hunt) Indeed he was, and so many other boys have been or are being, cheated out of their boyhoods. That has *unintended* consequences for the rest of their lives.

Dr. Reynolds laments, "When there's a dollar to be made there will be somebody there to make it. Even with kids… One of the reasons I love working with kids who've got special needs—behaviorally disorder kids, ADHD kids—is because they are the most interesting, creative, outside the box kids. That's what's special about them! You take a kid like that… you put a kid like that on medication, all that stuff that makes them cool and interesting, it is all sectioned off so they can focus. It is like a mental straightjacket. Now they can do their homework, and they can pay attention, and they can sit docilely in class, but all the stuff that makes them interesting—GONE! And the parents know this. That's why they say, 'My child's personality has changed when he's on medication.' They no longer get emails from the teacher every day. She's happy. 'My child's grades have gone up. So I'm happy.' But nobody is stopping to ask, 'What is the effect on this child's personality development?' These medications shrink these big personalities… shrink to fit. All that stuff that makes these kids wonderful and special, where has that gone?"

Dr. Azerrad brings it back to the culture:

> …parents are taught to reward bad behavior with more attention – and that's nonsense. Many of the most popular child-rearing books repeatedly urge parents to hold, soothe, comfort, and talk to the child who bites, screams, throws, breaks things, or otherwise behaves in obnoxious, infantile

ways. Commonsense and truckloads of research argue solidly against this practice. Yet these experts seem to be unaware of the well-established fact that children do what gets noticed, that adult attention usually makes behavior [to] occur more likely, not less. The result is that the "terrible-two" behavior begets the even worse terrible threes, fours, and fives followed by a diagnosis and then – all too often – pills.

Dr. Reynolds would agree. "If parents find their way here, by the time they've gotten to my clinic… We don't do medications here. We don't medicate children. By the time parents have gotten to my clinic, they have been through all kinds of medications, all kinds of different therapies and special education. For them it has been a nightmare… to the point where I think of changing the name of the clinic to The Clinic Of Last Resort. I can tell you, if you actually sit down with these parents and listen to what they have to say, and then help them to develop the tools that they need to provide the right environment at home, these kids don't need medication. But the parents seldom get that kind of help because it is not that readily available. There are not a lot of people who do what we do here."

Reynolds grieves over that paucity in mental health services, and the mentality that "medications fill the gap." I asked if that was a matter of insurance companies finding it more difficult to compensate mental health services than to pay for drugs. "Exactly," said Reynolds. "That's the insurance companies' protocol. Anything outside of those protocols the insurance companies say, 'Go knock yourself out. If you want to pay of those services, go right ahead. We're going to pay for medications.' So that's another roadblock. Insurance companies fail to compensate for treatment other than medication-based treatment. For example, when a child is having trouble, a parent comes to me saying, 'My child is having trouble in school. His teachers are constantly reprimanding him. He's constantly being in detention. I get emails every day about his behavior.' I often go out to the school. I'll call a PPT (Planning and Placement Team) meeting, or have the parents call for the meeting, so we can all talk about it. And I'll set up a plan that the teachers can implement that gets the child on track. But the insurance companies don't pay me to do that. They reimburse whatever they feel is the cheapest, most expedient way to solve a problem. 'Hammer the kid with medication. Problem solved.' The kid is a zombie sitting their stoned, but he's no longer a behavior problem. Everybody's happy."

Dr. Sally Satel, psychiatrist, resident scholar at the American Enterprise Institute, and co-author of *One Nation Under Therapy*, blames much of the current aberrant social behavior on *therapism*, "not the same things as therapy per se, which can often provide real benefits, but a damaging mindset [that]... 'pathologizes normal human emotion, promoting the illusion that we are very fragile beings...'" That mindset includes the concepts that competitive games in school kill self-esteem, that we—fragile helpless creatures that we all are— can only reach full potential via a soft and cuddly world, and that criminals and wrongdoers are "victims of malign[ed] social forces, entitled to... empathy... compassion... and... our tax dollars." (Thornton) These convictions, seemingly enlightened and compassionate social concepts, as we've seen, play into the hands of social engineers, corporate accounting departments, and an entire array of scallywags and confidence men.

The expose of the Biederman scandal came to light in 2010. Four years later the number of kids being drugged into docility has not decreased! Worse yet, as we have seen, if a parent refuses to give a kid declared ADHD his prescribed drugs, the state can take custody of the kid, force the drugs down his throat, and jail the parent.

I cannot help but think of Dr. Azerrad's description of poor parenting as anything but an analogy for our transformed society. Those who have behaved badly, those who've kicked and screamed and bitched the loudest, are the ones who've been rewarded with attention, which has reinforced their tantrums. Soothing talk, political pandering and appeasement beget an increase in obnoxious and infantile behavior. Although many are aware of this, the pitfall of democracy is that leaders, in exchange for power, can pander comfort. This leads to poor policy decisions, which in turn leads to ever deteriorating social conditions and greater needs, which leads to stronger and more intense demands, bitching and screaming, which in turn requires more soothing, pandering or medication. Supportive industries and bureaucracies sprout, grow, strengthen, mature and propagate with their primary motives being profitable self-perpetuation. It is a vicious cycle; symptomatic of a society and culture that has derailed.

Gender Inequity

At the moment I am thinking of the demeanor of the intelligent and beautiful TV host, Mika Brzezinski. If there is something she doesn't agree with, she treats it with open contempt. Her attitude feels almost like Rene Descartes' pronouncement, "I think, therefore I am," except with Brzezinski it seems to be, "I am a woman, therefore what I say is true." The assumed postulate is: Being a woman, thus being part of a victimized class, makes my statements incapable of being false, and further makes them unchallengeable. In this manner she bullies listeners. Mika's presentation does not invite give and take. There is no, "I agree with you on this; let me think about that; I'm not sure item three is correct." What it invites is a defensive attitude in an arena where she holds all the power. This limits the exchange of ideas: dialogue and rational thought be damned.

Many public figures, particularly from the political left, seem to adopt this attitude. They deal with the world through displays of anger and dissatisfaction, and they use this as a tool and a weapon to get their way. Then, even when they have gotten their way, they continue to wield that weapon because it has become their *modus operandi*. To me, it is a strange way to interact with the world.

A dear family friend has succumbed to that approach. She is a top executive, very successful. On Christmas Eve, a few years back, I met her for a drink at the Hartford Club. I said, "How's it going?" "She said, "Well, I'm really tired of having men telling me what to do. And that includes you." This was Christmas Eve. I was stunned. I'm thinking: How do I handle this? Do I get up and walk out? Do I confirm, acquiesce and condone? Do I throw my drink in her face? So I said to her, "How about those Red Sox?!"

She went on. "You know, when I walk into a meeting I have to get rid of my purse; I have to get rid of my briefcase; and the guys have nothing. They look at me as if, because I'm a woman, I'm supposed to get the coffee." Her attitude was almost venomous. I'm thinking: Where did you get this? When you were growing up your father and I used to ask you what you wanted to become. You'd answer "President of Delta Airlines," and we'd say, "Good. Go for it."

Then she said, "I got a text from _X_ (a cousin) which said, 'Merry Christmas to you and _Y_ (her ex of seven years).' You know

129

what I told him?! 'I've been divorced for seven years. I've moved on. You should too.'" I said, "I don't think your cousin meant any harm, or anything hurtful. He probably just wasn't thinking, except that he does think enough of you to send you those wishes.'" She couldn't accept that.

Her girlfriends have the same attitude, and they reinforce one another... in misandry as in misery, one loves company. I'm astounded that growing up in her family she developed these attitudes. She wasn't coddled. She wasn't given extras because she was a girl with two brothers. Where did this animosity come from? It was there before her divorce, although it definitely got worse with the divorce. Her brothers kind of roll their eyes. She has never said it was from this, that, or the other thing. It has settled down but that may be more a matter of wishing to be conciliatory and polite, than a change of attitude. My apologies to her: I love her dearly, yet I am using her as an example of this predetermined feminist attitude that women are oppressed because they are women.

I raced with a girl who was a trainer for the local university hockey team. She wanted to sail with us. There was another gal on the crew. The difficulty that developed was that if they were criticized or told to do something in a different way, they would take offense. Their assumption seemed to be, "You're telling me that because I'm female, and you don't think I'm capable." This became a real issue. On a race boat there are always directions. It is not criticism. There is a hierarchy: the captain, the crew boss, the tactician, etc. Things need to be done in a particular and proscribed manner, and the whole crew needs to work like a well-oiled machine.

When my son Paul raced with us he said, "Dad, it's amazing. I get on this boat and each guy goes to his position and they start setting up the boat without anybody saying anything. One guy hooks up a snatch bock and runs a line through, then gives it to the next guy without saying anything, and that guy takes it and runs it to wherever it needs to go."

But these two women just had an attitude and assumed that the rest of the crew didn't think they were capable. When we were going to do the Bermuda race—there were nine on the boat but we could only take eight—the guys didn't want her. They didn't want to spend five days, twenty-four hours a day with her. I worked with her in the hospital, and I was, "Well, you guys know..." They were, "NO! If you bring her, we're not going." That was the level of animosity that developed. It seems to be a microcosm of a much broader social condition.

The cerebral cortex of men's brains works back and forth while in women's brains it works side to side. Women talk things out. Men don't talk but still communicate via their movements and actions. A guy can just hand another guy a tool without saying, "Here, take this. You can use it to do this. When you do... And then..." With guys, the other guy just takes it because the gesture has communicated the needed information. Whether you're on a race boat or construction crew, guys watch, see voids, automatically fill gaps. Our teamwork style is different than the sisterhood's compassionate cooperation. Females, being more verbal, need to verbalize what they are doing. Perhaps—guys not realizing women need verbal clues, and women not realizing that guys by nature don't—women surmise that men are not operating fairly with them, and men conclude that women can't handle the tasks. Sometimes it is as if the genders are speaking two different languages, and neither realizes that the other does not understand their native tongue. So they speak louder in their native tongue as if that's the solution. When the problem isn't solved resentment follows.

The attitude, *They're not operating fairly with me because I'm a woman,* misses the reality of the differences in the languages we speak. One gender has a computer operating system built on Android, the other is based on Apple. They don't communicate even if there is no real clash between the two; and there is no innate clash. One not getting that communication interprets it as being shunned or put down or oppressed. The reaction to being shunned, et cetera, is anger and resentment. Anger and resentment fester to become reactionary ideologies.

The politics of gender versus equal education for boys and girls is a reactionary ideology. The passage of Title IX of Education Amendments, signed into law by President Richard Nixon on June 23, 1972, was the culmination of the women's movement of the 1960s. It was followed by the Gender Equity in Education Act of 1993. Many very positive and wonderful events and trends occurred because of these laws. As mentioned earlier, I'm a fan of UConn basketball, and particularly of the Lady Huskies. Women's scholastic and college sports programs would not be where they are today without Title IX. That is only one, although possibly the most visible, of the many important accomplishments of the Acts.

The acts, in general, as written, are pretty gender neutral, a la: "...provide a gender-equitable education to elementary and secondary school students..." and "...access progress in achieving gender equality in education." Less visible are the detrimental effects caused by legal interpretations which declare girls to be an underserved population. This affects not just men's minor sports programs, but boys in classrooms nationwide. Keep in mind those regulatory movements are co-occurrences with the DSM diagnosis of ADHD—as multipliers in the attack on boys.

Book after book, after lecture, after article, are filled with the negative results of the anti-male/anti-boy trends. A few of the most poignant: Camille Paglia (*Sexual Personae*), Christina Hoff Sommers (*The War Against Boys*), Suzanne Venker (*The War On Men),* Louann Brizendine (*The Male Brain*), Helen Smith (*Men On Strike*), and Sally Satel (*One Nation Under Therapy* (co-authored with Sommers)). Each of these authors, all women, all rational feminists, convey poignant and detailed accounts of how, when, where and why the ultra-feminist movement has damaged not just boys and men, but American culture as a whole.

Paglia: "Primary-school education is a crock... It's oppressive to anyone with physical energy... They're making a toxic environment for boys. Primary education does everything in its power to turn boys into neuters." Ms. Paglia continues by describing the emphasis in high schools as being on female traits—sensitivity, socialization and cooperation; and terming college as "...all about neutralization of maleness." Political correctness has deleted the models of manhood from the lives of many boys; resulting in a current class of political, financial and institutional leaders with fragile values at best, possibly with no values at all.

On the women's movement Ms. Paglia claims feminists like Gloria Steinman or Naomi Wolfe, and societies like the National Organization for Women (NOW), have erred in their promotion of gender as merely a social construct; and has accused some proponents of no longer seeking "equal-opportunity feminism," but of striving for quotas and protection as due compensation for their victimhood. The women's movement should abandon "the 'nanny state' mentality that led to politically correct speech codes and college disciplinary committees..." (Weiss, on Paglia) and perhaps pay more attention to the horrors afflicting women worldwide, from rape in India to honor killings in Muslim countries.

Sommers: I place more emphasis on Sommers here because of her exposés on the contradictions of gender-equality and the inequitable treatment of boys in school. She is also critical of the extreme political stance of some in the women's movement. "I have sought to make a clearer distinction between the humane and progressive women's movement and today's feminist lobby," she writes. "The lobby too often acts as a narrow, take-no-prisoners special interest group. Its members see the world as a zero-sum struggle between women and men... The current plight of boys and young men is, in fact, a woman's issue. Those boys are our sons; they are the people with whom our daughters will build a future. If our boys are in trouble, so are we all."

Sommers has examined numerous schools and school programs—those that work for boys and those that denigrate their humanity. She describes how Aviation High School in Queens, NY (a magnet school with an 85% male enrollment) emphasizes the male qualities of "... organization, precision, workmanship, and attention to details... The world of aviation—and classes with a lot of hammering, welding, riveting, sawing and drilling," she states, "seems to resonate more powerfully in the minds of boys than girls." Aviation rates in the top tier of all American high schools, but it is under attack. "...The common sense explanation," Sommers says, "is that sexes differ in their interests and propensities..." yet the American Association of University Women (AAUW) and the National Women's Law Center claims "...The vocational programs offered (at these and similar schools) correspond with outmoded and impermissible stereotypes on the basis of sex." The American Civil Liberties Union (ACLU) has labelled this "invidious segregation." Sommers comment: "What they saw at [these schools] is not 'men fully alive,' it is [to them] gender apartheid."

The Gender Equity in Education Act, which declares girls as an "underserved population" has been used to gain hundreds of millions of dollars [yes, as always, follow the public money because that defines political power] in grants "to study the plight of girls and to learn how to overcome the insidious bias against them." Reviewing DOE reports Sommers found that "girls were doing far better than boys," and that they had higher aspirations than boys, took more Advanced Placement tests than boys, out preformed boys in reading and writing, and enrolled and matriculated in colleges more than boys. The latest figures that I've seen indicate the current freshman class nationwide is 63% female, 37% male.

"Contrary to the story told by the girl-crisis lobby," Sommers writes, "the new study revealed that by the early 1990s, American girls were flourishing in unprecedented ways. ...far from being timorous and demoralized, girls outnumber boys in student government, honor societies, and school newspapers... and generally outshine boys on almost every measure of classroom success." A program for shortchanged-girls helped them close the 'science gap.' "But what is hard to understand is why the math and science gap launched a massive movement on behalf of girls and yet a much larger gap in reading, writing, and school engagement created no comparable effort for boys." Nor has the growing college attendance gap. "Today, women in the United States earn 57 percent of bachelor's degrees, 60 percent of master's degrees, and 52 percent of PhDs."

Sommers points out that "By the middle of the 2000s, the precariousness of boys and young men in American schools was one of the most thoroughly documented phenomena in the history of education..." yet the National Women's Law Center and AAUW not only ignored these exposes, they seemingly reveled in them. AAUW executive director, Linda Hallman, said in 2008, "Our adversaries know that AAUW is a force to be reckoned with, and that we have 'staying power' in our dedication to breaking through the barriers that we target..."

The results: no programs for boys. Grades, as we've previously noted, often reflect a teacher's perception of a student's general behavior, and in general, boys have poorer grades than girls even if they score as high or higher on standardized tests. This is not just a grade school issue, although that's where it begins. Higher grades open up AP and Honors classes, and this put girls, in general, in better positions to get into college. It starts in kindergarten and sets the boys back for their entire lives!!! As Sommers' puts it, "...our educational system may be punishing boys for the circumstance of being boys. And it is a punishment that can last a lifetime."

Recall Camille Paglia's comment about NOW claiming gender is a social construct; or as Sommers put it, proponents of the agenda believe that "sexual identity is learned by observing others." Of course ignored are the gender specific anatomy and brain structures formed in utero, differentiating male from female by the hormonal cocktail the fetus itself creates. The belief that children can "adopt either gender identity to suit the ends of equity and social justice…" is utter nonsense. Worse, it is one of the roots from which has grown an ethos that denounces and pathologies normal boyish behavior. Claiming that typical and traditional boy-behavior is learned, that boys have been indoctrinated to emulate the aggressiveness of their elders, and that the differences between boys and girls are not innate or physiological but cultural, allows radical elements of the women's movement to attack the humanity of men, and to demand laws essentially requiring the re-education of boys. As Sommers puts it, "Gender scholars have spent the past twenty years trying to resocialize boys away from such 'toxic' masculine proclivities… resocializing boys to play more like girls has been part of the gender equity agenda for several decades."

Resocialize?! Reeducate?! Again, Sommers: "Boys today bear the burden of several powerful cultural trends: a therapeutic approach to education that valorizes feelings and denigrates competition and risk, zero-tolerance policies that punish normal antics of young males, and a gender equity movement that views masculinity as predatory. Natural male exuberance is no longer tolerated."

To me, and to many of the men I know, it feels as if NOW, the AAUW, the ACLU and other p.c. groups wish to open reeducation camps for any male who has absorbed dreaded male characteristics. If only boys could be transformed into more passive, less competitive and less daring creatures, then the men they become will be easier to control, and all will be right with the world. Damn! What a way to look at the world! Then, of course, along comes the reprobates—me, the authors mentioned, a host of others—like curmudgeons sounding the alarm to younger generations. The battle is engaged.

But the situation on the ground is much worse than most realize. More factors: The Gilligan escapade at Harvard, along with the Valian affair at Hunter College, remind me of the Biederman scandal. Again it is Sommers, with her concentration on boys in school, to who we turn for a delineation of these accounts. Briefly, PhD Carol Gilligan's field of research is adolescent development with an emphasis on gender theory; her core belief is that children must be freed from "oppressive gender roles." With these thoughts in mind she studied a group of girls and found them to be at special risk due to being silenced, tortured, personally diminished, forced underground, and "distressed because the system was biased in favor of boys." Like Biederman, Gilligan became a leading voice in her field: highly respected, considered one of the initiators of gender theory, an important (and well-funded) academic. She was a prime mover in transforming the "girl crisis" into a civil rights issue where girls were classified as victims of rampant discrimination. Her study and follow-up pronouncements became founding blocks for equity in education laws and many ensuing regulations.

Yet, in the 1990s and 2000s, as the education gap was widening, Sommers notes, "…with girls well in the lead, boys became objects of neglect while the education establishment focused on rescuing the afflicted girls." This concept is often denied, challenged or dismissed. Sommers gives us these statistics: there are special federal programs designed to improve the skills of girls in mathematics because "boys have consistently outnumbered girls by up to 10,000" in advanced placement math courses and tests. However, there are no programs designed to improve the skills of boys in biology, history or English where "girls have consistently outnumbered boys…" in AP testing by, respectively, 32,000, 56,000 and 206,000. "Why," Sommers asks, "don't the lower male numbers count as disparity and underrepresentation?" Then she answers, "Because they do not fit the shortchanged-girl narrative promoted by the women's lobby. Unfortunately for boys, that narrative has been adopted by the federal government and other influential quarters of the American educational establishment."

With reality slapping some academics in the face, Gilligan's research became suspect. First, she studied only girls. Perhaps, had she studied both genders she might have found that adolescent boys suffer many of the same insecurities as adolescent girls. That is not a question she asked. Perhaps, also, the insecurities of girls have little to do with male aggressiveness, or male anything. A Girl Scout study, mentioned in of all places Parade Magazine says, "...of 8- to 17-year olds, one-third of the girls who said they didn't want to be leaders attributed their hesitancy to a fear of being disliked by their peers."

When Gilligan's studies were challenged [all scientific studies, to be accepted, need to be reproducible] she refused to supply either the raw data from her research, or any other supporting evidence. The foundation, the legal structure upon which gender equity laws have been built, rests on quicksand. Additional confirmation supplied by Sommers:

> The Metropolitan Life Survey of the American Teacher 1997: Examining Gender Issues in Public Schools. ... During a three-month period in 1997 various questions about gender equity were asked of 1,306 students and 1035 teachers in grades seven through twelve. ... What [the study] found contradicted most of the findings of Gilligan, the AAUW, ... "Contrary to the commonly held view that boys are at an advantage over girls in school, girls appear to have an advantage over boys in terms of their future plans, teachers' expectations, everyday experiences at school, and interactions in the classroom."
>
> The Horatio Alger Association of Distinguished Americans... study... 1998... ...contrasted two groups of students: the 'highly successful' ...and the 'disillusioned.' ...the successful group in the 1998 survey is 63 percent female and 37 percent male. The disillusioned students... nearly seven out of ten are male.
>
> In 2000, the Department of Education published its comprehensive analysis of gender and education, *Trends in Educational Equity of Girls and Women*... "There is evidence that the female advantage in school performance is real and persistent."

Unfortunately, other academics—Women's Studies and Gender Studies proponents particularly—have been complicit in reinforcing and skewing the issue. For example, ultra-feminist professor, Virginia Valian of Hunter College avers, "We don't accept biology as destiny... We vaccinate, we inoculate, we medicate... I propose we adopt the same attitude toward biological sex differences."

We don't accept biology?! Good Grief! Biology is basic. Repeat: Biology Is Basic. Claims which contradict the most basic blocks of reality are at best nonsense, and more probably malicious, insidious, and a view into a warped mind. Still parents pay good money to have their children indoctrinated into this anti-reason rubbish!

Unchallenged, the influence of *reformers* and *resocializers* increases. Teachers and administrators like Graham Seekamp and his vice principal are becoming few and far between. Parents tend to trust their schools, and to be too busy putting food on the table to delve into such issues. And kids who complain are often singled out as trouble-makers in need of reprogramming.

Thank God some people are watching. Sommers response to Valian, "We vaccinate, inoculate, and medicate children against *diseases*. Being a typical little boy or girl is not a pathology in need of a cure..." Ms. Sommers, you are an American hero. Thank you.

Suzanne Venker is another acute observer. "Feminism," she says, "didn't just change America's understanding of sex and gender roles. It changed the very meaning of life. It took the spotlight off what matters—relationships and family—and put it where it doesn't belong, on money, power and fame."

The assault on boyhood occurs in stages. Set-up by denial of normal behavior [rough and tumble, etc.] in elementary school, the second wave hits as a boy's body is being deluged with testosterone at the end of the *juvenile pause*. From approximately nine or ten to fifteen or sixteen the blood hormone level of T in boys skyrockets 2000%. Louann Brizendine writes "...male brain circuitry, with its billions of neurons and trillion of synaptic connections..." goes live. These are the growth spurt years, the years when a parent finds that the pair of size 8½ Nikes bought yesterday need to be replaced with a pair of size 10s today. There is nothing similar in advertised *total body makeovers* to compare to the reworking of a teenage boy's body during puberty. It is so extreme it hurts. And it is exhausting and confusing. The little boy who only a few years ago was wearing a bunny rabbit costume on Halloween is now transforming into The Hulk. Muscles, bones, testicles, penis all get larger; the voice drops; hair sprouts; some boys have been known to add two inches or more to their height overnight. Few sci-fi films portray such ferocious metamorphosing, time warping and dimension shifting as the real little-kid-yesterday-man-today growth that adolescent boys experience.

Thought patterns, too, change. The sexual-pursuit circuits in these creatures' hypothalamuses grow, according to Dr. Brizendine, "...more than twice as large as those in girl's brains. The male brain is now structured to push sexual pursuit to the forefront of his mind." Yet teenage boys are being told by school officials and school policies that there are no differences between male and female, that traditional gender identities are oppressive, and that females are victims of traditional educational practices and therefore deserving of special considerations. No wonder more and more boys are finding the school environment unfriendly. Venker states it simply, "...male bashing has become par for the course." This sometimes overt, sometimes latent animosity drives boys to withdraw. A growing number are dropping out.

There are heroes in this battle, and the picture is not across-the-board bleak. Dave Larson, the superintendent we met earlier, told me about his program established to get more first-generation poor and minority males *to want* to go to college. "One of the most successful programs was the Wesleyan Upward Bound program," he said. "This program would take a group of promising kids—probably 50::50 male/female—and the kids would go to Wesleyan University during the summer. They would go on an Outward-Bound kind of program for the first two weeks to help them bond into a group, and then have classes. During the school year they would go back to Wesleyan one afternoon each week where they would receive guidance and extra help. If we want to address the problem we can't simply demand they come to class.
Extra effort and extra resources are necessary to deal with today's issues."

Like Aviation High School, the Upward Bound program engaged students in a manner most high schools don't, won't or can't. Larson supplemented the program with other efforts. He recognized that schools don't exist in isolation. "Some of the reasons kids weren't doing well in school was because things weren't going well at home. These are still kids—16, 17 years old. You can't leave them to their own devices. As a society you have to work with them. In many cases these kids were going home to a single parent. That parent may not have a high school diploma; may not know how to negotiate through our system; and likely doesn't understand the value of an education. I got one of our retired social workers; I got some grant money, and we hired him. Before a kid could drop out, I required a parent and the kid to meet with him. They talked about why the kid wanted to drop out. If all else failed we had great catchment programs—Alternative Ed program—at the church on the Green, including a night program for kids who were working during normal school hours, and a day adult program for older kids. These programs didn't have the rigidity of a high school. We offered the federal ABE (Adult Basic Education) where a kid could get a high school diploma. If we got kids into these programs, they weren't drop-outs. They were alternative programs… and they were successful."

Problems that affect the *Yang*, affect the *Yin*. Larson expanded on how the helping hand of social programs has become the intrusive hand of foisted dependence. "I think welfare perpetuates welfare because it says to too many young 15 or 16 year old girls, 'Go off and get pregnant, and we'll give you Section 8 housing, we'll give you food stamps, we'll give you a stipend. This is your job. Raise the kids.' Now we're into third, fourth, fifth generations of single moms having kids, and perpetuating that cycle." Often this is with no men around the house, no male influence, or at least no responsible male influence. "I think kids growing up need both male and female influences."

I asked, "Where are the men in these communities?"

Larson answered, "Out having sex with these women, having fun in their lives, but not taking responsibility for what happens to the children they sire."

I asked, "Dave, why is that?"

He answered, "Because our society, our government programs, allow that to happen."

So it is happening, at least in part, because it is enabled. If you pay people to act a certain way, why be surprised or upset if they act that way? I pressed Larson about programs for boys and young men, for that vulnerable segment of the population, particularly amongst minorities, that we are losing. Is there and equivalent in housing, or to women-and-children…

"Other than Section 8 housing and some job-training programs, I don't think there's much out there for boys. We're not giving them the help and the structure they need. Not just in school, but in society. We discount them. And it is something like 80% of the people who are incarcerated are high school dropouts. Young women get more from the government because they have the children."

"So the baby is what tips the scale?"

Larson nodded. "Yes. She has the responsibility for the child. A lot of these kids don't know who their father is. I may be over-generalizing, but I think our governmental policies towards the poor aren't working. Not that we shouldn't have policies and programs to assist. We have to help poor people. That's a given. People talk about American schools failing. Our schools are not failing, but public policy is. I think it's the way it's been structured. The structure perpetuates the problems. The girls get pregnant. They get help. There are no programs to assist the father, to encourage him to stay around and support the children. In reality, it's just the opposite."

"Unintended consequences of trying to do the right thing," I said. "These are side-effects, and unfortunately, as in medicine, side-effects may be disastrous."

"I think, "Larson concluded, "it is ultimately a matter of how we deal with the poor in this country. First of all, when a poor woman is pregnant, she doesn't get the proper pre- and post-natal care so the chances of something happening to those children that will injure them is elevated. These kids live in rents where there's lead in the paint and in the pipes, so you get those problems. Often they don't have transportation. They don't have jobs.

"It is our public policy makers in this country that have totally turned the other way from effectively dealing with poverty. There's no reason why people should go hungry or not have proper medical care in the richest country in the world. People try to point at the schools and say they are at fault, but it starts before the schools. It starts while kids are in the womb, or even before that. Our public policy makers want to deal half-way down the pipeline. They don't want to deal at the beginning. I think if we dealt with the problems starting there, we'd be much better off."

Drugs are a major problem for humans in utero. Labor and delivery associates tell me stories of welfare women on drugs, using sex to get keep up with their habit, having their fifth, or sixth, or seventh child—with each infant being taken at birth by DCF (Department of Children and Families) and placed in foster care. It is illegal for the state to force the woman to have her tubes ties without her granting permission—it is her right to choose. I told Larson the story. He responded, "What is that costing society? What is that costing these kids?" Often these kids have been damaged in utero. The state raises them, which tends to be a very different upbringing than that afforded in a two-parent traditional household. To me this is child abuse—severe, pre-birth child abuse. But no one calls it that. No one arrests the mother. No one goes after the father or the drug supplier. This is an example of what Larson meant when talking about the beginning of the pipeline.

Victimhood: A Chip On Her Shoulder

Earlier I wrote that I did not know where a dear family friend developed her venomous attitude toward me. But I do have suspicions. She was indoctrinated into a culture of victimhood by an educational system which believes there is an innate prejudice against women, and is given over to using the gender binary to define all females as victims while simultaneously denying the existence of that binary. Her education in subject matter was exceptional, but her indoctrination in worldview was and remains highly flawed. Victims—exploited by whomever or whatever they identify as the oppressor, be that a white western European traditional patriarchy or The Man—righteously and adamantly resent the source of their struggle. Where traditional Buddhists recognize life as struggle, American ultra-feminists teach girls to see life's tribulations as class conflict. As the fathers and husbands of my generation worked and struggled to keep food on the table, a decent roof over their family's heads, and tuition payments flowing to educational institutions, we were portrayed as emotion-tyrants. The harder we worked and the more we kept our heads down and noses to the grindstone, the more we ignored this cultural revolution; and by doing so, the more we facilitated it. It is no wonder to me anymore that this dear friend is venomous. She has been thoroughly inculcated into the beliefs, if not the jargon, of class warfare. But why? By the time it was impressed onto her psyche, it had existed elsewhere for decades. More than existed—it had already become institutionalized.

Mindsets are often trans-generational. When my 18-year old granddaughter (son's daughter) returned from college I asked her, "Where do you get your news?" With an air of sophistication she said, "I read the Huffington Post." I said, "Maybe you might want to read something to give you the other side of the story. Let me send you a subscription to the Wall Street Journal." She shot back, "I wouldn't touch that rag!"

Her education in the arena of public policy has been punctuated by emotional wording: for example, the opposition is the 'Nazi Republicans.' This kills me. Sometimes it is hard to keep up enthusiasm when you feel as if you are being bombarded from all sides. I want to say to her, "You, women of your education and generation, don't seem to recognize that when you accept the role of victim, or convince others that they are victims, you are actually victimizing yourself and them. One who is in control of his or her destiny is not a victim. One who believes he or she is controlled by others may believe in their victimization. The first person is empowered; the second person—recall that behavior is consistent with self-image—disempowers him or herself. Implementing self-empowerment is the polar opposite of establishing yourself as a victim.

Boys are emergent men. It seems that the most radical end of the women's movement believes if boys, incipient men, can be controlled and transformed, all the plans of the movement will fall into place and women will no longer be victims. That may sound extreme but consider Maureen Dowd's remark in *Are Men Necessary?* "Now that women don't need men to reproduce and refinance, the question is, Will we keep you around? ...the answer is... We need you in the way we need ice cream—you'll be more ornamental." Or reflect on the words of Maria Shriver in The Shriver Report—"...no longer a man's world... Emergent economic power gives women a new seat at the table—at the head of the table."

Suzanne Venker describes the ambient cultural story the movement foists: "...woman are victims of a patriarchy and therefore lack basic civil rights. ...there are no real differences between women and men other than their private parts. ... To achieve gender equity...

all we have to do is raise children differently—you now: give girls trucks and boys dolls, that sort of thing—and promote different cultural messages..."

Venker understands the politics and pathology of public victimhood. "The push for so-called gender equality (the modern catchphrase for "women's rights) sounds so right and fair you wonder who could be against it. That's the thing about feminist ideas: on the surface they sound innocuous. ... But gender equality isn't about equality at all. It's about creating a new world order. It's about upending human nature, as if this were possible, and making the sexes interchangeable. ...divesting America of traditional gender roles is what the sexual revolution is all about. ... The modern notion of equality doesn't raise women's status. It lowers it by cheapening women's value to men."

Seeing oneself as a victim may be more damaging than being victimized by an outside force. A similar paradigm exists within the Civil Rights movement. Main-stream activists, Martin Luther King, Jr., for example, stood for equality under the law and for self-empowerment. But latter day charlatans—Jesse Jackson, Al Sharpton, et cetera—these guys play the race card to create victim self-images within their followers. They do not lead people to better themselves but lead them to behaviors which are self-destructive. Former Secretary of State Condoleezza Rice said it this way:

If you are taught bitterness and anger, then you will believe you are a victim. You will feel aggrieved and the twin brother of aggrievement is entitlement. So you now think you are owed something... [You are] on a bad road...

People who identify themselves as victims, or as being in a victim-category—this could be by race, ethnicity, gender, age, political or legal status (as in the case of many class-action lawsuits), work (labor or labor unions which use the premise of victimhood as a motivation and/or negotiation tool)—tend to have a mentality that says, you've been putting us down, therefore, to reinstate fairness to all and for all be brought to an equal level, we will tear you down. This is the righteous vengeance in victimhood. So—CAUTION: when it comes to gender politics, beware the woman who perceives herself as scorned!

Responsibility vs. Aberrant Masculinity

Instead of protecting they exploit; instead of providing they plunder; instead of building they destroy. Why? What factors aggravate, and what factors inoculate, against boyhood excursions into malevolence?

Back in the 1950s, in either fifth or sixth grade, I recall receiving my first Boy Scout pocket knife. It had multiple blades but was pretty basic, nothing as fancy as a Swiss Army knife. The sides were black and textured as if wood, and there was a silver oval insert on one side—stainless steel, I think now—inscribed, I imagine, with *Boy Scouts of America*. I was so proud the first day I wore it on my belt to school. Some of the older boys had them. Some wore them every day, though as I look back on it, most of my friends stopped carrying them after an initial period, only wearing them on days when we had a scout meeting after school. But that first day... Oh, the Glory of being a Boy Scout! It was a ritual marking of the passage to the next level; the acceptance and realization of being *one of the older boys*; a symbol to self and to others that I accepted the responsibility that went along with carrying that knife.

A half century later we seem to be telling students that we do not and cannot trust them with a pocket knife because they are not trustworthy. What does that mean? Not the knife, but the loss of that ritual passage, and the loss of trust? What is the fallout from such an attitude?

Recall that behavior tends to be consistent with self-image, that self-image is derived from the story we tell ourselves of ourselves, and that personal story comes to us via ambient cultural story. These policies which convey a lack of trust are components of the new ambient cultural story. They impact behavior.

The destruction of boys and boyhood, and the denigration and elimination of traditional rituals and rites of passage, have been caused by a series of complex, multifaceted, interconnected, and often insidious attacks. These assaults were ignited by the righteous feelings and beliefs that women in traditional cultures had been marginalized and victimized. Movements grew; and corporate, academic and government bureaucracies emerged to fulfill the demands for action. Their confluence of interest reinforced the one tacit goal: tame those wild beasts, those aggressive males, so that others (as if others somehow means inclusiveness) are never again marginalized or victimized! These movements and bureaucracies exceeded all early expectations; yet as Paglia, Sommers, Venker and others illustrate, many of the ultra-feminists claims about boys and men—the very foundation of the demands for action—have been proven utterly false.

So what? What happens when boys are no longer trusted, or when they are not allowed to be boys, when rough and tumble hero-play is outlawed, and when even writing about violently opposing evil is banned? What happens when their essential humanity is denied by indoctrination, domination or chemical castration? What happens when they are reeducated into a wussified culture where the only acceptable outlets for their energies are organized sports—either played or watched, or video games—the more violent the better?

Accomplishments and the Loss of Hope: Striving for great accomplishments, as we've mentioned earlier, is a typical male trait. It is also a typical adolescent dream and desire; and it begins with toddlers testing themselves against their environment. Recently I watched a video of a friend's 19-month old grandson. The boy, his hand high in the air, was attempting to walk a slackline—a two-inch thick rope loosely strung between two posts, sagging to about six inches off the ground. And he did it, for several steps. Then he fell off. He got up and did it again. And again… a smile from ear to ear. And again. It is almost impossible to overstate this male need for accomplishment. It is part of our biological imperative; part of competence and competition; part of what Camille Paglia calls male "…extreme-risk-taking and mono-focused, maniacal obsessiveness…" It is uncommon in women, and is the reason, Paglia notes, that there "…are no female Mozarts."

We are back to asking, what happens to a boy, or to a man, when he is blocked from striving to do great things with his life? The biological imperative does not dissolve. Being accountable, responsible and productive, and being a contributing member of society is consistent with providing and protecting. These are the things that lead to a life filled with deep personal meaning and satisfaction. Aren't these our goals and our wishes for our children?

If thwarted often enough, over a long enough period, the boy, or the man, loses hope. When hope is lost depression ensues; or aggression. Depression or aggression redirects the mono-focused, maniacal, obsessiveness of boys. If not deadened by drugs, or destroyed by indoctrination into alien customs, these traits produce something dark. It is in this way that poor policy and lamentable laws cause bad behavior. Drive and drive thwarted beget of men both most Fortune 500 CEOs and most convicts in our prisons.

We seemingly have a conundrum. Although seldom said in these words, today's politically correct thought is: We must destroy boys or we are willingly allowing them to destroy girls. Many of us recognize that there was, and for some it still exists, a traditional manner of civilizing the ogre innate to masculinity, and that the conundrum is a false premise. Sommers writes, "All societies confront the problem of civilizing children—both boys and girls... History teaches us that *masculinity without morality is lethal*. But masculinity constrained by morality is powerful and constructive, and a gift to women..." The emphasis is mine. I also would alter the last clause to read: and a gift to the human species.

Sommers continues: "We have a set of proven social practices... traditional... character education: to develop a boy's sense of honor and to help him become considerate, conscientious, and gentlemanly. The approach respects the boy's masculinity and does not require... [him to play *girlie games,* and] does not ...make a seven-year-old boy feel ashamed for playing with toy soldiers..."

Do you recall when a boy was trustworthy; when a boy was loyal, helpful, friendly, courteous and kind; when a boy was obedient, cheerful, thrifty, brave, clean...? If you don't, those are the words of the Boy Scout Law: A Scout is: "...and reverent." Reverent?! ACLU leaders have nightmares over that last word; and PC politicians likely lay awake at night thinking of ways to outlaw it.

Traditional values controlled the most-base impulses of boys and men by developing systems or codes of ethics and morals which each individual was supposed to learn and follow. They were designed to set limits and parameters, and to guide kids as they were growing up. PC denied the traditional values and denigrated traditional ethics and morals thus contributing to a societal breakdown. In some instances PC went further, essentially outlawing traditional practices and programs. The ensuing unleashed and uncontrolled natural aggressiveness and spirit of boys then foisted the need for the new bromides and different kinds of control—ones which were external and institutional. In order to control boys and men in the PC age it became necessary to deny the nature of masculinity—the very humanity of men, and to restructure maleness into girlie-men.

I do understand where people on the left, or people in education, are coming from, when they say boys are rambunctious and need to be control. We agree. You cannot let a school or society devolve into *Lord of The Flies*. Boys cannot be allowed to go completely crazy. Families, schools, society in general need both a structured system to control, and to teach self-control. Civilization needs laws and ethics and codes of conduct; but those laws, ethics and codes, to be effective, need to be in harmony with our biological imperatives.

I come back to scouting (I grew up as a Boy Scout, and I became head of the executive committee for the local troop when my sons were that age), but there are many, many groups which have stressed similar codes. "On my honor, I will do my best, to do my duty, to God and my country, and to obey the Scout Law; To help other people at all times; To keep myself physically strong, mentally awake, and morally straight."

But... Holy Shit, Sherlock...! PC practitioners gag on the very thought of one being kept morally straight—as to some ears it sounds like an attack on gender identity, and an attack that will eventually lead to banning a women's right to choose... like what kind of mind-control are these Scout leaders perpetrating?! They are being exclusionary of the fantasized seven-year old transgender person. They are a precursor to military service and raise boys to become soldiers. And they are not Girl Scouts. Exclusionary, innately biased, unequal... the Boy Scouts therefore must be destroyed. [Just a side note: this movement to eliminate Boy Scouts erupted in the late '60s and '70s as an element of the anti-American involvement in the Vietnam War, and has been going on for nearly five decades!]

What role did the Boy Scout Promise, and the Boy Scout Law play in the socialization of boys? Wasn't it an educational system or a training system designed to develop self-control of base impulses? Isn't it better for boys to control themselves than to have external forces press them into non-male behaviors against which they will likely rebel?   What are the long-term ramifications of putting down these codes? If you delete a code from a culture, what are the ramifications of not replacing it with an equal substitute? What happens to boys when they are forced to be more 'girlie'? And why do they put them down anyway? The more one looks into the topic, the more one speaks to families of boys so persecuted, the more frustrating it becomes; and the frustration is amplified by the general lack of recognition that all this is happening.

Great traditions—codes of good sportsmanship, of gallantry, of respect—have been built up over centuries, and have successfully trained boys, adolescents, and young men, bringing them into adult cultures as virtuous men—and as gentlemen. The term *gentlemen*, and all its usage connotes, is not simply a label but is a description of a mode of behavior. A gentle man treats life and circumstances gently. A gentleman lives by a code of honor. A gentleman does not cheat, lie or steal. A gentleman minds his manners. There is a reason for teaching and honoring gentlemanly characteristics. Although we may all love a rogue, there is a threshold that should not be crossed. Elevating the anti-gentleman—the charming cad, the conniving but smiling thief, the celebrity or sports star *bad-boy*— to hero creates models boys will emulate. Who do you wish your kid to follow—Davey Crocket, Johnny Tremaine, Dan'l Boone or Eminem, Russell Brand (arrested at least eleven times, a heroin and alcohol addict), or Kayne West? How about the neighbor's kid? And who do you want your daughter to date… or marry—Albert Einstein, Martin Luther King, Jr., John F. Kennedy or Joseph Biederman, Anthony Wiener or Al Sharpton? Who should be their cultural icons?

On cultural and religious rituals: Again we all love the iconoclastic scallywag who bucks the system; the energetic Jack Black in *School Of Rock*, or the inspiring Robin Williams in *Dead Poets Society*. Rituals and codes almost seem made to be broken; but they cannot be broken, and teenagers cannot define their identity or test their limits by breaching them, if they no longer exist. Ritualization has meaning to the individuals and to the cultures. Denying or destroying rituals has consequences. Sometime the consequences are unintended; sometimes removing a ritual creates a vacuum and a different ritual fills the void. It is not always easy to project the resultant effects. In the lives of youths, has removing the religious ceremonies that honor a loving god allowed Gothic blackness to fill the void? Columbine, Colorado comes to mind, but I confess I do not truly know the details of that incident, so this example requires deeper investigation. I know a lot more about Boy Scouts: does maligning scouting, or The Boys Clubs of America, or the teaching of the seven deadly sins, or any of the numerous programs designed to let boys be boys within a disciplined environment, enable the growth of bad behavior, of low self-worth, of the rise of street gangs? As a society we should be seeking answers to these questions.

On honor and honesty: Can there be honor without honesty; trust without truthfulness (recall that trust is an element of all successful relationships), responsibility without provide and protect? The male virtues of duty, honor, valor, striving, competing, disciplined aggressiveness and patriotism—are values which control behavior. If we are no longer allowed to teach values but instead promote PC girlie-men as the solution to behavior-control, the virtues and values cease to exist. At what cost? Why do PC proponents believe that their de-masculinizing boys will result in 'better' behavior anyway? I think it is because they have a very shallow understanding of the male mind. There is no contradiction between being hard-assed aggressive and being soft, kind and respectful. See the following description is of U.S. Navy SEAL Adam Brown, a SEAL Team 6 Operator, who was killed in Afghanistan in 2010: "Tough as nails on the battlefield, but a teddy bear of a dad and a loving husband." He is a hero to emulate.

On patriotism: There was a time—many of us lived through it—when patriotism was considered wrong. Patriotism was evil, insidious because of its exclusionary properties and belief that somehow we were better than others. How, in a global world could American people with all their faults be exceptional, be better than the citizens of any other nation? Again we come to a clandestine confluence of interest with multiplying effects—what destroys boys is good for girls and is good for the world. It is not and has not panned out that way. I now sometimes worry that, because of all the attempts to emasculate American males, if we were invaded our men would no longer be able to put up the necessary strong resistance. I know this is overstated. I know there is still a core of American boys with tremendous physical and mental strength. I know there has been great changes in weaponry requiring much smaller armies, and thus only a core few may be adequate. But I still worry. As male characteristics are increasingly denigrated, the ability of outside forces to take over the country seems to be enhanced. And just a thought: where is the equity in depending on the few, the proud... and letting everyone else skate?!

On the need for heroes: Recently I read an article about the success of films based on the lives of heroes. In every culture there is a need for both this type of story, and for real-life true heroes. Without the latter we are vulnerable. I've included the qualifier "true" before the word "heroes" because, unfortunately, the word hero as it is used today has been horribly diluted. Attitude that denigrates competition, that declares everyone in grade school a winner (or their self-esteem might be damaged), have infected the term. We do have heroes in everyday life, but just showing up should not earn one that title. Recall the NY Times article about the 50::50 marriage and the recognition that beyond the warm, capable, dutiful husband there was still a need of a man in the hormonal sense. Attempts to deny that role, or to disrupt boys maturing into that role, may be moderately successful, but beneath the modern mantle of political correctness there is still the need for men. There is still the need for heroes; for those who provide security and protection; for those who do the heavy lifting and the dirty work. Morality and personal integrity are built upon stories of the hero, upon "Truth, Justice, and The American Way." I think the historic and the current success of books, movies and games based upon heroes and their actions is a reflection of a basic, species-specific and genetically-initiated cultural need.

On the adolescent desires for freedom: There is no such thing as freedom without personal responsibility. Without personal responsibility one is dependent upon others for the functions necessary to maintain life. Dependency implies restrictions. Independence defines freedom. Think of the extremes of life—the newborn solely dependent upon the mother, or the patient on life support solely dependent upon caregivers—in neither case is the individual responsible and free to act on his or her own. Indeed, think of the adolescent with surging hormones rebelling against parents and "the system" to establish his own identity—essentially becoming free to be responsible for himself! That happens and is less traumatic when the shift is gradual, when the individual is given and accepts responsibility in incremental steps throughout boyhood. It happens unless the natural and gradual process of acceptance of responsibility is hijacked by outside forces—by gangs or cults or con men or restrictive political policies which portray independence as a burden which only they can alleviate. "Let us help you. Let us guide you. If you do it our way and give yourselves over to us, we will support you. If you'll only become a unit of our village or of the Borg Collective, you will have all your needs met, and you will be free of responsibility." But being free of responsibility means being a slave or an indentured servant of someone else.

On sharing: A code of conduct is very different from the regimentation produced by institutional rules and regulations. Under the first, controlled freedom thrives and social trust is reinforced; under the second, despite the perception of freedom, control of the individual thrives and social trust atrophies. Regimented kids learn what sharing is, and they are told they must share with others; but they do not necessarily learn how to share or to want to share. Coerced sharing seldom becomes innate, and often feels contrived or fake. Institutionally forced sharing, like unreasonable taxation, spawns resentment. However, in those who learn how to share on their own, who develop from experience a sense of their interconnectivity with others—think here of the kids on the street playing stick-ball and making up the rules to their own games—sharing does become innate. In boys, it is reinforced by, and reinforces, their natural inclination to provide and protect.

On unbalanced social programs, bad laws and bad behavior: Elements of bad behavior include irresponsibility and the denying of accountability for how one's behavior affects oneself and others. If a law or a social program removes responsibility and accountability, it follows that the law or program are causative factors of bad behavior. The most tragic effect is perpetrated upon the individual whose self-image or personal identity withers. When the social order breaks down far enough, boys see themselves as worthless, as throwaway beings; striving, accomplishment, and contributing lose their meaning; punishment becomes irrelevant; and bad behavior becomes customary.

Boys, you are meant for more than this: Albert Einstein once wrote, "Changes of view are continually forced upon us by our attempts to understand reality." From ancient codes to today's most sophisticated brain structure and mechanism analysis techniques, we are seeing that reality is forcing us to change, or change back, our perspectives on what boys are, how boys should be seen, and how reared.

Boys are genetically programmed to strive, to accomplish, to contribute. It is the source and core from which males derive meaning. When boys are not allowed to strive, not allowed to perform pre-provide and pre-protect behaviors that are normal male traits, they develop in aberrant ways. In Part VII we will see how this plays out in adulthood; but to boys, and to all who nurture boys, know this... the universe and our species has chosen them for great things. Let them strive, let them discover, let them accomplish.

Dr. Jeffrey Rabuffo

PART V: The Doctor Is In

Men, Medicine, Prostates, PSAs, PCa, and the T-Bomb

Introduction

Men are frequently accused of not taking responsibility for their own health. One reason, particularly in regard to prostate cancer (PCa) and other male disorders, is a lack of awareness of incident rates, causes and treatment protocols. Other reasons: disinformation, and no societal or media support. Men's health doesn't seem to be on anyone's radar screen.

The American Cancer Society estimates that 30,000 American men will die from prostate cancer this year. That's a pretty high number for a disease many health advocates and professionals claim men die *with*, not *from*! The incident rate of prostate cancer and the mortality rate from the disease are roughly equal to those of breast cancer, yet last year National Cancer Institute statistics showed more than double the research money, $631 million to$ $300 million, was spent on breast cancer research compared to prostate cancer research.

In this part we will turn our attention to our male machinery, to prostates, PSAs, prostate cancer (PCa), Low-T, ED, testosterone replacement therapy (TRT), and the T-bomb. We will also look at the impact of stress on health, and the interconnectivity between the destruction of masculinity and men's health. All this will needs to be seen against the backdrops of mind and body, and of the physical-social-political environment. Modern PC culture, despite assertions to the contrary, seemingly is no better at allowing guys to handle stress and all its adjunct complications, than the taciturn John Wayne culture of yore. Why?

But first, let's look at physicians, then at the characteristics of the male patient. For many years I was on one side; I now find being on the other quite enlightening.

Characteristics of Physicians

Every doctor has a story, and of course I do too. Our training is long and intense. There are protocols to follow. There's a hierarchy of command. Some of the lessons we learn are not medical, but are lessons in life. Our story shapes us; and the commonality of experiences creates a degree of common characteristics, a medical community. This helps and this hinders health care.

I did all of my training at Georgetown University, first going to college there, then on to Georgetown University School of Medicine. I did my internship at Mercy Hospital in Buffalo, New York, and obtained a residency and fellowship nomination in urologic oncology at Roswell Park Cancer Institute, also in Buffalo. In 1966, Uncle Sam and the draft intervened. Instead of my going to my residency I went into the United States Air Force. I spent two years at Keesler Air Force Base in Biloxi, Mississippi, and was scheduled to be discharge from the service in October 1968. I anticipated going back to Roswell Park for my residency, but, unfortunately, that program had a July 1st start date, and the cancer institute would not wait for me to be discharged. They gave my position to somebody else. I went back to Georgetown. I loved the school, but more importantly at the time, the length of its residency was one year longer than that required by the American Board of Urology. That meant that even though I would start my first year in November (five months late), I would be there seven months longer that the requisite time demanded by the ABU. So I was able to start my first year of residency in November 1968. That 'year' was only seven months long, but the over-all time was more than enough to satisfy the requirements.

There were other benefits of going back to Georgetown, besides getting a great education. It was a well-known hospital used by the rich and famous of Washington DC. I participated in the care of many of these individuals, and learned about the power they could wield. I also learned they were human beings, that they had the same fears and concerns as the rest of us. Two were daughters of a very high ranking administration official; one was the new coach of the

Washington Redskins, Vince Lombardi; another was a very famous general involved in the conduct of the Vietnam War. The Secret Service was always concerned about hospital security. Typically it would allow only Chiefs of the sections to do routine tasks. As a resident I transported one of the daughters on a stretcher, and I drew her blood, while Major General, Dr. Walter Tkash, the White House physician, oversaw the whole process.

One thing I learned from those experiences was that if you want the best care you should let the people who do it all the time take care of you. While the Chiefs may have the credentials, they may also be far removed from the finesse required to do a routine job well. There is a right way and a wrong way to transport a patient on a stretcher; there a right way and a wrong way to draw somebody's blood. Not doing a task for an extended period of time lets one's skills rust. In the operating room this becomes a critical concern.

I also learn that while famous people reacted to their health situation pretty much with the same angst, denial, or questions as all patients, the medical staff reacted differently—including, at times, me. I had a brief conversation with Mr. Lombardi. I was thrilled. Same thing when I was in the emergency room and Sonny Jorgensen, the famous quarterback of the Washington Redskins, who was bought in with a broken shoulder blade. While he was waiting for his x-ray I got his autograph for my kids. My boss didn't think that was appropriate, but my kids loved it.

The common denominator amongst these famous people is they were all very nice, and all somewhat nervous. These experiences taught me not to be intimidated by the rich and famous. In future years when I took care of someone of this stature, I made a point not to be daunted. It made my job easier, and I sincerely believe they got better care.

I also learned a bit about politics—low-level politics. The daughters of the president, and Coach Lombardi were in adjoining rooms. They had arrived at almost at the same moment. A *big* uproar broke out between the hospital administrators—who should get the first welcoming bouquet?! Administrators really do worry about these things. The discussion was long, drawn out, and somewhat heated. They solved the problem by delivering welcoming flowers to these patients simultaneously. Aha! So... that's the way not to offend somebody important. And, in reality, it went very well. Administration is to medical care as traffic lights are to automobiles—it keeps the units that are doing the work from crashing into each other.

I had a patient that I operated on at the Washington, D.C. Veterans Hospital. I spent time there as part of my surgical rotation through the various hospitals in the District of Columbia. It was October and this fellow needed surgery to correct a problem he had as a result of an injury in the war zone. I discussed the procedure and process with him, and he asked if he would be able to be home for Christmas. Home was Savanna, Georgia. I saw no reason why that would not happen so I assured him he would make it home. Things did not go as well as I expected. His healing took much longer than I'd anticipated. Still, he was ready to be discharged on December 23d. The VA transportation officer called me and told me there were no flights available. I thought: I'm in Washington; I have a very famous veteran who wishes to be home for Christmas; and there is nothing medically stopping him from travelling. What could be a better story than getting this guy home? So I called White House, talked to the operator, told her my problem. She very kindly listened to my concerns, but I thought that was the end of the line. Shortly the phone rang back and it was the White House transportation officer who asked where the patient was going and when he wanted to go. Soon he offered six flights to Savannah on Christmas Eve. What could be better? I was excited. I told my veteran patient that I had succeeded in getting him a flight home. He was ecstatic. Off he went on the morning of the 24th; and off I went for Christmas break.

When I returned there was a very large box of pecans and a thank-you note. There also a phone call from the VA transportation officer. He was livid. I had gone over his head. Whoa! I was not expecting this. If anything I was expecting some praise for solving the problem. I told him I thought the goal was to get the guy home for Christmas, and that I didn't understand why he was upset. He thought I was being sarcastic, screamed a few nasty things, and slammed the phone on me. I told my professor. He asked me, "What lesson did you just learned?" I already had the belief that one should always do the right thing, so it wasn't that. And I had learned much earlier about being a team player, so it wasn't that either. It had more to do with gaining an understanding that some of your teammates might only believe in teamwork and doing the right thing if it makes them look good. My professor looked at me, chewed on his pipe, and smiled.

One more example: I was Chief of General Medical Services at Keesler Air Force Base when the base ran a disaster drill—one which a few colleagues and I originally thought was an actual calamity. Mostly everybody else on base knew the drill was coming, and they had prepared their responses in advance. The raters gave the base high marks, but I didn't think the drill gave the command a realistic assessment of basic capabilities; so my colleagues and I staged a severe, multi-vehicle truck and bus crash—unannounced! We covered several "victims" with ketchup, simulating blood. Then we called for disaster response. Our disaster exposed weaknesses in the base's preparations and organization. We got into some trouble but were vindicated a few weeks later when Biloxi got hit by a tornado. Five people were killed in town, but the base responded superbly. The changes that had been instituted because of our unannounced disaster turned out to be the right ones, and I like to think we saved a few lives. Eventually I received an unofficial commendation from the hospital commander. It was dedicated to the *Ketchup Kids* in recognition of the ketchup we had poured all over our pseudo-victims. The commendation is still on my wall.

Being in the field of medicine these many years, I have, of course, interacted with thousands of physicians. Physicians, in general, are not leaders—not in the sense of leadership as we described it in Part II—not goal oriented, not focused on the broad mission, not able to dismiss emotional side-effects. Physicians are care-takers and rule followers. This is a good thing. I think that's what we want and need in physicians. We want and need someone to care about us.

I've found that the physician-leader, the strong businessman-physician who will be innovative and change the status quo, or who will fight insurance companies and/or hospital administrators for what they believe is right, generally are held in contempt by other physicians who may accuse them of "just being interested in money."

Most physicians, as I said, are rule-followers. In this, they are almost neurotic; usually obsessive. They worry. These are all things patients should want in their physician. You want him to worry about you. You want him to obsess over your condition. You want him to do the right medical thing.

But as a group, physicians are not necessarily leaders. That shows up in the way medicine and health care has evolved. As a group, doctors are not fighters. They tend to be quiet, introspective people. In American medicine physician competence is a highly esteemed quality. Following the rules is a side effect of the quest for competence; and stepping outside the box exposes one to allegations of incompetence.

That's part of the reason why insurance companies [and the government] have been able to take over the business. We will talk more about this consequence in The Doctor Is Out, more about there being managed health care but no managed dentistry, no managed law, no managed real estate, and no managed automobile maintenance. People in other businesses tend to have a different view of the world; and the world tends to view them differently than they view physicians. What is it about medicine that allows, even encourages, this?

I had a conversation with a colleague, a psychologist, who said to me that physicians, because of their training, missed out on part of their emotional and psychological development. "You know," he said, "the trouble with you guys is: when college was over everyone else went out and got an apartment and started partying, and started working in the real world. You guys had four more years of school, then a year of internship, then three or four or five years of residency. You were in your mid-30s when you finally came out and looked up. You missed that whole part of your emotional development. That's why you guys are the way you are."

I suppose there is some truth to that. Of course one would want to factor in the self-selection process of people who choose this path to begin with. This psychologist friend rubbed it in. "You're not businessmen. You know how to follow rules because that's what you've been taught to value, and that's what leads to your success. You don't know how to go outside the box, you can't push the envelope. You only know what you think is the right thing to do. And you have contempt for anyone, including your partners or patients, if they don't follow medical rules and don't do the right thing."

Grasp this physician-mindset. The rules say that the patient should take such and such medication. And they say if he doesn't take the medication the book or the protocol prescribes, then he's not going to get better. And if he doesn't get better, then I'm in trouble because it is my job and my responsibility to get him back to health. Because of this sense of duty, and I've seen it many times, the physician is seldom open to alternative treatments or alternative medicine. He's going to follow the rules, and he's going to angst over the patient who rebels, or the colleague who defies the norm.

I had a guy, an engineer, from one of a local defense plants. Quite often this man had to travel to Turkey. He had a problem with his prostate which complicated his traveling and interfered with his job performance. His prostate had become colonized with bacteria growing within the gland. No matter how many antibiotics I gave him, the infection wouldn't go away. He had had radiation treatments for prostate cancer; and one of the rare side effects of such is the formation of crystals along the urethra where it passes through the bladder. This seemed to be the loci of these recurrent, severe infections. I tried treatment after treatment, talked to other specialists, all to little avail. Finally I consulted with an infectious disease specialist who found a possibility in an obscure paper. "Why don't we inject the prostate directly with the medication?" There was <u>no evidence to say that it would work</u> (remember these words), but neither was there evidence to say that it wouldn't work. I presented the concept to this guy and he said, "What do we got to lose?" I answered him honestly, "I haven't a clue. If you're willing, I think we should try it." He agreed, so instead of giving him more pills, I injected a series of potent antibiotics directly into the prostate. It worked. He was happy. I was happy. The infectious disease specialist was happy. But my partners were not happy with me. They had never heard of this and were very critical. I asked, "Why was it wrong?" They answered "There's no evidence to show that it works." In their minds it bordered on voodoo. I said, "But it just worked, so that's evidence. And there was no evidence saying not to do it."

Recall, the physician mentality says there are rules you have to follow and if you don't you're a *bad doctor*. That is a pervasive attitude. That's one of the reasons why there is so little change in the way things are done; or why change in medicine comes slowly. It can be like pushing a battleship with a canoe.

In 1847 the Hungarian physician, Ignaz Sammelweis, began insisting that physicians and midwives wash their hands before touching patients. At the time this was not a cultural norm.
Still he warned that women were being infected during childbirth, and that these infections led to many mothers dying shortly after the event. There was no evidence that said washing hands was going to save lives, but Sammelweis did it anyway and insisted that others do it. For this he was ostracized. Slowly people realized that fewer women were dying... evidence.

That's what I mean when I say physicians are rule followers. You go in, or I go in, and we say to our doc, "I'm not doing this." The physician is going to feel threatened. People say, "Doctors like to control things." I don't think it's a power trip, or an ego trip. I think it is fear. If they don't control what's happening, and if they feel responsible for you, their patient, and if you get sicker or if you die, they're going to blame themselves. Particularly if some authority figure says, "Your patient didn't take this medication as he was supposed to." If you reply, "Well I told him to but he refused," they'll counter, "You didn't try hard enough."

That's part of the neuroses that physicians have. It is always the physician's fault. And we know that. We feel that. Lawyers use that when they attack us in court. It's our fault if someone dies. We are the caregivers. It is not supposed to happen on our watch. If someone dies it is because of something we did, or something we didn't do that we should have done.

Physicians are not infallible

I once saw a patient die in the operating room. One of my colleagues was working to repair the collection system of the kidney of a middle-aged woman. The kidney has two essential anatomic functions—one to filter body fluids and produce urine, the other to collect that urine so it may be expelled from the body. This patient had a stricture or blockage in the collecting system due to scarring from a previous procedure, making this second operation necessary.

The original surgeon had not done anything wrong. He had followed rules and procedures, but the procedure had not worked. It had nothing to do with his skills, but had something to do with individual variations—in this case her lumbar vein was in an abnormal location.

During the second procedure, the previous scarring had further distorted the normal anatomy and had hidden that vein in a clump of scar tissue. The vein was not visible, and during the dissection the vein tore and profuse bleeding occurred. The vein also retracted to the inside of the muscle surrounding the kidney cavity.

Every urologist knows what to do in this situation, and my colleague followed protocol. He called for additional help. The anesthesiologist started a second IV. A nurse brought an additional suction apparatus to the table. There were a lot of hands in this person... the anesthesiologist, the nurses... we had people running around hanging blood... There was the sack of intestines packed off to one side, and there in this space which was about four or five inches wide and about eight inches deep, down in the bottom of this hole was the bleeder. We couldn't see it. The hole kept filling with blood.

Larger sponges, a foot square, were packed into the cavity wall to apply pressure to stop the bleeding. That didn't work. A third suction was brought to clear the field so the surgeon could identify the source of the bleeding. Even with multiple suctions, we could not keep the field clear, and an additional surgeon was called in.

This was all happening quickly, within minutes. The anesthesiologist was pushing fluids into the IVs to support the patient's blood pressure. Twenty percent of one heart's output flows through the kidney; all of one's blood passes through the heart every minute; so one fifth of a patient's blood flows through the kidney every minute. That's a lot of blood. The surgeon knew he did not have much time.

We had three suckers but couldn't keep the field clear. We pack the hole with surgical sponges. That wasn't enough. We were doing everything that we'd been trained to do in this situation; and the team was performing perfectly. But we could not find the source of the bleed. Even with all the packing and all the sucking, because of the way the vein retracted, we couldn't clear the area enough to see it.

At five minutes the patient's blood pressure bottomed out. The anesthesiologist could not bring it back up. It was a very surreal moment. Everyone present knew what was happening, people were doing what they needed to do, but nothing was working. Every surgeon knows that every procedure is risky. Following all the rules reduces the risk, but some occurrences cannot be avoided. This was such a case. When the anesthesiologist said, "We're losing her," I felt a chill and a sense of dread. I had never felt it before, and never since. Part of me was saying, "I know where this is going." The other part of me was still working. And, of course, there was the beeping in the background. The stress in that OR was palpable.

In spite of all the expertise, the patient died on the table. The operating surgeon, the one in charge, was absolutely devastated. He had done everything he could, had followed all the rules and guidelines. In this case it just didn't work. When it was all over I just stood in the OR. There was stuff all over the room: IV bottles and blood on the floor and sponges that are really big rags full of blood. Debris. It almost looked like a battle scene. It was just... I can still see it... vividly... but at the end it was like I couldn't think. I didn't know what to do. I knew what had happened. I had not witnessed that before. I was stunned. While it was happening my training had kicked in; but when it was over I could barely move.

After the death the surgeon and his team went to talk to the family. The family knew, going in, that the procedure was more risky due to the previous operation. Everyone understood that, and also understood that if the surgery was not done the patient would have lost kidney functions and been on permanent dialysis. Given the alternatives, the patient, the family and the doctor had agreed surgery was the best choice. But being intellectually aware of risks, and experiencing the devastating consequences of one's decisions in real life are very different. The latter is a hard emotional burden to bear.

Few people realize what goes on in the mind of a surgeon while he is in the operating room; seldom is the stress acknowledged. When someone dies, the physician—not the equipment, not the nurses, not other staff—becomes the focus of blame. The physician is the captain of this vessel: the buck stops here.

When a traumatic event happen during a procedure, particularly if he loses a patient, he may suffer from the symptoms of PTSD that are similar to other high-risk professionals—policemen, firemen, airline pilots, ship captains—when a situation goes awry and injury or death is sustained.

Other professions and industries have protocols to handle these events. The airline industry, for example, is frequently held up as a model for quality control vis-à-vis the medical profession. When there is a traumatic event involving a plane and its crew (think Shelley Sullenberger and the Hudson River) the industry removes the crew from service and evaluates them for emotional symptoms including PTSD. They cannot return to duty until those issues are resolved. The *infallible* surgeon, on the other hand, is expected to return to duty right away. Hospital and even the physician's colleagues pay almost no attention to the possible emotional side effects of these events. A recent article and JAMA suggest that changes may be coming to this thinking.

In the above case I think the family was somewhat comforted when they realized how distraught the surgeon was. He was not arrogant. He did not attempt to blame someone, anyone, else. He accepted the responsibility for the decision and for the outcome.

In the days and weeks which followed he mentally beat himself up attempting to conjure up a scenario in which he did something different, some little motion, some twist of the wrist. *If only I did... If only we tried... If only we had...* But all the conjured scenarios produced the same results. They had done everything right but the patient died. He felt responsible, guilty. Guilt is the core emotion which binds the symptoms of PTSD.

Days later the family expressed their irritation. Irritation became anger; anger progressed to lawyers; lawyers lead to a lawsuit. In Connecticut, in order to bring a malpractice suit, one needs to find a doctor who, after looking at the records, will say it's possible a mistake was made. The family's legal team couldn't find a doctor to say that. A number of doctors reviewed the records; and each one concluded no mistakes were made. I think that showed that everything that could have been done was done. The family tried a different route. They went to the Department of Public Health. The department performed a full investigation. They too concluded no mistakes were made.

Most people don't know what goes on emotionally in a physician's mind, especially in the mind of a surgeon. We tend to keep, and are trained to keep, our emotions in check. It is a necessity.

It allows one to act and to make calculated decisions when treating patients. In all my years I've yet to see a patient or family fully realize the emotional burden doctors and surgeons carry. The death of a patient is a traumatic event which the surgeon relives much like a soldier reliving the death of a comrade in battle. The above incident will stay with me forever.

Hey Doc, Listen up!

Physicians are trained and programmed to accept responsibility for the lives of patients. With all this caring and obsessiveness one would think doctors would be great listeners, but many patients complain that their doctor doesn't listen. Physicians are trained to interview but they are not trained to believe their patients; they are trained to listen, but very often they dismiss what they hear. We will get into the difference between personal medicine and statistical medicine, the art of medicine and the medicine of metrics, in a later section, but for now let's just look at a few more peculiarities of the profession.

As I am now older and seeing medicine from the other side of the fence, that is seeing the medical profession from the patient's perspective, it has become important to me to participate in my own healthcare. To date, I have not been to a physician who has said to me, "What do you think you have?" or "What do you think we should do? How do you want to approach this?" Nor have I had a doctor affirm that what he is seeing is a snapshot of my health, and what I am bringing to the discussion is a feature-length film. It leaves me feeling, or wanting to snap, "Hey, I'm not stupid. Don't treat me as if I am. Listen up. And don't reduce the problem to a two-word description."

Some doctors seem to convey a feeling that says, "Listening to you is a chore. I'm the expert. I know what's going on." As I am now usually the patient, I think it should not be a chore, *because physicians don't know a whole lot.* Pardon that blasphemy! Most doctors think they know more than they know. Generally they have a massive amount of information, an incredible amount of knowledge, but medical knowledge is transient, and the core information of every specialty is constantly expanding. Yesterdays' accepted practices and theories are continuously being discarded; continuously being superseded by newer, more complex procedures and understandings.

Half of what I learned up to only five years ago has been proven to be specious. The quest for competence becomes elusive, while simultaneous influences on physicians from outside the field—from political, legal, financial, academic, and pharmaceutical interests—escalate.

My first insight into we-don't-know-everything happened while I was in medical school. At that time you are studying, memorizing, challenging yourself and your fellow students. One of our professors pointed out that knowing the book doesn't mean you know the subject. "Medicine," he said, "is an evolutionary process." As if fate wanted to hammer that point home, one of my team members was a forty-year old female dietician. At that time this was quite rare. We, younger, male students, asked her why a dietician would want to go to medical school. What we were really asking was, "Why the hell are you in medical school?" We treated her with respect, but our thoughts weren't as kind. She replied that she thought many of the diseases we were seeing were due to what people eat—very prescient for the time. We boys chuckled. We *knew* that wasn't true. In our heads we were all going, "Yeah, right!" Of course she was visionary, and as most everyone now knows, what we eat plays a major role in just about all disease processes.

Another example: I work out in a local gym, and have been doing so for nearly two decades. Most of the serious gym rats drink protein supplements while they exercise. Most of these guys are lean and muscular. I started drinking them, too. A few years ago I mentioned this to my physician during my annual physical. He indicated to me that I should know better, and that I should save my money because "...everybody knows those supplements don't work." To be honest, I don't know if they work or not, but I know the guys in the gym are superb specimens of humanity. "Now Jeff..." he's patronizing me, "...now Jeff, you're a physician. You know better." Huh?! I was a bit dumbfounded. When I started supplementing with natural protein shakes, I think I got better results. Maybe there's science to it, maybe not. But it sure seems to work. Maybe it only works because I think it's going to work and that gives me a boost and I work out harder.

Think of the implications of that "Huh?" I am a physician. I have practiced medicine for decades. I have known thousands of doctors. And I think, of my own personal physician, I'm not fully comfortable with the characteristics of this guy. I don't question his professionalism, his degree of caring, or his level of knowledge. I like him, he is a friend. But he doesn't think the way I think. I think his mental box is too small. And he doesn't really pay attention to what the patient (me) is saying. If he would only take some time and explain to me exactly why I'm wrong—instead of condescendingly just telling me my belief on this or that is wrong—it would go a long way in alleviating my dissatisfaction. His behavior is characteristic of many, not all, physicians; many, not all, know what they know, and they fit what you tell them into their box.

Physicians want to hang on to what they know, and what they've been trained to know. That's one of the reasons why medicine changes slowly. Physicians aren't perfect, and they aren't gods; as a psychiatrist friend says, "I'm not God. If you want God, that's extra."

I had surgery last year. It required a pre-op procedure with which I was uncomfortable. The doc walked me through it, explained everything he was going to do and why he was going to do it. He worked with me and let me convince myself that this was necessary. At the post-op visit I was very happy. It was easy and so well done. So, I have run into physicians who I think are more reasoned with their patients. I think I was one. Being on the other side is an education.

Characteristics of the Male Patient

"I'm a guy. I don't talk about my disease because it isn't polite to talk about testicles in public. Besides, it's not wise to signal weakness. Jackals circle the clan waiting for the frail to stumble. A man on his knees invites attack."

Is that *old thought* or is that a genetically triggered characteristic of male behavior?

Earlier, when we elaborated male traits, we said when a guy is in pain, or when he gets sick, the man thing for him to do is to grin and bear it, to man up, or to crawl off into a cave and lick his wounds. Men do tell themselves "Put up with it! Don't cry." They may even have the attitude, *Don't take pain meds. Sit there and suffer.* It's a common initial reaction. But when men hurt, when pain becomes chronic and disease symptoms express with ferocity, all bets are off.

In many ways guys and women are no different when it comes to handling disease. Perhaps the biggest difference is you don't see many guys going into a nursing school class or to a chamber of commerce seminar to talk about themselves being victims of their illness. We also are less apt to look for compassion from our brotherhood, and are more apt to follow, or to worry about not being able to follow, our delineated traits. Our problem-solving/analytical brain structures move into high gear—and if a solution is not forthcoming, our stress skyrockets.

One patient, long after his initial diagnosis, told me, "When I was told I needed to be admitted into the hospital, I couldn't talk. It had nothing to do with my health. I made up some excuse, but the reality was there was so much financial pressure due to the economic collapse, I was sure... this was instantaneous in my head... I was sure I was going to lose my house. That was all I could think about. I couldn't say that. I don't know why. But I could see it. I could see how things were going to unfold. I was tearing up. All I could think to say was, *I cannot go into the hospital right now. I just can't do it. It is not possible for me to be admitted.* I put it off for a couple more weeks. I went to a different doc. I had the tests repeated. I was getting sicker and sicker, but I was working. And at night I was trying to get all our paperwork lined up so (my wife) would be able to follow it. It was not a matter of denial or of not hearing, it was a matter of projecting the outcome... losing the house, being out on the street, being a loser. It came pretty close to that. What kind of man..."

Taking care of men can be a real challenge. Men tend to internalize emotions; we know this. The initial act of burying emotions delays stress and anger, and allows a man to deal with the situation. Dr. Reynolds, whom we talked to at length about boys and ADHD, tells us, "...men tend to be less flexible than women. When things don't work out, they have a harder time adapting or adjusting to changing circumstances. Oft times they want to keep trying harder. It's the old saw, 'If at first you don't succeed, try, try again.' I see men beating their heads against the wall trying to make the same thing work. Women seem to respond to life challenges in a more fluid way."

It is stories like the one from the patient above—doctors seeing his overt continence but not knowing what is going on in his male mind—which lead to the idea that men don't care about their health, or that they don't take care of themselves. I said it before: Tens of thousands of my patients cared deeply about taking care of themselves, but often they hid it; and many, many times they put the concerns for their families ahead of concerns about themselves. Superficial medical and social perceptions skew conclusions away from reality.

Last year I was doing an interview with a female TV reporter. She said, "Thank God there's some guy who wants to talk about men's health. I'm sick of only hearing about women's health." She brought up the issue of men not caring, and I said, "They care a lot, but they don't have a vehicle, a cultural mechanism, which encourages it. If men didn't care, I wouldn't have had a practice for forty years. My office wasn't filled with zombies waiting to die."

Still, it is true that guys beat themselves up over getting sick. When a guy says, "I don't have time for this crap!" he is really saying he wants the problem fixed; he wants to get on with his tasks. Consider the characteristics of being physical, of needing to achieve, needing to be competent, self-sufficient and competitive. Being sick is not simply a blow to the body, it is a blow to confidence, to self-mage. Being sick, being incapacitated, being in a state of declining health is stressful. When men are faced with a situation that to them is threatening, they first try to rationalize it away, then they try to analyze or intellectualize a way out. Finally they attempt to come up with a plan to solve the problem—all while keeping their emotions in check or hidden. One can't think himself out of pneumonia, diabetes or cancer, but the male psyche, at least initially, thinks otherwise.

We'll talk about additional medical complications of stress below, but for the moment consider that many behaviors of the male patient are mechanisms aimed at stress reduction and at the maintenance of traditional capacity. These mechanisms may include initial denial, pain justification, and purposeful ignorance (as in the act of ignoring). A side-effect of these mechanisms is they tend to lower cultural demand for information, thereby exacerbating the situation in which information on male conditions is not readily available. Society interprets this to mean men don't care about themselves.

Recently I read a short article on eating disorders that said it is a widely held belief that only women experience these conditions. Although men suffering from symptoms of the disorder knew something wasn't right, it was only after they "suffered a crisis, or required emergency medical help, that they realized… they were sick. The men often said they were slow to seek help because they didn't know where to go, or they feared they wouldn't be taken seriously."

Pain justification is an interesting phenomenon. Two year or so ago my back began acting up. The pain began slowly, steadily increased in intensity and duration, and became quite severe. I didn't know the cause and imagined various serious scenarios. I had an MRI. Because of the location of the pain, and because of my age, the doctor concluded that it was spinal stenosis. That didn't make sense to me, and it did not alleviate my concerns (we'll talk about age-related diagnoses and misdiagnoses in Part VIII). I sought out a second, and then a third opinion. One element of pain is fear, the fear that something awful is going on. The last doctor focused in on a mechanical issue, a pulled and torn hamstring which was affecting my spinal alignment. It was an "Aha!" moment. I recalled twisting and pulling that muscle while out trail running, but I'd discounted it and didn't made the connection because the back problem had had a long-delayed onset. Once I understood the pain I got used to the idea it was there. Some days it was more intense than others, but I no longer fretted over the cause. I knew it's there. I knew why it was there. It became part of the background noise of life. The sensation of pain hadn't changed, but my mind interpreted that sensation differently.

When something awful *is* going on: chronic illness and severe, persistent pain are game changers. They cause the patient's vision to tunnel. That is, the breadth of one's focus and thought narrows, and it becomes difficult to see the sides of the path we are on or to take in the broad vistas of our surroundings. Time, too, foreshortens. When one is in pain, when one is nauseous, to interact with others, even loved ones, is difficult. Achievement, striving, fun and enjoyment are subjugated by the immediacy of unrelenting discomfort; and projection into the future—the most basic element of hope— deteriorates.

Our Male Machinery: T, Low-T, ED, TRT, Prostates, Peeing, PSAs, PCa…

Anyone who reads a newspaper, watches television, goes online, or is a football fan knows October is Breast Cancer Awareness month. The ubiquitous pink that has come to symbolize the disease—from dyed women's tresses, to stylish ties donned by news anchors, to shoelaces on the cleats of NFL behemoths—is everywhere. By Columbus Day pink has seemingly managed to crowd out autumn's dazzling hues.

But something else is missing from this palette. How about blue? Not Big Blue as in the NY Giants, but the blue standing for prostate cancer awareness. September, although virtually unrecognized, is Prostate Cancer Awareness month.

Advocacy groups like the Susan G. Komen Foundation have done a marvelous job promoting education and research to combat breast cancer. Their work—including the nationally recognized *Race For The Cure*—symbolizes a grassroots effort to save lives, and it has resulted in increased survival rates. They are to be commended.

The public education surrounding prostate cancer (PCa) isn't, and has never been, commensurate. The statistical rates of diagnoses and death for PCa are very similar to those of breast cancer. One in eight American women will develop breast cancer; one in six American men will develop PCa (not the one in two as is sometimes reported in the media).

An odd, cultural quirk exists which causes some men's advocacy groups to argue that prostate cancer is not a deadly disease, and that those who contract it will die *with* the disease, not *from* it. That claim is problematic. Complicating matters is the further debate over how the public should view prostate health. Some of these same advocacy groups claim that a highly accurate, simple and beneficial procedure, the Prostate Specific Antigen (PSA) test, should not be administered at all. These groups believe that the test leads to more invasive, and likely needless, procedures—procedures, they assert, that do more harm than good.

What's going on here? Let's start with a short history of testosterone (T).

Suspicions of a substance that effected masculinity go back thousands of years, and experimentation with testicular tissue transplants pre-date the American Revolution. By 1889, over a century before the FDA approval of Viagra, it was recognized that injections of testicular extracts reinvigorated mental and physical abilities. Forty-six years later T, testosterone, was finally isolated as the elemental component of the extract. Then in the 1940s Dr. Charles Huggins, a physician and researcher at the University of Chicago, demonstrated a link between hormones and prostate cancer (PCa). At that time, a diagnosis of PCa meant a prognosis of pain, hopeless deterioration and death. Huggins showed that castration and estrogen administration reduced the severity and spread of the disease; and he thus concluded that if female hormones could control the disease, male hormones must the cause. His early results lead to a series of articles describing PCa activation by androgens (T), and PCa inhibition by estrogen. These discoveries are considered to be the birth of cancer chemotherapy; and in 1966 Huggins was awarded the Nobel Prize in Medicine.

Huggins' conclusion went unquestioned for nearly fifty years, and it became the foundation for the idea that you could not give guys testosterone for old age infirmities because that would cause prostate cancer. That was reinforced by the cultural thought: Why would you *want* to give old guys testosterone just so they can have sex. Then it was discovered that T supplementation increased muscle mass, reduced body fat, and increased the ability to concentrate. People were still saying, "That's well and good, but it causes prostate cancer." Finally new studies found that T does not cause prostate cancer. What now is suspected of causing prostate cancer is a lack of testosterone.

Going back to the studies by Huggins: it has become clear they were not actual studies but only anecdotal observations on less than ten individuals. To determine that the prostate cancer was decreasing Huggins measured a chemical called acid phosphatase. This is the blood chemical we used to use to determine if prostate cancer was present, or if it was under control—high meaning present, low meant under control. It turned out that the test was so indefinite it was worthless.

The point is almost everyone believed that acid phosphatase was *The Test*, but this premise was wrong. Studies in the '90s found that people who had prostate cancer had low testosterone levels; and patients with higher grades of PCa had the lowest T levels. In one study involving radical prostatectomies (removal of the prostate) due to high-grade (aggressive, more apt to metastasize) cancer, T levels were checked before and after surgery. T levels were found to be consistently low.

That was the moment in science which led people to reconsider testosterone replacement safe and efficacious. And, of course, that was quickly followed by drug companies and their marketing departments—you've got to love marketing people... these are the ones who have popularized ED (erectile dysfunction instead of impotence), and who developed a campaign around Low-T. The marketers go through a litany of: "Do you have this? Do you have this? Do you have this? If so... take _____," and they fill in their product name.

Guys would come to my office and ask about testosterone replacement therapy (TRT). There are some side-effects like acne and swollen ankles, or if you have sleep apnea it can make it worse. So I would talk to them about it, but the thing that always bothered me about it was that it was becoming *The God Molecule*. As in: "Take this. If there is anything that is going to make you live forever, this is it." You always have to wait for the bomb to drop, and, as we shall see, it did.

Recall when they first began doing HRT (hormone replacement therapy) studies on women with menopause—they gave them estrogen and progesterone. Then, all of a sudden, the incidents of breast cancer went up. The media got hold of that and pretty soon women wouldn't take their prescriptions. Thousands stopped cold-turkey. Many suffered hormonal deprivation side effects like vaginal dryness, mood swings and hot sweats. Several years later a study done at Yale University concluded, "We never said it was the estrogen. We said it was the estrogen *and* progesterone in combination that cause it (the increase in breast cancers and heart problems)." Additional studies found that the negative effects were more prevalent when the therapy used synthetic estrogen (derived from the urine of pregnant horses) and synthetic progesterone (progestin), and that using bio-identical hormones did not have similar correlations with breast cancer or other complications. So the attitude toward female hormone replacement therapy is now beginning to swing back. The jury is still out as to whether these types of results may apply to different forms of testosterone; still the incident shows the potential danger of hormonal manipulation. We don't always know what's down the road.

An aside: estrogen and progesterone are both derivatives of testosterone—or vice versa. The molecules are exceptionally similar. Progesterone is higher during pregnancy.

Anyway, when I would talk to my patients about T replacement, they often ask about side effects. I always went through the acne and swelling, et cetera; then added, "But you have to keep in mind what happened with estrogen. Everyone thought it was great: women were going to live forever, have beautiful skin, great boobs; then they found out it caused breast cancer."

So, I was waiting for the bomb to go off regarding testosterone and TRT... and it did... kind of anyway. But first, let's get back to the benefits of testosterone. I think this is interesting from a medical perspective. Starting at about thirty-five years of age, serum T levels begins to decline about 1% per year. As men get older and T levels drop there are certain infirmities that occur that were thought to be due to *old age*. Older guys—hypothetically at sixty our T level is down to 75%—begin to develop osteoporosis, lose height, and tend to hunch or be bent over. Muscle mass decreases, and we develop fatty breast tissue and a big belly. The older guy has less strength, less sexual desire. His body fat percentage increases. He's more likely to be depressed and less likely to be able to focus on specific tasks. Quite often I've heard friends or patients say, "It's hell getting old!" I usually joke that it is better than the alternative, but only in serious conversations do we discuss the alternative.

Briefly, guess what happens when muscle mass is increased and body fat is decreased? There's less heart disease, and there's less diabetes. There's better bone strength and better focus, which means more accomplishments and less depression. And there's a stronger libido. Those are some of the benefits of T, so why not take it? Why not... well... yes, it is more complicated and complex than that. There are numerous factors to consider, and there are alternatives. I'll explain in a minute, but first... perhaps you have to go!

On Peeing

"I recall when everything was tight and we could shoot straight," a friend once said to me. "This goes back to when we were little kids—maybe six, eight, ten years old. There was a woodshed behind my father's house, and nobody could see behind it. The roof at the back of the shed was maybe six feet high. We were small, you know, maybe three and a half or four feet tall, and that meant our crotches couldn't have been more than two feet off the ground. We would stand back there—at one time or another every boy from the neighborhood—we'd stand there, take aim, and see who could pee up to the roof. Sometimes, some of the streams arched over and reached almost to the middle of the roof! That's the kind of range we had at that time. It was kind of a bonding experience. Now these same guys joke about taking Viagra just so they don't dribble on their slippers." I think that's funny, but there is some truth to the fact of a weaker stream.

Another amusing anecdote: when I was in practice I would guess what questions would come from different personality types. If a guy came in with a plastic pocket protector and a tie clip, he was likely an engineer, so I'd expect something technical. One of the most common questions was, "Why, sometimes, doesn't the stream come straight out?"

"Well," I'd say, "the urethra is flat, like this." With my hands I'd indicate horizontal. "When it gets to the end of the penis it's like this." I'd indicate a 90-degree turn to vertical. "So the conversion of this-to-this incorporates a spiral, and that's why it comes out straight. It's like rifling." In the military, in basic weapons training, there was an adage instructors used with recruits to teach them proper nomenclature. It went something like, "This is my rifle (holds weapon high), and this is my gun (grasps groin); one is for fighting, and one is for fun." I rather doubt many of the instructors realized it, but both barrels have a type of rifling.

"But why NOT straight. Why, sometimes when I stand at the toilet, does it come out split in two streams… one on each side?"

We've all done that dance trying to get both streams in the bowl before finally have to shut it down and start over. The split stream usually indicates there is some secretion residue at the end of the urethra, or there's something stuck. If you've recently had sex, there might be swelling. That's usually what it is. And assuming that it is not actually something serious, it's just a matter that the spiral mechanism gets disrupted. It happens to everybody.

Back to Basics

Weighing in at all of one ounce (about 30 grams) it might seem that the prostate gland garners big attention for its size. Even its size grabs headlines. Located south of the bladder, north of the muscles of the pelvic floor, and west of the rectum (about where Colorado would be on the diagram below), the prostate is a three-layered structure responsible for producing the vehicle-fluid for sperm cells (from the testicles) which, during ejaculation, is potently propelled by the muscles of the prostate into the urethra and spewed from the tip of the penis.

On the diagram below, note the spatial relationship of the anus/rectum to the prostate; this allows your urologist access for digital exams and other procedures.

The urethra descends from the bladder, passes through the prostate, and continues on to the penis. Where the urethra traverses the prostate there is a series of one-way valves or ducts which first begin to open during sex, seeping pre-seminal fluid as a lubricant, then are thrown wide open by the forceful contraction of the gland's muscles at ejaculation. These ducts are closed during urination preventing urine from entering the gland; and during ejaculation the muscles of the prostate (along with the bladder sphincter) close the urethra above the gland preventing urine flow during coitus.

The gland is structured in layers like a baseball, but functions more like a small factory. Its core, the *transition zone*, wraps around the urethra. This structure is the shipping and receiving clerk compiling incoming materials, and opening and closing the ducts. Surrounding the core is the *central zone* (like the rubber covers around the cork pill of a baseball). This is the staging area or loading dock where sperm from the *vas deferens* (sperm duct) from the testicles, stores from the seminal vesicles (essentially mini-warehouses), and prostatic secretions are prepared for shipment. About the central zone is the *peripheral zone*. This tissue, like the cotton and wool yarn of the baseball, makes up the bulk of the gland (about 20 grams). It is the fabrication facility consisting of smooth muscle fiber and prostate-fluid production cells. The prostate fluid, a thin, milky, slightly alkaline liquid contains many enzymes, including prostate specific antigens (PSA). The fluid is both the vehicle and the protection river for sperm cells. It is essential for male fertility. The entire gland is

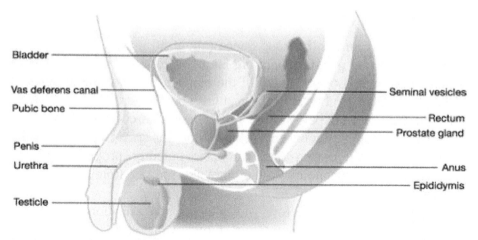

Location of the prostate gland

encapsulated in connective tissue—a la cowhide!

As men age the transition zone tends to enlarge with benign, non-cancerous, growth. It is this growth that most commonly restricts urine flow from the bladder. Most prostate cancers occur in peripheral zone tissues.

An additional function of the prostate is to convert testosterone into dihydrotestosterone (DHT), a biologically more active form of T.

PSAs

As noted above PSA, or prostate specific antigens, are produced in the outer or peripheral zone of the prostate gland. In guys, this antigen circulates throughout our bloodstream. The acronym PSA is often used to mean the test for detecting blood levels of this chemical compound. It is not an expensive test. The significance of that fact will become apparent shortly as it is relevant to the controversy surrounding administration.

The PSA is a simple blood test that can be given at any time of the day, and does not require fasting. In my opinion it should be part of one's annual physical exam—starting at the age of fifty-five, or earlier if the patient has a family or ethnic history of prostate cancer. It is unclear if family history is important because of common genetics or because of similar familial behaviors, but either way having a first-degree relative (brother, father) with PCa correlates to a risk rate 2.5 to

7.7 times higher than having no affected relatives. Risk declines if the affected relative is second-degree (uncle, grandfather), and more so if the relative is more distant. If the family member contracted the disease before age 50, one's risk rate also increases. Some guidelines require the cessation of the test at age 70, citing life expectancy averages versus the average time for the disease to become lethal. That is the equation responsible for the idea that men die *with* the disease, not *from* it.

The purpose of the PSA test is to allow your physician to detect prostate cancer in its earliest stage so it can be treated and cured. This method of testing has been available for about twenty years. It is an effective diagnostic tool, yet some physicians (and insurance companies and government bureaucrats) continue to debate its value. The American Board of Urology and the American Board of Oncology both recommend it; yet the American Academy of Family Practice feels the test leads to unnecessary surgeries and other treatments, and does not recommend it.

Let's put this in perspective. The PSA—the actual test not including the office visit, blood draw labor, facilities overhead, transportation of blood to the lab, etc.—costs approximately $10. Yep, ten bucks. That's it. We are not talking here about something that is going to break an insurance company or a government health program. So that is not a concern—unless someone is worried that they may have to pay for treatment if disease *is* found! With people frequently changing insurance providers, delaying detection may be financially beneficial by kicking the can down the road until it is someone else's problem. More on the economics of this below.

The PSA test is simply an indicator which shows if there is an abnormality in the prostate. If the antigen level in the blood is elevated it can be due to one of three things: a benign enlargement of the prostate, an acute infection of the gland, or prostate cancer. At this point a frank discussion with your physician is necessary. Depending on the degree of elevation and on family history one may choose to repeat the PSA. Repeated high or rising levels indicate a prostate biopsy should be ordered to determine the condition that exists.

The biopsy is a trans-rectal procedure which is moderately uncomfortable, but not particularly painful. I've heard patients describe it as someone pushing a staple gun up your ass and shooting a staple into the prostate. To one not seeing the tool, the sound may be similar. There are no staples, but a thin biopsy needle does fire forward and retract seemingly in an instant. [As an aside, women going through breast biopsies don't have it much better. Some describe it as lying face down on a torture-table with a hole in it that has a vice which squeezes the breast to prepare it for the biopsy gun.]

Most biopsies come back negative; about 30% come back positive. By comparison, 17% of breast biopsies are positive. These rates factor into the controversy, but realize that when a woman receives a negative results her reaction, and the reaction of those involved with her, be they family or the sisterhood, tends to be, "Pheew! Thanks God." When a guy receives a negative result from a prostate biopsy the common reaction from others is, "See! That was unnecessary."

If the biopsy comes back positive the treatment options depend upon the grade of the cancer, and the age and overall medical condition of the patient. A low-grade prostate cancer can be watched. For this we use the term *active surveillance* (AS). AS requires semiannual PSA testing, visits to the urologists, and repeat biopsies—usually every other year. Approximately 85% of patients with low-grade cancer do well; 15% do not. That's the reason for the close observation. Keep this 15% in mind. If the grade of the prostate cancer is moderate or high, then treatment options might include radiation in the form of radioactive seeds (Intensit-modulated radiation therapy or IMRT), hormone therapy, radical prostatectomy (usually preformed robotically), or some combination of all three.

The use of the PSA test does require discrimination. The treating physician must determine, before ordering the test, if the individual will benefit from the results. If a patient is elderly or suffers from other comorbidities, the test may not be appropriate. The use of the test should be discussed with the patient and his family.

Saying that, I strongly disagree with critics who state that doctors would need to screen 1,000 men to save one life; and use that statement to deny testing. First of all, even if that were true, so what?! We put seatbelts in millions of cars at considerably higher cost to save less than one life per thousand. That really is, or should be, beside the point.

Left undetected prostate cancer advances and can cause great pain and suffering. I have seen this too often in my practice. PCa is not a harmless disease. As noted earlier 30,000 men die each year from PCa; and there are nearly 300,000 new cases annually. Critics of PSA testing ignore immutable facts. Since the advent of PSA testing the death rate from prostate cancer has dropped 30% to 40%; and the incidence of metastatic prostate cancer as the initial presenting symptoms has decreased by nearly 80%! Why would we not want to have, and use, this valuable diagnostic tool? Critics also cite the downside of treatment which can include loss of urinary control and erectile dysfunction. Really! These are problems we can deal with—*if you're alive!*

New advances in biomarker testing are just now coming into more common use. We'll talk about them below.

A word on PSAs and cost: As mentioned, I lobbied the Connecticut State legislature to pass a law forcing insurance companies to pay for PSA screening just like they were paying for mammograms and Pap Smears; and for that I was pretty well beaten up in many of the state's newspapers. It got pretty nasty. Corporate representatives would cuss about costs rising. I'd counter that they should go home and see what happens when they tell their wives they're against mammograms. It was unpleasant drivel. I could not believe that it was only about money. Recall the cost of the test is only about ten bucks. It is relatively small, and it is short-term. In the long run the test is far cheaper than the alternative. If a guy has metastatic prostate cancer we give him a drug mixture called ***Lupron/Casodex*** which basically blocks the action of testosterone.

The cost of just this standard medication: $6,000 per year!

It got to the point where I was saying to the corporate reps, "If you want to save money tell your employees we can accomplish the same thing with an operation that cost 800 bucks. We'll remove their testicles. That gets rid of the testosterone. That'll be the end of it. And remember to tell your potential employees too, that if they come to work for you and they get prostate cancer, you'll only authorize that they be castrated?" That didn't go over big, but that was the point. There was, as noted above, more to it than just the initial cost, but that's really all people were hearing or reading in the of the media. No one publically spoke about kicking the can down the road. No one openly said, "If we don't test for cancer, we don't have to pay for cancer care." No one acknowledged that since a large percentage of people change insurance companies annually, there was an economic incentive to wait and let the PCa care be someone else's problem.

Our governor, however, was behind our proposal. Because I was largely responsible for the text of the law, then Governor John G. Roland asked me to be at the signing. During the signing, he turned to me and said, "Dr. Jeff, this is really a good thing you've done. My father had prostate cancer. This would have helped him."

PCa

Prostate cancer (PCa or sometimes symbolized as PC[a]) is, quite simply, cancer of the prostate gland. Like all cancers, prostate cancer involves abnormal tissue growth. Different forms of PCa, with varying growth rates and different prognoses, form in the different and diverse tissues of this tiny, multi-layered, multi-functional gland. PCa can be silent and slow moving, or aggressive and nasty.

Angiogenesis, the process of growing new capillary blood vessels, is an essential and natural biological mechanism the body uses to grow new, or repair damaged, tissues. Our bodies, the amazing machines that they are, regulate this vessel-growth process by continuously generating and adjusting a meticulous aggregate of chemical growth and inhibitory factors. When these factors are out of balance trouble ensues; and abnormal growth, either too much or too little, occurs. Abnormal angiogenesis is common to many diseases; and it has been shown to play a central role in the progression of advanced prostate cancer. It is unclear whether or not this rapid overgrowth of capillaries is present at the onset of PCa, or if it is a resultant of early cancerous cells secreting angiogenic growth factor proteins that stimulate the blood vessel growth necessary to provide oxygen and nutrients to cancerous tissues.

The progression of PCa can be slow or rapid, the disease can be localized or can have metastasized, and treatment protocols as noted above, range from active surveillance to surgery. Understanding the above basic mechanisms should be an important step in a prostate-cancer patient's decision process.

In my practice, if a patient's biopsy came back positive, we would have *the cancer talk*. I would explain that we first needed to ascertain the full location of the cancer, and identify the specific form and aggressiveness of the disease, before we determined which treatment option to follow. A certain percentage of prostate cancers are not aggressive, and I would say, "We can do watchful waiting."

I'd further tell him, "Okay. Here's the deal. You have a low-grade, low-volume cancer, so you would be a perfect candidate for active surveillance. BUT..." I always gave this great emphasis, "...you need to be aware that the statistics say that within ten years, fifteen percent of this kind of cancer is going to progress to metastatic disease. So there is a risk, and it is a serious risk. We can be watchful. We can repeat PSA testing every six months and look at the trend. If the number doubles in less than three years, that's evidence of clinical progression which means we'll be dealing with a riskier situation." Then I would ask, "What do you want to do?"

I don't think that is a fair question to ask someone who has cancer. It's like asking, "Do you want to roll the dice?" but it is part of the proscribed protocol. I would try to put it into the real world for them. "What I'm asking you is kind of like, 'Would you walk across 5th Avenue in New York during rush hour, against the lights, if you knew that sometime in the next ten years you had a fifteen percent chance of being mangled by a taxi cab; or would you wait at the intersection for the walk light? The walk light is the treatment." Most guys would answer, "I want to get treated. I don't want to have a ticking time bomb inside of me."

A few years back the federal Public Service Task Force (USPSTF) claimed that PSA testing was doing more harm than good, and recommended against doing the test for any reason. This group is comprised of epidemiologists who do not practice medicine. Their recommendation led to the advice that those with low-grade, low-volume prostate cancer should *not* be treated because 85% of them were going to do well. The American Urological Association (AUA) responded by recommending active surveillance, and by challenging the USPSTF to explain the science behind their position. The Task Force declined to do so. With other physicians from the Urology Political Action Committee (UROPAC) I went to Washington to press a number of senators for a bill which would require the USPSTF to provide their data. Our effort became a clause attached to a bill to repeal Obamacare, and it died with that legislation.

What seemed to be lost on the USPSTF was the fact that although 85% would do well the *other* 15% would *not* do well. Their disease would progress and they would suffer. Of course, physicians do not know who will be in the 85% and who will be in the 15%. The USPSTF also ignored the fact that African-Americans have a 40% higher incident rate of PCa than the general population.

I've had a number of patients who decided to be watched; and who, after the third or fourth year, showed up with advanced disease. They'd be pretty upset. I'd remind them, "We never said it wouldn't progress. We said the chances are that it probably wouldn't progress." But put yourself in their place. Try to feel what they were feeling. They had just being hit with traumatic news. Their original decision had been based on statistics. As a physician I did not, and could not, make that decision for them; it was not up to me to decide from what disease they were going to die! But the Public Service Task Force, and the attitude they promote that PCa is a disease you can live with and won't die from, be damned! For 15% that's not true. That's absolutely not true. And it's tragic.

As mentioned, new advances and new tests are just now coming into more common use, and they look to be better diagnostic tools than just the plain old-fashioned PSA. The Prostate Health Index or PHI is a mathematical formula based on three serum PSA elements: total PSA, free PSA and 2.Pro PSA. It is considered a better indicator of the presence of clinically significant/high-grade PCa, and also a better prognosticator of the disease's progression during active surveillance.

PCa3 tests use an alternate indicator of prostate cancer. One, the PROGENSA PCa3, analyses urine for a fusion gene (TMPRSS2: ERG RNA) which is present in half of all prostate tumors. This diagnostic tool is specifically used when PSA is high but a biopsy has been negative. If this test is positive a second biopsy is indicated.

It is suggested that these new diagnostic tools will lead to fewer, not more, biopsies. Biopsies, too, are being updated and are becoming more accurate, switching from the previous norm of ultrasound guidance to new methods of MRI guidance.

What agencies, insurance companies, or medical groups approve the new testing methods and/or biopsy procedures is still a work in progress.

Treatments: Most guys agree that they should get treated. After AS, treatment options include hormone therapy (as with androgen biosynthesis inhibitors), radioactive seeds therapy (with radioisotope radium-223), anti-angiogenic therapy (a form of chemo); and radical prostatectomies. Hormone, seed and chemo are generally considered less onerous than surgery. If you're an older man, you may do well with radiation or a combination or radiation, hormone, and chemo; but if you're younger, say 65 and under, statistics suggest that the surgery is favorable in the 15- to 20-year timeframe. Surgery may mean partial or full removal of the prostate, and may be proceeded by and followed by other therapies.

All therapies have side effects. I always explained to my patients that these are chemicals we're putting into your body. Modern chemos, hormone supplementation and balancing, and radioactive seed implants are far more targeted than similar therapies of only a decade ago, but they are still going to do things we don't intend. Hopefully they will also do the things we want.

A few years back I was at an NFL dinner/ fund raiser for prostate research. Cornerback Mike Haynes of the New England Patriots got up and talked about the immediate aftereffects of prostate surgery—leaking and impotence. It is likely that it is the fear of those two conditions which is behind most guys' decisions to avoid surgery, or even to avoid all treatment options. At another lecture I was talking about the consequences of surgery including bleeding and infections. One of the audience members called out, "You mean complications." "No," I responded. "Not really. These are consequences. We expect them to happen. Complications are unexpected. Mislabeling consequences as complications promotes the belief that one should never have a radical prostatectomy because you're going to bleed and leak and lose your erection. Those are short term consequences. They are not reasons to forego needed surgery." Gentlemen, rein in your fears and put your male problem-solving mechanisms to work. Seek solutions. We can deal with and correct those consequences... but only if you aren't still kicking.

Prostate Pain

Not all pain, and not all high PSA levels, mean prostate cancer. Bacterial infections are one of many possible sources. Others include non-bacterial chemical inflammation which might occur if there are chemicals in the urine, or if there is faulty ductwork allowing urine to seep into the prostate. Pain may also be triggered by auto-immune responses to previous infections, or by nerve damage.

The condition is called prostatitis, and it can be chronic or acute. Guys would come into the office and they would be very uncomfortable. They might describe having pain by the prostate, or in the region, and they might say "It won't go away." Some of these guys were really hurting: "Oh my God! Oh my God! Doc, we gotta do something." Sometimes we could find the cause of the pain, sometimes it was elusive. Someone came up with the term, Prostadinia, which is just a fancy name for prostate pain. Sometimes it was phantom prostate pain—that is, it was caused by a neural pathway to the brain previously established by the body in reaction to a past disease or infection to trigger the sensation of pain, yet in the wake of the cessation of the disease the nerves were still sending the message. Sometimes pain "in the prostate" is caused by inflammation of the pelvic muscles, particularly levators which hold everything in down below. It they to go into spasm, that spasm can be causing the pain. In these cases, instead of giving a patient antibiotics or pain meds, we'd give him a muscle relaxant, usually two milligrams of valium, which is a very low dose, and the pain would go away.

We would need a series of textbooks to go into all the types and causes of prostate pain, to delineate all the symptoms and treatment possibilities. This section is only meant to make the reader aware of the complexities of prostate cancers and pain, and to emphasize how important it is for one to have a personal physician one trusts. In later sections we will discuss the fallacies of the growing walk-in clinic approach to medicine. Given the complexities of the human body within an even more complex physical and chemical environment, it can be easy to treat a problem with the wrong solution.

Tactics: Prevention and Prostate Protection

Testosterone, as we've seen, is a powerful hormone. Eighty years since it was first isolated, it continues to inspire research and controversy. Currently there is a study going on at Yale University to determine why testosterone levels decrease. Is it due to aging? Is it due to something in the water or food supply? In Connecticut, all male physicians including me received a letter requesting that we sign up. If half the physicians do sign up, the number of subjects in the study will be approximately 4,000. That's a decent number for a research study. But just as important as the size of the subject population is the design of the study. What are they looking for, and how are they going about looking for it?

As the Elis look for the reason why T declines, we might wish to consider factors which keep it from declining. We've mentioned some of the benefits of normal T levels, and the seeming tie between PCa and truly low-T (hypogonadism, not necessarily the Low-T of big pharma's ad men). Hypogonadism is certainly age related, with 39% of all men over 45, and 50% of men over 80, being affected; but correlation is not causation so it is not possible to simply blame it on age. High blood pressure and high cholesterol also correlate with lower levels of T; as does obesity, diabetes, positive HIV status, AIDs, and opioid use. Let's look at some factors.

Exercise, particularly high-intensity exercise, increases T-levels via the sacrogenic creation of testosterone. This is the muscle itself actually making the hormone. As you exercise the muscle synthesizes testosterone which in turn increases muscle tissue, allows for more exercise and for even more muscle creation—an elegant, synergistic loopback system. This testosterone is not related to testicular or ovarian functions (ovaries also make testosterone) or to the adrenal gland.

Diet and obesity are additional considerations. Reports tell us that school age obesity has grown to approximately 40% and that adult obesity rates are even higher. We could have an extended discussion on the causes and consequences of this, on what is happening to our food supply and to our eating habits, but let's restrict ourselves to this: if one has excess body fat (adipose tissue), one elaborates a chemical substance which converts testosterone into estrogen. We know that PCa correlates closely with hypogonadism, and we suspect that this T conversion in the obese is behind their higher incidence of PCa. Think about that for a moment. Reflect back to what is happening to boys in elementary school who are being reined in from rough and tumble play. The suppression of their physical nature may set up a lifetime of reduced activity and an increased propensity to be obese. Draw your own conclusion.

Diabetes is another disease that causes low serum testosterone. Behaviors, diet and blood-sugar levels all interact. When you exercise you need calories for the energy to do the physical work. Exercise essentially drives blood sugar into your cells to meet this need, so your blood sugar levels go down. Arthur Ashe, the great American tennis player, was a diabetic. They used to say—this was years ago—that when he played tennis he didn't need insulin because the intense exercise itself would reduce his blood sugar.

Your body first burns sugar, then it metabolizes and burn fat (body fat or adipose tissue). When you're burning this fat the action of insulin is blocked because you can't burn fat and sugar at the same time. If you are constantly replenishing blood sugar with high glycemic-index foods, your metabolism never switches over to burn stored fat. Indeed, it converts some of that sugar into more stored fat. Obesity is one result; a second is insulin-resistance. If your blood sugar stays up that is basically the definition of being diabetic. Metabolism under these circumstances destroys testosterone. That effect, along with the adipose tissue conversion of T and the resulting fatigue due to low-T becomes a vicious cycle.

Over the years numerous vitamins, minerals and/or supplements have been touted to either increase T or to protect the prostate. Some have proven track records; some we thought were important have proven to basically be worthless. Think about this for a moment: If you go to your local supermarket and get a head of lettuce, and if you don't eat it in two or three days, what does it look like? If you're lucky you might have a little grocery store with very fresh produce because the produce manager goes up to the farmer's market every day, but then; do you shop every day? Most of us don't. We chow down on various levels of chemically-preserved, highly-process food. And even much of our non-packaged food has been raised on depleted soils. As a nation we do lack needed nutrition.

About 15 years ago there was an article in the Journal of The American Urological Association which talked about the nutritional basis of cancer. The author went through all the different nutrients one needs—like lutein for the eyes, vitamin A for the bladder, et cetera. He went on to say that our food was so over-processed and so old by the time we get it that the nutrient value was diminished. He was a big proponent of taking vitamins. I was skeptical, but I am no longer. But be careful.

For a long time it was believed that the nonmetallic mineral selenium lowered one's risk of getting prostate cancer. This was based on the recognition that farmlands in the East and in the Pacific Northwest have much less selenium than farmlands in the center of the country and Southwest, and that the incidence of PCa is lowest in the areas where selenium is highest. Several huge, controlled studies—one by NIH tracking 20,000 physicians for about ten years—were undertaken. The conclusion was: selenium produced no significant results regarding one's probability of contracting the disease. On the other hand, another study conducted not with mega-doses but with the over-the-counter multi-vitamin, Centrum Silver, showed a reduced incidence rate of PCa of 11%. That was one, relatively small study, but it shows promise. For years the supplement saw palmetto seems to have shown positive results in helping to control benign prostatic hyperplasia (BPH), the non-cancerous enlargement of the prostate which causes some men problems with urination by squeezing down on the urethra. Saw palmetto is the plant form of *Serenoa repens*. A 2011 double-blind study using 369 subjects, published in *The Journal of the American Medical Association* (JAMA), reported that men in the experimental group, those receiving the saw palmetto extract, actually experienced less improvement (although the degree was statistically insignificant) than men in the placebo group. The study size was small, and the question of efficacy is still open.

At the moment you might be asking, "Well then, what does work?!" Well, how about sex, masturbation and fantasy! And garlic and scallions! And ginger, oregano, rosemary and green tea!

We need to ask, and answer: What long-term effect does orgasm/ejaculation have on the prostate gland? Does it indeed have any effect? Do men who have more frequent orgasms either by masturbation or intercourse have less prostate cancer compared to men who, for perhaps religious or cultural reason, seldom have orgasms? Are there any long-term effects on testosterone levels via fantasy? Do T levels increase because of fantasies, or vice versa, do fantasies increase because of higher T levels? Perhaps this psycho-physical complex works in conjunction. Are there health consequences, positive or negative, from daily or weekly orgasms? Does high T equate with better health? We already answered that, didn't we? Does this change as one ages—not the T level but the benefits of higher or lower T levels? Is it possible to say our fantasies keep us healthy?

Men's Health magazine reports that an Australian study of 2,338 men found that men who took themselves in hand at least five times a week had a 34% lower likelihood of developing PCa by age 70 than men who abstained. Six or more time per week did not improve the percentage. The lead author, Graham Giles, Ph. D. conjectured, "Seminal fluid contains substances that are carcinogenic. Regular ejaculation may help flush them out." If he is right, how might that correlate with exposure to Agent Orange (AO)? The VA automatically compensates American veterans of the Vietnam War who contract prostate cancer with a 15% disability rating on the presumption that the cancer has been caused by exposure to this defoliant. I don't believe there have been any studies comparing ejaculation frequency, dioxin (the chemical contaminate in AO) exposure and PCa. Previous exposure to AO has been shown to be a significant predictor of rapid biochemical progression (PSA-doubling time) after radical prostatectomy, but to be statistically insignificant in PCa onset.

But back to fantasies: neuro-psychiatrist Louann Brizendine tells us that, "True arousal for men typically starts in the brain with erotic thoughts or images." ...not sure she really needed to tell that to most of us! Fantasies, thoughts and images get us going, or as she puts it, "That's all it takes for a man's brain to send signals down the spinal cord to the penis to start an erection. ... The male brain's sexual-pursuit and arousal circuits must [however] be primed for action by testosterone in order for him to function."

Do you see where this is going? Erotic thoughts flip the on switch, testosterone primes the pump, the circuits kick into gear and the machinery, amongst other things, produces more testosterone which stimulates erotic thoughts. That may be the male's most basic circular circuitry of all, and it is healthful. Have you ever gotten one of those SYBST emails… you know, Send Your Buddies Some Titties, with photos (images) of beautiful topless women? There's usually a punchline about this being healthy for you; but it's really not a joke. It is healthy. It raise your T level which lowers your PCa risk, keeps your prostate from enlarging, increases your muscle mass, decreases serum cholesterol, et cetera, et cetera. It's more healthful to look at female breasts in the physical world, at least from a T-production perspective.

Going back to the question I get from patients and from guys in the gym: "What can I do to get my wife to have sex with me?" Well, all wives are different, but feel free to tell yours, Dr. Jeff says, "If she wants to keep you healthy, she should show you her breasts, and make love to you often."

A penultimate tactic: Do you like to cook? Why not throw together a nice stir-fry with ginger and garlic and scallions to taste? An article in the Journal of the National Cancer Institute reports that daily consumption of ten grams of garlic or scallions (about three cloves or two tablespoons respectively) reduces the risk of PCa by 50%; and a study from the Center for Holistic Urology of New York found the growth of prostate cancer cell in their lab to be lowered by 78% when the culture was exposed to a mixture of ginger, oregano, rosemary and green tea. Perhaps tomato sauce with garlic, oregano and rosemary *is* a health food; but a word of caution—go easy on the pasta. Like all grain-based foods pasta spikes your blood sugar levels. Too many *nice'a bowls* like grandma used to serve, coupled with a sedentary job, is likely to lead to increased adipose tissue, which is likely to lead to… Well, you get the idea.

The alternative to diet, supplements, exercise and fantasy is testosterone replacement therapy—TRT. TRT works; in some case, maybe too well. We'll get to that, The T-Bomb Affair, in a moment.

Testosterone for this therapy comes in the form of skin gels, injections, patches, pellets implants, and oral applications. About 70% of guys on TRT use the skin gel which is typically rubbed onto shoulders and absorbed through the skin. Doctor- or self-administered injections account for 17%; and slow-release skin patches for another 10%. Oral T and implanted pellets make up the remainder.

Guys would come into the office and request testosterone shots. They'd say, "I think I have Low-T. I have fatigue. I'm weak. I have no sex drive." I always told them, "I'm not going to give it to you until after we know your T-level." We've noted this before: testosterone is a potent substance. Despite the impression one might get from Low-T commercials on TV, the use of TRT is not, and should not be, like going to the pharmacy for an over-the-counter drug. If a guy's testosterone is normal he should not receive more via TRT. If he's fatigued, experiencing low libido, et cetera, we need to look for other potential causes. Proper assessment includes a medical history and physical exam to determine the source of symptoms, and to rule out illness which might be the cause. Many of the guys I talked to were long-term patients. I knew them; I knew their medical histories and the results of their most recent physical exam. Some exhibited signs and symptoms consistent with androgen deficiency, some did not. We would request a blood draw to be taken in the morning when T-levels are normally at their peak, then evaluate the results against all the other data. If the T-level was unequivocally low, we would then proceed. It is a bit more complex than what I'm saying here, as we would also attempt to differentiate between primary and secondary hypogonadism while being aware that low-T is often a symptom, not a cause, of something else going on in the body.

If T was low and all else fit our criteria, I'd give him a shot. The shot would last for three weeks. Then I'd have him return and we'd evaluate the results. Sometimes guys weren't sure. I'd ask, "Did you have more energy? Did it improve your sex drive?" Sometimes I'd have to give them a second shot. After the second shot, if we determined it helped, we'd re-measure their T level to see if it was up. If it was up I'd switch them to one of the medication, perhaps Axiron which is like a roll-on deodorant. If that worked I'd see them in three months. If it was still working I'd monitor them every six months.

The choice of medication was often driven by cost. If a guy could come to the office and get a shot of testosterone—I think it was twenty bucks per cc—insurance usually covered the expense. If you had State of Connecticut health insurance, it covered all the therapies, so guys would usually opt for something like AndroGel, one of the gels that is rubbed on and absorbed through the skin, because of the convenience. These other treatments tend to be more expensive than injections, with some running about $400 per month. So the choice was driven by cost and insurance coverage.

I give the pharmacy industry credit for informing the public about testosterone replacement therapy. In the appropriate hands it is a good tool. Alternate drug companies have come out with a rash of T-boosting supplements. Their ads are sometimes over the top. "Hey, you... I hear you can't get it up. I hear you can't lift your car or jump over tall building with a single bound. You can't sleep. You can't think. Your wife no longer thinks you're a man... Take this. Rock Hard'n'Roll..."

Patients used to ask me about these supplements all the time. I'd say, "I don't really know what's in it so I can't tell you that it works. The FDA doesn't scrutinize the supplement industry. Some may be potent, some may be rice powder. Sometimes the effect, if there is one, may be strictly a placebo response. I can't even tell you that it's not toxic. It might be great. It might be a con job. Be careful."

For a moment think about the phenomenon of the growth of both pharmaceutical TRT and the T-supplement industry from a social perspective. There is obviously a need, or a perceived need, that guys are attempting to fill. And it is increasing. TRT became a big part of my practice—maybe 10%. That's a big number! There is a need for this therapy to be economically feasible; but why is there such increasing demand? Is it simply a matter that guys like having erections, or will pay to have more confidence in the bedroom? There are many potential causes of hypogonadism: one may be a general pattern of increased stress experienced by American men. Keep this in mind.

The T-Bomb... or Dud; and The V-Bomb, too

With the popularity and growth of TRT came the questions, as we mentioned earlier, about why, or why not, give it to older guys. First it was, it causes prostate cancer; then better research showed that to be erroneous. The next round of thinking was we'll have a bunch of feeble, old codgers mindlessly running around wanting to have sex. But the effects tended to be far more beneficial: more muscle mass and less body fat so cardiac health improved and the incidence of diabetes dropped; better mentation; improved blood sugar metabolism; and greater capacity to exercise. And yes, their sex drive was revived. Hurrah! Hurray!

This was all developing concurrently with the advent of Viagra. In the early days, when it was said that men didn't need testosterone for erections, the brochure for Viagra instructed users that they had to be excited for the drug to work. At that time I would tell my patients, "Don't take one of these and go to the Stop'n'Shop and expect it to work." I had one guy who said to me, "You gave me this, I took it, and nothing happened. I took a shower like two hours later and I got this erection, and I couldn't do anything about it because I was in the shower. You didn't tell me not to take a shower." I'm thinking, *Really!* I said, "The obvious thing is to bring your wife into the shower with you." He was like, "Ahh... Oh," then smiling, "Okay."

It was the marketers of Viagra, not wanting to use the term *impotence*, who came up with the phrase Erectile Dysfunction or ED. The testosterone ad men followed up with Low-T. So now you can say Low-T in public. I think this is good. Guys used to be embarrassed to bring it up, so it would go untreated. No one ever used to talk about ED or Low-T. I think the first guy to say it on air was Phil Donahue. He brought it up on TV. Wives listened to it and talked to their husbands, and the bandwagon for treatment began to fill.

Now, fast-forward to early 2014. New studies on TRT began showing that guys who take testosterone have higher incidents of heart attack. Guys in the gym began asking me about long-term side effects. As I used to tell my patients, I'd say, "We don't know of any, but as you know, drugs are chemicals that we put in our bodies and sometimes they do things we don't expect." I'd use the example of estrogen replacement therapy for women. Estrogen helped menopausal women with hot-flashes and vaginal dryness. Then they found out that it caused breast cancer. Then it was found that it wasn't the estrogen but the combination of estrogen and progesterone in the early formulas. But the media got hold of the idea that estrogen was causing breast cancer and many women stopped using it. Many switched to alternatives—bay leaf or something.

There were two studies supported by NIH and the VA that showed TRT increased the risk of heart attack. One study showed that in the over-65 age group, in the first ninety days after starting TRT there was a significant bump up in incidence. In the under-65, there was also an increase, not as large but still statistically significant. The FDA announced, there *might be* a problem, and they were going to look into it further. Their announcement said: We are not telling you to stop taking the drug, we're saying that it might be a problem and you should talk to your doctor. We have previously approved all these hormone replacement therapies, so you can continue to use them because we don't have the evidence to show that it really is a problem.

As soon as those studies were published, the Medical-Legal Complex picked up the issue. Almost overnight there were ads on TV trolling for class-action clients. "Have you or a loved one had a heart attack or a stroke, or if a loved one has died, and if you or your loved one has taken testosterone, the FDA has warned that there might be a problem. Call the offices of Attorneys Flim & Flam. Protect your legal rights. You may be entitled to compensation."

When I first saw that I thought, "Geez, they haven't even determined there's a problem." But, of course, those attorneys were lying in wait—modern day ambulance chasers—looking for a class-action gold mine. The downside of their ad blitz is that it scares patients. Some stop TRT, which may be worse because they are losing the benefits of the therapy.

On first seeing the articles, my thoughts were, guys receiving TRT are feeling so much stronger and so much more alive, they are going out and doing more strenuous activity. In some cases these activities are more strenuous than anything they've done in years. They are exercising, playing basketball, skiing, but without the pre-training period required after sedentary careers. That may be the reason for the increase in heart attacks, not the fact that testosterone has some sort of direct causative property.

One potential legal factor is drug-company advertising that implies that if you have this list of symptoms—fatigue, etc.—it is due to Low-T. They have not gotten the message across that it might be due to other causes. But if you go to the doctor and you have these symptoms, as we noted above, he's going to check your testosterone. He's going to evaluate your physical health. And he's going to monitor your response to the TRT. I've attempted to imagine who would give T when not needed. Lawsuits and class-action TV ads imply that doctors would. I wouldn't. I didn't. The physicians I know wouldn't. Trying to think like the people who make these accusations, I come up with the guys that maybe would do that are salesmen. You know, "well, you don't need a new copier (or phone or car), but I've got this new one which is *so* much better." That might be the way some salesmen think, but physicians are not salesmen. They aren't, and shouldn't be, paid for moving product.

Politicians get all upset if a doctor goes out to dinner with a drug company rep as if the rep is going to brainwash the physician. But really what the drug companies do, is they invite you out to dinner, they have a speaker come, and the speaker talks about a new drug—what it does and what it doesn't do. So, instead of a you get a steak. So what! It becomes part of our education. But seen from a politician's perspective, if a physician is invited out to dinner, it is a bribe to curry some sort of quid pro quo favor. That's the world of politics. That's how they behave. That is not the world of the traditional physician—the rule follower. That is not how we behave. Anytime you are looking at criticism, you need to look at the critic. Sometimes he or she is telling you more about their own underlying morals than the morals of those they criticize.

The T-Bomb turned out to be a dud. First, a group of professors reviewed the original study. It left many of them scratching their heads. The conclusion, they pointed out, doesn't match the data. For one thing, one of the non-testosterone user groups was comprised of women. By late 2014, Renal & Urology News was reporting on a study of 25,420 men, 25% of which were taking TRT by injection and 75% were non-testosterone users. The results:

> ...testosterone therapy... was not associated with an increased risk of heart attack. In fact, patients [who were on TRT, and] who had a higher probability of cardiovascular problems, had a 30% lower rate of heart attacks than patients with the same probability of cardiovascular problems who were not receiving testosterone therapy.

First T was harmful, then it was beneficial, then it was beneficial and maybe harmful. What I always told my patients: Everybody is different. Any chemical we prescribe that we anticipate to be beneficial may have negative side effects in some people. That's why we monitor you. And you should also be monitoring yourself. Call me if you think a problem is developing.

The V-Bomb is exploding right now, and the firms of Attorneys Flim & Flam, and Attorneys Konman and KaChing, have been quick to place ads in primetime: "If you have taken the little blue pill, and you have developed melanoma... ca-ching... ca-ching... you may be entitled to financial compensation... ca-ching... ca-ching." My apologies to the reader. Sentences like that erupt out of frustration over lawsuits, not science, driving medicine. Much more on this in the next section. The Viagra-melanoma link has yet to be resolved. I don't see the preparation of class-action lawsuits as helpful to the truth.

Viagra, and other ED meds, have their place. In my practice many guys felt Viagra opened up a whole new world for them. It was kind of like the effects of air conditioning opening up the Southwest to real estate development. Without air conditioning Las Vegas would still be a small, dusty, cowpoke town with a few good bars and a bunch of slot machines. The mechanical improvement changed the social environment. So to with guys and Viagra.

When you're young you don't have any problems with erections. When you get older some guys want Viagra. The desire, of course, is fueled by advertisements (the newest one with a sensual woman lying on a bed talking directly to the viewer about pleasing his honey); and by a cultural myth that has developed around the subject. It is, of course, also fueled by the fact that ED drugs are, at least partially, effective. If they were not effective there would be no $2 billion per year industry, no cultural myth, no advertising. Still, the problem is, if the wife or girlfriend is not interested, ED drugs don't work. What works well is a woman that wants you. I've had patients who got divorced, or who maybe hadn't had sex for a long time because their wife was ill, and when they got into a new relationship they were having sex all the time—<u>without pills</u>. Age was not a factor. I'm talking about guys in their mid-60s and mid-70s who would come in and say, "I don't need this anymore." There are guys that do need ED drugs, but for many the key is the desire of the woman. Sometimes guys recognize this. The drugs can force challenge into the relationship; as in, "It's not me. My tool works just fine. It's you. What are you going to do about it?!"

There is an organization called *Even The Score* which is backed by the pharmaceutical company Sprout, that is petitioning the FDA to approve flibanserin as a treatment for Female Sexual Dysfunction (FSD). Sprout has argued that the FDA approved Viagra in six months, but has failed to approve a drug that addresses "female desire." (The FDA has approved nearly two dozen drugs that treat vaginal dryness or pain during intercourse.) The misplaced fact in the argument, however, is that "Viagra addresses male desire." It doesn't. It only assists with the fluid mechanics.

The point is, low libido in women affects men; and low libido in men affects women. Remember, men need intimacy; men express themselves physically; to men physical touch is an emotional expression; and not being touched is interpreted as rejection. A positive sequence for a guy is to 1) find someone to whom he is attracted; 2) to find out if she is attracted to him; 3) if she is attracted and willing—the smile or come hither look followed by other clear sign, then let the biological fires of passion ignite. Problems arise—and this is a legitimate female complaint—when a guy, first date or in an established relationship makes little difference, over steps the bounds of propriety. Sometimes feelings of rejection lead to aggression. That's a no no. That's abuse.

Stressed Out and Limp

Low-T and ED may be symptoms of mental and physical fatigue caused by stress. Both fatigue states, according to Suzanne Venker, "affect the same region of [the] brain—the anterior cingulate cortex," and "mental stress significantly affects physical performance."

Indeed, unresolved chronic mental stress affects our bodies in hundreds of ways; and the more severe the stress, the greater the affect. Hopelessness equates with early heart attacks; chronic stress correlates with IBS, Crone's Disease and ulcerative colitis; the in ability to cope elevates blood pressure and blood sugar levels, and leads to obesity. The immune system is suppressed. Mentation becomes cloudy. Stress leads to behavioral changes: lack of exercise, depression and repressed anger. The culmination of factors reduces T-levels and makes one more prone to PCa and other diseases and conditions related to low-T.

Our world today seems, for many, far more stressful that at any time in the past three or four decades. The economic difficulties of the past seven or eight years have exacerbated emotional exhaustion. I've seen this in patients, in friends, and in guys in the gym.

How guys deal with stress determines the severity of physical and chemical reaction in the body. If a guy is restricted in the ways in which they can deal with stress, if he feels trapped and frustrated and problems remain unresolved—and if he represses it all—his health will suffer.

I recall one study about aftereffects of the ending of the Apollo Space Program. Many of the engineers were laid off, and within one year 25 percent had heart attacks. That was a huge percentage of myocardial infarctions in a small, well-defined population. The men had kind of lost their identity. Other problems piled on. Depression and immune system suppression followed, along with unhealthy coping mechanisms like excessive drinking, smoking and lack of exercise.

Psychologist Robert Reynolds, whom we met earlier, says, "The way in which I see men changing has not been necessarily positive. I think society has become more stressful, and the demands on people in general are much greater. Financial demands, family demands [kids, divorce, incompetent bosses]… rather than these issues strengthening men, I see men breaking down. I see men losing their way." Problems met, challenges faced and overcome strengthen an individual. These are our heroes; these are the robust, wind in their faces guys we admire. As Reynolds notes, "If you think about the traditional male of the 50s and 60s, he was the strong silent type. I don't see too many of them anymore. Keep in mind, I see a skewed sample—men who come to me with issues in their lives that aren't working. But I see men [in general] as being broken by the stresses and challenges of life."

In *The War on Men*, Venker identifies another cause of stress: "Over the past four decades, America has witnessed a profound change in marriage and gender relations—for the worse. And while there are definitely a handful of reasons for the fractured family unit, the most significant phenomenon to rupture marriage was feminism. In the span of a few short decades, the movement managed to demote men from respected providers and protectors of the family to superfluous buffoons."

Recall one of our early thoughts: "I'm a guy. I don't talk about my disease because it's not politically correct to talk about testicles in a public forum." I wonder how much that too adds to the level of stress which in turn diminishes health. It may be unintended, but elements of political correctness harm men in unseen ways.

Stress: frustration, depression, and hopelessness affect behaviors. In complex combinations inflammation increases, testosterone production decreases, and overall health is hurled into a descending spiral.

Conclusion

Prostate cancer, to date, has no public profile commensurate to breast cancer. A lingering general lack of public awareness and misinformation still surrounds this malady. We need to do more to create a greater awareness of the issues facing men. We need more than a month dedicated on paper to raise public awareness of PCa; more than a month to spread the word about prostate health; more than a month to affect changes of attitude which will allow men to openly and frankly talk about these issues. Recently I founded **The New England Men's Health Initiative** to give these issues a vehicle to bring them into the bright light of public awareness. Please visit our site: drjeffsays.com. You do not need to be from New England to participate.

PART VI: The Doctor is Out

The Business of Medicine

One of my pet peeves is that most physicians won't stand up for themselves. When it comes to taking charge of the business end of medicine, doctors traditionally have been submissive. I do not necessarily mean the finances of a private office; but more how charges, compensation and distribution of funds are determined in what we now call the Healthcare System.

Earlier, when we talked about the characteristics of physicians, we noted that physicians tend to be rule-followers who think inside-the-box, and caregivers who fear failure and what that might mean to the health of their patients. We said that much of this was good because the doctor then had the patient's best interest at heart. We further noted that most doctors, as a self-selected group (that is they chose and worked hard to become doctors), tended to hold a level of contempt for the commercial aspects of their profession. I did. I once thought physicians shouldn't be in business to make money, but should be in business to take care of people—making money would be a by-product of this effort. That was a general attitude held by most physicians of my generation: *If you are focused on compensation, then you are not focused on patient care.* It was almost an obsession. For many years focusing on, or even casually talking about, business earnings and profit was a taboo.

I think most patients also believed that a *good* doctor did not, and should not have, cared about money. That attitude hasn't ebbed. In fact it is stronger than ever. Think of your own reaction to news stories you read or watch about doctors voluntarily going to third-world nations to work in clinics for the indigent. Be it *Doctors Without Borders* or Senator Rand Paul, M.D., don't you admire them for the work they are doing at least in part because it is without compensation?

Don't get me wrong: some people are attracted to the profession because they expect to become *rich doctors*, but college, medical school, internship and residency is not a get-rich-quick scheme. Few con men are willing to spend a dozen post-high school years in school for the privilege of starting out on the ground floor.

Not long ago I taught a Family Practice course at a local hospital. During one session I asked the residents, "What are you going to make?" One of the new docs said, "I don't know. I don't really care about money. I just want to take care of patients." I said, "That's great. Can you come to work for me? As a urologist, having a family doctor in the practice would be impressive. You could help with diabetes and blood pressure patients and conditions like that. I'll teach you urology, and you teach me family medicine. I'll pay you twenty grand a year." She gasped, then blurted, "I'm worth more than that." I said, "That's really my point. You do think about it, but you don't allow yourself to acknowledge your own thoughts. You don't know how to express it without feeling crass. You won't allow yourself to say it; and you feel embarrassed and ashamed if you do say, 'I'm worth a hundred and fifty grand a year.'" She bit her lip. She wasn't alone.

The tacit taboo against talking about the business end of medicine, coupled with a passive ignore-*ance* of responsibilities for the financial superstructure of the profession, have led to serious side effects. These consequences and ramification are playing out, and not just on patients and physicians. They have, and are, enabling others to take charge of American Medicine, and to define the continuing evolution and configuration of the American Healthcare System. In my lifetime we have gone from private practices to managed care to the *big box* corporate model, all while allowing lawyers, bean counters, insurance companies and politicians to run the show. Physicians have become pawns. The Doctor is out.

A Brief and Limited History of the Business of Medicine In America

Let's step back and look at where American Medicine was fifty or so years ago, then look at the route we've taken to get to where we are now. The road traveled has been the composite of all the vectors expressed upon the profession. Identifying those forces will allow us to project the future—the positives and the negatives—of American Healthcare.

In February of 1972, while I was Chief Resident in Urology at Georgetown, I wrote a letter-to-the-editor of *Time Magazine* in response to an article they had published. At the time only a small percentage of American physicians were women—the figure was down in the single digits, but it was growing. The Time article recommended that our medical system rearrange itself so that women physicians would be able to get home early enough to take care of children, to cook dinner, or to do other tasks.

My letter was short. I said, "Physicians need to be around when disease happens. You can't structure a disease. You can't schedule a disease. You have to be there when it happens. That's how we, as doctors, learn about what is affecting the patient. If you're not there at that time you're not going to discover, or uncover, the problem or its cause. This is a situation that the physician herself should not, and cannot, tolerate." Time published my letter. My boss read it, and for the whole next week I was the boy wonder!

Basically what I was attempting to point out was, if you want to be a physician you have to be a physician. Being a part-time physician doesn't work. Suggesting that the way to increase the percentage of female physicians was to cut the hours they would have to work ignored the fact that this would have a negative impact on **patient care**. Although often unrecognized, those highlighted words are at the heart of much of the debate over healthcare. To me, and to many, patient care is the core *raison d'être* of the medical profession. Its optimization is the ultimate criteria against which all decisions should be measured. We will come back to this concept over and over again in this section, as so many policies and programs which now structure the business of medicine seem to devalue, degrade or disregard the concept of **patient care!!!**

Another trend in medicine which began accelerating fifty or so years ago is the movement to divide and segregate patients into *populations*. Many years ago, if you were sick, you just "went to the doctor." He was down the street, or down the block, or downtown. His office may have been in his house, or perhaps several rooms in amongst the stores and row houses of Main Street. There was a waiting room, the exam room, his private office, and perhaps a small lab room. He practiced alone; perhaps his wife served as his nurse and receptionist. Hands-on patient care was a necessary diagnostic procedure. Often these offices looked like Norman Rockwell paintings; and sometimes little girls did hold out their toy dolls while the doctor listened to the doll's chest with his stethoscope. More than one of my elderly patients told me of 'bad' times when they were children, of their parents paying the local doc in vegetables or other homemade items. These images are nostalgic, yet certainly also archaic when contrasted against the great leaps forward in science and medical technology since that time.

With those images in mind, it's interesting to see how medical care has evolved, and how and where it has devolved, into our current healthcare system.

Specialties: The explosion of knowledge, and the rapid acceleration in the cost of medical devises and equipment, along with patient demand, necessitated the creation of specialties. If your child is sick you likely will take him or her to a pediatrician. If you have a teenager he may go to someone who specializes in adolescent medicine and focuses on the complex issues common during puberty. Between the ages of 16 to 20 a young man's file is usually transferred to the regular family doctor, who is now referred to as a primary care physician or primary care provider (PCP). We also have gynecologists who have taken over the care of women, and who additionally are classified by insurance companies as primary care providers for women. There are cardiologists, endocrinologists, gastroenterologists, internists, oncologists, urologists, et cetera, et cetera, et cetera. A procedural outgrowth of this has been the segregation of people into disease, trait, or statistical populations. It's interesting to note that there is no category defined as men's health specialists. It appears that every segment of the population, except men, now has specialists they can access.

Men usually go to their family doctor or PCP—who generally provides excellent care. But the questions arise: Why is this so; and why don't women go to the family doctor?

The reasoning behind the move to specialty medicine seems to be that specialists have more focused knowledge about particular physiological systems than generalists or primary care providers. That's valid, but it still doesn't answer the question: Why do women use a specialist for concerns handled by PCPs? Perhaps it is an outgrowth of the emotional discomfort of being examined by a male going back to the time when few physicians were women. Likely it is also a natural progression stemming from women going to obstetricians—who provide care to them during pregnancy, birth and postpartum follow-ups—to continue with the same Ob/Gyn physician for their general health care needs. Perhaps as part of the women movement's objective of redefining women as separate from men, women lobbied for and won their particular specialists. With that win came the acquiescence (and thus coverage) by insurance companies to allow specialists to handle general care. That last point is important—kind of a follow the money theory—because without funds no segment of medicine remains existent.

Men do not have an equivalent pregnancy-specialist-to-general-health progression. I would see young men for vasectomies or various testicular problems, but once the issue was resolved they would go back to their family doctor. They did not stay with me or any other urologist for general care.

Not long ago I had a conversation with one of the administrators for an organization of primary care physicians in Connecticut. He was quite proud of the fact that they were putting together *accountable-care organizations* so they could *manage populations*. (I've put those phrases in italic because they have become buzz-words in the healthcare industry.) I was told that an accountable-care organization was a tool so that physicians could manage high blood pressure, heart disease, diabetes, women's health, et cetera. I asked this administrator, "Why don't you have a plan to manage men's health?" He was intrigued and said he'd get back to me, which he did. During his return phone call he indicated that the accountable-care organization had no interest in men as a population at this time.

I still have a tough time understanding his response, as prostate cancer, which occurs approximately as often as breast cancer and has a similar death rate, is generally ignored by accountable-care organizations. Many insurance plans tout their women's health programs, as do many hospitals. Men's health just does not seem to be as important.

I'm not sure why, in this new system of healthcare, women get to be a managed population and men don't, but the consequences of that kind of decision has led to very specialized care for women and for children, yet, unfortunately, not for men. I recall a meeting sponsored by The American Urological Association that I attended some years ago. Dr. Bernadine Healy, the first woman to head the National Institutes of Health (NIH), spoke about funding for prostate health. She mentioned that women were lobbying for larger and larger amounts of research money to go to breast cancer. She looked at us and asked why we weren't doing the same. Frankly, most of us didn't have a clue that research money was a product of political dynamics.

Over the years many of my male patients felt their concerns were ignored by *people*—using that word to mean society in general, or the frequency of media coverage of the topic—and that they were not allowed to talk about their concerns even with family or friends. Because of that they had delayed seeking help for symptoms, the equivalent of which would have sent their wives or girlfriends quickly to the doctor.

When the PSA test became available, I lobbied the Connecticut state legislature very intensely to get them to require insurance companies in Connecticut to pay for this test, exactly as they were paying for mammograms and Pap Smears. I didn't know if the lack of attention to men's health was a monetary decision on the part of the insurance companies, a political decision because male voters don't expect their senator or representative to espouse a position on men's health, a general lack of noise by men, or the whole idea that we men don't talk about our testicles in public, but you would think that in this day and age even men would get the timely care they need when they need it, and without a fight. This does not seem to be the case. We just are not *a population*.

Money Moves To Takes Control

Concurrent with the growth of specialty medicine and the conceptualization of patients as populations has been a change in the way medical professionals are paid. Recall the Norman Rockwell image? At that time going to the doctor was pretty much a cash business. I used to hear about doctors making house calls, and they'd pull a wad of bills from their coat pocket that was four inches thick. It was mostly ones, but for many men at the time a dollar was several hours pay, and a $10 medical bill could upset the average family's weekly budget.

Insurance companies came to the rescue. They could ameliorate a family's concerns by collecting premiums and establishing communal funds to be used when needed. Doctors tended to see this as a wonderful development. It not only guaranteed they would be paid, but it alleviated any need to dun a patient (to most caregivers a most unsavory activity). "Let that be the insurance man's responsibility," was the tacit attitude. Then, as insurance became customary, doctors increasingly, although somewhat naively, delegated more and more of the financial management of their businesses to insurance companies. These companies took their cut, *reimbursed* practitioners for their services, established their bureaucratic structure, and grew.

The other day someone asked me, "Why do physicians get reimbursed? Why don't they just get paid?" I explained: With insurance, if you have a loss, say if your car is stolen, they reimburse *you* for the loss from a pool of funds collected for that reason, and you go out and buy a new car. That's where the term reimbursement comes from. Medical or health insurance is a bit different. To health insurance companies doctors are providers. The payment to providers also comes from a money pool, but the payment system isn't quite the same. Health insurance doesn't pay money back to, or reimburse, the person who paid the premium; and that person doesn't go out and purchase a replacement body part or repair service. Health insurance companies pay providers directly. They also *manage care* and determine what a provided service is worth—X dollars for a colonoscopy, Y dollars for an appendectomy, Z dollars for a sniffles visit. For the provider, this is different than being paid as the sole proprietor of his practice by his patient. It is also different than being paid as an employee of the insurance company, or as an employee of an institution such as a hospital or clinic. We'll see how those dynamics come into play a bit later in the evolution of the healthcare system.

As the clout of insurance companies grew, and grew, and grew, they found it necessary and beneficial to essentially take control of the business of medicine. By doing so, they said, *healthcare financing* would lower costs and provide higher quality service. Perhaps it was an unforeseen side effect, perhaps not, but the new system slowly weaseled its way into the doctor-patient relationship. Most physicians willingly entered into the pact, agreeing to allow insurance companies to determine reasonable and customary fee schedules for virtually all services. Insurers would keep 20% of the revenue, and doctors would be assisted in creating more efficient fiscal models that would allow them to deliver quality care and still stay in business.

That was the plan, or at least the sales pitch. It didn't quite work out that way. At least as early as twenty years ago columnists like Tom Donlon of Barron's were calling the "higher-quality, lower-cost" model a myth. And it remains a myth, but now one wrapped in a conundrum, obfuscated by an enigma, and called a law.

Doctors continued to deliver quality healthcare; medical, biological and physiological sciences continued to advance and developed wonderful, but often more expensive, technologies and procedures; and doctors formed groups or organizations to manage services more efficiently, and to meet the goals and demands of insurers. Insurers often did not uphold their side of the bargain. There were a number of reasons, including corporate greed and/or corruption, but chief amongst them was the fact that they simply couldn't. The stated goals, or sales pitch, were not just unrealistic, they were impossible.

Complicating the process was the facts that each insurance company had its own fee schedule, and seldom did the schedule specify exactly what was expected of the doctor. From the physician's business perspective this led to uncertainty and chaos. Physicians or physician groups essentially became the insurers because they accepted the financial risks not only for their own medical infrastructure, procedures, and practices, but also for the financial success of the now intertwined physician/insurer venture; while insurance companies, via micromanagement techniques, dictated care decisions thereby essentially becoming the "doctors." Failures were inevitable.

I want to be cautious here. The tremendous costs involved for an individual with a complex medical problem—be it a rare cancer requiring surgery and individualized chemotherapy, or severe physical injury sustained in a car wreck—become prohibitive for most people. The pooling of funds is a necessity; the justification for insurance is that it allows the catastrophic cost of a statistically rare event to be ameliorated by spreading it out over a larger population. The line differentiating catastrophic cost from acceptable cost is constantly shifting. Some might argue it is defined by deductibles and co-pays. Consider the following hypothetical examples:

1) To treat John Q. Public's rare, metastasized bladder cancer costs $250,000, well beyond John's ability to pay; but only one in a million members of his insurance pool will develop this disease. The cost per member to cure John is 25-cents—easily affordable.

2) The cost to treat Jane Doe's flu symptoms are $400—much of that being either facility overhead or the insurer's administrative fees. Jane is in a pool with 100,000 others; of which 16,000 will seek treatment this winter for the flu. The distributed cost is now $64 per pool member.

3) George Jones is a member of Group Z, a pool of 250,000 insured, and he is eligible for a $450 physical each year. Ninety five percent of the members of Group Z will take advantage of this service costing each member $427.50.

Note the progression and value to each patient, and the cost to each member of the insurance pool. Johnny Q's prohibitive costs were immense, but for members of his group the cost was negligible; whereas Georgie J's value was barely worth the effort, and in fact if the insurance companies fees were extracted the cost would have been $360, thus, with insurance, actually costing George $67.50 more!

Of course there are more factors involved. Without insurance coverage for physicals the percentage of pool members who would see a physician each year might drop precipitously; the serious conditions these physicals uncovered in early stages would be missed, and the cost of later-stage treatments would likely top the cost of the physicals.

Still, these examples illuminate some of the problems in the healthcare debate, and might help us separate reality from rhetoric.

Beyond the conundrum that exists when attempting to establish *the line* between financially imperative coverage for catastrophic events and discretionary coverage for common or inexpensive treatments is the enigma of the access threshold. When I was a general medical officer in the Air Force I ran a clinic and emergency room which handled 12,000 patients per month. This was back in the days before we had a lot of the technical equipment—EKGs, et cetera—that we now take for granted, so usually a physician saw each patient. Most patients came in with minor or very minor ailments. The problem was, there were so few of us and so many of them; and the patients were neither responsible for payment nor accountable for self-care. That experience gave me great trepidations of any system without an access threshold. That is, when care is free many people will come in for conditions from hangovers to stubbed toes, that they would elsewise take care of themselves. Even worse, some will come in as a way to avoid work or duty.

When systems become overwhelmed patient care deteriorates, serious conditions receive less attention than they deserve, and doctors burn out. In the civilian world co-pays and deductibles are used to limit frivolous visits for those who pay for their own insurance. Paying for one's own insurance is not universal, as employers use health insurance as a benefit to attract workers, or government programs essentially pay the co-pays and deductibles for others.

Back to the insurance industry/doctor conflict: as insurers became more and more powerful, physicians developed larger groups. Theoretically this would allow them better management, more efficient use of resources, and grander economy of scale. The larger groups would also create greater leverage for physicians to influence insurance company determinations of coverage, and to negotiate reimbursement rates with insurance companies. Very large groups, fifty or more physicians, had some success; and they had that success because the marketplace for insurance was open and competitive.

But there were still problems. Recall that physicians tend not to stand up for themselves, and that they generally do not speak the financial language of business. At one time I headed up a group of over three hundred Central Connecticut physicians. The head of a local Chamber of Commerce called me and asked, "Can you tell us, which are the best insurance companies? We really don't know. Just give us a list of the top three." I went to my group and said, "This is a great opportunity. We can work with the businesses that are buying the policies for their workers; the policies from which we are eventually paid." The group couldn't decide to provide the list. It was not a matter of not knowing the best three insurers. The docs just didn't want to get involved. They saw this as a terrible conflict of interest. "Oh, you can't tell them which insurance companies…!" I countered, "Why not? The insurance companies don't hesitate to tell the businesses owners who they consider to be the best doctors." In retrospect, I shouldn't have added, "The insurance companies have no clue who are the best doctors; their recommendations are based on who they perceived as the most cost-effective physicians. That's not necessarily a recommendation patients should seek."

Note here: from a business perspective, doctors and the medical services they and their staff provide *are the product* healthcare consumers (patients) purchase. Insurance companies, although they sell the product by selling peace of mind, are simply the managers of the financial end of the business. A problem arises when the manager becomes the gate-keeper restricting patients from obtaining the products they need. As head of a large physician's group, I was able to have one of the larger insurers thrown out of Middlesex County for what I will call inappropriate behavior—a combination of being overly restrictive (not allowing patients access), and not fulfilling contractual reimbursement as agreed.

Recall, the health insurance market place was open and competitive. As a group we had options. The CEO of that particular insurance company and I had a meeting. He asked, "What can I do to regain your trust?" I said, "Nothing. You've had all these years, and the only reason you're here is because we've pulled the plug on you." He said, "What do you mean?" "I said, "You don't have a product to sell anymore. Patients bought your coverage to get my group. They didn't buy you to get you. They only got you to get us. There are other companies that deal with us and our patients fairly."

Everybody else in the meeting looked at me and gasped. Most doctors didn't realize the extent of the machinations of this gate-keeper; nor did they understand the strength of their own bargaining position, or the fact that competition amongst insurers was a check on corporate shenanigans.

In our area, insurance companies consistently raised the premiums they charged individuals and employers, and they told everyone the reason was because healthcare costs were always increasing. I had a conversation with the president of another local Chamber of Commerce. He said, "You guys..." meaning our physicians group, "...keep raising your prices!" I said, "Sam, the way it works is the insurance company tells us what they're going to pay us. We don't set the price. This is managed care. Managed care is managed cash. They manage it." Then I asked him, "If they're not managing the premiums in a way you approve, and they're not managing the care in a way you approve, what are you paying them for?"

With most public officials, and with most business leaders, that kind of questioning about healthcare didn't exist. I said to one of the business group execs, "When you get twelve cases of toilet paper, someone in receiving opens a carton and make sure that what's in there is what's supposed to be in there? But you guys don't open up the healthcare agreement to see what's covered and what's not covered. All you do is base your decision on price. When you base it on price it's like you're selling heating oil to your customers at 50-cent a gallon, then coming to me, the supplier, and expecting me to cover you when it's costing me $3.00 a gallon. That doesn't work."

The naiveté of both doctors and consumers continues to this day, and, as we will see, it is continuing to enable shenanigans that have severe repercussions on patients and patient care.

Another side effect of the move to insurance-managed healthcare was the change in physician focus. Remember, physicians were never taught business, and, generally, they seldom focused on money. We said, or at least I said, this was and is a good thing. But now physicians *are* driven to think about the money. They still don't know how to account for their value—few will say, "I fixed this guy up and returned him to being a productive member of society, that's gotta be worth X amount." Worth in a managed-care system is defined by insurance-company reimbursements. If the reimbursement is not adequate to keep the doors open, the heavy financial pressure causes the doc to worry, and the more one worries about keeping the doors open, the more one's focus turns to money.

That's element number one in this change in focus. A second element—this goes into the shenanigan category—is when insurance companies arbitrarily deny payment for treatments by saying the treatment is not medically *necessary*. Often the decision is not substantiated in science. Again the doctor is forced to think about money. Many physicians find creative ways to go around these decisions in order to get patients the care they require. Sometimes the insurance companies just arbitrarily deny a payment for something that is acceptable and that is in their coverage agreement. This mechanism seems to be the whole crux of some insurance company strategies to increase profits. These companies are not benign providers of better medicine or better health care.

A third element is more indirect. Insurance companies rate doctors, or groups of doctors, on efficiency scales. This is very complex, but simplified it looks something like this: Theoretically the insurer sets the premium rates they will charge subscribers (patients) based upon the medical procedures that they will approve (those included in the subscription agreement). Via actual analysis the insurers know what each procedure and each office visit cost them, and they know how many procedures are done. Low-cost high-frequency procedures are usually approved allowing the insurance companies to make more profit based on the premiums they charge. High-cost procedures, especially the newest ones, are frequently denied or "reviewed." This is a decision process based on cash flow analysis, not on patient care. If one physician does many low-cost procedures and another one does more high-cost procedures the physician that does the most low-cost procedure is rated highest, even if the use of the high-cost procedure is more medically appropriate. To steer the physician towards the low-cost alternative the high-cost alternative is frequently deemed not medically necessary.

Groups are also played-off against each other. An insurer might tell the head of a group, this other group does 12% more of X-procedure; how come you guys do so few? Doctors are thus directed toward doing high-value procedures; that is they have to think about how much money a procedure costs, how much it will net the financial overlord, and how it will affect their own compensation. That's a downward spiral. It has been resisted by many doctors who grew-up in the old system; but as new physicians come on board they've never experienced anything but this new commoditization of medicine. They are less apt to object.

The Corporate Model

Hospitals took the next step in the commoditization of medicine. Instead of being the non-profit community- or religious-based service centers of yore, they structured themselves as for-profit corporations. (In some states these corporations are owned by insurance companies. Sometimes there is a complex, dual for-profit/not-for-profit structure which allows the institution to take advantage of both systems.) In and of itself the for-profit corporation is not necessarily negative. Advances in medicine and sophisticated technical and chemical procedures are costly—very costly—and the for-profit model has been much more adept at keeping pace with these advances than most not-for-profit institutions. But there is a snag. For-profit corporations *must* focus on money—that's part of a corporate charter; and bondholders and shareholders expect and deserve a return on their investment. Big-box corporate models claim that good care is a by-product of financial success. This stands the old model on its head—where financial success was the by-product of good care.

Many large hospitals have adapted well to this corporate solution: They deliver a decent return to their investors, pay their executives millions of dollars, and rigidly control how much they pay their employees. Said in a more skeptical manner: the more efficient the crew, the higher the executive bonuses! At least fifteen of Connecticut's top hospital executives are compensated in excess of a million dollars annually, and some have packages in excess of five million. Perhaps they're worth it. In a competitive system you have to pay the best to get the best. But when I hear nurses or staff complaining about monitoring equipment that is old and often on the fritz, or of bed sheets used so many times they are filled with holes, I shake my head.

Those are relatively minor concerns. Understaffing from ICUs to Labor & Delivery centers creates potentially perilous situations; but it cuts cost. Recently, while out grocery shopping, I ran into an ICU nurse with whom I had worked. "Here's what's happening in our hospital," she said, and she went on to explain about a new grid-scheduling for nurses. "You come in, you're scheduled to work, but if the census [number of patients] is low, they send you home. Sounds good, huh? You can take the day off. But it's without pay unless you take a vacation day."

What it meant to her was, she had a job, and a good job at which she was highly skilled—she was a terrific nurse—but now she didn't know from week to week how much money she'd make. Making the situation worse, she explained, "...they send you home because the computer says there aren't enough patients in the unit, but the computer doesn't factor in how many people are waiting in the ER. Since there is minimal staff in the ICU those patients in the ER can't be transferred up, so they have to keep them down there. So the ER gets clogged up. Then, maybe, they call us back in. Our day off isn't even a day off." And patient care, perhaps an even higher personal priority for nurses than for doctors, suffers. That leads to frustration and lack of job satisfaction.

Hospitals presidents tend to be people who were not trained in the corporate world but were trained in the not-for-profit world, so they bring in consultants who impose their thoughts and methods. Hospitals are notorious for doing this. These consultants are seldom doctors or nurses, but are often corporate MBAs. Their approach is to ask: How can I save money? That's their primary criteria. They answer their question with, "We'll cut the work force hours by 20% and that will save 20% of the cost of labor." In a hospital setting it just doesn't work that way—but note, the hospital president by using consultants has insulated himself from the results of these decisions.

The overall cycle has been something like this: health maintenance organizations (HMOs) or insurance companies took over the health insurance marketplace; they cut reimbursements to doctors and to hospitals; hospitals responded by cutting beds and by letting a lot of nurses go; the nurses found job elsewhere (maybe working for a school system... someplace where the weekly income was steady).

With variations and local differences, this cycle has been repetitious. A decade ago, in an attempt to cut costs, many nurses were laid off; but soon the hospitals or the HMOs found that that didn't slow the flow of patients, so they needed to put more beds back into circulation and they needed more nurses. But the nurses were no longer there. To get them back they raised the pay scale. The cost-cutting was short-term. In the long term costs went up.

My first wife was the assistant head nurse at the obstetrical unit at Georgetown. This was in the early 1960s. She took home $50 every two weeks. It wasn't much, but we were all doing good things—taking care of those babies—and that patient care was the motivation. At the time, as we've noted, doctors and nurses weren't very money savvy, and, of course, you didn't have layers and layers of bureaucracy and management all needing to get paid, and you didn't have the hospital having to make a profit for its shareholders. Now, fifty some odd years later, an assistant head nurse in an intensive care unit makes over $100,000 annually, and well she should. She's well compensated, she's very knowledgeable, she's high-tech, and she has a massive amount of responsibilities and accountability.

Cost cutting, over the long run, has often caused extremely costly disasters. Over and over again this has happened, and it is particularly costly in labor and delivery units where cutting back on staff eventually causes a mistake resulting in a fetal demise. Lawsuits over the loss of an infant are emotional and heart-wrenching. Settlements tend to be very high when the mistake, the medical malpractice, is shown to be rooted in the lack of proper staffing. After the settlement the staffing goes back up, but then the process begins all over again and the administrators or consultants or bean counters again begin to pare away the staff to 'save money.' And they do; in the short run! That's one of the biggest problems: they are focused on the short run and not on patient care or the longevity of the hospital.

Of course, the hospital insures itself against losses, so the settlement does not affect the institution in one lump sum which could put it out of business. The medical-malpractice insurance company has been collecting premiums and pooling funds for just this possibility. At one time I thought how horrible it must be for the insurer to have to pay out such exorbitant amounts. That turns out not necessarily to be the case. The more an insurance company pays out, the higher premiums it is allowed to charge; and as their fees typically are based upon a percentage of premiums, their profit over the long run increase.

With the people imposing all these rules and regulations not being the people who have the accountability for patient care, the morale amongst the staff at many hospitals—these were places where most of us felt we were part of a team, part of a family—in recent years has plummeted. Another nurse told me it has gotten so bad, because of the pay insecurities, that nurses are fighting amongst themselves about who is going to go home and who is going to stay. Cooperation is in the trash can. Asking for help may engender the response, "That's your problem, Sister. I don't get paid to help you." People are at each other's throats. I have heard similar stories from unionized and non-unionized hospital staffs, and from physicians who practice at the VA hospital in West Haven. Animosity affects patient care... but grid-scheduling appears to be cost effective.

In a competitive system one would anticipate that these problems, over time, would self-correct. Quite simply, if your patient care deteriorates, patients will seek care elsewhere, thus to stay in business your patient care must improve. But if entry into the system is limited (thereby reducing competition and making it not truly a competitive system at all) corporate management is enabled, if not facilitated and protected, in these abuses.

Coexisting with pay insecurities and grid scheduling is the feeling that patient care is becoming secondary. For many healthcare workers patient care is, and always has been, their primary motivation for entering the field. When that primary award for work is devalued—that is, when one is constrained from giving excellent patient care—the worker (physician, nurse, technician, et cetera) becomes frustrated, the teamwork deteriorates, and the individual tends to seek an alternative place of employment. But again, this paradigm shift is happening throughout the healthcare system, so one's move is often retrospectively seen as jumping out of the frying pan and into the fire.

Another consequence of this evolution has been that physicians, who at one time survived both administratively and financially on their own, are now becoming employees of hospitals. From a strict financial perspective that seems fine. "Pay Doctor Rabuffo a salary of $120,000 per year; that should keep him happy!" But a different problem emerges—the physician is then no longer bound solely by the Hippocratic Oath. He is now beholden to hospital rules and regulations—which are often in place primarily to control costs and increase profits.

Here's the thing I see coming: if you are now a hospital employee and you are working for a corporation, then you have to follow the corporation's rules. So if you think some x-ray or drug or treatment is necessary for your patient, and the hospital disagrees with you, then who do you act for? If you're the physician and the hospital tells you (which may be because this is what the insurance company is telling the hospital), "No, we don't want you to use this drug," or "We don't approve of you ordering that MRI," and you really believe, based upon your training and experience, that the drug or test is necessary, it becomes a Hobson's choice. If you act upon the behalf of the patient, you put your job at risk; and if you act on behalf of the hospital you put the patient at risk.

As we've said, physicians are trained to obey rules, but typically they also chafe at micro-management. By nature their focus is not on business but on what is best for their patient—that's not only what they studied to become physicians, but that's what they study continuously as physicians constantly updating their knowledge-base by reading each new technique or study in their specific field. So how they react to the financial management saying you cannot, or should not do X or Y procedure no matter how appropriate you think it is, becomes both personally problematic and a policy issue.

To be fair, in private practice there have always been physicians who were torn between the needs to meet the bills of their practice and the duty to their patients. That, however, is qualitatively different than a physician who is put in this spot because a corporation requires him to maximize its profits by using less expensive procedures or generic drugs versus what he knows to be more appropriate treatments. In the first case the doctor is interacting directly with the patient and experiences up-close and personal any negative affects suffered by the patient; in the second case the corporation essentially despotically dictates treatment by the numbers with no personal contact and no personal investment in the specific human being who is the patient.

At the individual level the physician wants to live by the code: First, Do No Harm. He wants to stand up for his patient. But in the corporate world, if an employee refuses to follow directions, he or she is subject to termination; so vigorously standing up for his patient might cost him his job. It might even destroy his ability to be hired by another hospital and thus cost him his career. Decisions become even tougher for young physicians with families to feed and heavy college loan debt.

One might think that physicians or physician groups can and should remain independent of the corporate hospital; and certainly many physicians wish to do just that. But that's not what's happening. In the business world corporations often grow by either beating their competition (better and cheaper services), by out-selling their competition (taking over the market by various means which might include sophisticated marketing and underpricing which causes the competition to collapse), or simply by buying up the competition. This later practice of corporate hospitals buying up smaller medical practices has become widespread.

One thing lost is a patient's ability to go *here or there*; that is, in a realistic sense, the patients lose the ability to choose. The hospital, as a business, has become a monopoly. Once the hospital is the only game in town, it can charge whatever its administrators want, and the services can be as good or as bad as the administrator deems acceptable. This, of course, is within limits set by another vector in the equation—state and federal regulators. Hospitals do give up some control to regulators in exchange for the tremendous direct and indirect backing provided by state and federal programs. Below, we'll look at the mutually beneficial confluence of interest that has resulted; but recall, we saw in 2014 what can happen when administrators shirk responsibilities or fake compliance with regulations—the VA Medical Center in Phoenix, Arizona being the glaring, and repulsive example.

The reader should know, all of us experienced physicians, and all the experienced nurses too, talk amongst ourselves; and we ask, "When the time comes, who's going to take care of us?" We foresee what is coming down the pike... and we are frightened.

The Rise of Hospitalist and Physician Extenders

Concurrent with the expansion of insurance, the shift to managed care, and the development of the big box corporate hospital, has been the rise of the hospitalist and the creation of auxiliary medical centers.

In Connecticut we have had a shortage of primary care physicians because primary care reimbursement by insurance companies is terrible. Few people are attracted to unviable or unsustainable careers, so many of those who took this path have branched into other areas. In response to financial pressures the remaining primary care physicians changed the way they practiced. It used to be one got up in the morning, went to the hospital, saw his patients that were there, and then he went to the office. He'd also take emergency calls and emergency calls at night.

Because reimbursements were so bad, PCPs stopped going to the hospital. By staying in the office they could bring in more revenue and remain viable. The primary care people also stopped delivering babies for a similar reason—the malpractice insurance became too onerous. So primary care practices basically became office-based.

This is analogous to when I was in the Air Force. As a general medical officer I didn't have hospital privileges. If I had a patient in the hospital, a staff internist took care of him. In civilian hospitals some of the staff internists became the new specialty, Hospitalists. In most hospitals today, hospitalists take care of the admitted patients of primary care physicians. Hospitalists are employees of the hospital, so they are salary-based as opposed to fee-for-service based. As noted above, this raises questions of allegiance for a physician. In general I don't think hospitalists are as productive as fee-for-service based physicians, but in saying that let me add, I know a number of hospitalists, and most of them are wonderful doctors who over time experience a great variety of diseases and develop a tremendous knowledge base. Typically, with an old-style fee-for-service physician, if his patient needed him to be in the hospital, he was in the hospital for however long was necessary. With hospitalists being employees they deal with all patients who need them during their shifts. Then they go home. The patient group is taken over by the next guy. This guy may also be extremely capable, but a number of studies tell us that most medical errors in hospitals occur during or just after a shift change. That's the downside of the new paradigm.

Secondly, with these guys being employees of the hospital, when a hospital charges for their services they use hospital coding versus physician coding. A recent example in the Wall Street Journal explained: If you go to your cardiologist for a follow-up visit on your heart attack, the code will be 99213 for the office visit. The physician gets paid approximately $75 for that appointment. If, on the other hand, you go to the hospital, the hospital is allowed to use a different coding system—one specific to hospitals; and instead of that visit being an out-patient office visit, it becomes a hospital-based outpatient cardiology evaluation. The procedure is the same, but the price is triple. This is good for the hospital, and the insurer passes the cost on after removing its fee, but the final payer—be it an employer, an employee or the taxpayers—takes the hit. So, the primary care people don't go to the hospital anymore, and care is increasingly hospital-based. Night call is now run by emergency rooms and floor physicians. Because of the coding, and the powers that hospitals have, costs are trending up, not down. In a period where *everyone* says they are striving for affordable medicine, perhaps *everyone* does not have the same motivation.

Complicating the situation, hospitals generally have needed, and still need, primary care practices to feed them. Hospitals make money on admissions. If they did not have primary care physicians that were loyal to them, they could not survive. So hospitals have done everything possible to boost loyalty and admissions. Some hospitals created their own Family Practice Residence Programs which they hope would yield family practice physicians who would stay in the local area and become part of their feeder system. That might alleviate the PCP shortage if reimbursements allowed their practices to be financially viable, but as we will see, many PCPs have had to shift to an alternate system.

None of this, of course, is about medicine. It's about the financing of medical care... the business of medicine. If the business of medicine is unhealthy, medical care and the entire medical care delivery system fails. The great debates over the past decade often seem to confuse medical care with the economics of the delivery system. If we were talking automobile maintenance this would be the difference between the skill of the mechanic and the quality of the parts he uses versus the earnings of the dealership. As a consumer you are likely to be more concerned about the first, aren't you? Keep that in mind.

Another cost-control tactic—seemingly sold as a way to help physicians deal with an enormous number of people—has been the development and expansion of physician extenders. These are physician assistants (PAs), nurse practitioners (NPs), nurse anesthetist, and various types of medical or surgical technicians. They are analogous to corpsmen or medics in the military. When I was in the service I was very impressed with those guys. They were well-trained, knew what they were doing, were efficient, and most knew how to handle the level of authority they were given.

As the civilian healthcare system evolves, first contact and access into the system is more and more via PAs or NPs. The billing for their services is less than for a physician. Most doctors' offices will have two physician extenders per doctor. It's not a bad system. Sometimes a crossover is used. This is a tactic doctor's offices use to remain viable. If the patient is seeing a physician's assistant, and the doctor then pops in, the office can bill as if it were a doctor's visit. It's a way of getting around diminishing insurance reimbursements.

Although PAs, et cetera, generally do not have the training and education of a physician, some become exceptional. As in the military they take on, or are forced to take on, responsibilities *above their paygrade*; but unlike in the military they often do not have the legal authority to perform at that level. I have also seen RNs put into tenuous situations by hospital administrators wishing to control costs by using less expensive personnel. Responsibility without authority is tremendously stressful, and a high percentage of people put into this situation either emotionally burnout or physically become ill.

As exceptional as many physician extenders are, there are limits. Often when I used to talk to these people in the emergency room, what they generally lacked was depth of experience, insight and judgment. I could tell by the way they talked that they were reporting what they saw, but often they really didn't know how to interpret it, or what the consequences of it might be. There are, of course, many grades and levels of this.

So, the physician extender system *is* a great system... that is, until it isn't! PAs and NPs may, and do, make mistakes physicians would not. But my real concern here is less with the quality of these people—as I've said many are tremendously impressive—but with a system that is purposely taking shortcuts supposedly *designed* to reduce costs, but in which the costs are increasing, and most of the increased fees are going to the non-medical end of the business. Seen from another angle, insurance companies have responded to the services of PAs and NPs by ratcheting down reimbursements. I'm not certain where the increased premium dollars are going, but it seems to be to the people we've all had to hire to do the additional paperwork required by the unending increase in regulations. All these vectors, and more, precede the Affordable Care Act.

Surgi-Centers and Walk-in Clinics

An entrepreneurial response to rising costs (and another vector in the healthcare equation) has been the establishment of surgi-centers, and the changes they have produced. These centers are independent, streamlined units designed to operate cheaper, faster and better than the old, lumbering hospital OR system. The concept has had ramifications far beyond what was first imagined; and, as you might expect, the hospitals, at least in Connecticut, fought the development and approval of this competition.

Private people and independent businesses built these centers. Sometimes called outpatient surgery centers they were designed to do the most common procedures, not the most complex surgeries. If you wish, think of this model as analogous to taking your car to a Jiffy Lube instead of going to the dealership. The dealership can pull the engine, rebuild the transmission, or replace faulty wiring harnesses, but if all you need is an oil change you don't need the capacity of the dealership.

Hospitals, as businesses, fought this intrusion as they saw it cutting into their profits, but hardheaded guys like me fought back. We got the approvals, built and equipped the centers, and began operating. The hospitals, seeing money going elsewhere, fought back using all the tactics corporations often bring to bear upon competition. Many centers were bought out. Seeing the need for, and the viability of, such centers, some hospitals built their own Jiffy-Ops either within or adjacent to their own physical plant; and then adopted some surgi-center practices. These were great advances for the big box corporations—forced upon them by smaller shops filling important niches efficiently and effectively; but, most times, the large corporations continued institutional thinking rather than entrepreneurial thinking.

The big question for surgical centers was, "Who's the customer?" To the layperson this may seem odd. It is not the patient. The patient is the doctor's customer. For the surgical complex it is the doctor who is the customer. So the more cases a physician does, and the more efficient he is, the more a center caters to him. Hospitals, on the other hand, tend to have a different approach. They think that because they are doing good things, that's all that they have to do. Efficiency lags. The time between cases can be half an hour or forty-five minutes. Cases can run late.

I once did a study. Ten percent of my patients were booked for the operating room. The room wasn't ready, or was running late, 20% of the time. This resulted in a 30% reduction of my business to the hospital—because I couldn't get my patients in. The hospital's response was, "Well, we'll see them anyway." That could be in a week, or two weeks. The hospital saw it as just pushing out the business and the revenue over a longer period of time, even though they had a constant base expense or overhead. Also, if a patient was pushed out two weeks, it meant the doctor was not seeing someone else at that time. I think hospitals (hospital administrators) mean well, but I think they need to learn better business practices in order to be more efficient, and therefore deliver better medical care to more people. When competition is limited, and it may be limited by corporate practices or by the onus of over-regulation with which only the largest corporations can comply, better medical care to more people becomes a subordinate criteria.

Independent surgical centers, run properly, have shown great success both medically and financially; and just as in auto maintenance where the quick-lube businesses became the model for brake centers and other specialty services, surgi-centers have become the model for numerous walk-in clinics and independent "emergency rooms." The development of these facilities comes with new potential problems. Clinics and walk-in centers tend to be less personal than "Your doctor's office." Less personal means the physician or PA or NP likely doesn't know you. Staying with the car analogy, your body may need a specific tweak that you and your doctor previously discovered; one that, when you explain it to the PA at the walk-in clinic he looks at you as if you have three eyes. Cheaper medicine is not necessarily better medicine. On the positive side, smaller clinics can be supported by neighborhoods where hospitals require cities. Run properly and with compassion it might almost be as if we are bringing back those Norman Rockwell physicians... but with all the modern medical and scientific advances.

Another vector is the change in physician attitudes that correspond to the change in the delivery system. Older guys don't like what's going on. In my experience the goal of the older physician, and really that of many current and young physicians, was, or is, to do good medicine. Yes, the old-timer was concerned about his business, but he had a very personal mission: I'm a doctor. I take care of people. That's shifting under the new systems, be those free-standing clinics or Emergi-centers, or overwhelmed hospitalists, to: I'm a robot facing a conveyor belt doing a job on units. Patient bodies consist of parts. The job must be done as the units go by or the conveyor belt will back up. Such medicine is cold and less personal.

This may sound like an exaggeration. It isn't. But it is also not so simple. The caregiver is still a caregiver, and his primary motivation is still be to deliver quality patient care, but there's a growing difference between the mature physicians and the younger physicians. I've seen this time and time again.

When I was in practice I was always the last one out of the office, whether I was the one on call or not. And I'd always go over to the hospital to look at X-rays or see a patient, even though we had a call schedule and other guys could do it. You could question whether that was a good thing or not—I was very anal-retentive about it—but most of my generation of physicians behaved like this. There was call, but if you weren't on call you were still involved. And if somebody needed help and they called, you would go. One did not say, "I'm not on call. I'm not working tonight." That was never ever an issue. So my generation has some contempt for the younger generation because they don't seem to have that characteristic. For us it was a profession; almost a calling. For them it seems to be more of a job.

I had a conversation with Bob Kraft, the owner of the New England Patriots. I had been invited to a cocktail party because his charitable organization, The Kraft Foundation, was doing something about prostate cancer. I met his cardiologist, and we had this same conversation. After residency there are fellowships. He said, "I had my fellows... When I was in training, if someone came in with a heart attack, you stayed with him, even if you weren't on call, even if you had to stay all night to make sure he was okay and stabilized. But these guys, they're like, "It's five o'clock. I'm going home. I don't know if that's good." Like me, he was uncomfortable with the idea that you would just leave your patient to someone else because you were going to take care of your needs. You were going to go home and eat a normal dinner. We were trained that you were completely committed to the patient... wherever... whenever... and we were proud of it.

The new generation may not care as much, but my generation also didn't like the fact that the insurance companies were intruding on our ability to fulfill our need to provide that kind of patient care. We would be really, really committed to the patient. Amongst my colleagues there was a camaraderie about this. We all understood what we were each going through, and there was a lot of support. I remember the one time we lost a patient and I felt so absolutely awful. My buddies said... we all sat around the locker room, and one said, "Yeah, I remember I had this case..." It bothers you. You revisit what you might have done, or could have done or should have done. All those possibilities! But we had a support system in medicine. So you could get through the tough times. We would stay up all night doing whatever we had to do. Back when we were in training there were morning conferences, and if you dozed off, your ass was in trouble. The boss would come in, and you'd have to recite everything about that patient—his blood work, his X-rays, and such. And if you didn't do that, you might not get moved on in the training program. So there was tremendous self-discipline. If the other guy wasn't doing that, we learned to hold him in contempt because the right thing to do was what we were trained to do.

As mentioned, most medical mistakes seem to happen during the hand-off period when the nurses and doctors change shifts. Now there are more shift changes because the doctors don't work 36 hours. They work 12. So in that 36-hour period there are two additional shift changes, times the number of people who are working, so there are a lot of shift-change occurrences which means a lot of opportunity for mistakes. I don't know which is better, but my generation felt that our way was better. I think the patients did to, because they related to you as their caregiver. Now hospitals have hospitalists who take care of patients and who work set schedules. When they go home, the next guys take over. This is part of the conveyor belt mentality as if people were comprised of interchangeability parts. There's less personal connection, and that causes less confidence. You walk in and I don't know you. You're telling me what to do, but it might not be what the other guy said. That's part of the system change that I don't think is good.

In medicine, as in the military, the individual at every level is important. The great Prussian strategist Carl von Clausewitz once said, "Is there a field of human affairs where personal relations do not count, where the sparks they strike do not leap across all practical considerations?" Paraphrasing his answer we might say, "The personalities of *physicians and nurses* are such important factors that in *medicine* above all it is vital not to underrate them." When a physician becomes just another worker at a clinic, or just a paid employee at the hospital, the value of his personality is discounted... and it becomes as if the interchangeability of parts is not just patient organs but the medical machine that work on them.

Two more examples: the first is from Bob Kraft's cardiologist. We had this discussion about what we were seeing. He said, for physicians that are now coming up, medicine is a job. In the old days, where you and I were dedicated to making sure the patient was okay, for them, "It's five o'clock. I'm going home." Another comes from the chairman of the Department of Urology at Georgetown. He was a medical student when I was the chief resident. Not long ago he told me similar stories about his current crop of students. He said, "I can't get these young guys to talk to the patients and examine them. All they want to do... they're all very computer savvy... all they want to do is examine the data and look at the X-rays on the computer. They don't want to examine the patients. They don't want to talk to them." Perhaps the young guys are doing what they are supposed to be doing, but there's less personal interaction. They have less people-skills. For them it seems to be, "answer the question; enter answer into computer. That's all that's needed." If the patient is in pain the attitude is, "we have to do another test (and enter that result into the computer also)." You wind up with more tests, and with prescriptions which may not be needed.

So, the attitude of the younger physicians is they are less involved with the patient and more involved with the data. Remember, physicians in general are rule followers, and the new rules say you have to do what the data says.

Statistical Medicine, Metrics, Matrix, Evidenced-based Medicine Oh My! Oh My!

Nearly everything in healthcare is moving away from personal medicine and toward data- and statistics-based diagnoses and treatments. As a way of introduction to the topic, consider the following: if you reach 75 years of age your life expectancy is 11 years. That is, 50% of all 75-year olds will die before they turn 86, and 50% will live beyond 86. The current guidelines for colonoscopies in most policies say if you are 75 you do not qualify to have a colonoscopy because you have to live more than eleven years for society to statistically gain a benefit from your colonoscopy.

We are talking significant financial numbers here. According to the National Colorectal Cancer Roundtable, "It is estimated that between $12 and $14 billion are spent every year on colorectal cancer treatment in the United States, with Medicare bearing more than one-half of these costs." That's a lot of money (but works out to be only $43.75 per American). Still, it seems someone has figured out that colorectal cancer left undetected and treated later, or simply left untreated, kills the victim, on average, in or after the eleventh year. This is a similar discussion to the one we had about PSA testing, but the cost of a colonoscopy can be 100 times the cost of a PSA test.

A recent article in JAMA (Journal of the American Medical Association), tacitly said, "Wait a minute, maybe we shouldn't base these decisions on age, but on longevity." The author cited the example of two guys who were 75: one who smoked three packs of cigarettes a day, didn't exercise, had cholesterol off the wall, was diabetic, had high blood pressure, and was obese—a guy who, based on his lifestyle and personal physical qualities, likely would not last more than another three or four years; the other guy didn't drink, didn't smoke, ate right, had a body mass index of 22.5, and ran three miles before breakfast each morning. The second guy's projected longevity might be well beyond eleven years. Should he get the colonoscopy? According to statistical guidelines, he should not. The benefit to the system of managing everyone as a statistic is it does not have to pay for the colonoscopies for the half of the 75-year-old population that will live beyond 86 (a $6 to $7 billion dollar swing for Medicare). Another article, this one in JAMA Advisory, reports on the cost of only the diagnostic procedure (not follow-up treatment for the disease) and states, "Elderly Americans may be getting too many colonoscopies, increasing the risk of adverse effects and wasting Medicare an estimated $500 million each year..."

Of course, under these guidelines, the other guy or the other half of the 75-year-old population that may live beyond 86 (and maybe to 106), does not get the medical care he or they should. In the short run this is cost effective. Once one factors in the cost of treating late-stage colon cancers that could have been detected earlier, the savings become questionable. I've yet to see a study that also factors in other, indirect costs to society of these patients dying earlier than they would have had they received care; or the converse 'benefit' to society of no longer having to pay their social security once they're dead.

Statistics have their place, but basing medical decisions on the work of insurance actuaries does not deliver optimal patient care to the individual... and in the end every patient *is* an individual. Despite all the talk about improving the quality of care, and using *the numbers* to prove this is happening, old fashion patient-centric medicine may be both more efficient and more cost effective.

Talking about *the numbers* and proving *quality* is the realm of medical metrics, kind of a new soft-science in which the doctor fills in (or hires someone to fill in) the checkbox lists developed by the statisticians, as if the checkboxes themselves were somehow patient care! Dr. Victoria McEvoy, a PCP and assistant professor of pediatrics at Harvard Medical School, in her article *Why 'Metrics' Overload Is Bad Medicine*, notes:

...we have had every aspect of our professional lives invaded by the quality police. ... Since it's so difficult to measure things that are worth measuring, questionable measures are used to satisfy demands for accountability. ... When a healthy child visits, I must complete these tasks while reviewing more than 300 other preventative care measures such as safe storage of a gun, domestic violence, child-proofing the home, nutrition, exercise, school performance, safe sex, bullying, smoking, drinking, drugs, behavior problems, family health issues, sleep, development and whatever else is on a patient's or parent's mind. ... the endless box checking and scoring takes precious time away from doctor-patient communication. Not one of my patients has lost a pound from my box checking.

There is a difference between *collecting metric data* (which when collated from a population produces a *matrix*, a visible pattern of measured affects within a community) and the diagnostic technique of *matrix medicine*. Think of this latter as a paint-by-the-numbers canvas. As each color is added onto its designated spots a picture emerges. So too with medical matrix data for an individual patient. As qualitative points are added—everything from blood chemistry to CAT scans to height, weight, age, medical history and very sophisticated test results— the matrix spits out a diagnosis. This really is no different than what doctors have been doing for centuries—observing an array of symptoms and coming to a conclusion as to the cause—except today's ability to observe via hundreds of available diagnostic tools produces so much information that a computer can be a useful tool in handling the plethora of data. Indeed companies like IBM are developing special computers and programs to provide diagnoses and treatment courses, as they describe, from combined "data integration, analytics, and coordination of care capabilities... that offers a personalized, 360-degree view of the individual to facilitate outcome-focused care."

Ah, but even this can be fraught with problems. Recall above the chairman of the Department of Urology at Georgetown saying of today's medical students, "...they're all very computer savvy... all they want to do is examine the data and look at the X-rays on the computer. They don't want to examine the patients. They don't want to talk to them." Perhaps someday we'll get to the point where doctors will have incredibly accurate, handheld sensors like Dr. Jim 'Bones' McCoy on Star Trek, but until that day it helps to say to the patient, "So, Joe, what hurts?"

The Problem With Evidenced-based Medicine

Evidence-based medicine, or EBM, is an emerging trend which purports to enhance decision-making by emphasizing the use of evidence from well-designed research. The implied concept is based on the idea that doctors have been treating patients in certain ways with no evidence to support those treatments. My initial response to EBM was, "What the hell do you think we've been doing?" The way I was taught... you leave medical school with a strong knowledge base, and then you constantly read, go to conferences and lectures, and you never stop upgrading that knowledge base. So I found myself chafing at EBM suggesting PSA testing was not supported by evidence; and it occurred to me that EBM runs into trouble when it operates on negatives.

Dr. R. Scott Braithwaite of NY University School of Medicine wrote about this in *The Journal of the American Medical Association* (JAMA) more than a year ago. There are six words he says he hopes he never hears again. They are: "There is no evidence to suggest..." as in: We don't do this test, operation, procedure, et cetera, because *there is no evidence to suggest* that it works. Dr. Braithwaite points out there are many things in life for which we have no research-based evidence. For example, there is no evidence to suggest that looking both ways before you cross the street saves lives. It's common sense. We know it works. But there is no study to prove it. There's no evidence to show that if a guy has a gastrointestinal bleed he is better off going to the hospital in an ambulance versus a taxi. Obviously you want to get the patient there as quickly as possible, but the variables of each particular situation are more likely to determine the proper decision than are any number of studies—no matter how well designed.

Braithwaite adds that the words, "there is no evidence to suggest" can be deceptive and may lead to false and perhaps fatal "inferences for clinical decision making." He continues, "We further contend that, applied to the interpretation and application of pain research—such as relating to the use of opioids analgesics for chronic pain—those 6 words also can encourage poor quality pain management and inexcusable patient suffering."

So what is really going on with the EBM trend? Of course there are good elements to it... of course we want to make our clinical decisions based upon evidence from well-designed research, but, as Braithwaite notes, "The absence of evidence is not the same as evidence of absence." Just because we haven't seen, or haven't documented something, doesn't mean it is not there. (Or just because the statisticians didn't create a checkbox for it doesn't mean it doesn't exist.) EBM seems designed to disregard wisdom, intelligence, intuition, and experience. That's what most doctors of my generation have operated on. If you define wisdom as the accumulation of knowledge and insight based on experience... that's what fathers and grandfathers and older doctors have just because they've been around a long time... you are left with data points and checkboxes, and a program designed by someone using statistical averages to determine patient care. That may sound great. It may be hyped to the hilt, but we've seen it before. People are individuals. Statistics are for populations.

So EBM feeds into the conflict between statistical medicine and personal medicine; and where we're headed with American healthcare is toward statistical medicine, because the evidence is going to say, you know, 64.3% or 81.372% of the people don't need X, Y or Z—so why pay for it? The "no evidence to suggest" question really should go back to the elementary tenets of the philosophy of science and the impossibility of proving a negative, but that's a discussion for another time.

EBM, along with statistics-based medicine, metrics, corporate-medicine and insurance-managed medicine all trend away from patient-centric care, and all are driven by money. But there are other trends in medicine, exciting advancements which actually hold the potential for great efficiency and effectiveness which base care and treatment on the individual patient's genetics, and which are based on science. If the business of medicine is care and healing this would have been, or should have been, our focus. Unfortunately, in the public realm, healthcare has become almost synonymous with systems that control payments, costs and reimbursements.

A Word On Medicaid

I recall a number of Medicaid programs with the State of CT that were put together to assist low-income people, but where the reimbursements were so low most physicians just refused to participate. In my group, my practice accepted Medicaid patients because we felt we should. They needed our care; that was our primary motivation. In most of these programs the co-pays were $35. Now you take someone who has no money, and they were not going to pay the $35. So what was happening was, we would see the patient, he wouldn't pay the $35, we'd say okay, and we'd get paid $25 by the state. If the patient had paid the $35 the total reimbursement was $60 which was okay... enough to keep the lights on, but without the $35 the reimbursement was so small the group finally had to stop accepting anyone who had not paid a previous co-pay.

Another thing, and this was common, was that people on Medicaid had an absentee rate for appointments around 35%. They just didn't show up. No calls. No cancelation. Nobody really knows why, but 35% is a significant portion. As the number of people on Medicaid increased, and as more people who were scheduled didn't show thus leaving empty patient-visit slots, the managers said, "If they don't show up we're not going to reschedule them." Again note: this is not about medicine but about financing.

If Money Is Running the Ship, Legal Is In the Chart House, and Political Is On the Radios

More than 55 years ago President Dwight Eisenhower warned the country of an emerging Military-Industrial Complex. The trends of the past 50 or 75 years have also resulted in a Medical-Industrial Complex which likely also would have given Eisenhower the willies. Actually this latter has become much more than just a medical-industrial complex: it is more like a Medical-Industrial-Insurance-Legal-Political Complex. Money powers the engines; Legal sits in the chart house navigating; and Political, including Political Correctness, has usurped communications. Let's explore these vectors.

Overriding all the many aspects of the business of medicine— private practice, medical groups, clinics, corporate hospitals, drug manufacturers, distributors, and insurers of every stripe—are federal, state and local rules and regulations, and armies of attorneys bent on making sure every act and action is in compliance and documented, or is attacked for not being so.

Every element of medical care, the medical care delivery system, and medical care financing must comply with ever-expanding legal and political requirements and mandates. Often these laws, rules, regs, and requirements strangle healthcare. Sometimes it seems that the only aspects of the entire system that are healthy and thriving are the financial, legal and political bureaucracies that grow like cancers on American healthcare, that metastasize to reach every organ, and that are fated to eventually destroy and kill the host.

Legal is multi-faceted: decisions from lawsuits to legislation to court interpretations impact every aspect of the business and practice of medicine. Earlier we mentioned about the law firm of Flim & Flam, and how suits and settlements are not just costly to the system, but how medical practices and procedures—developed by scientists and perfected by years of physician-experience and use—may be altered by a single claim. We also touched on a few legal elements when talking about insurance. Let's see how a few others have exacerbated and/or enabled the development of the medical-industrial complex. This section, necessarily, will be but a cursory review. When finished, we will add all the composite vectors we've described to see where we are in American healthcare, and how this has brought us to the ultimate bureaucratic overlay known as ObamaCare.

Consider the patient who had a hip replacement five years ago, and who goes to the dentist to have his teeth cleaned. Because of the potential for bacteria from the mouth getting into the blood system and infecting the site of the implant, patients typically took an antibiotic bolus prior to the dental procedure. For years it was considered proper to apply this practice in the twenty-four months following surgery, and then, if the surgery was successful and recovery full, to anticipate the implant to be so encapsulated as to be essentially immune from this cause of infection. But someone, somewhere along the line, long after the twenty four-month period, developed a site infection. The results became the recommendation that the antibiotic bolus be taken prior to any dental procedure for the remainder of the patient's life. There are no inquiries made of the specific patient's implant health, just a new blanket regulation; despite the fact that unneeded antibiotics may also cause health problems.

Practices and procedures change. Someone claims a commonly used medical device caused undisclosed pain and suffering in their personal use; a jury of their peers agrees (if it even gets that far) and the use of the device is essentially banned (a result as likely to occur from insurance companies withdrawing coverage as from any legal barring of the device). All those who may have benefitted from the device no longer have the option. The science behind the causality of the rare failure of the device is seldom as pristine as the emotions of the plaintiff. The legal decision hasn't changed the medical realities. Bans, new rules, more guidelines ensue—all requiring more documentation and signatures, more computer data entry and checkboxes. And someone has to check the documentation and signatures, the computer data and the checkboxes to make sure they have all been properly executed. If not, there will be fines. So the physician's group or hospital or clinic has to have a department of checkbox compliance to avoid fines; and the regulators need to have checkbox auditors to find non-compliance (so fines can be levied and they can *earn* their keep).

The class-action suit: previously we saw what happened with the T-bomb. "If you or a loved one... you may be entitled to compensation..." turned out, in this incident, to be a dud. But it is a pretty good example of just how quickly Flim & Flam, PC can hit the TV airwaves and troll for class-action clients. The T-bomb case is not over; as I write this, ads are still being run; potential compensation for attorneys and victims is highly motivating. The potential fallout: people become frightened to use treatments which may be beneficial to them; or conversely, they may seek alternative treatments which may be less beneficial or have out and out undesirable side effects.

The rise of political control over the business end of medicine is a direct resultant of public (often political) criticisms of presumed business practices in medicine. This goes way back! With each business *advancement* there's been someone there demanding to control what's going on. As mentioned earlier, politicians used to get all upset if a doctor went out to dinner with a drug company rep. Certainly there were instances of improprieties, but I believe they were rare. Still, once made public and reported in the media, politicians sought to control this relationship. As said, what the drug companies began doing was to invite groups of physicians to a dinner to hear a knowledgeable speaker explain the particulars of a new drug. Yes, it was a commercial for their product, but is that an unreasonable way to educate a professional group about a new product? Accepting a dinner invitation did not mean a physician had to prescribe the drug any more than test driving a car at an auto dealership means the consumer must buy the car. The era of distrust in *Big Pharma* had yet to arrive, but, as noted, legislators saw the practice differently. As said before, the sense of mandatory quid pro quo is part of the political world. It is not part of the world of the traditional physician. In that same vein, political lobbyists also tended to be different than drug company reps. Both may educational elements to their pitch, and both may be rewarded if they are successful, but where the sale is usually the goal of the salesman, the political lobbyist often wants to cultivate continuing future personal benefit.

Anytime one looks at criticism, one also needs to look at the critic. Keep this in mind whenever you hear someone condemning a system. If changing that system gives them more control over it, the need for change may be manufactured, and the motivation may have little to do with actual needs. Again, as said earlier, sometimes criticism tells you more about the critics own underlying motivations and morals than the motivations and morals of those they criticize.

Dr. Daniel F. Craviotto, Jr., an orthopedic surgeon from Santa Barbara, California wrote an opinion piece for The Wall Street Journal in April of 2014. Like so many physicians today, he has experienced the problems of political and legal control of the business of medicine, but in addition he has made a case for doctors declaring independence from bureaucratic madness. One element he points to is the Medicare/Medicaid demand that physicians use specific electronic health record (EHR) systems or have their reimbursements, already low, cut further. The EHR (this is analogous to the Bloom Board in education) creates immense amounts of make-work. Dr. Craviotto explains that he spends two hours every day filling in blanks and checking off boxes "…just so I can be paid and not face a government audit." Like so many, he complains about the work being less efficient and less fulfilling—but it is now the law.

> I don't know about other physicians but I am tired—tired of the mandates, tired of outside interference, tired of anything that unnecessarily interferes with the way I practice medicine. No other profession would put up with this kind of scrutiny and coercion from outside forces. The legal profession would not. The labor unions would not. We as physicians continue to plod along and take care of our patients while those on the outside continue to intrude and interfere with the practice of medicine.

Public attitudes and perceptions feed the problem. Recall when we spoke of image, self-image, and ambient cultural story; and of how story came about, and how it ends up controlling individual and public behavior. One of the things we said is that story creates self-image and behavior tends to be consistent with self-image. I wish I could interrupt the TV shows, commercials and exposés that talk about healthcare plans and that show videos of doctors in scrubs or with stethoscopes around their necks. The audio will say, "…the hospital…" but those docs have nothing to do with running the hospital. They may set up medical quality control, but when it comes to pricing they're not even in the picture. When you're talking about healthcare costs, don't show images of doctors. It's a false image that propagates the idea that healthcare costs are up because of doctors, and that isn't true; yet decisions are made, policies are set and laws are passed as if it were.

Politicians have tried very hard to shape the image of healthcare as if healthcare were one entity; and they have suggested that all that has to be done to make healthcare work is to come up with the right formula so everything will click into place. But healthcare is complicated, complex and involves so many elements it is not just impractical and undesirable to portray it as a monolith, it make sensible decision-making impossible. Healthcare is not one business but multiple businesses. The different businesses deal with far-ranging elements. There is no medical reason to try to hammer them all into one box.

Over the years an entire constellation of influences from commercial and political groups have grabbed hold of healthcare in order to make money. Medications (Big Pharma) has played a role. As all sorts of new medications have become available, the medical-industrial-insurance-legal-political complex has become more and more commercial, and more and more powerful, and there has ensued a tremendous push to sell, sell, sell! Today, for each and every malady people are encouraged to go to the doctor and get a drug. A caveat: Big Pharma has done and is doing amazing research, and it has and is discovering new, highly-effective, wonder-treatments—often less expensive and less invasive than those in previous use. Blanket criticism of Big Pharma is as inappropriate as most biases. Saying that, there are certain trends in the public use of pharmaceuticals—Americans use more prescribed drugs than any other people on earth—that are driven by money and advertising, not by physical need.

If you look at the flu season, every doctor will tell you the flu is a virus: drink plenty of fluids and get plenty of rest. But what you see on TV is, "The incidents of flu are rising. Go to the doctor." That's fine, but there is a cost. And the value of the office visit is questionable. Some physicians have told me they prescribe antibiotics for the flu. It's the wrong thing, they know it, but they'll say, "I do it because the patients demand it. They believe they need it."

Why? Who's convinced them of this? Every year there are stories about 40-year old guys or mothers of three who delayed but finally went to the hospital with the flu, and two days later they were dead. The implication is, if you don't go to the doctor, you're going to die. Death from the flu is an aberration, but it can happen. It is very rare. Perhaps someone's immune systems can't fight some viruses, or someone has a compromised defense, but these are uncommon circumstances. Uncommon circumstances don't sell billions of dollars' worth of drugs. So the medical-industrial complex now markets directly to the entire potential patient population, and attempts to convince everyone of the need for whatever product they are peddling at the moment. It's more than *convince*. Convince is the traditional role of advertising. Now it is more like scare. The CDC lends *compassionate credence* by making it virtually antisocial or anti-patriotic to be a renegade from the crusade for *herd immunity*, and to not to get a flu shot, or not to dampen symptoms by taking either prescription or over-the-counter drugs (which may or may not work, and which may elongate the period of symptoms or even create more severe problems—i.e. cough suppressants may increase lung congestion which can lead to dangerous complications).

Mass media marketing about the flu is but one example; direct advertising is something else. At one time drug reps used to come to the office and educate us about new products. Well in good. They would check back with us to see if we'd prescribed the new drug, and how it worked for our patients. Even better. Now reps go to the pharmacies to find out if physicians are actually prescribing their drugs. They go to all the pharmacies and find out not just if I prescribed it, but who all the patients are... then they market the drug directly to the patient; you know, here's a $10 coupon for your next order, or here's a pass to the local gym. Marketing is optimized, patient care is secondary.

When allergy season comes pharmacies make millions of auto-phone or robo-phone calls to potential buyers for these products. This is another type of direct-to-the-consumer advertising... part of the marketing world knowing everything about you... and it also can be threatening. "You don't want to wait for your symptoms to come... Be prepared. Refill your prescription today." This is not necessarily bad; but this type of marketing likely does lead to more medications being sold—which of course is the goal. The problem becomes one of over-medication—as noted before, putting any chemical in your system is going to mean it bathes every cell in one's body even if is prescribed for only the cells of the right little toe.

When doctors took care of their own families, they didn't prescribe an unending list of medical chemicals. Traditionally people didn't seek or get medical care unless they absolutely needed it. But now, a product of marketing and creating an ambient cultural image of better living through pharmaceuticals, people are ingesting prescription and over-the-counter chemicals like candy hearts on St. Valentine's Day. We are spending more money because of this change in behavior, but we are not necessarily a healthier population, nor are we necessarily getting the medications we do need.

A look at how drugs are chosen by medical insures is revealing. An insurer has a list of approved drugs. One might think a drug has been approved because the insurer's in-house medical consultants have looked at it and said, "Oh, these are the best drugs for these conditions." But what really happens is the insurer deals with a middleman, perhaps a distributor, who deals with various manufactures. The insurer negotiates a price. A hypothetically example might go like this: "We can get 100,000 Lipitor pills at a penny each," but then they find that, in the long-run Crestor is cheaper. As a physician I'll get a letter saying, "We have determined that Crestor is a better medication for your patients, and you should switch to prescribing it." Some people think it is based upon medical evidence, but seldom is the case. It's based on finance. Is it the same drug? No. Does this cause confusion? Yes. Hospitals, too, have their own inventories of drugs, and their own approved lists. If a patient goes into the hospital and has been on one drug, he may be switched to the other for no medical reason. And when he goes home, his discharge instructions may be different from those given by the specialist he's been seeing. This is all about money, not about medicine or science, and sometimes it causes complications.

Government programs mesh with these new systems, or vice-a-verse, and the effect is cumulative. Take Silver Script, Part D Medicare: it goes—here's the drug, here's the cost to Medicare, here's the cost to you the consumer, here's the cost to the provider, here's the total cost, here's your out-of-pocket cost. It is a computer printout of all these different numbers. As we get older the marketers surf for patients to sell their wares. The computer gives them the ability to identify individuals—and it knows not only all the things you've bought in the past but all of the things you've even looked at on line. Computerized-marketing thought basically says, "Aha! We can sell this consumer X, Y, or Z. Let's hammer him with notifications." Okay, so what? That's what salesmen are supposed to do, isn't it? But this type of marketing— tapping into data bases that hold vast amounts of personal information, databases that are legally mandated and which force consumers to disclose information—fringes on invasion of privacy ethics (which is why there are so many unreadable disclosures attached to just about everything today). This is all at the margin of free-market capitalism, and freedom of speech. Why I say this is, that at the fringe, it may overstep the line allowing the consumer to choose freely to buy or not to buy, by using scam-and-scare tactics. Instead of educating a population to the benefits of a product, knowing the individual consumer's purchasing habits and other characteristics allows marketers to tailor campaigns which to pinpoint fears. The collusion of government and industry encourages psychological dependence upon not just drug use, but upon a culture which promises the avoidance of risk and anything that might be unpleasant—including the flu or hay fever. It is not limited to medications. This is symptomatic of the nation moving away from principles of self-reliance, self-confidence, mutual trust and independence. The real problem, of course, is that the promises of risk avoidance, et cetera, cannot be kept; and when a people lose their ability and self-trust, they become more vulnerable to the likes of Flim and Flam, PC, and political conmen.

When Politicians and Special Interest Groups Get Involved: AIDS

Not long ago I was in a general discussion with a liberal friend about politics and medicine, and the conversation turned to the onset of awareness and the public response to AIDS. I said, "You know, the first political disease was AIDS." She said, "What do you mean?" I said, "AIDS was a very, very infectious disease. At that time, in the

State of Connecticut, if I tested you for gonorrhea and the results came back positive, the next day somebody from the state health department would be knocking on your door, and they were going to ask you who you've had sex with, because they were going to want to investigate your partners and make sure that they got treated. But with AIDS, because of the politics associated with the Gay Rights Movement and their demand for privacy, what happened in Connecticut and most other states was, you couldn't test anyone for AIDS unless you had their permission. That's fine. But if you did test and it did come back positive, you couldn't tell anybody. You couldn't tell the health department. You couldn't tell the wife or the boyfriend or the girlfriend. This was 30 years ago. This enabled a very infections disease to spread. It spread so extensively, the statistic given in the early days of the epidemic suggested that by the year 2008 every surgeon in America would be infected."

My friend said, "Well, you don't understand. The reason gays didn't want everyone to know was because people were highly prejudiced against gay people." I said, "I do understand that, but the consequence of that behavior allowed the disease to spread and many gay men died because of it." She shot back, "No, you don't understand. Gays were being locked up and killed. It was like a witch hunt." I shook my head. I wasn't sure where she'd gotten that bit of information. I said, "But infected people were out infecting non-infected people, and as a public health issue it was less of a concern what was happening to individuals than to society. The public health goal was to save civilization."

Today we're more aware of epidemics and possible pandemics, but the controversy and conflict between individual rights, privacy, and public health is still being played out. Ebola, measles, the flu have all recently been in the news. The difference is the degree of political special interest; and there still exists wars between politics and science as if laws and political pressure can change reality.

AIDS, the narrative goes, was originally spread by one flight attendant who became infected, it is suspected, from a monkey. That doesn't mean sex with a monkey, but somehow he came in contact with this animal and he got the virus. He was a very promiscuous gay man who was going around having sex with lots of other guys—something like 800 or 900 guys—and, of course, the disease expanded geometrically—or in today's jargon it literally went viral. The story may have some inaccuracies—AIDS has been traced back much earlier—but the story does hold lessons we should have learned.

In the beginning of the epidemic physicians and public health officials didn't really know what they were dealing with. Men were showing up with two very rare diseases, one being this weird, amebic pneumonia called *pneumocystic carinii,* and the other being a skin cancer called *kaposi's sarcoma.* A couple of doctors—I think one at San Francisco General and one in New York—began to sound the alarm. Via chance conversations they compared notes: "Hey, I had a case like this…" and it grew, and along with researchers at the CDC they finally tracked it to sexual transmission within the gay population. SF was one of the hubs. Gay men hung out in the bathhouses—there was a gay liberation movement happening—and men were freely having sex with each other. The bathhouse was the meeting place. It was not uncommon for a gay man to have sex with three or four or more partners in the bathhouse on a single day.

But AIDS was not like a cold or the flu. One didn't have sexual contact one day and symptoms appeared a few days later. The disease was just coming up on the public health radar, and within both the medical and the gay communities it was still misunderstood. As pieces of the puzzle began to emerge some—maybe the CDC—suggested that the bathhouses be closed. The mayor responded, "You can't do that. It'll going to kill the economy. It's going to kill my reelection." The Gay Rights Movement responded that they were being singled out, attacked and discriminated against.

Researchers still didn't know just what they were dealing with, but they were tracing it to a viral agent, and thought it might be hepatitis C. They didn't have a test for the viral agent but they had a test for hepatitis C. The Red Cross checked some of its blood supply and found that some blood was positive for Hep C. It was proposed that all the blood supplies be checked, but Red Cross officials objected. "No. You can't do that. That's our business. Blood is our business." So it wasn't done as early as it might have been, and blood transfusions became a source of the spread of the disease.

A third thing happened to slow the advance. Bob Gallo, a scientist at the NIH, was working on the cause of AIDS in competition with a group in France. The guys in France were probably the ones that discovered the HIV virus, but Gallo thought he had another virus that caused the syndrome. There was a political conflict between the two, and the French researchers were saying that Gallo's specimen was contaminated from their specimen, and that what he was doing was stealing their research. Eventually they sort of settled it: Gallo didn't admit he was wrong, and the French said, "These things happen." They shared the discovery, but the fight caused additional delays in developing protocols and treatments.

The research approach was: viruses come with a protein coat and contain DNA; they attack your cells and inject their DNA into you cells; your cell is then reprogramed to make more viruses. A guy named Rous discovered that the mechanism could actually work backwards, meaning that the cell could infect the virus using RNA, and that the sarcoma virus was a retro-virus. When Rous reported his findings, some in the scientific community laughed at him. Others said, "That can't happen." But Rous showed it happening with the chicken sarcoma virus. That's how the AIDS virus works. Until this was accepted, most research was pursuing non-productive paths.

The fear of HIV/AIDS, the discrimination against gays, and the politically motivated antidiscrimination movement did little to protect public health. Finally, with the development of highly-effective antiretroviral drugs and new treatment protocols, the politics of the disease begins to abate. Treated people could lead healthy lives with HIV. But had it not been for the fact that politicians and pundits didn't want to pinpoint gay men, they would have been able to control this disease a lot sooner; fewer men would have suffered, and fewer would have died. A deeper discussion on the topic can be found in *And The Band Played On* by Randy Shilts.

Getting back to the discussion with my liberal friend I said to her, "You don't have to give up your ideals to recognize that political pressure and special interest pressure can, and often does, create corruption or at least circumstances which are counter-productive to society. In fact, your ideals and my ideals are very similar. We both want the same kind of things for society, for our children and grandchildren. And we both want to see all Americans receive decent patient care—care which is compassionate, effective, efficient, as non-obtrusive as possible, and affordable. But when policies are skewed by political or monetary perspectives for ulterior motive—left or right—

they break action from reality and responsibility the resultants. What is left if the wake is a destroyed society cluttered with the flotsam and jetsam of ordinary lives.

ObamaCare: Killing Us Softly With His Song

All these vectors with all their forces pulling in a multitude of directions have culminated in an attempt to consolidate healthcare, the healthcare delivery system and healthcare coverage (finance) under one immense, bureaucratic roof... without eliminating or replacing any existing levels of bureaucracy! The Affordable Care Act (ACA), or as it is called ObamaCare, does not make the system more efficient, more effective, or more equitable. It does incorporate several meaningful reforms, but these could have (and should have) been incorporated into the existing system without building a new, unwieldy superstructure. What we are witnessing is a systemic stage IV disease—the final attack destroying a potentially amazing system. Concurrent with the attack are true medical and scientific advancements which are being used to cover errors and bad policies; and an American spirit of resilience adapting to and making the best of a bad situation.

The good: the ability of young adults up to the age of 26 to be covered under their parents' insurance appears to be a godsend for many entering, or attempting to enter, the job market in this difficult economy; increased mental health coverage, particularly in light of the rash of school shootings by people suffering with mental illnesses; and the removal of coverage restrictions for prior existing medical conditions.

The number of people covered: when the White House first proposed ObamaCare a major selling point was that all American citizens would have access to the healthcare insurance they need. Particularly benefitting would be those who would not, or could not, pay for coverage; but also the public pocketbook because those newly covered under this partnership of government, insurers and healthcare providers would cost less than a system in which the use of hospital emergency rooms as free clinics was funded indirectly at public expense—that is, ObamaCare would make order out of chaos and save money.

The numbers, in all their iterations, have never added up, and it's not easy to ascertain what is actually happening due to the partisan nature of many government and private reports. We are a nation of 320 million people. For some time the stated goal for the ACA was to sign up 6 million *newly-covered* people; and within about a year of the initial rollout, some say that goal has been reached. Others pointed out that many of these newly-covered have previously been covered under Medicare or Medicaid or some other insurance, and that the number of newly *no-longer-covered* equals any gains made. That is, according to some, the ACA is, quite simply, a colossal folly.

This is important: the healthcare delivery system did have problems; and reforms were required. Adding 9,283 auditors (at the yearly cost of $1.9 billion) but no physicians is perhaps the clearest gage of the ACA structure—bureaucracy over patient care—but we'll hold off on that for a moment.

The chaotic rollout of the new program, and the ensuing intense cacophony over that fiasco, hid deeper problems. We'll ignore here the $650 million original cost and the $300+ million repair bill for the computer system built by Canadian political cronies of the current administration, as that near billion dollar cost is actually pretty small compared to the cost of establishing and maintaining the new bureaucracy. This latter subject received little media exposure during the rollout period. It is not just the governmental oversight bureaucracy costs that we should be looking at, but the costs incurred by the entire system.

The ACA adds a layer of bureaucracy over the existing bureaucracy of managed care. Insurance companies work with massive amounts of data in their actuarial base in order to come up with premium prices. These companies are not charitable organizations rushing to donate their expertise to the health of the nation. Rather they are like any other corporate business whose first goal is to make money. Simply put, insurers looked at the projected numbers under the ACA as they would any other risk, did the math, and came up with policies and premiums they could provide under the new system and still make money. They did this in three ways.

First they created plans with premiums higher than the previous premiums for similar plans. For those that might have difficulty paying these premiums, the government (taxpayers) under the ACA will step in and subsidize the payments. Insurers realized that the subsidies would not cover their full risk; so the companies added higher deductibles. What this means is patients pay more out-of-pocket before their insurance kicks in, thereby reducing insurance company liability. The figures we're seeing for the new deductibles appear to be in the $3000 to $5000 range. In a society full of people who cannot afford to pay $50 or $150 for an antibiotic prescription, the idea of $3000 deductibles seems counter-intuitive, but the actuarial numbers work.

There is an insurance company called Golden Rule that for years based its products on low premiums and high deductibles—essentially selling catastrophic coverage. These were great products for the few who could afford the scenario, but most families were not in that situation. Some families, however, would buy these policies and gamble that no family member would have an illness or accident that would force them to come up with the cash. This is not a viable alternative for most people, or for the public in general, but it is a situation to which many more are now being subjected to under high-deductible ACA plans.

Secondly, insurance companies act in a monopsonious manner. A monopoly is when a company uses its size to control the market; a monopsony exists when a company uses it size to control its suppliers. In this example, physicians are the suppliers of services to insurance companies. In Connecticut one of the major insurers, in response to ACA financial demands, announced the dismissal of approximately 2500 physicians from their approved list. The company said that they were selecting the most efficient physicians so that they could keep costs under control.

In my experience running a large independent practice association, I found that insurance companies collected a massive amount of data—much of it erroneous for the purpose of gauging physician efficiency. It is very difficult to extract data that is accurate when you use only claims. Using claims might suggest a correlation between the data averages and physician efficiency, and it might imply causality. But correlation is not causality. A high correlation exists between cancer patients and right-handedness, but to suggest that right-handedness causes cancer is invalid. Firing thousands of physicians based upon claim data and implied efficiency is equally invalid. The results of this firing (if it goes through) will be thousands of patients without a physician. Other states are seeing similar problems. Most physicians are already completely booked with patients and it is ludicrous to suggest that the remaining physicians will have the capacity to cope with this additional patient load. When a patient does gain access to a new physician, there is an enormous amount of data from the previous doctor/patient interaction that now needs to be digested by the new physician who, as we said, is overworked and overburdened. Transfers of this type do not bode well for accurate care… and so much for more people being covered!

A third problem is the obscurity of actual payment of fees to physicians. Many physicians across the country have balked at the low fees paid by Medicaid or other state plans. It is not that physicians are greedy. As we've seen, in this new environment they have been forced to become more business-aware. When a physician sees that low fees will not allow him to fiscally continue in practice, he makes adjustments. I have surveyed a number of practices, and no one is certain what their reimbursements will be in either the short term or long. Remember, physician's practices are small businesses. These businesses have to meet payrolls, pay for employee health benefits, pay taxes. In addition to all the other overhead items, the doctor also has to pay for medical malpractice insurance. Connecticut has the fifth highest medical malpractice claim rate in the nation. I am certain that most people in Connecticut do not believe we have the fifth worst physicians in the country. What we more likely; we have the fifth most active legal community in the country. The ACA has done nothing to address tort reform and other pressures on healthcare.

As a retired physician, in many ways I am divorced from the hubbub of ObamaCare; but in several ways I am not. I cringe at what is happening. Politicians and businessmen complain bitterly about the "healthcare crisis," but they seldom differentiate between medical care and healthcare financing. Medical care, despite all these gyrations, is still pretty damn good.

The current bureaucratic overlay does not inspire confidence. People are frightened by what is happening in healthcare, and projections of the current program increase anxiety. Physicians wonder who will be taking care of future patients. A January 2015 report by the Congressional Budget Office (CBO) projected numbers for ten years hence, and suggested that 24 to 27 million Americans who were uninsured in 2010 will have health insurance coverage by 2025. That sounds great, doesn't it? Again, however, the numbers don't add up. There were an estimated 30 million Americans without health insurance in 2010, but the CBO projects that there still will be between 29 and 31 million "nonelderly" Americans without medical insurance in 2025. Huh?!

The good news is, all this new coverage will cost, again according to the CBO and the Joint Committee on Taxation (a group of members from both houses of Congress), only $50,000 per covered individual! Wait...! Oh... and that's only the cost to the taxpayers. It doesn't include what the individual pays in insurance premiums or deductibles... only the government's portion for implementing the ACA and paying for its guarantees. Over all, the government will spend just a hair under two trillion dollars over a ten-year period. It will raise about one third of the funds from penalties, fees and new taxes; but the other two thirds... well, pony it up Mr. Taxpayer. It's only about $50,000 per insured individual (okay, that's a mere $5,000 per year—what a bargain!)! And... (repeat) there will still be about 30 million people uninsured!!!

As insane as this may sound, it really is not a surprise. It is simply standard, bureaucratic mechanics. The bureaucracy supports the bureaucracy, grows the bureaucracy, protects the bureaucracy. Unfortunately there are other, very real consequences of establishing this super-structure bureaucracy that impact individuals and society far beyond the usual discussion of healthcare reform.

Stresses, like regulations, are cumulative; and every regulation adds a pang of stress to someone's life. Unresolved stress is harmful to human health as it causes systemic inflammation which manifests via many and various ailments. As local, state and federal agencies escalate their production of regulations, the general well-being deteriorates. This is not to say regulation isn't necessary. Some regulation, of course, is necessary; but when a guy says, "They're driving me crazy," or "They're going to give me a heart attack," or "They make me sick," he is describing reality. The words from The Declaration of Independence, "... and the pursuit of happiness..." weren't used by whim. Tyranny, autocracy, and oppressiveness are bad for your health—unless you are one of the elite, the autocrat, the dictator, or the oppressor. So a law, no matter its stated purpose, that increases the dictatorial powers of the state will have unexpected, unintended, and difficult-to-measure side effects.

When I was in active practice and treating patients who were working, paying their bills and raising their families, I never heard a comment akin to "I can't breathe." But when a guy was laid off, behind on his bills, and there was stress at home, that sentiment, indeed those exact words, were common. This had nothing to do with race or ethnicity. It had everything to do with the economy and the individual's financial status. Feeling oppressed, feeling under the gun or behind the eight ball affected their sense of well-being and their health.

Consider what has happened to small business in America in the past eight years. It almost seems as if the government is running a war against the economy—not just the medical care sector. Despite the often glowing reports of economic recovery, a recent report from Gallup Chairman and CEO Jim Clifton "revealed that 'for the first time in 35 years, American business deaths now outnumber business births.'" (Hall) The numbers are significant. Out of 26 million businesses in America, nearly 77% are businesses in name only—that is they have no revenue, no workers and no customers. The remaining 23% (about 6 million businesses) employ 100 million Americans; with only one third of the companies (2 million businesses) employing five or more workers. This latter sector is contracting. As Clifton puts it, "I don't want to sound like a doomsayer, but when small and medium-sized businesses are dying faster than they're being born, so is free enterprise. And when free enterprise dies, America dies with it." (Hall)

The bureaucracy and regulations set up under the ACA are causing businesses to cut back, be aborted or be stillborn. That in turn destroys employment opportunities. Non-government jobs are dwindling. Despite published figures for unemployment (at this writing officially 5.6%), the workforce is at its lowest participation level in 50 years. Many of the gains won by the women's movement over the past six decades have been reversed; but the segment of the workforce that has been most affected is young men—just out of school or just out of the military. Many of these guys are being underemployed. Without real job creation via business expansion there is no place for them to go, and they lag—highly educated and/or highly experienced—in unemployment or underemployment limbo.

Gallup's Clifton states in another article, this one titled *The Big Lie: 5.6% Unempolyment,* "If you, a family member or anyone is unemployed and has subsequently given up on finding a job—if you are so hopelessly out of work that you've stopped looking over the past four weeks—the Department of Labor doesn't count you as unemployed. That's right. While you are as unemployed as one can possibly be, and tragically may never find work again, you are **not** counted in the figure we see relentlessly in the news... Right now, as many as 30 million Americans are either out of work or severely underemployed... Say you're an out-of-work engineer or healthcare worker or construction worker or retail manager: If you perform a minimum of one hour of work in a week and are paid at least $20—maybe someone pays you to mow their lawn—you're not officially counted as unemployed... If you have a degree in chemistry or math and are working 10 hours part time because it is all you can find—in other words, you are severely underemployed—the government doesn't count you in the 5.6%... It's a lie that has consequences, because the great American dream is to have a good job... in recent years, America has failed to deliver that dream... When we fail to deliver a good job that fits a citizen's talents, training and experience, we are failing the great American dream."

According to Clifton, only 44% of Americans, 18 years old or older (and not retired), currently hold full-time (30+ hours per week and a regular paycheck) jobs. That means 56% don't! ...the lowest rate of workforce participation in 50 years. It means a gutting of the middle class; it means a growing percent below the poverty level; it means a widening gap between the rich and the poor; and it means social mobility—the ability to elevate one's position through hard work and talent—is stifled.

All this is politics, and it isn't anything new. Over 180 years ago the big issue in American public debate was whether or not The Bank of The United States should be re-chartered. At that time President Andrew Jackson "... denounced the bank as an institution of privilege inconsistent with American democracy; as a monopoly which stifled free and fair competition; [and] as an enterprise which widened the gap between the rich and the poor..." (Lane) Those criticisms could easily be applied to the ACA. Despite the Supreme Court's decision that the ACA was constitutional if viewed as a tax, it certainly is inconsistent with democratic ideals as it rigidly institutionalizes an omnipotent bureaucratic system that in turn enhances insurance company and corporate hospital monopolies stifling free and fair competition. Although sold as affordable [the name of the act is a fabrication every American should find outrageous], and as if it would reduce healthcare costs, it is apparent as of this writing neither is true. The Wall Street Journal, reporting on the January 2015 CBO report states, "… the country's long-term economic outlook underscores what budget experts have long known: *The rising cost of health care is the single largest driver of the gloomy long-term fiscal outlook for the U.S.*" (Galston—my highlight) Under the ACA there are vast sums of money to be made by a few at the expense of the many; that is, the ACA is an enterprise which widens the gap between the rich and the poor in direct contradiction to its hype and selling points.

How often have you heard a politician describe a crisis and say, "We must do something."? That tends to be their standard fare. What we actually need are politicians standing up and saying, "We must undo something." If doctors told the kind of lies that seem endemic to politicians we'd all be in jail. Politicians and public office holders (and academics, too), should be forced to take an oath before being allowed to practice, an oath the equivalent of the doctor's Hippocratic Oath, "I hereby solemnly vow to First Do No Harm.

Dr. Jeffrey Rabuffo

PART VII: Culture Wars

Male Virtues Under Siege

I like to understand how things work. It's an obsession. I like to work puzzles, make connections, see how the various parts influence, interconnect and impact each other. It is likely why I became a physician—driven by the need to understand the complexities of the human body. When I first entered medical school I expected the puzzle to be physical, or physical-chemical-electrical. At that time I had not considered *outside* elements—environmental, dietetic, financial, political, or spiritual. Nor had it occur to me that the impact of these elements could be as great as, or greater than, the impact of pathogens, deficiencies, or hereditary physiological aberrations. Over the years, slowly at first then accelerating, that perception changed.

In this book we have been painting a picture of boys and men, of the basics founded in biology, of what manhood once was, and of how masculinity has been remolded. The consequences of the shifting landscape against which we've been cast amount to a clandestine, civil and guerrilla culture war. Men are in crisis: their values and virtues are disparaged; their health and longevity suffer; American culture is under attack from within; and a great blind of skewed stories hides these realities from the majority.

For more than a half century this culture war has been rampaging through virtually all American institutions, creating new institutions and new bureaucracies, changing not just the fabric of American society but re-sculpting the American spirit.

A Man's Made Outta Mud... But It's A War On Women

Let's examine the current state of The War On Women. The reason this is important is the concept implies that non-women are the antagonists, the wagers of attacks and oppression, and the benefactors of spoils won in battle. Can it be so?

A close friend tells the story of him and his wife attending Parent Effectiveness Training (P.E.T.) classes about thirty five years ago—shortly after their first son entered the terrible twos. The course was taught by an ex-Protestant, Anglo-Saxon American woman, a thoroughly modern, ideologically correct WASP. The host household was the mansion of a wealthy Jewish businessman and his very lovely and social wife. The walls of the drawing room were papered in gold foil; the master bedroom suite with its enormous and well-appointed bath was at one end of the structure, and their three-year old daughter's suite was at the other end. The lucky little girl had not only her own room, but she had two well-equipped playrooms—one for physical games (kind of a gym), and one for more sedentary behaviors (reading, a dollhouse, TV). The host had generously sponsored the classes. He and his wife were worried about their daughter's "acting out" and "emotional distancing from them."

Over the eight-week course the P.E.T. instructor went through her standard litany of cause and effect, and of corrective behaviors: Active Listening, Effective "I Messages," No-Lose methods for resolving conflicts, et cetera. She seldom missed an opportunity to insert a dig against the dads. Never once did she mention, nor did she seem to even take note, that the host's little girl was essentially isolated in her charming canopy bed every night (50% of her existence), thus allowing mommy and daddy to play at their 1980's equivalent of Fifty Shades of Gray.

Toward the end of the course my friend, a normally soft-spoken, second-generation Italian-American, found himself subjected to a more vitriolic ration of the instructor's thoroughly modern, feminist beliefs about child rearing and about the oppression of women by men—particularly in America during her life and knowledge-span (seemingly all the way back to her mother's generation). Women had been trapped inside homes, forced to cook, clean, raise the children, interact with the help. They were not allowed to work. A 'good' husband gave his wife a stipend; but before the 1960s most women had no money or property of their own. They also had little true authority, and that which they possessed was derived from being the wife or daughter of a banker, lawyer, manufacturer, or doctor.

My friend took her digs personally and found her accusations offensive. He could take it no longer. "I don't recognize what you're talking about," he said. "My mother... she was the eldest of eight, of immigrant parents... graduated Normal School (two-year teachers college) in 1932. She headed the nursery school programs (small at the time) for the entire county for the next eight years. My father's mother had a grocery store—probably going back to 1918 or 1920. I had aunts who owned apparel stories in the 1950s and others who were executive assistants. All the women in the family were strong. They didn't depend upon anyone for their authority."

The instructor was dismissive. "It could only have been that way if the businesses were in the husband's name... ...they could only have been that way if... blah... blah... blah... the man... blah." My friend became hot. To the instructor he said, "You base all this women's rights stuff on conditions which maybe exist in your ethnically-limited life. Maybe that's the way it was in your family... but you don't know anything about most Americans—men or women. You have no idea how most men worked. And you don't have a clue how families work." Then he turned to the host. "Think about your parents or your grandparents," he said. "If your daughter were living with them, where would she be sleeping?"

The example spurs various thoughts—beyond the thought that my friend might, at times, come across as a Neanderthal. Without denying the plight of women over the ages, and simultaneously without denying the wonderful advancements earned by the Women's Movement in the 19th and first six or seven decades of the 20th centuries, let's look at the lives of most men—not just the elite. We could do a historical review but for simplicity let's limit ourselves to the post-Civil War, or even the post-World War I period.

Most men worked menial labor jobs. Most men worked six days per week. Many of the jobs they worked were dangerous, and many men were injured. In my father's generation it seemed that at least half of all men were missing part of a finger or hand—lost to a milling machine or tractor or a steam shovel. Men worked in factories, in fields, in mines. They dug canals, laid railroad track. They cut stone, built bridges, roadways and highways. The jobs were strenuous, dirty. Few women worked these jobs. If most women didn't have the choice to work outside the house, most men didn't have the choice to stay home. Often the male jobs paid so little the life men were able to provide for themselves and their families was subsistence level or only a little better. Things did not change much for men until after World War II when, corresponding to increased education levels (22% high school graduates in 1910 to nearly 90% by 1960), growing mechanization, and burgeoning national prosperity, the majority of men broke away from manual labor. Women too advanced during this period—with their men, and on their own.

Today, for many men that's one source of the rub when they hear women bitching about being oppressed, about there being a War On Women. Those claims, digs, bitchings or accusations, they feel, "Have nothing to do with me. I'm being lumped in with the oppressors. How prejudiced is that?!"

The War On Women historically has had a financial element, but seen from the perspective of immigrant-Americans from the mid- or late 1800s on, the war has been a War On People—a class conflict, not gender-based combat. To many immigrants the amazing thing about America, indeed the great attraction of America, was the potential for the social mobility of individuals—male or female—and of families. Hard work, initiative, and a plan—my father had a saying: *Plan your work and work your plan*—could lift ones social and economic status. It was not automatic. It has never been automatic. And it didn't and doesn't always work.

Recall the folk song *Sixteen Tons*. The lyrics by Merle Travis went: *Some people say a man is made outta of mud; But a poor man's made outta muscle and blood; Muscle and blood, skin and bone; A mind that's weak and a back that's strong...* and the chorus, *...I owe my soul to the company store...*

There have been company towns and mill towns where the business owners had set up systems—the company store—to keep people in debt and essentially indentured without end. There have been labor practices like the Padrone System where immigrants rose on the backs of their fellow countrymen. There have been connivers and con men. And there have been laws and government programs that enabled local monopolies—companies, mines, banks—essentially buttressing the elite and condemning the common man to subsistence living. The vast majority of men bore these burdens, and their women and their families, wittingly or unwittingly, shared these burdens.

Many men, hearing the current rhetoric about the War On Women, scoff. It is not because they are oppressors; it is because they have never oppressed, but have themselves been oppressed.

Really?! you ask, as if what I just wrote is blasphemy. What about wages, glass ceilings, CEOs, wealth distribution, professional degrees, sexual harassment, et cetera, et cetera, et cetera? Well, let's look.

77 Cents: He makes more because he's a man...

We all know that a woman, compared to a man, earns only 77 cents to the man's dollar. We thus know, as many politicians have highlighted in their speeches, that American employers discriminate against women. This was reinforced in the 2015 State Of The Union messages and at the 2015 Academy Award ceremonies. It is part of our ambient cultural story.

According to a Bureau of Labor Statistics report, in 2013 the median weekly earnings of women working full-time were 82.1% of that of their male counterparts. Aha! There's the proof... but... note— the median weekly earnings number does *not* account for the number of hours worked! BLS defines full-time employment as 35-hours per week. According to the same BLS report, more than a quarter of all male workers spent 41 hours or more per week on the job compared to less than 15% of female workers; and better than twice as many men worked 60+ hours per week as opposed to women. In the medical professions, young male doctors work on average 500 hours more per year (the equivalent of 12½ 40-hour weeks) than young female doctors. [As of 2010 one third of all physicians in the U.S. were female, and the percentage has been steadily rising. The total number of doctors has changed only slightly. As older male physicians retire, they are being replaced in large part by younger female physicians who work less hours. The total number of doctor-hours is declining. This "doctor shortage" is a serious, but seldom mentioned, healthcare issue.]

Accounting for hours worked instead of median weekly earnings, women earned approximately 90 cents for each man-dollar. So... well still... that's discrimination isn't it? But wait... other factors come into play. Women, particularly those with children, more often than men, work at jobs which allow telecommuting or other

257

flexible arrangements. These jobs tend to pay less than jobs which demand more rigid work schedules. [As an aside: remember that little boy who was so antsy in first grade he couldn't settle down and everyone but his dad wanted to put him on ADHD drugs; he's the same person who now at 30 or 35 is highly focused on his 60-hour per week job.]

Women, more than men, also leave jobs during child-rearing years resulting in shorter work-experience records when they reenter the labor force. Adjusting for those additional factors brings female earnings to within 5% of male earnings.

Other dynamics eliminate that gap. Christina Hoff Sommers points to a study by Georgetown University's Center on Education and the Workforce which compares the chosen college majors of men and women. The study shows that men outnumber women in all but one of the top ten most remunerative fields (eight of these majors are in engineering all populated more heavily by men; women outnumber men only in Pharmaceutical Sciences and Administration). At the same time woman dominated nine of the ten least remunerative majors. As Sommers puts it, "Much of the wage gap can be explained away by simply taking account of college majors. In the pursuit of happiness, men and women appear to take different paths."

Equal pay for equal work has been the law of the land since The Equal Pay Act of 1963 "prohibit[ed] sex-based wage discrimination between men and women in the same establishment who perform jobs that require substantially equal skill, effort and responsibility under similar working conditions." If discrimination were the cause of women were being paid 77 cents on the dollar the courts would be clogged with suits over these violations, employers would be paying large fines, and some would be doing jail time. The fact is: the courts are not thusly clogged. The accusation is one of the *big lie narratives* often used for political gain. What do these lies mean to men, and what effect do these lies have on us?

Sexual Harassment: Doctors, Duke, Dartmouth, Wesleyan & Dis-accomplishment

In The Beginning: As a surgeon, to me there wasn't anything better than the nurse that knew what she was doing. There wasn't anything better than that. If that nurse called me and said, "Come quick. Your patient looks like shit," I would be there ASAP. On the other hand if I was working in a tough situation with a nurse that didn't know what she was doing, I could lose it. I wouldn't be disrespectful, but I'd let her know about it. Sometimes medical emergencies necessitate loud, commanding orders. Sometimes younger nurses took offense. In the operating room where there was no political correctness—*it might be the last place in the world where there's no political correctness*—this seldom happened. We told each other dirty jokes; we got very close, you know bending over the patient there were remarks about different parts of our bodies touching… it was just a very real situation. No one took offense.

But picture this. I'm trying to put a catheter down this guy's penis. He had a stricture. For this procedure you put a coat hanger-like wire—that's the best way to describe it—inside the catheter, which is flexible, to make it stiff. Then you shape it so when you get it to the bladder you can flip it so the catheter goes above the prostate rich that tends to block the insertion. For the patient this is a very painful procedure. I got good enough at it so I could get it done in less than 30 seconds. If I needed something, I would say, "Get me a… whatever." There are certain things that the nurse needs to do, and this one time the nurse didn't have a clue. Not close to a clue. So this one time… here I am, the guy is screaming, there's blood all over the bed, and I go, "Get me…" and she's looking at me, and she has no clue what I'm talking about. I can see she has no clue—that's a problem with her training—but right now my duty is to the patient, and I'm sorry but I really don't care about her feelings—those are a secondary concern. Right now we have to focus on the patient and the procedure. She's looking at me, angry, her lips are pursed.

Son of a gun, she took offense to my reaction to her not knowing what to do, and she reported me to the director of nurses. I got called down to the office of Big Sis. I explained, "I raised my voice but I didn't yell at her. I didn't demean her. I didn't call her stupid (even if that's what I thought). I was upset because it was a tense situation. I wasn't going to start singing, 'I needed this and I needed this now.'" The head nurse said, "Well, she's young." I said, "I'd be happy to meet with her and explain the procedure to her. I don't want her to go and tell all her friends, 'Rabuffo is a son-of-a-bitch who doesn't like women.' And if she's there when we do a similar procedure, I want her to know what to do." If I had been in the same situation and had loudly commanded an older nurse, the older nurse (without today's insecurities and defensiveness) would have snapped back at me just as brashly, "Okay. I'll get it."

The point is: this newer attitude, this taking of offense at being told to do something in a work situation, this feeling that one is being criticized because one is female but not because one isn't doing the job right, this is a destructive mindset which not only destroys talent and capabilities, but creates medical crises. It will never be corrected as long as the victim-attitude is reinforced.

I guess, once in an operating room, I did have a similar situation. Modern operating rooms have what is known as computer-order entry. Where you used to say, "Get me 50 of Demerol and give it to this guy cause he's having a lot of pain," now, with computer-order entry, you can't just say that. You have to type it in. But I've got gloves on. Similar situation: I'm hunched over this patient trying to get a catheter in. The guy is writhing in pain. I turn to the nurse and say, "Give him 50 of Demerol." She says, "You have to put the order in." For one second I freeze, stare at her in utter shock, then say, "You've got to be *effin* kidding me!" There was an orderly in the room and I said, "Go get someone to come in here to help us out."

Again, an old-style nurse, one who had trained before all this feeling-oppressed started, would simply have handled the situation. I recall one situation when an older nurse called me (from an upper floor) because this guy's blood sugar was low and he was beginning to have seizures. She called and said, "We just got the labs back. His blood sugar is 30." I said, "I'll be right up, but you've got to give him x, y, z sugar solution." She said, "You know, I'm not supposed to do that." I said, "I know, but you know how to stick a needle in an IV. Give it to him. I'll write the order when I get up there." She did, and by the time I got there the guy was stable. It was about two minutes. But it was a critical two minutes to the patient. A political correctness issue didn't take place, but had it been a younger person that might well have been an issue.

Along with political correctness, there are all these new regulations which younger nurses are told they must obey. They are being told you can't do this, or you can't do that, because if you do it's a potential lawsuit or it doesn't meet (government or insurance company or corporate) protocols. Most people are unaware this is happening in medicine. When we forget political correctness and the many regulations brought on by the political world, we all do things in times of urgency that need to be done at once. We *want* to make the situation work. When it is a matter of either you do it or something bad happens, you do it. It's that simple. Or it used to be. You didn't sit there and say, "I'm not going to do it because I'm not trained, or I'm not certified, or it's not in my job-description." Sometimes one may not have been trained in a specific procedure but he or she may have experienced a similar situation before. Coupled with strong base knowledge, one extrapolates and acts. Yet, seemingly, that spirit is being eroded and replaced by, "I'm not going to do that; I've been told I'm not supposed to do it; It's above my pay-grade; If you yell at me, I'll report you for sexual harassment."

Such are the unintended consequences produced by the current PC atmosphere in which sexual harassment accusations are one tool of those who perceive themselves to be victims. Efficiency and effectiveness ebb. Patients are put in peril. But this is overlooked in the name of equality. I have seen it in my medical practice and in the hospitals, but the incidents to which I've personally been exposed are child's play (unless you were the guy on the table) compared to what has happened elsewhere.

The Escalation: Rape is a very serious and sensitive topic, yet the politics behind it are as abysmally misleading as the 77 cents on the dollar myth. The purposeful distortion of stories and figures amounts to another attack on men.

Most readers are likely aware of the 2006 Duke University "lacrosse case" in which three white members of the men's lacrosse team were falsely accused of raping Crystal Gail Mangum, a black student from another university who was working as a stripper. The players were indicted on charges of first degree forcible rape and kidnapping. Prosecutor Michael Nifong, early on in the investigation, labeled the alleged assault a racist sex assault and a hate crime. He pursued every possible angle from that assumption. The circumstances in which the alleged incident occurred were sordid and did not bode well for the players—a drunken bash at an off-campus home during spring break for players who had to remain on campus for team practices. Based on circumstantial evidence, the accusations by

Mangum, and further statements by Nifong, university officials suspended the entire lacrosse team and forced head coach Mike Pressler to resign. The lacrosse schedule for 2006 was cancelled. Those actions by the school convinced many that players and coaches were guilty. Thousands of threats were made on their lives; players were hounded and pressured by court officers attempting to coerce confessions. The team was vilified in the press Relations between the university and the city of Durham deteriorated.

Without recapping all the details, evidence soon mounted supporting the stories of the players and showing purposeful tampering with the facts by the prosecution. Within a year Prosecutor Nifong, who may have originally seen the case as a personal political steppingstone, was disbarred for systematic abuse of prosecutorial discretion, a conspiracy to commit malicious prosecution, dishonesty, fraud, deceit, misrepresentation, and lying about DNA tests. The local police department was castigated for circulating posters in the immediate aftermath of the incident which presumed the guilt of the lacrosse players. Thirteen months after the incident, not only were charges of rape against the players dropped, but the judge declared them innocent of all allegations. The accuser was not charged with false accusations as defendants declined to prosecute. The defendants, and other players from the team, did successfully sue the City of Durham, NC and Duke University.

The events surrounding this case are extreme, but they are illustrative of a mindset that has taken hold in America, and that seems to be becoming official policy both on college campuses and in the political mainstream. These attitudes lead to public vilification of those accused; punishing them before they are convicted or even officially charged; then essentially trying the case in a media circus. It results in guilt and conviction by accusation. As part of this syndrome, members of a *victim class* are automatically awarded credence, and members of the *oppressor class* are automatically deemed guilty. Women accusing men of rape are to be believed, defended and consoled. Men being accused of rape are to be immediately distrusted, sequestered, and condemned. Due process is cast to the wind.

Even after being exonerated, presumptions of guilt remain. In the Duke case one might cite *The Price of Silence* by William D. Cohan. As explained by Dorothy Rabinowitz in the Wall Street

Journal: "Mr. Cohan is regularly at pains to make clear: *These were white sons of privilege, from families who could pay for their excellent defense lawyers.* ... [To the author] apparently, true justice is served by... writing ... [a] book attempting *to restore the taint of guilt and suspicion on three young men who had been cleared.*" (My highlights.)

The Duke community is far from being alone in its rush to judgment and prejudicial attitude against men. At Dartmouth College in Durham, New Hampshire proponents of the all-men-are-beasts mentality have escalated the war. In the spring of 2014 student occupiers commandeered the schools main administration building demanding their 72-point manifesto be adopted. As described in a column in the Wall Street Journal, *Oppressed by the Ivy League*, Dartmouth President Phil Hanlon invited the students to discuss their ultimatums, to which the protest leaders responded that talking will only lead to "further physical and emotional violence enacted against us by the racist, classist, sexist, heterosexist, transphobic, xenophobic, and ableist (sic) structures at Dartmouth... our bodies are on the line, in danger, and under attack."

Wow! Talk about being victimized, these poor students with their exceptionally privileged $65,000/year education-lives certainly have it bad. *Oppressed by the Ivy League*, goes on to illuminates how, led by History Professor Russell "Dartmouth-is-White-Supremacy-U" Rickford, the protestors expressed: contempt for free expression, open debate, and due process; how their anger and resentment could not be pacified; and how "reality is not an admissible defense." I want to scream, ARE YOU KIDDING ME?! but the reader can decide for him or herself if this attitude is anti-educational, anti-intellectual, anti-reason, anti-liberal, and/or anti-liberty.

How does this affect the politics and the procedures regarding men on that campus? Dartmouth has created a new Center for Community Action and Prevention to deal with sexual assault and violence. Headed by Amanda Childress, the center is charged with determining the institution's sexual assault policies. So far, so good, except that Childress is on record as asking, during a conference on college sexual assault issues, "Why could we not expel a student based on allegations?" A repeat from above, *due process is cast to the wind,* but now we should add, it is being purposefully, maliciously and prejudicially cast to the wind.

University offices, panels, centers and/or committees are being or have been set up across the country to decide who should be expelled upon allegation—not to decide who should be expelled upon substantiation of allegations. Professor Gordon E. Finley, Ph.D. puts it this way. "...men are stripped of all due process and cross-examination rights... ...the Progressives want to remove the investigation and prosecution of sexual crimes from the venue of the police and courts and rather transfer these responsibilities to unqualified but ideologically sympathetic administrative units..." I'm thinking, that perhaps the Center For Community Action might interpret "requiring criminal complaints be filed with police" as the equivalent of requiring reality to be admissible! Horrors!

Oh, but of course, virtually all victims of these accusations are men. Similar stories in the national media mention Brown, Swarthmore, Auburn, UVA and many more of the nation's 4300 two- and four-year schools.

One in Five

Rape *is* a very serious and sensitive topic. Students, in particular female students, certainly do have a right to be protected from their testosterone-crazed classmates. As many politicians have note—indeed the number has even on the White House website—one in five (1 in 5) college women become the victim of a coerced sexual assault. That is the justification for Centers For Community Action, and for college judicial panels capable of expelling male students on accusation alone. Students, as Ms. Childress noted, "have a right to safety."

The problem is the figure is not only unsubstantiated, it is false and may be false by a factor of at least 100, and perhaps as much as 700 or even more. Those are not percentages. If they were noted as percents the figures would be 10,000% to 70,000%. Those are pretty big errors. Where does the one in five come from?

The Center for Disease Control has reported that 1 in 5 women will be raped over their lifetime, but adds that most rapes occur to women under-18 years of age (prior to college). A University of Colorado (Denver) criminology professor adds that women who do not attend college are 30 percent more likely to be raped than those seeking a degree. The Department of Justice's National Institute of Justice (NIJ) reports that approximately 1 in 5 college women experience some form of sexual assault during their college years. Sexual assault, however, by its definition may include anything and everything from a man *or a woman* calling a woman a derogatory sexual epithet, unwanted ogling, flipping her the bird, attempted forced kissing, engaging in intimate encounters while intoxicated, or brutally and cruelly assaulting and raping her. Let's look at some hard numbers.

In 2013 there were 20,642,819 undergraduate students enrolled in universities in the U.S. Of that number, according to the U.S. Department of Education, National Center for Education Statistics, 56.8% (11,725,121) of all students, were female; and of that number 7,234,623 were full-time students.

The total number of crimes reported to police or school security agencies—including everything from rape to having one's cell phone stolen—was: on campus 30,400; and off campus 35,657. All college and university on-campus and off-campus crimes have been required to be reported under The Clery Act of 1990, and statistics are thus available for 25 years. The probability of anyone being the victim of any crime on campus is about 1 in 680; off campus 1 in 580; and either on or off campus 1 in 312.

The number of **forcible sex offenses** reported under The Clery Act in 2013 was 3,300. Let's assume that 100% of these crimes were perpetrated by males against female students, and that 100% of them were rape. Using the number of all female students, and dividing it by 3,300, the results is 3,553—leaving one to estimate that in any single year 1 of every 3,553 college females is raped. If that number is divided by four years (assuming students stays in school on average four years), the results is 888 or the probability of being raped while one is in school is 1 in 888. If one wishes to cook the books a bit and use only the number of full-time female students, these probabilities increase to 1 in 2192 per year, or 1 in 548 over four years.

It may be argued that the Department of Education isn't getting the full picture, and that rape—even in this time and atmosphere when reporting is promoted and encouraged—is still under reported. Connecticut's senior senator and master of the photo-op, Richard

Blumenthal, recently sponsored the Campus Accountability and Safety Act to make sure that colleges and universities don't allow "staggeringly prevalent sexual assaults" to be "...sweep... under the rug."

Well, let's not sweep anything under the rug. Pick a number. Are there two rapes for every one reported? Three? Four? Five? If it is five, and we use only full-time students, the probabilities become 1 in 438 (0.002283) each year or 1 in 110 (0.00909) over four years. That differs from the 1 in 5 claim by factors of either 87 or 22.

Rape is a very serious issue. The allegation of rape is also a very serious issue. The purposeful distortion of stories and figures amounts to nothing less than an assault on the dignity and character of men; and the skewed painting of men as a horde of rapists is an attack on their values and virtues. How do you think false accusations affect men? How does it affect their self-image; particularly the self-image of our younger generation? Decisions, programs, and/or laws created from false data and built upon false premises inevitably produce unintended consequences.

The Camel Gets His Nose Inside The Tent: "Oh Master, It's cold out here..." begins the Arabian fable about a desert wayfarer who, little-by-little, is forced from his tent by his smooth-talking beast of burden. The story suggests that by allowing small, innocuous concession one enables larger transgressions from which unwanted consequences follow. And so it seemingly is on the campus of Wesleyan University in Middletown, Connecticut.

For background: the Division of Health Interview Statistics of the Center for Disease Control and Prevention, extrapolating from a 2013 interview sample of 34,557 American adults, determined that "96.6% of adults identify as straight, 1.6% identified as gay or lesbian, and 0.7% identified as bisexual. The remaining 1.1%..." either didn't answer the question or checked that they identified as "something else."

With this data for perspective, and with the camel's nose in mind, here is the next stop in the progression of gender politics. Like Dartmouth, Wesleyan prides itself as an institution which champions diversity, inclusiveness, opposition to sexual discrimination, gender equality, student safety, and sexual freedom of expression. In its admirable effort to protect female students from sexual assault and "gender-based power dynamics," the university first ordered its all-male fraternities to admit women, then six months later decided to terminate at least one fraternity's housing program for not making a reasonable commitment to "residential co-education."

Concurrent with the latest round of attacks on the fraternity system the university began promoting housing options for "LGBTTQQFAGPBDSM" individuals: that is for lesbian, gay, bisexual, transgender, transsexual, queer, questioning, flexural, asexual, genderf (sic), polyamourous, bondage/disciple, dominance/submission, and sadism/masochism students. [*Really. I'm not making this up. When I first read an article on this I thought it was a spoof. Wesleyan is located in the same town where I practiced for decades. Over the years I've treated many students from the university; some were amazingly bright, some incredibly arrogant. This story reflects on only one element of the school; but the reflection is not pretty. See Nazworth or Haverluck in Sources, or google Wesleyan LGBT or LGBTTQQFAGPBDSM for verification. I do find it a bit amusing that they left out of their alphabet an N for neutral, a third-gender category recognized by the University of Vermont.*]

The administrations' reasoning behind having women live in fraternity houses is a bit convoluted. Concerned about rape on campus (one might assume that at least a few Wesleyan professors and administrators trust the 1 in 5 myth) and reasoning that frat parties facilitate forcible sexual assaults:

> ...because fraternities are male-exclusive and the possessors of some of our campus' largest party spaces, they explicitly and implicitly cultivate a gender-based power dynamic that privileges men, the hosts, over women, who are among the guests. This power dynamic engenders sexual assault because women are institutionally encouraged to 'repay' men for their hospitality, often with sex, and men are institutionally provided with a control over their guests, especially women...

officials of the university have surmised that having women reside in fraternities would eliminate "the gender-based power dynamics" which encourages sexual assault. (Nazworth)

Okay, I guess. But let's think back to our opening premises—biology is basic, and the gender binary is complimentary, not oppressive. To me, the camel's nose in this instance is confusion, or perhaps the purposeful exploitation of the confusion between biological gender and intellectualized-emotionalized gender identification. This is a culture war being waged against men and against masculinity. We've seen that it starts with little boys being drugged for rough and tumble play. We know that male::female college ratios have flip-flopped. Now it seems men are being singled out and told they cannot have housing or social gatherings unless they are gay, bisexual or willing to be dominated or beaten.

How can one imagine that the banning of fraternities (male-social group housing) while simultaneously promoting gay, lesbian and sadomasochist social-group housing is not prejudicial to men? Or that it won't have a negative impact upon their studies, careers and lives? Academic loads at schools like Wesleyan can be challenging. Discrimination such as the above puts male students at greater risk for failure. Replacing discrimination against a minority—be that sexual, racial, religious or any other category—with discrimination against the majority is *not* a solution to discrimination; yet in the Wesleyan example we seem to have the 96.6% being abused by the 2.3%. In the long run, actions like these will limit the future contributions of men to society.

Thus is the state of American college campuses; the atmosphere in which our future leaders—male and female in academia, business, medicine and public policy—are being steeped. Everything is pointing to: masculinity is unacceptable/femininity and all-other gender identities are acceptable. This does not bode well for a positive future for men or women. When the politics of diversity become the politics of divisiveness, the product of those policies are not inclusiveness and equality but pettiness and an increase in segregation, intolerance and hate.

The master has been driven from the tent. Can the situation get worse? Let's look at...

The Curious Case of Benjamin Babinski

"I know a superintendent of schools," says Dave Larson, the past Executive Director of the Connecticut Association of Superintendents whom we met earlier, "who lost his job because he came into a school office, stood behind two seated secretaries, and put a hand on each woman's shoulder as he looked at their computer screens. A third secretary, not the ones he touched—neither of those two objected—filed a sexual harassment charge."

A more upsetting case is that of another superintendent, one Benjamin Babinski.

Larson identified Babinski as a personal friend. "I was kind of like his father-confessor," Larson said. Babinski came to America as a young boy—the son of Russian Jews emigrating from the repressive Soviet communist state. By all accounts the Babinskis did well in America; the family grew, their warmth and generosity became well known. Benjamin became a teacher, then an assistant principal, principal, assistant superintendent, and was finally chosen as the superintendent of schools for a medium-sized Connecticut town.

Benjamin Babinski is not this man's real name. I have decided not to identify him as his conviction and official punishment (a 30-day suspended sentence and a $15.00 charge for court costs) are at odds with his crucifixion in the local media. There is little to be gained by dragging his name back into the ordeal he experienced for nearly three years; the consequences of which still haunt his life. That being said, I want to be clear that Benjamin Babinski certainly is partly to blame for the tempest which swept him out of education. He seems to have been a man living, at least in his own mind, in an ancient culture; one he never fully understood no longer exists.

Larson says, "Ben grew up in a Russian-Jewish family. They came to America at the time of the pogroms in Europe. They were a family of huggers and kissers. When he sees me he hugs me and kisses me. He hugs my wife. He hugs my granddaughter. He does that to people." Larson further explains that this is a very European affectation, one that is even more exaggerated and more enthusiastically expressed in Babinski's ethnic background. "He hugged teachers and school principals. One of the principals objected and filed sexual harassment charges. The poor bastard... It was high profile. It was in the papers, on TV... But that's how he grew up. That was how men acted in his family. We're in a period where that's unacceptable. If you do that you get arrested, dragged into court, maybe lose your job, your career. Today a superintendent needs to be as chaste as Caesar's wife."

The newspapers were far less kind in their assessment of Babinski. Repeatedly they printed stories about Babinski being charged with two counts each of fourth-degree sexual assault and second-degree breach of peace. Babinski, they said, had been charged with inappropriate touching and kissing of female principals. When the state dropped the sexual assault charges and one breach of peace charges, the papers seemingly implied that the plea bargain that had been struck (pleading guilty to one charge of breach of peace) was a deal with a predator made solely so the town could move on with the hiring of a new superintendent. With the case closed, one paper printed:

> Any doubt... [that] the incidents were blown out of proportion has been erased [by the release of a police report that indicates] ... Although other female school workers said they did not mind [Babinski's] embraces, the superintendent, who had ignored complaints about his remarks and contact with women... offered to resign to prevent the charges from becoming public. The report describes [Babinski] repeatedly touching the buttocks of the two women who filed the complaint, as well as hugs and kisses on the lips.
>
> The... school board's only choice was to remove [Babinski]. His misconduct was compounded by his being these women's superiors. They feared for their careers... if they complained. [His] behavior was not misunderstood as overly affectionate... The superintendent repeatedly engaged in misconduct—sexual harassment—that he should have known was impermissible.

Note, the media story does not say Benjamin Babinski *allegedly* "touched the buttocks of..." It reports this as fact, even though Babinski maintained before, during and after the proceedings that he was innocent. To the paper his misconduct and sexual harassment are fact. The paper also averred this was not a case of "he said, she said." It gets away with these statements because of the legal results. At the close of the case Babinski's attorney indicated that the superintendent could no longer fight the powers that had been deployed against him, and that was the reason he accepted (plead guilty) to the reduced charge.

When I read the stories, I thought something was missing. All the reporting, and even the police report, didn't tell what actually happened. An element of the case and of the entire proceedings was oddly, or perhaps not so oddly, left out. What were the actual negotiations that took place, and what (or who) was the power center driving the deal? What forces were mustered and brought to bear against Babinski? What forced him to throw in the towel?

From these questions you may ascertain why I changed the superintendent's name. I believe there is a strong possibility that Babinski was coerced into the plea bargain—essentially entering a guilty plea which cost him his job, career and reputation—because there was no possibility of him matching the resources that the state was bring to bear against him. If he did not fold and comply with the state's demands, he faced the threat of graver consequences.

The Babinski case does not stand alone. Benjamin's behavior may or may not have been inappropriate, but it seemingly has gotten to the point where accusations are enough to condemn a man. Should that man decide to fight, he had better be prepared for the full weight of the state—powered by taxpayer dollars. He must also be prepared to be exposed on the nightly news and in the daily press, accused—even if the wording is couched in legalese to avoid liability—of awful actions and sinister motives. His picture will be on the Six O'clock News; a reporter will be filmed knocking on his door; his neighbors will be interviewed. As long as the media can get someone to say it, they can report it without fear of liable: "Aw gee, we've lived next door to that guy for twenty years. I always liked him. I never knew he was such a creep!" And the accusers—very often their identity is *protected*! Accusations, carried on page 1, seemingly become proof of criminality. The media becomes the judge, jury and crucifier. Acquittals, if that is the case, will be carried on page 21 beside the ads for used cars.

Let's look at the power center. In the Babinski case one axis likely was the Connecticut Commission on Human Rights and Opportunities (CHRO--pronounced char-row). CHRO is a department of 74 people with a budget of over $5.6 million (at the time Babinski was charged—since then it has increased by 13%). Virtually all states have similar commissions. Dave Larson noted that CHRO "is the biggest pain in the butt for anyone who has to run a business. A woman can go there and make a claim that something was done to her because she is a woman. CHRO will pick it up and run with it."

CHRO does not operate in a vacuum. Once a complaint is accepted, the office can enlist the assistance of numerous state agencies. "They have a battery of lawyers," Larson continued, "who will make your life miserable. You have to jump through all these legal hoops. You have to hire lawyers to protect you. The person making the claim isn't paying for the CHRO attorneys; but you'd better be able to spend a lot of money. That's my observation."

CHRO is funded by taxpayers. The state's attorneys are funded by taxpayers. Prosecutors are funded by taxpayers. CHRO defines protected classes as (amongst others): sex, and sexual orientation or gender identity or expression. Public Act 11-15 states: "...public schools have an affirmative obligation to prevent and respond to harassment and bullying that is based on the protected class of the victim..." and further that "Failure to address harassment or bullying based on the protected classes... can lead to liability for the school district..." Complaints can be brought before CHRO, the State Board of Education (annual budget approximately $3.5 billion), and the U.S. Department of Justice. Charges, accusations, prosecution and/or defense can be expensive for towns. The costs, or the possibility of them, essentially encourage and motivate municipalities to shun the accused and settle as expeditiously as possible.

"A disgruntled person," Larson recalls, "will come up to you and say, 'I'm going to go to CHRO and file a complaint.' I didn't used to see this as an issue of the feminist movement, but they are the ones who induced this into the laws, and we are now dealing with the bureaucracies that the laws built. Any time you have a bureaucracy, it is going to self-perpetuate. It's their livelihood. It's their job. You know, the attitude is: 'We gotta make sure we get the cases. We gotta keep this commission going.'"

Commissions like CHRO actively seek out cases—which is right; but they also actively develop cases which may be questionable or have little foundation. The later, due to the bureaucratic motivation of self-perpetuation and growth, and due to the current ideological motivation spawned by elite elements, sometimes becomes *making a mountain out of a molehill*. Once a complaint has been filed and a case started, there are many positive reinforcements for caseworkers, attorneys, and bureaucrats; and much of this is coupled with feelings of self-righteousness and indignation. Thus the overwhelming power of the state can be brought to bear upon these actions; and usually the accused, with only personal resources, is totally outmatched. In those cases the accused might accept a plea bargain agreeing to unsubstantiated or possible even false guilt simply because the alternative will be far more devastating. The legal system follows due process but resources are so lopsided the results are the equivalent of having a *kangaroo court*; the proceedings seem legit but the outcome is not based upon evidence or fairness. Let's give this a big, one toe up, and call it *A Negative Babinski*.

Crossing the Threshold: Gender-baiters

Traditionally, in exchange for provide and protect men expected love and care from their mates. In some cultures, and within elements of others, love and care morphed from a biologically normal and necessary *quid pro quo*—part of the complimentary gender binary—into various degrees of demand for dependency and servitude. When and where that happened women were indeed oppressed. Throughout history that has been the valid justification for fighting back. The advent of the pill, as mentioned before, changed everything. It created the great female emancipation—the normal and necessary *quid pro quo* was no longer normal and necessary; returning love and care came to be seen by some as oppression. The new view elaborated into The Women's Movement. We are now nearly six decades since that inception.

With so many victories and so many positive changes for women over those decades, why the continuous negativity? Why the continuous defensiveness? Why is there a need to skew the story from reality? At what point does advocacy for women cross the threshold from ensuring equal rights to where the rights of men are subjugated and the humanity of men denied? Why do some advocates feel they must bash everything masculine? And why do politicians pile on?

I would like to make what I believe is an important distinction between advocacy and attack. Advocacy groups are pro-group. They support the causes and issues of the members. That is legitimate. Activists who attack everything that is not-of-their-group are radicals, and they tend to have ulterior motives. When we assess a group's leadership or that leadership's aims, we should first know whether it is indeed an advocacy group or if, in reality, it is an attack group.

This may be speculative: It seems to me that the attitudes of some of the women who were chafing at historic roles, who were liberated by the pill, and who powered the feminist movement of the 1960s, became frozen in time. The behaviors, philosophies and processes which led to successes in the '70s and '80s ossified. The thrill of victory and the experience of power became addictive. These are the women who became the ultra-feminists, the radicals. Their attitudes and actions have not abated even though the pendulum has swung far in their favor.

Perhaps some of the extremists were not secure enough in their new identity to say, "I am a woman and I am okay." The only way they could feel okay was to contrast themselves with men, and to put men down. Not all women did this, of course, but for some reason that attitude gained public prominence and political affiliation. Radical feminism is a media story; successful women—not so much. Radical political positions built upon opposition to perceived oppression attract donations and votes; complimentary gender roles—not so much. Those appointed or elected based upon radical gender positions continuously reinforce the cultural story of oppression—the stories of success just aren't as sexy... nor are they as saleable to publishers or producers. To bolster and maintain personal status, ultra-feminists became the equivalent of race-baiters. I will thus call them gender-baiters.

Gender-baiters, dependent upon the continuation of the conflict, cannot acknowledge equal pay and other gains without putting themselves out of business. To stay in business (and not to disrupt their brains with the cognitive dissonance of contradictions) equality of opportunity needed to be replaced with equality of outcome. Even then—as we've seen with boys in school, college matriculation and graduation rates, and post-graduate degree percentages—with the pendulum swung well in their favor, radical or ultra-feminists have either denied or ignored the positive results and have continued to pursue policies as if nothing had changed in half a century.

Doesn't that make you want to ask them, "Hey, why feel victimized? Why not instead feel thrilled at your achievements? Why not celebrate? It seems to us guys that you ultra-feminists don't think much of us men. Do you have to put us down to build yourselves up? Do you need to show contempt for us in light of the fact that you now have great jobs, make tons of money, can go off anywhere on your own, can party, get drunk, pick up guys, have one-night stands?!" There are no limits.

If equality is the ideal, subjugating the rights of either sex is wrong. Where that happens it needs to be identified and extinguished. Our aims should be to bring things into balance, and to restore an honest society un-skewed by political gender-biases and gender-based lies.

I have more questions: If there is a War On Women, who's waging it? If one identifies *the who*, then he should ask: Why? Who's benefiting? Who's defending their turf? Are the stated targets of this war the real targets of the attacks, or are the stated targets collateral damage in a war with unidentified or hidden objectives?

I don't think the average woman is waging a war on men, and the average man is not waging a war on women. The real assaults come from ideological and partisan elites of one ilk or another: sometimes from academic partisans with specific worldviews and the arrogant claims that they know exactly how all things should be. Radical ideological elites tend to pontificate, and they tend to want to coerce society to live by their conceptions. The also tend to have, or to be connected to someone else's, financial scheme—to what many now call *dark money*. Find out whose benefiting; follow the money; follow nominations for political offices; follow political financials. Whether it is composed of male or female, academic, social, financial or religious zealots, doctrinaire elites want to channel how people live. They want to limit the roles of men and women. They want to limit what people can earn (or at least what they can keep). In that way—even if they are selling human rights, minimum wage, or a chicken in every pot—they can control others. It has become a war of oppression against the individual and against the people; but it is often sold in the terms of class victimization.

Those victimizers, we are often told, are evil white, males of traditional Western societies; and that evil needs to be opposed, broken, and cast on the dung heap of history. To the radical this is not just a battle, it is a revolution. One should make no mistake, the radical has entered into this war as if a military force with the aim of fundamentally transforming traditional society. They do not limit their attacks to the things most of us might agree should be, or should have been, overturned. For the radical it is not enough to gain equality. The radical wants to transform the entire system and "win" the war by reducing to ash everything she or he sees as representative of *the traditional, the other, the non-me.* Ultra-radical feminists have and are using a scorched–earth campaign with the vague concept that a new society will rise from the ashes, and it will be created in their own image.

I think it was Gloria Steinem who came up with the term *male chauvinist pig.* Radical feminism is as chauvinistic as the worst male chauvinism of yore. Its goal is not to put the movement in charge, but to benefit specific leaders of the movement; and to do this the target of opportunity is the average Joe—starting from the time he is an infant. These leaders are Machiavellian and manipulative. Sun Tzu would be proud of their tactics for they haven't needed to fire a shot. We've seen how the radical and rabid minority of ultra-feminists have stacked the deck effecting education and sexual harassment laws. They have formed teams of attorneys, nurtured media outlets, lobbied for laws, built enforcement bureaucracies, and changed the ambient cultural story thereby convincing a majority of people that all of this has been done in the name of fairness and equality.

The phrase The War on Woman has become a shill, a diversion, a subterfuge. It is allowing a very small army—an ultra-political estrogen mafia with allied males—to wage a War on Men, a War on Culture, a War on People, and a War on Personal and National Identity. The radical is not looking for equality; she or he is looking for dominance. This "…second wave of feminism," as it is called by Paul Joseph Watson, "…deliberately confuses gender roles and makes young men apprehensive about exercising their masculinity for fear of being overbearing or aggressive towards women."

We men, in general, do not want to wage a war against women, and we don't want a war waged against us. We want to be allies in all aspects of life. We want to recognize natural differences, not beat up one side or the other for being different. But that is not the case in this culture war which declares masculinity irrelevant; which aims to destroy the vestiges of male values and male virtues in the name of equality; and which benefits in wealth and power the elite of a specific socio-ideological caste.

It comes back to "Who is waging this war?" doesn't it? And why? Some call this a social movement. In reality it is an old fashion con shrouded in false ideals and lead by extremist and their true believers. Like the communists of decades ago, the leaders look at their followers as *useful idiots*. The concept of A War On Women in reality is a component of an ideological war on people designed to control the population. The strongest potential opposition is men; therefore the main attacks must be against masculinity.

Who wants this to happen? Who is benefitting from it? Are there political advantages to specific elites? Not just convincing women that men are the enemy, but convincing racial minorities that the racial majority is the enemy, or ethnic minorities that English-speakers are the enemy, or any economic class that everyone more wealthy than them are the enemy? The War on Women is part of someone's class warfare ideology. Why are we allowing them to divide us for their own advantage? Both sexes end up being the victims of false narratives and deceitful ideologies.

A threshold has been crossed. There may be no turning back. Cumbersome bureaucracies cement false gains in place.

The Rise of the American Apparatchik

Over the past several years I've talked to many people, men and women, who have, or who are, getting out of the business they have been in for much of their adult lives. Again and again I heard them repeat a demoralized mantra, "I can't go back there. I can't take it anymore. I can take the red tape." Often the language was coarser; the speaker utterly disgusted. He or she couldn't take the ever-expanding regulations; couldn't take being put in a position where their best efforts were continuously thwarted. They'd just had it. Without saying it in these words, they were reacting to the rise of the American Apparatchik.

Ah-pa-ra' chik: a Russian colloquialism; a full-time, paid agent of the apparatus; a functionary; one who holds a mid-level bureaucratic or political position of responsibility. The term implies lack of quality, lack of care, poor attitude and incompetence. It also suggests a tenured-like status—one whose occupancy of position is guaranteed or one who cannot be removed except by extraordinary means. As used below (when capitalized) I also mean it in a collective sense—a group of functionaries, bureaucrats and middle managers who have come to infest institutions of government, medicine, education, finance, and many, if not most, other elements of society.

A word of caution here: not all government workers are part of the Apparatchik. Indeed, most are not. I don't say this out of fear of retribution; but out of the recognition that to lump all government employees together is as naïve and as prejudice as the worst racist or sexist bias. Also, by using the term Apparatchik I do not mean to imply an enormous growth in bureaucracy. Although various state and many local governments have burgeoned, over the past three decades the number of people in the federal workforce has barely changed despite a growing American population. This may partly be due to technology and automation reducing the need for manpower; or it may have to do with tens of thousands of non-government contractors having assumed the duties of government employees.

The rise and growth of the American Apparatchik is not a simple numbers game. It is a shift in attitude, a shift in mission, and a shift in power centers. The attitude shift is fueled by laws and regulations, by commissions and bureaus, by righteous beliefs in policies and programs that don't produce the results on which they were sold, by worldviews skewed from reality, by federal patronage and cronyism, and by selfishness and avarice. To be accepted into an Apparatchik one must buy into the narrative that established the system. If that narrative is false, it makes little difference; only allegiance to the narrative is important, only it will insure acceptance and perpetuation. Having and keeping the job becomes one's primary mission; doing the job gets lost in the paperwork—the paper life. Results are secondary to compliance. Power results for the capacity to approve or disapprove what others do; and to punish those who do not comply.

Apparatchik implies a willingness to use any and all resources and powers at the disposal of the functionary to force results acceptable to the narrative, and to the approval of his or her superiors. Functionaries—often timid and smiling—tend to be furtive and duplicitous. They are the ones who have figured *out how the system works*, and how they can make it work for themselves. Wielding the powers of their positions, they become government- or institution-authorized bullies. He or she also tends to be disliked by subordinates and distrusted by superiors. The more institutionalized society becomes, the more power is seated in the Apparatchik, and the more robust the functionary-class becomes.

It is not just in government. We saw this in education in the case of Benjamin Babinski, and we will look at what it did to Graham Seekamp. When I retired fifteen more doctors in my group also left the profession. All were younger than me, in their mid-50s to early 60s. They could take it no longer. This seemingly has happened in the mortgage industry, in real estate, and in financial services. It seem to me a wave of great dissatisfaction has swept the nation; it seems as if people are switching because they are looking for something that makes sense; something that says life still has meaning; someplace where the meaning of their job hasn't been reduced to a check in a box.

In medicine—this is growing as we look on—Obamacare regulations have mandated over 10,000 government auditors. In turn medical practices, hospitals and related businesses have had to add hundreds of thousands of employees to guarantee compliance with these new laws and regulations. This is at great expense to the healthcare system, but the Apparatchik is not concerned with cost-effectiveness. It justifies it existence in terms of fairness, protection of equal access, and compliance oversight. Ignored is the unfortunate circumstance that not a soul has been to patient care.

When the task at hand (patient care) is primary, the task is usually well done—in fact, usually very well; but if the task becomes of secondary importance, quality drops. Under these circumstances job satisfaction also declines. This produces disgruntled worker and devious bureaucrat willing to sabotage the system or inflict pain on others as vindication for their fruitless position.

In some hospitals it seems the primary mission has become compliance with rules, regs and protocols. Recently I was talking to an old colleague about the ruckus caused by an event in a specific unit at a regional facility. Doctors there, I was told, were furious and ready to revolt; and the nurses were distraught and anxious. All this over a unit manager had become so obsessed with compliance—including employee equality measures—that patients were put in severe danger. The final straw that set the doctors off was a patient who likely suffered irreversible brain damage—the results of the unit manager meeting goals by using undertrained staff—but she had been able to check off all compliance boxes.

In the field of education, the American public school student population increased by 96% from 1950 to 2009. During those same years the increase in teachers has been 252%, meaning a better student::teacher ratio exists now than in the post-WW II years when baby boomers began entering kindergarten. In that time frame administrators and non-teaching staff also increased—by 702%. The increase in this last category accelerated over the past two decades as the education apparatchik ballooned. Teacher Graham Seekamp described the current snarl of bureaucratic compliance:

> With Common Core they've restructured the way teachers are evaluated. Someone at the capitol wanted to make sure that we were getting rid of the bad teachers and just keeping the good ones. But the way they've decided to assess us is unrealistic, and takes a tremendous amount of time—time that would normally be spent on making lesson plans and preparing lessons so your classroom runs better. We now have to document everything we do and prove that what we're doing works and justify why we're doing it... taking up huge, huge, huge amounts of time. To implement it we have this new computer program called BloomBoard. It comes out of the private sector. Whoever sold it to the state... they're making money on it. Once the state adopted it, it meant we all had to use it.
>
> All the big rules and big programs we have to follow are made by people who have never been teachers. These people sit in the legislature. They haven't been to school since they were students. Everybody has to do what they say, and a lot of that, at the classroom level, doesn't make sense.

According to the BloomBoard website, "Great teachers are essential to improving student achievement. Unfortunately, providing the personalized feedback and training necessary to nurture and grow effective teachers has traditionally been difficult and expensive." That is the way the program is sold and it certainly sounds good and reasonable. Perhaps if it is used wisely it is a terrific tool, but Graham's experience is likely common.

It's a tool to help administrators figure out what teachers are doing at all times, but the onus falls on the teacher to input the data. First it was insert your goals into BloomBoard. Then ever so many weeks you had to look at the data from these mandated tests and see if the data was matching your goals. Then you had to collect "relics," things that prove what you're doing. Taking pictures of kid's papers, taking pictures of lesson plans, and inserting them all into BloomBoard, compiling this giant portfolio. Then you had periodic reviews with your administrator where you reviewed the BloomBoard documentation to understand how the data was being used and to assess whether or not you were meeting your goal. Then they'd ask, "If you're not meeting your goal, what are you going to do to turn this around so you'll meet your goal?!" BloomBoard became a full time job.

The intension is likely pure, and systems like BloomBoard can be very effective when used properly, but here the bureaucratic structure that had been set up was aimed at a secondary mission of education. It took too much time and energy, and it destroyed teacher creativity and individual initiative. This is common to many bureaucratic functions. The micro-management can be measured, checkboxes can be checked, documentation can prove a job well done... except what is being measured is not the valid and ultimate criteria of either great teachers or a great educational process. Graham continued,

People were going home at night completely spent. I literally had no time to plan lessons because I was constantly trying to prove that I was worthy of being a teacher. Isn't that what I went to teacher's college for? Isn't that what my degree and certifications are for? Haven't I proved that over the previous 15 years? It made no sense. I've been teaching 16 years. I came this close to going to the office and saying I can't do this job anymore. It's impossible.

Not only was it taking up huge amounts of teacher time, every teacher at every level needed a minimum of three observations (by an administrator). With every observation there was a preconference; and then there was a formal post-conference where everything was typed out and signed off on the dotted line. We have sixty some teachers in our school. We have only two administrators. You do the math.

One loci of the problem is nothing new but something that has been debated in an untold number of ways over the past 325 years or more (at least back to the Glorious Revolution of 1688). Is the government responsible for the happiness of its citizens? What should be the government's role in human satisfaction? Should the government intervene in every complaint? Or should the government practice benign or constructive neglect like the parents of my friend, mentioned above; and should it avoid injudicious giving and destructive nurturing as M. Scott Peck suggested to the minister?

The ultimate side effects and unintended consequences of enabling unfocused, mis-focused or irresponsible behavior—even for the most pure motives—are the rise of a self-defeating bureaucratic culture which attacks and destroys the virtues and values of the past. As we witness an ever-increasing nanny state being built with bureaucratic layer laid upon bureaucratic layer in the name of help, verification, protection and oversight, we are also seeing a society brought to a standstill by cumbersome regulations so numerous they act like red traffic lights set up at ever intersection.

Numerous conservative commentators have blamed these effects on "an entitlement culture," but I believe it is less the actual entitlements and more the growing co-dependence between the enablers and the enabled. The Apparatchik doesn't work for men. Men want to get things done. They want to accomplish things. Recall the adage *women cooperate, men compete.* Unless men have been indoctrinated in the new, politically correct culture, they want to compete, to strive for excellence, to be competent, and to complete tasks. The Apparatchik is cumbersome. It doesn't want to get things done, and it certainly doesn't want to get things done quickly. Cooperation is a goal in and of itself. Solutions are not. Solutions, solving problems—the big problems, not the small ones inside the big ones—puts functionaries out of work.

Perhaps the most devastating outcome of the culture war is the damage the growing Apparatchik does to the host society. Bureaucrats and expanding bureaucracies affect a society in much the same way that the corrupted cells in the disease primary amyloidosis affect the vital organs of a patient. In that illness aberrant cells move into the heart, liver and lungs, and displace functioning and productive tissue with benign but non-productive fibrils. Eventually the non-productive mass becomes so copious the organs cease to perform and the patient dies.

Will this be the fate of America? If we raise non-production above the esteem of primary production, if the evaluation of workers becomes more important than the product of their work, won't that strangle the country?

The final product of the Apparatchik will not be insuring equality, safety or fairness, but more likely will be the appalling dismantling and destruction of the American Spirit of independence and self-reliance, the curtailment of the pursuit of happiness and property (except by the elite), and the subjugation of the individual by the weight of the system. Liberty and freedom are in their death throes.

A Rent In The Social Fabric

We have mentioned this before: to be successful every relationship and every society requires trust. If there is a breakdown in the trust between husband and wife, or father and son, the relationship fails. Similarly if there is a breakdown in the public trust—between the people and their institutions, or simply between people in general—the society fails.

Recently I was talking to an old patient, a businessman, who said to me, "We used to do business face-to-face and on a handshake. Even if we had a contract the real agreement was man-to-man. I can only recall being screwed once. Then things changed. Now our contracts are four times longer and they're ironclad. Plus there are fifteen more pages of disclosures. Now everybody is looking for an edge, an advantage. That's a nice way of saying they're all out to screw you. And they do."

His plaint equates to a breakdown in public trust at a most basic level. When that happens... well, let me back up.

I've mentioned earlier how witty nurses could be with their off-colored jokes and foul language; how they'd call the trans-rectal biopsy instrument a Black n' Decker Pecker Wrecker; or how'd they joke in the OR, giving back or initiating exchanges that might make a Marine blush.

Those were the days, really not very long ago, of camaraderie and trust. In the OR it got pretty intense because what we did was intense. So the jokes and quips were outlets; stress-relievers. There was no harm meant by them. It brought the unit closer together, and that meant the unit worked more efficiently.

Now you have people thinking, "I better not tell that story, or I might be charged with sexual harassment, or maybe with creating a hostile or unfriendly workplace." When everyone is on guard camaraderie and unit bonding are interrupted. One side-effect of laws designed to prevent anyone from feeling uncomfortable is a breakdown of trust, which in turn causes a breakdown in the relationship between co-workers. That has further ramifications, thus it becomes both effect and cause.

The collapse of trust creates a constellation of behavioral changes in individuals and in society; and the degree of the collapse can be matched to the degree of aberrant behaviors within different segments of society or during different time periods. These changes can be seen across a broad spectrum of social components —from academia to business, from medicine to the military, from town meetings to national elections. Everything is influenced: marriages and families, homes and property, individual and national debt, race and race relations, aggression, xenophobia and the pursuit of happiness.

A teacher or principal or superintendent avoids hugging a student or co-worker. Sexual harassment charges are avoided, but so too is affection. Human beings thrive on affection. As affection decreases, so too does trust. This sets off a cyclone, a descending spiral. Women accuse men of not being sensitive, not showing their feelings—or of not having feelings. Men withdraw. Author Helen Smith in *Men On Strike* says:

> "…men aren't dropping out because they are stuck in arrested development. They are instead acting *rationally* in response to the lack of incentive society offers to them to be responsible fathers, husbands and providers. …men are going on strike, either consciously or unconsciously, because they do not want to be injured by the myriad of laws, attitudes and hostility against them for the crime of happening to be male."

Trust between guys, thrust within a society in general, breaks down when you have regulations which define all behavior, and which dis-incentivizes trust. You can't show feelings. They can't show feelings. The custom of drinking or getting drunk with someone you don't know in order to establish trust has been legislated out of existence... you're more apt to end up in jail or in court than to end up with a friend.

When government regulations overshadow every aspect of business and of life, it is essentially as if the government is saying to the citizens, "We don't trust you. We have to look at everything you do; we have to read every one of your emails; we have to record every one of your phone calls; we have to set up surveillance cameras on every street to watch you... *you are not to be trusted*." In his mind the citizen responds, "You say I'm not trustworthy. If that is so, if I'm not trustworthy enough to take care of myself, I must not be responsible for myself—or for anything. Take care of me." The state then smiles, "Yes, we will take care of you," and adds in a whisper, "just a notch above the subsistence level. You will be a ward of the state, and our indentured servant."

Society is a biological entity. One expects safety and security (herd protection) from one's social entity. If one no longer trusts the greater group, he is not going to rely on it, but instead will attempt to protect himself, his family, his sect. That leads to fragmentation which further destroys the cohesiveness of society.

In addition to distrust, surveillance—I don't want to call it spying—alienates people from the group and makes the feel that they are being targeted. Even worse, those that want to maintain their status quo within the group are hampered by the fear of being caught doing something which might be construed as unacceptable. Do you recall the image of the guy in the office? A superbly constructed, well-dressed, delightful woman walks in. He is hardwired to look. Somebody with a smart phone snaps his picture as he's focused on her butt. They upload the photo. Suddenly he's a bad guy. He's staring at her body; he's a pervert; he doesn't respect women; he's sexually harassing her; he's a dirty old man. It makes no difference that the response was automatic. One sensing that he cannot express his full range of thoughts and emotions traps energies inside. Ultimately they erupt. They are destructive to self if aimed inward, or to others if aimed out.

I think this all goes to the very top of our national leadership. What we have is a trickle-down scam society. It used to be that citizens pretty much trusted the guys at the top—think about General Eisenhower, then President Eisenhower. There probably wasn't anyone who was more trusted than him... Kennedy a bit less, LBJ, less, Nixon less,[does anyone recall Ford?], Carter less... had the country not been as strong as it was at the time he likely would have done more damage than he did. Followed by Reagan... some people didn't like him, didn't like his policies, but the trust in his leadership was higher than most in the list above. It dropped under Bush I, dropped precipitously under Clinton, moved up during the early Bush II years, post 9/11/01, then wavered and tumbled, and now is in complete freefall.

There is a carryover in trust from the top of a society to the bottom. We are seeing scams and scandals again and again—and we are seeing a trickle-down scam mentality where everybody is out to scam everybody else. Recall also that trust and the expression of trust are factors in creating personal story. One who is distrusted internalizes that trait into his or her self-image, and his or her behavior tends to reflect the self-image of being untrustworthy. Individuals and societies who are not trusted become not just untrusting, but become devious. This is a sickness, a psychosis.

With this rent in the social fabric one doesn't automatically trust one's neighbor; one doesn't even automatically trust people within their own family. Administrations in some schools have gotten to the point where if a child repeats something said by his or her parent, authorities can go after the parent. It's reminiscent of Hitler youth, and all those communist societies we used to despise; it brings to mind all the tyrants who used youth against their parents, neighbors against neighbor. Turn someone in to the government over anything and be rewarded. This completely destroys trust amongst people. When that happens—when this rent in the public trust becomes deep—you end up with a society that is less trustworthy and less responsible, and less accountable. That society then wants to be taken care of; wants others to be responsible for them; sees others not fulfilling their needs; feels great dissatisfaction. It's not a very pretty society. It sounds like some Third World nation, but I'm afraid that is where we are heading. It will require great leadership to reverse this course.

A new term (at least to me) has entered our lexicon: *The Paper Life*. Friends have been slipping it into conversations; academics reference it in articles. Using the term shortens the need for explaining what they are enduring on their job and within their personal lives. The term is symbolic and symptomatic of the breakdown in public trust that corresponds to the explosion in regulations and the ebbing of self-reliance and the spirit of independence.

The paper life is the way we now document actions taken. The reasoning behind it is a CYA (cover yer ass) mentality, a defensive response to the overabundance of regulations and penalties. It is aimed not at accepting responsibilities but at avoiding any possibility of being blamed and penalized. It is a hospital unit manager checking off all the right boxes despite improper patient care being delivered. It is also a doctor forced to lie to either protect himself or to protect his patient. He checks off a box—the never-ending box-checking—stating such-n-such which he knows isn't real but knows it is the only way he can get the approval to treat his patient in the way he's convinced the patient needs. The physician is forced to compromise his ethics; the rule follower suffers angst; the doctor opens himself up to legal actions and recriminations; the man's job satisfaction dissolves.

The paper life also promotes risk and responsibility avoidance; which in turn furthers the fractionalization of society by decreasing the individual's ability and desire to contribute to the success of society. As Dave Larson put it, "to want to make the nation work," or as Graham Seekamp noted, "People still want to do the right thing. It breaks down when they feel powerless, and can do nothing but what is required by regulation." Put another way—the imposition and stress of the tons of paperwork dumped into every facet of our lives triggers resentment; resentment triggers sabotage and elicits a 'F**k You' response.

Dissatisfaction and distrust—spawned by the ever-increasing layers of bureaucracy designed to oversee and enforce every-increasing regulations—are driven by social agendas, monetary incentives and disinformation. When one has an agenda—and it makes little difference if one is an academic, a researcher working for a pharmaceutical company, a social scientist advocating for a government program, a political activist backing his or her party, or a corporate bean counter pursuing the bottom line—one tends to discover data which supports that agenda. This may not be malicious, or even conscious, but conclusions, supported or not, are often false. The very best scientific procedures are subject to experimental bias. Introduce agendas and monetary incentives and the conclusions from those procedures become suspect. We'll return to this in a moment.

More than ever Americans distrust government and institutions. The 2014 General Social Survey conducted by a team from the University of Chicago reported that only the following percentages of Americans had *"a great deal of confidence"* in the these institutions:

The Supreme Court	23%
The Executive Brach	11%
Congress	5%
Banks	15%
The U.S. Military	50%
The U.S. Media	7%

Note: those trusting the media to get the story straight were at an all-time low; and those fully distrusting the media were at a record high.

Why? What has so destroyed the public trust? Scandals (*too inconvenient to carry two cell phones*)? Idiocy (*we'll just throw together this 2000-page law that will impact one sixth of the economy, enact it without knowing what's in it, and...*)? Debt (*your portion of the public debt now stands at $54,620. So does your son's. And your two-year old grandson's*)? Purposeful disinformation (*al qaeda is finished; you can keep your doctor; the reform is affordable; the economy is well on its way to recovery*)? The list is finite but is so infuriating it would take infinite patience to document. Let's look at one example: employment/unemployment.

In the late winter of 2015 much of the media reported a drop in the unemployment rate to 5.5%—a seven year low. The post-WW II average, according to the U.S. Bureau of Labor Statistics, is 5.83%. The 5.5% represents 8.7 million people out of work.

Well, Hurray! We're #1! Doin' Great! Except... there's a nagging feeling the numbers have been cooked. The percent of people in the workforce is at a 37-year low. In February 2015, according to the BLS, the potential labor force (16 years old and older, not in the military or incarcerated) was 249.9 million; 157.0 million had jobs or were actively seeking employment; and 92.9 million adult Americans were not participating in the labor force. That last number includes retirees (about 55.9 million), leaving 37 million people who may be stay-at-home moms or dads, people who simply do not want to or need to work or who are working in the underground economy, and all the people who are out of work and who are so disillusioned that they are no longer actively seeking employment. If that last category is one quarter the 37 million it numbers at 9.25 million. Add that to the official 8.7 million unemployed (and to the 157.0 million labor force total) and the unemployment rate looks like 11.4%

I would suggest my estimate is closer to reality, or at least closer to what most people are sensing. Couple this with underemployment and it leaves people shaking their heads. One month last fall (2014) the media reported the creation of nearly 300,000 jobs during the previous month. On fuller analysis the new jobs actually totaled closer to 725,000, however job losses of 425,000 reduced to creation to the net figure. Looking a bit closer one found that nearly 350,000 of the lost positions had been full-time jobs with benefits; but only some 30,000 of the created jobs were in this category. Nearly 90% of the new jobs were part-time or temporary, and without benefits. But the official unemployment rate dropped.

Comments by politicians touting the drop, and reportage by media outlets cheerleading the announcement, add to the creation of the credibility gap. Knowledgeable guys hate that hype. It exacerbates the rent in the public trust.

Concerns like the above are not new. In different forms we Americans have been dealing with them for centuries. Many of the controversies of the early years of our republic dealt with government expenditures and the national debt as they related to government control over citizens (i.e. lack of freedom and liberty). Writing about the political squabbles of the late 1820s and the 1830s Carl Lane noted, "Debt [to President Andrew Jackson] meant dependence upon creditors, and *obligation of the majority to a minority, a burden on the many to the advantage of the few.*" The emphasis is mine. Today we talk about the growing gap between the rich and the poor, or the 1% and the 99%. The meanings are the same. Lane additionally described Jackson's position, "Borrowing tempted government to overspend and to expand beyond its legitimate sphere. Debt, in brief, corrupted government... public indebtedness was the mother of abusive power..." The author mentions Thomas Jefferson's influence on

Jackson, "…dependence begets subservience and venality, suffocates the germ of virtue, and prepares the fit tools for the design of ambition."

The national debt, wiped out under Jackson, returned quickly and has never abated. Crises and war have expanded debt, and more recently social programs have added to its expansion. American national debt grew zero to approximately $8 trillion in the 175 years from 1837 to 2008, and in the next six or seven years has more than doubled to $18 trillion. With each increase there has been a corresponding increase in dependence upon creditors, a heavier burden on the majority to the advantage of the minority, and greater arrogance and abusiveness of power by elected officials and the apparatchik who licks their boots.

Increases in dependency and heavier burden mean not just less political freedom, but they mean all freedoms have been mortgaged; they mean the pursuit of happiness (being able to keep the fruits of one's labor and initiative) has been leashed; and they mean that the average man's capability to compete to strive for competence and for excellence, … to provide, to protect and to prosper have been hampered and limited. Is it then any surprise that America's trust in government and institutions is at an all-time low?

But so what? So what if we the people are no longer as free as we once were, as our idealized projections of ourselves might fantasize us to be? So what, if in exchange for universal health care (a misnomer, one of the big lies as we've seen, essentially an abusiveness Apparatchik, a system established for the massive profits of the few with lip-service benefits to the many) we, as a people, have become more subservient. So what if the very heart of our virtue has been asphyxiated leaving a diverse and disparate society with each sub-sect clawing at every other just to breathe?

SO WHAT?! Are you kidding me?! We are Americans. We are better than this. When we, as a society, again believe, as Dave Larson put it, in "making the country work;" when we again believe in E pluribus Unum—one out of many—one people looking out for each other, that's when we will again be a healthy and happy nation. That's when the rent in the public trust will be healed.

Unfortunately, the course that has been set is taking us further from, not nearer to, that destination.

The Real War On Science

I don't like idiocy. I don't like a lack of common sense. I don't like information being manipulated. I don't like it when someone proclaims they are pursuing truth, but if the truth is inconvenient they block that path and choose an alternate course. I don't like these things in others, and I really dislike it if I catch myself skewing reality because of one prejudice or another.

Science, to me, is the quest for truth. It is seldom an easy journey. All sorts of things can get in the way, and history is full of examples. Medicine and medical research are no exception.
In recent years much to do has been made in the media and on campuses about The War On Science, about deniers of "accepted science", and about skeptics of one scientific theory (actually most of the time these are hypotheses) or another. Many of the arguments are political. Acceptance of some of these theories holds tremendous monetary value extrinsic to the actual science—that is, funding and the businesses associated with results may be worth millions, billions, even trillions of dollars. Often political assertions exhibit little understanding of science, scientific principles, or the difficulties and pitfalls faced in experimentation and theory formation.

Accepted Science and *Settled Science*, as used by politicians, are nice catch phrases, but they are the antithesis of *Science*. In the words of Albert Einstein, "Science is not and will never be a closed book. Every important advance brings new questions. Every development reveals, in the long run, new and deeper difficulties."

Today I am reading a story about "punishing deniers." It makes me think I am living back in the time of Pope Urban VIII, back nearly four hundred years. In 1633 Urban VIII had Galileo Galilei arrested for promoting heliocentrism, the idea that the earth revolves around the sun. The theory was not new. It had been published by Nicolaus Copernicus in 1543 in his book *On The Revolution of the Celestial Spheres*. Ninety years later, with the scientific revolution of the Renaissance heating up, and with authority feeling challenged (the church had banned heliocentrism decades earlier as false and contrary to scripture), Urban VIII threatened Galileo Galilei with punishment—torture, imprisonment and being burnt at the stake—for daring to challenge "accepted beliefs." Galileo was to be put on trial at the Inquisition headquarters of the Holy Office.

Pendulums swing. Science attacks traditional authority. Pendulums swing back. Someplace in the middle there is a truth; but also dark areas of the unknown, and gray areas of the believed to be so that will later turn out to be false. In medicine science strikes back at "science" for promoting accepted truths which should never have been accepted, and which hold little truth. "Much of what medical researchers conclude in their studies," writes Jacob Brogan in a 2010 article in The Atlantic titled *Lies, Damned Lies, and Medical Science*, "is misleading, exaggerated, or flat-out wrong." Brogan's exposé is disturbing—not so much for the specifics but for the patterns of bias and deceit he describes. It becomes all the more upsetting in light of what we've discussed about the Apparatchik and other bureaucracies, and about the loss of trust and trustworthiness. We will not confine our thoughts only to medicine. Once the patterns are understood, we'll extrapolate into other areas of inquiry.

Brogan's piece centers on Dr. John Ioannidis, C.F. Rehnborg Professor in Disease Prevention, Professor of Medicine, Health Research and Policy, and of Statistics at Stanford University. Ioannidis is a meta-researcher, and "one of the world's foremost experts on the credibility of medical research." (His investigations launched the *evidenced-base medicine* movement which I believe has been, to some extent, hijacked, and the original intent besmirched—thus my criticism in The Business of Medicine.) Ioannidis starts his questioning of medical research by asking, have pharmaceutical companies manipulated their studies to increase the appeal of their products? This reminds us of the Biederman Scandal of unreported compensation for ADHD studies, but here the pattern is replayed manifold and at greater amplitude.

The transgressions are not simple; and out-and-out falsification is less frequent than the engineering of experimental design to produce desirable, usable, and possibly advertise-able results. For example a study might purposefully avoid measuring "critically important 'hard' outcomes... such as survival versus death," but instead measure 'softer' data "such as self-reported symptoms." We see this in advertised medications when the voiceover says, "...many people reported relief in the first..." minute, day, week, month... (pick one you've heard).

Ignored in other studies may be data which indicates that factors other than the drug being tested may be responsible for improvements in test subjects; and in yet other research marginally positive results may be reported simply as positive giving a false impression of effectiveness.

Some studies are like good trial lawyers; they ask only questions to which the researcher already knows the answer. Brogan gives an example in which a pharmaceutical company study compares its new drug not to other effective therapies but purposefully to products "known to be inferior." Again you've seen the results on TV, "Xyz has been shown to be nine times more effective than that other brand!"

Malleable data and biased research designs are at the core of the distrust of Big Pharma; however doctors, hospital boards and insurance companies tend to trust published research. When studies are exposed, boards and companies tend to be insulated from criticism, but trust in caregivers, the only ones who actually interact with the patients, deteriorates.

Dr. Ioannidis, Brogan tells us, has been on a campaign against "misleading, exaggerated, and flat-out wrong," studies. "He charges that as much as 90 percent of the published medical information that doctors rely on is flawed." These pervasive flaws are the result of medical research being "riddled with conflicts of interest," caused by an obsessive need for approval of research grant money, and by a corresponding mutation of research motives.

Studies go wrong and science becomes dysfunctional when:
--questions posed (the hypotheses) are biased
--research is design to find specific results
--subject and control selection is not random
--data analysis is selective
--interpretation and presentation of results highlights only positives
--researchers are chasing career-advancing findings, not truth
--selection by scientific journals is based on a Wow-factor
--money is used to suppress opposing studies.

Brogan writes:

> We think of the scientific process as being objective, rigorous, and even ruthless in separating out what is true from what we merely wish to be true, but in fact it's easy to manipulate results, even unintentionally or unconsciously. "At every step in the process, there is room to distort results, a way to make a stronger claim or to select what is going to be concluded," says Ioannidis. "There is an intellectual conflict of interest that pressures researchers to find whatever it is that is most likely to get them funded."
>
> … To get funding and tenured positions, and often merely to stay afloat, researchers have to get their work published in well-regarded journals, where rejection rates can climb above 90 percent. Not surprisingly, the studies that tend to make the grade are those with eye-catching findings. But while coming up with eye-catching theories is relatively easy, getting reality to bear them out is another matter. The great majority collapse under the weight of contradictory data when studied rigorously.
>
> … In the paper, Ioannidis laid out a detailed mathematical proof that, assuming modest levels of researcher bias, typically imperfect research techniques, and the well-known tendency to focus on exciting rather than highly plausible theories, researchers will come up with wrong findings most of the time. *Simply put, if you're attracted to ideas that have a good chance of being wrong, and if you're motivated to prove them right, and if you have a little wiggle room in how you assemble the evidence, you'll probably succeed in proving wrong theories right.* (my emphasis.)

Oh my! Proving wrong theories right?! Ioannidis' meta-analyses found that 30 to 50 percent of "the most acclaimed" medical research was questionable. This is the state of medical science in the second decade of the 21st century. It is a state in which money, political perspective and prestige sway researchers from the truth. That is the real War On Science.

This is far different than what most commentators imply when they use the phrase. A more common connotation is that Christian fundamentalist's beliefs in creation and the age of the world are a war on modern thought; or anyone expressing skepticism of "accepted science" is assailing Knowledge.

We've see this mugging of science in other areas--in the assertions of inequality in wages, and in the hype regarding sexual assaults on campus. We've see it too in the accusation that the gender binary is innately oppressive, and in the supposition that gender identities are genders. There's no science to these claims. These are opinions. People are entitled to their opinions, but that doesn't make them correct. Claiming the opinions are based in science is an assault on truth, and as we've seen this is often an assault on men and masculinity. Michael Medved noted in a column titled, The Utopian Left and Its War On Science, "The Left... eagerly embraces laughably unscientific views on gender and sexuality, despite an abundance of well-researched and readily available research to contradict their convictions."

Pope Urban VIII might also be said to have been waging a War On Science. So too might it be said of former Vice President and founder of the Climate Reality Project, Al Gore. In the spirit of Urban VIII, Mr. Gore has proposed to "punish climate change deniers," and has suggested that political activists who do not share his view suffer legal consequences for voicing their perspectives.

As note numerous times earlier, one must *follow the money* and look to see who will benefit from proposed policies. Let me say here, I am not a proponent of burning fossil fuels. They are dirty and require a great deal of cleaning and scrubbing to keep particulates and pollutants out of the air. I am not an engineer so this is just opinion, but to me photovoltaics and new storage systems (like the Tesla batteries being developed for home usage) show great promise not only for clean energy but also for individual independence from power companies and from bureaucracies develop to monitor and regulate the power grid. We're not there yet. As technology improves and these products enter mass production, market forces may send my oil-burning furnace the way of the horse and buggy. I hope so.

But right now we must deal with oil and gas, and we must understand a bit about them in a historical sense as that should impact our scientific perspectives. Advocates tend to ignore:

1) that as European populations recovered from the plagues of the 14th and 15th centuries, people—needing warmth—deforested

nearly the entire continent (creating one of the impetuses for exploration and the founding of the New World—the search for trees. As an aside, accepted science in 1345 said the plague was caused by a great pestilence in the air attributed to the conjunction of three planets.);

2) that from discovery, Western Europeans settlers in North America denuded much of the land of trees (creating one of the motivations behind the slogan, Go West, Young Man, Go West);

3) that the discovery of oil at Oil Creek, Pennsylvania in 1859, and the subsequent switch to oil as a fuel reduced the demand for wood as fuel and is the single most important factor in the reforestation of Europe and eastern North America;

4) that Mr. Gore's "putting a price on carbon" means treating carbon emissions as a commodity (or more accurately—emissions would be quantified, a charge would be levied per unit, the unit would be the commodity; allowances to emit units of carbon would be tradable). The carbon-commodity exchange (think soy beans and hog bellies) would become the largest commodity exchange ever (think in terms of trillions of dollars per year), actually trading more value than all current commodity exchanges combined (in comparison Eddie Murphy's orange juice ruse in *Coming To America* would be like finding a soggy dollar bill in the gutter); and

5) that in citing the "science" behind the models (hypotheses) of global warming/climate change, the deforestation of the central Asia landmass is often ignored. That deforestation began in earnest in the 1960s and accelerated thereafter. Without tree cover solar insolation heats land to higher temperatures, the air above the land then heats and rises creating currents. When the landmass is the size of central Asia, the rising currents significantly alter global air currents. By 1970 this biogeophysical effects was so great it distorted both the southwest and northeast monsoons across all of Southeast Asia. Trees also fix CO_2 ameliorating carbon emissions. It is not a matter that a large body of scientific inquiry hasn't been done in the area of forest modification of geophysical energy flux, it is a matter that many activists pick and choose their data, and even their results, and exploit only those studies which support their political activism. With the amount of money involved, one would be hard pressed to believe experiments don't have built-in biases, or worse; and that some data is

misreported and other data is deleted or suppressed from publication ala Climategate.

So a second front in the real War On Science may be being waged by the very people who are most loudly screaming there is a war on science. If it fits into what they think is politically correct, and you attach to that the ability to attack the people who don't agree with you, that that's a very powerful weapon. When a man challenges these *settled science* assumptions, others like Al 'Urban VIII' Gore are there to threaten and punish them.

History instructs that threats of punishment are often realized. Galileo Galilei, for example, was found "vehemently suspect of heresy," and placed under house arrest for the remainder of his life.

Political Correctness: An Insidious Artificial Sweetener

It started with words; one here, one there.

If you're a urologist you know and you use the word *micturate*. Or at least you did. In school your urology texts had sections on micturition disorders. At some point twenty or twenty five years ago someone in the hospital system decided it was an inappropriate term, and we were told we could no longer use it when talking to patients.

At first I laughed and made fun of the new rule—just some silly detail, someone with a bug up there rectum—but soon the list of forbidden terms began to grow. Don't say bowel evacuation. Don't say this, don't say that. I found the directives intrusive and annoying, and I challenged the wordlords, "What are we supposed to say?" They answered in serious tones, "Use every day language."

As a urologist I often talk to people about their sex habits. I queried the wordlords, "Should I ask, 'Hey, did ya get laid last night?'" They didn't think that was funny. In fact, they thought my question inappropriate, even though I really was seeking clarification. Well... maybe I was trying to show them just how ridiculous they were being, but I felt it was less appropriate to talk to my patients as if they were ignorant or stupid than it was to use relatively common anatomical and medical terms, and to define those terms if necessary. I considered that part of *patient education*. The wordlords considered it intimidating, perhaps even hostile.

In the end I lost. The mechanisms controlling what we say grew stronger and began to invade every aspect of life in America. Oh, pee and pooh! (Yes, those *are* considered appropriate terms!)

At the gym the trainers have had similar experiences. One explained:

When you're trying to get your client to do a certain exercise, and you are trying to help him feel a certain muscle, you cue the person. Let's say we're doing a leg exercise. I place my fingers on the guy's knee to isolate his focus on those muscles. But now it's like, "You can't just go and put your finger on somebody. First you have to ask, "May I touch you?" You've already established a rapport with this guy as his trainer. You're there with him talking about muscles and joints and things that are moving, and you just touch the person in flow with the exercise. If you stop and say "Oh, can I touch you?" you've just created an awkward situation. You've interrupted the natural flow of exercising and you've put up a wall between the two of you.

Even with female clients, once you have that rapport and they understand that all you're talking about is working a certain muscle or muscle group, and you're trying to get them to feel it... I've never had an issue. I've trained people for over twenty years and I've never had anyone ever complain. I don't think it's an issue unless you make it one.

And that's the point. It's not an issue until and unless you make it one. Any single issue can be made to sound legit, or all important, or the root of abuse. But issues are not principles—not consistent, coherent and complete codes of conduct or ethics. When one isolates an issue, or a word, and attacks its contemporary usage, it is usually pretty easy to make it sound ugly. This is similar to isolating a small target in war, then bringing overwhelming firepower against it. The strategy almost always produces a win. With enough skirmishes won, the enemy will wither; when the enemy withers, the war can be won.

Political Correctness, of course, is not restricted to terms like micturate, or to behaviors involving bodily contact. It is a weapon in the War on Culture. In the words of British author Theodore Dalrymple, Political Correctness "...attempt[s] to reform thought by making certain things unsayable; it is also the conspicuous, not to say intimidating, display of virtue (conceived of as the public espousal of the 'correct,' which is to say 'progressive' view) by means of a purified vocabulary and abstract human sentiment. To contradict such sentiment, or not to use such vocabulary, is to put yourself outside the pale of civilized men…"

In our model of story, PC is a way of changing individual and cultural story, thereby changing individual and cultural self-images and the behaviors that are consistent with those self-images. PC is a tool in a long-term campaign to fundamentally transform our lives, to change our beliefs and attitudes to correspond with those of the wordlords and other elites. It is part of the power grab: limit input, limit thought, channel self-image, then watch as people emerge from metamorphosis as compliant units. Once accomplished, the elite will not need to use force.

Women, too, have been harmed and hoodwinked: One highly-successful friend said, "We were sold a bill of goods. We were convinced we could have it all." The women's movement did not only result in women being able to work, which was great, but for many it resulted in women having to work. And most jobs, like most jobs that are held by men, are not particularly glamorous or fulfilling. Some women have risen to become CEOs of major corporations or institutions, but for most, again like for most men, the job is controlled by others, by bosses, and women are workers, drones, cogs in someone else's machine—so much for liberation! "We were told we could have it all," says my friend. "We could have careers; delay childbearing until we were well-established. For me and for many of my friends we delayed too long. It is more difficult to get pregnant when you're forty than when you're twenty-five, and the risk of birth defects increases dramatically. A lot of us feel we were pressured into making these choices by a public attitude which looked down on motherhood. I postponed trying to have children and then found it was too late for me." For my friend this was a continuity of life issue. She has had "a wonderful life… but when it's over, it's over."

Guns and gun control: The issue is not the guns. With the mass shootings of the past several years we're beginning to hear more and more that it is a mental health issue. It is a matter that the perpetrators are nuts. Now think of the cause of their mental illnesses. Think of this in connection with what we said in the War On Boys. If these terrible acts are primarily mental health issue, and the PC reaction is to restrict boys even further, won't that create more mental health issues? In this light, laws and regulations enacted to conform to PC beliefs will actually exacerbate, not reduce, the problem. Behaviors of this sort by legislators or executive branch officials—making things worse in the name of making them better—is psychotic.

History hijacked: PC is invasive and pervasive. A while back I watched a National Geographic special about John F. Kennedy and his early years. I had forgotten about his experiences in Poland in 1939 when Nazi Germany was negotiating a non-aggression treaty, just before its tanks rolled across the border. It was an event which shaped JFK's worldview. During WWII he may or may not have been a terrific naval officer—there's some legitimate debate about his actions as commander of PT 109—but his service and his previous experiences made him a strong supporter of the military. That never wavered. A few nights after the first program I watched one about the war in Vietnam. The production claimed that in 1963, just before he was assassinated, JFK was about to withdraw U.S. forces from Southeast Asia. That seems to be the prevailing wisdom, but research shows only minor evidence to back it up, and shows much greater evidence to the contrary. Much of the historical narrative of that war has been hijacked and warped by people wanting to make the narrative back their political position. It is not the only history being warped. The problem is often national decisions are made relying upon distortions. This is tragic. Basing actions on anything skewed means you are relying on an unreal world and reacting to unreal circumstances. The products of actions taken under such circumstances are unlikely to match the forecasted, desired or expected outcomes.

Political correctness is an artificial sweetener: It tastes good. It seems good. You think it is good for you, but it has insidious short-term and long-term effects. Immediately upon ingestion, as you are sensing pleasurable sweetness on your tongue, your digestive system is signaled to produce enzymes, and insulin begins to flow to process non-present sugars. An imbalance in body chemistry ensues; true biological needs are not met. Carbohydrate cravings caused by frequent usage result in behaviors that cause weight gain, and the 'unused' enzymes in the gut create digestive disorders. Confusing the process is false story—teachings and advertisements—that tell us artificial sweeteners help reduce weight. A sickly, deceptive feedback loop is established.

Political correctness does the same to the body politic. The skew from reality results in cumbersome regulations which further imbalance the body causing cravings for ever greater regulation to counter unintended consequences. Real needs are not met. The weight gain of new rules and regs forms a dense matrix which binds the organism. Said more simply, one symptom of PC is societal bloating and constipation.

Every facet of American life has been assailed. We've seen it in medicine, in education, at the gym, amongst working women. It has had tremendous effects on the economy. Most people do not realize that the financial systems became so bogged down with regulations, the regulations themselves were a major element behind the slow and still lagging recovery.

Righteousness, Justification and Vindictiveness: So I say, "Harrumph! Micturate on PC!" Hmmm! Not very nice of me. And I'm a guy who prides himself on his good manners, a guy who enjoys and expects others to be mannerly. But the weight of PC has made me angry—and I'm thinking revolt is not just important but is essential. Exposure of PC is important because the PC wordlords and behavior police often seem to simply be enforcing good manners. How could anyone object to that? But that's simply the righteousness and justification behind their assaults. It is not the reality.

The beating heart behind the PC chest is a hateful and fearful child which must strike out and destroy anyone and anything which opposes it. Adversaries are attacked not for their public policies or proposals—PC must appear fair, open and democratic—but instead for personal flaws, if they can be found, uncovered and exploited. Want to remake an institution in your own image, go after the leaders. Don't like the military because of its culture of integrity and tradition of honor contrasts so strongly with your arbitrary conceptions designed to enhance your own powerbase, then take down your top generals for private trysts that seem puerile compared to the scandalous and tawdry affairs of the political class. With these men of honor sullying their reputations and shattering their credibility prevents them from mounting a challenge to authority. (More on attacking the military below.)

PC is a tool: In the hands of a tyrant PC is frightening. It is a North Carolina prosecutor bullying students; it is campus safety councils expelling men on accusation, or administrators determining social-group housing from unsubstantiated figures. PC is an ultra-feminist's offensive designed to diminish men. It is a politician wanting to punish those with thoughts contrary to his or her own; it is a mega-billionaire buying up the media to control what stories are told, and how the American media tells them; and it is the systematic altering of education content at every level so that schooling teaches only "approved" story, turning education into indoctrination and campuses into reeducation centers. PC ultimately is a weapon in the war on culture used by a coalition of disparate political and financial forces under a tacit confluence of interest pact to advance their subversion of constitutional freedoms, inalienable rights and the spirit of self-sufficiency. It is almost as if the mind of America has been hacked and an insidious virus implanted.

The contradictions of PC are apparent: It is the policy and practice of the PC practitioner: to promote religious, racial and ethnic diversity at the expense of religions, races and ethnicities which he or she does not approve; to promote gender-identity equality at the expense of biological gender; and to promote freedom of speech and expression but only if that speech and expression is within approved parameters, and said with approved words; and to fit science to ideology and worldview instead of fitting their ideology and worldview to science. In reality, PC is a system of intolerance, and a warping of truth and reality.

Talking about words: Word restriction becomes very serious when one can't say Islamic terrorist; or can't say that the Islamic State of the Levant is Islamic; or can't describe illegal aliens as such but must replace that term with undocumented workers whether the illegal person is working or not. The restrictions may seem minor or pathetic but they have legal consequences, as when one describe small cell terrorist attacks as workplace violence and the victims lose legal status which would provide relief (as at Ft Hood). Not having been allowed to say micturate now seems pretty insignificant—but was it?

Each paragraph above deserves to be backed up with facts, figures, incidents, and anecdotes but that would take volumes. I ask the skeptical reader to keep the ideas in mind and compare them to events as they unfold.

Covert Adjustments: Peasants Are Practical

A peasant will do whatever he needs to do to stay alive, to protect his family, to be able to grow his rice or ply whatever may be his trade. That was a conclusion drawn by a patient who had been a Civil Affairs officer in Vietnam. If the communists controlled a district, and if they demanded, on threat of death, a share of the man's rice, the practical peasant shared his rice. If the demand was to go to a reeducation sessions, he went and listened to the communist political officer. If Allied Forces kicked the communists out of the district, the peasant would show allegiance to the new power. In my patient's words, "Peasants are practical. In order not to break, they bend under the weight of overwhelming force."

His anecdotes from Vietnam are reminiscent of stories I've read about how Italians acted during WW II when different armies were sweeping back and forth over their country; and of more contemporary stories of Iraqis and Afghanis.

The worse situation for a peasant was when both competing forces were strong, and control of the district was in dispute. In those cases the practical peasant showed allegiance to whoever was, at the moment, closest; yet he also kept that allegiance as covert as possible so if the other side swept back in they wouldn't know of his previous show of loyalty, and hopefully they wouldn't punish or kill him and his family for aiding and abetting the enemy.

In America we don't usually think of ourselves as peasants, yet we are indeed in an analogous situation. The ideologues and the financial elites in power, and those struggling to gain power, are like two clashing armies striving to control the district, and attempting to make all inhabitants conform to their dogmas. For many, practicality comes into play—we bend in order not to break.

In light of the aggressiveness of PC attacks, the crushing weight of regulations, and the systemic paralysis caused by bureaucracies and the Apparatchik, many men have made overt or covert, active or passive, adjustments to protect themselves, their families and their friends. From the outside the adjustments are tiered: some men have found ways to cope within the system; others have learned how to manipulate the system to work for them; there are those who have develop channels that circumvent the system; and those who have dropped out altogether. Every path has ramifications for those taking the trek, *and* for those who do not.

Working within the system businessmen (and businesswomen) have developed and opened the walk-in clinics and Surgi-centers we previously discussed. These are practical solutions to complicated pressures, and they are answers to the questions: "How can doctors stay in business? How can we remain independent of corporate hospitals? How can we adjust, restructure, and comply with all the new regulations, and still survive?" It is not just the medical profession but all professions and occupations have reacted to laws and restrictions, figuring out ways to make things work. Some toe the line, others tiptoe along the edge.

There is a not-for-profit clinic here in the state. The team they've set up is similar to a for-profit clinic—doctors, physician assistants, nurse practitioners, pharmacists, social workers, et cetera—but the guy running the clinic is a master at obtaining financial grants and finessing the system. One technique used by some not-for-profits is to pay out all funds that would be, in a commercial enterprise, profits. Pay the directors, pay the building owners, pay your brother/father/son/uncle/nephew/wife. The money has to go someplace; it's just that, with a not-for-profit, it can't go to shareholders. Some of these clinics, as you might suspect, have a reputation, within the profession if not with the public, of being a bit outside-the-law.

These ideological wars or, if you prefer, these culture wars, have been going on in western societies for a long time. In 1949 Winston Churchill warned his nation, "If you destroy a free market, you create a black market. If you make ten thousand regulations, you destroy all respect for the law." It seems to me that America avoided the brunt and the ramification of these conflicts for much of the 20th century. Perhaps I was too busy to take note. But I have been taking note for the past decade.

As regulations have become more onerous, and as tax obligations (or the perception of tax obligations) have become weightier, men have sought alternative paths to wealth or simply to subsistence. In doing so there has been an uptick in black market activities and in the underground economy. Recall our speculation above on real unemployment rates. Regulations may have changed, but people are still people. Men want to be self-sufficient unless that drive has been beaten or schooled out of them. How many men work off the books? How many women run undeclared childcare centers in their homes? How many people pay cash so the worker can avoid declaring that revenue as income? How many people covertly buy or sell legal products so they don't have to put up with the hassle of sales tax or EIN numbers, or a thousand other laws and forms? Undoubtedly there has always been an element of this in the economy, but, as Churchill's quote suggests, it grows when free markets suffer greater and greater restrictions; when monopolies are unwittingly developed because only the largest companies can comply; and when the public trust is at an all-time low?

Once an underground economy takes hold, and once it crosses a certain threshold, the national economy changes character. I saw this in Ecuador when we ran clinics for the indigent; and it can be seen in many third-world nations—bustling street-level markets (colorful and often attractive to tourists), but massive official debt oppressing individuals. These street markets do not contribute to national economies, and the vendors tend to be elusive and distrusting of authority. In the most severe cases black markets and underground economies, coupled with distrust in authority and officialdom drive people to trade in higher profit contraband items. At this extreme end of covert business and government distrust are the drug lords trafficking in everything from sneakers to heroin, guns to prostitution.

For those in the most dire straits practical says, "I have to get money someplace to survive. If I can't get it from work, I'll get it from food stamps, or welfare, or disability checks, or extended unemployment, or by joining a class action lawsuit. Somehow I have to get money." Since the economy took its nosedive in 2008 we've seem a doubling in the use of food stamps. Why would anyone expect something less?! I believe disability claims have increased more than 100%. It doesn't necessarily mean that twice as many people are disabled; it means that people are searching for a way to sustain their lives." Peasants are practical, but practicality has ramifications.

When government is not, or cannot be, trusted, when it is both corrupt and powerful, practical peasants seek to protect themselves and their families in fervent and fanatical ways. The mafia was born not as a criminal enterprise but as a defensive front against a contaminated state. Once peasants are outside the law, the switch to other forms of criminality is expedited and counter-cultures grow exponentially.

Think of all the Fergusons in America. I do not mean to disregard the terrible acts, but think for a moment about the social psyche that precedes violence. People are feeling worn down by the miniscule, by petty rules and regulations, by a culture and a government which they see as sitting oppressively on their shoulders, and by a main stream economy which is not working for them. It is unfortunate, worse, it is a tragedy, that the police have become the misguided symbol of this repression. But for a moment focus on all the pressures—including those caused by social programs which divide men from their families, and the cultural attacks on boys and men which leave males behind in education and jobs (single-parent households dominate the inner-city, and dropout and unemployment rates are highest amongst males in minority communities)—and add to this the fact that the outlets for repressed energies have been diminished by an economy which is bringing people down to only slightly better than a subsistence existence. Having two TV sets, or iPads and iPods, is not an adequate substitute for being able to walk without fear to a theater or even to the grocery store, or to go to a ballgame, or to hike a trail even if it is an inner-city trail (a la Skyline in Manhattan). The repressed energies of pent up populations, told and convinced they are being victimized by virtually everyone outside their community, naturally becomes explosive. Then peasants are no longer practical. Relentless degradation makes them vengeful. Violence ensues. The situation is analogous to Paris just before the French Revolution, except unlike Marie Antoinette, the first lady won't even let them eat cake! From this perspective Ferguson is a safety relief valve, but that valve is not big enough to drain off the festering resentments that are turning differing segments of the American population against each other. The greatest tragedy may be that the Fergusons of America becomes the justification for greater regulations, greater control, greater destruction of the family unit, and expanded oppression.

Finally there is the true dropout, the man who thinks and feels that nothing he does, and nothing he can do, has meaning. The attacks on his masculinity beginning with his being denied rough and tumble play as a four-year old up through him backhandedly being portrayed as a likely rapist in college have left him emotionally paralyzed. His life has been a game of Whack-A-Mole. Every time he's popped up and tried to work within the system someone—a teacher, a bureaucrat, a regulator—has smashed him over the head. His practical solution: he becomes the classic underachiever. He cannot be hurt if he doesn't exert.

Peasants are practical but in their need or desire to ameliorate the effects of PC lies, bureaucratic rules and regs, and the weight of the apparatchik, there is a social cost. From those on the edge of honesty to those dabbling with criminality, from those who deceive and cheat to those who are violent and explosive, and to those who are totally withdraw, their contributions to the nation, to their communities, to their families and to their own lives are greatly limited. In putting men down, the culture misses not just their *bad parts*, but their good part too. It is those good parts which, unleashed, have controlled the dishonest, the criminal, the cheating and the violence. It is those good parts which are meaningful in our lives.

Identity: Collateral Damage and The Death of The Average Joe

"What is your role? Everyone's telling us we're supposed to be head of the nuclear family, so you feel like you got robbed…" That is a quote from Hanna Rosin's article, *The End Of Men*. Teacher/social worker Mustafaa El-Scari is addressing a class of male students. He tells them there are four types of paternal authority: moral, emotional, social and physical. He does not include economic, but he does address that facet. "…you ain't none of those in that house. All you are is a paycheck, and now you ain't even that. And if you try to exercise your authority, she'll call 911. How does that make you feel? You're supposed to be the authority, and she says, 'Get out of the house, bitch.' She's calling you 'bitch'!"

This battle in the culture war in America is not an assault on women. It is a vicious attack on men, on male values and male virtues—in essence on our male identity. This is not simply an inner-city or minority crisis as the above quote might imply. It affects virtually all men to a greater or lesser degree. We've noted dozens of example and will not rehash them here. Instead let's look at the collateral damage.

What do these assaults do to the nature of men? If you do not care for the term *nature*, replace it with *personality* or *behavioral characteristics*. Biology is basic. That's a given. The three Ps are still wired in the male brain structure. After procreation, what happens to the man who has been essentially discarded, whose biological inclinations to provide and protect have been devalued by divorce or by social programs which have supplanted his role? I postulate that men seek alternatives, that some of these alternatives are meaningless or trivial, that others are destructive. For a young father displacement means life has lost its anchor meaning. He likely can't express it. He may not full realize it. The community about him seldom acknowledges his the loss. A young man shifts his focus and his loyalty to his favorite sports team or to the rulers of the local turf. His behavior may be covered by smiles or hidden beneath machismo and bravado, but his life has been trivialized.

Trivialization, this lack of meaning and lack of biological connection, is innately stressful. What are the long term ramifications of that stress on his mental and physical health? Men die earlier than women. There are many potential reasons. Men eat more steak or more processed grains than women, and generally have higher cholesterol; men are more apt to fight, to be injured, to be shot; they are more likely to take risks—especially after being displaced—and to be killed in accidents. The dual stresses of an attack on one's identity and the forced loss of biological value may be killing the average Joe.

We can postulate that this war on men is causative, but we need to check to see if a correlation exists between the attacks on identity and the health and longevity of men. I have not found a study which accounts for this phenomenon, and which controls for the myriad of potentially significant variables. We do know that as men go through adulthood the assaults on their identity are stressful. We know that stress suppresses the immune system. And we know that when the immune system is suppressed, the body is susceptible to more disease.

It is interesting that as the cultural story changed for women, as their identities and self-images changed, and as they entered the workforce in greater numbers, they began to suffer more heart disease.

Heart disease is now the leading cause of death in women. One might make the case (it has been made many times) that this increase in female heart disease is caused by the higher production of cortisol due to high levels of job stress.

If we can make that case, shouldn't we be able to postulate that male stress suppresses the immune system and results in shorter lives?

More importantly, we should make the case that attacks on male identity are the root cause of an altered cultural story which in turn has resulted in all the vast changes to culture that have led to the current asymmetrical state of our society. That's a mouthful, isn't it? But this *is* the method that the ultra-feminists have used, and are using, to force ever greater distortions and imbalances—to convince the masses of the 77 cents on the dollar inequity myth, and rampant rape on campus lie. Change and control ambient cultural story (even if you need to lie); that will change self-image (individual and societal) in specific ways you've directed; desired behaviors will follow because behavior will be consistent with the new self-images. Then laws, rules and regulations can follow to ensure compliance with the new paradigm (they too will be consistent with the new story and the new self-image. When the story is controlled the media has the power to disperse it and to give it credibility. That's a scary thought, because we usually don't see how or why the story changed, only the results of the change. We don't have a clue that the story may be purposely manipulated by elitist power mongers acting like puppet masters jerking our strings as if we are marionettes.

If we men are to impact cultural behavior (and the stress that is killing us), we must impact cultural story. To do that we need to correct the skewed narratives so that attacks on the values and virtues of men are defeated, and the cultural story is brought back into balance with truth and reality. If we don't...

We must ask: Is it possible to reverse the insidious and accelerating trends of the past half century? The answer: Maybe not. Certainly not if we peasants, we practical men, we natural problem solvers, simply continue to adjust to and accept deteriorating circumstances. Short term practical adjustments may protect self, family and friends, but they are tactical. Radicals think strategically. If we allow the strategic plans of the most radical element to go unchallenged, we lose. We lose our male identity; we lose our health; we lose our nation; and we lose our lives.

To impact the greater sphere, we need to engage, to enter the battle. Think of the ancient Greek philosophers warning that if good men do not participate in politics they will be ruled by lesser men. Throughout our lives we have kept our nose to the grindstone, have ignored or deferred or acquiesced to false platitudes and unfounded myths. To impact the greater sphere we need to get out heads out of the sand, to extend our expectations, to think strategically. Think of the nation's founding fathers creating documents to last hundreds of years beyond their own lives—that perspective, that perception and projection of the future produces hope. Hope relieves stress. We might even live long enough to see the beginning of the rebalancing.

But, only if we realize that we indeed are at a point where dishonesty and corruption are destroying the culture and the country. Why is everyone not up in arms?! Perhaps the reason is that "everything is changing," and that there is a confluence of interest amongst the manipulators and deceivers, the frauds and the hucksters. It is as if one groups tacitly says to the other, "I won't blow the whistle on you if you don't blow the whistle on me." Honor amongst thieves does not quell the rent in the public trust. Many of the things once consider corrupt are now legal. I'm thinking here of the scrapping of the Commodity Exchange Law in December 2000 which undid the Bucket Shop laws passed in response to the Crash of 1907, and the rescinding of the Up-Tick Rule in April 2007 that had been put in place to counter causes of the crash of 1929. The dissolution of those two acts, not the housing bubble, enabled the chicanery which brought on the Great Recession. The lobby for the greedy had worked their magic. Things that were once illegal became legal, and a pinpoint-elite was able to manipulate the markets to benefit themselves in wealth and power. They were also able to manipulate the story, to deflect blame and to scapegoat the world financial collapse onto less than 120,000 sub-prime mortgage holders (0.00171% of all U.S. mortgages) that were in foreclosure. Before 2007 what they did would have ended in jail terms; but after it ended up in a consolidation of wealth in the few at the expense of the many—a billionaire born every 20 hours!

Where this is all going, this new culture of institutional dishonesty and exalted avarice? I don't really know. The kids who were coddled... I don't think they were taught to look to the future. I think they are looking only at the now. So, to the question, "Where do they think this is going to end up?" I don't think they think that way at all. I think they see today, tomorrow, next month—what can I get. I don't think the thought occurs to them, "Gee, if I do this I'm screwing the country. I'm screwing civilization. These are heavy concepts. They take time and effort to even begin to recognize. That is very different from the manipulator thinking, "Great! I'm making a killing."

Old realities have been replaced by new myths, and the cultural story has never been the same. What is apparent to me is that these changes are happening in a system warped far from reality. I believe, had the system remained closer to the straight and narrow, the old attitudes would not have allowed this severe corruption to become endemic.

Not long ago my son asked me, "Do you remember the rise and fall of the Roman empire?" I answered, "I'm old but that was still a bit before my time. I am, however, aware of it." He chuckled. Then he told me a number of factoids from that time. At first I was pretty dismissive, but as I thought about it, I could see we are headed down this same path. Our institutions, like those of Rome, have become corrupt and detached from reality. It's scary because of what is happening now; because of the similarities. The path is strange. Male characteristics which enable them to protect are devalued, and the protectors of society are dismissed. The corrupt get all the money, but in the end the weakened empire crashes and it is taken over by barbarians. The Golden Goose is destroyed. The money of the elite becomes worthless, their power hobbled. What did they gain?

Standard Military Issue: One Life—Expendable

One of my favorite patients was a sailor stationed at the naval base at Groton. I remember saying to him, "You're twenty six years old, and you're the Fire Control Officer on the USS Dallas?!" He answered, "Yes Sir." He looked like a kid, but he controlled the highly sophisticated weapon systems of a multi-billion-dollar, nuclear-powered attack submarine. He was different from the college students and other young men I often treated. His posture was different; his manners were different; his focus was different. The military had given him responsibilities unimaginable in the civilian world, and he had grown into them.

Now, as this is being written, culture war proponents have set sight upon the U.S. Armed Forces. The military is being emasculated, warriors devalued, and the will to pull the trigger destroyed.

Up front I wish to say, I support women serving in the armed forces. I also believe gay men should serve. I do not believe any class or classification of citizen (other than by age) should be, en masse, exempt. I say this here so the reader does not misconstrue what follows.

One cannot write a book about the life of men without writing about soldiering, about the brotherhood of warriors, about men at their most noble and at their most vile. The philosophical precepts and the traditions of the American Fighting Man—soldiers, sailors, Marines, airmen and coast guardsmen—may be built upon the defense of the homeland and the high concepts of valor, freedom and liberty; but the nit and grit of soldiering and the attraction of combat to young men has more to do with the masculine imperative to protect, bonding, proving one's worth, being part of the action, and earning overt proof masculinity—the latter being particularly important when in search of a mate.

In this section we will briefly mention the basics, then turn our attention to the current issues involving women in foxholes, the rainbow brigades, the essence of recruitment, bitch-slapping the generals, and what biological value and expendability imply.

The mission of the military (and the reason we pay huge tax dollars to have the Pentagon) is the strategic defense of the nation. In order to accomplish that mission both defensive and offensive fighting capabilities are necessary. In this age of sophisticated and long-range weaponry, sophisticated and long-range defense capabilities and continuous vigilance are mandatory. So are boots on the ground. That phrase has become a cliché, yet it is seldom fully understood. Boots on the ground means control. One can have UAVs surveil the theater; one can fire rockets and artillery against targets; one can even bomb an area back into the Stone Age; but that does not mean one controls the area. Those are siege tactics. Those soften up the enemy. Boots on the ground means infantry. It means having Marines going house-to-house dispelling and destroying the enemy in a place like Fallujah, and thusly gaining control. Boots on the ground are up front and personal, and they are the ultimate weapon in war.

Threats are real. Many of the threats to the nation have roots which pre-date the existence of the United States of America; indeed, some pre-date the discovery of the New World. Many threats would exist if America and Americans were the most selfish people on earth or the most generous; the richest or the poorest; the whitest or the blackest; English-language dominate or multi-lingual; Christian, Jew, Moslem, Taoist, Buddhist or atheist. Threats happen not only because who we are, but also simply because we are; because we take up space; because others might covet this space and the natural and manmade treasures it holds. One can, or one's representative can, negotiate with those behind the threats, but negotiations—no matter how sincere--tend to be pathetically ineffectual when one is operating from a powerless position. With power, defense may be deterrence as during the Cold War and the theory of mutually assured destruction; or it may be interception as when the Coast Guard thwarts invading terror cells; or it may be projection as when our forces reach across vast distances to subdue attacks and stop them at their source. It is, of course, much more complicated, particularly when one has treaties and blocs and pacts with the devil. That's another book! Here let's concern ourselves with strategic defense, and how it is being impacted by social engineering.

There is a very significant push by various ultra-feminist organizations and other political and administrative forces for not only *gender diversity* in the military but for *gender equality and equality of opportunity* in ground force combat units. Currently woman can volunteer for, but cannot be forced into infantry, artillery or armor elements. This may soon change. We'll touch on the ramifications of that motion in a moment.

Recall the overlapping bell curves of characteristics that are in the introduction. Woman can be as hardhearted as the most callous grunt. That's not the issue. They can be ruthless, cruel, and atrocious. Limiting them from the ground combat arms has little to do with them not being able to pull the trigger and kill the enemy. Women have proven to be very capable of defensive fire and offensive butchery. One only need think about the all-women Khmer Rouge Nery battalions which were most feared because of their cruelty, slaughter and terror. If we plot the potential for cruelty on overlapping bell curves I suspect training quite easily could make the male and the female bell curves nearly identical.

Women also have proved to be very capable and highly valorous in other military specialties. They can be fighter pilot, they can drop bombs, they can pull triggers, and they can save lives. They can also do thousands of jobs military men have always done—from admissions clerk to mess sergeant to transportation specialist to UAV mechanic. But training cannot make women as fast as men; nor can it bring them to lift as much weight. Let's look at those characteristic—speed and upper body strength—and project the differentials onto a theoretical battle field.

Speed is important in combat. Shoot before being shot. The fastest man in the world ran the 100-meter dash in 9.572 seconds. The fastest woman in the world ran the 100-meter dash in 10.49 seconds. The women's record has stood for over a quarter century; the men's for about a year. More importantly the high school boy's record for 100 meters is 9.99 seconds—a full half second quicker that the fastest woman ever. The second and third fastest boys ran the race in 10.01 seconds. The eighth fastest boy ran a 10.15. In that race the guy who came in second ran a 10.18. Even in a small state like Connecticut the boy's high school record is faster that the fastest, best trained, woman in the world.

The very strongest and very fastest women are stronger and faster than many men. If we could find bell curves for a large sample, one suspects the third standard deviation of the women's curve would hits the second standard deviation of the men's curve. But the center of those curves—the speed of the average woman versus the speed of the average man—are still significantly separated. Were they not there never would have been a Title IX, for men and women would have always competed on the same teams at all levels. Perhaps it is testosterone's effect on fast-twitch muscle fiber.

As to weight: you cannot put the average woman on an artillery crew and expect her to lift and load 95-pound howitzer rounds for hours on end during a critical fire mission. If the crew isn't firing the infantry guys engaged with an enemy unit miles away get overrun and killed; and if the infantry doesn't stop the enemy they advance upon the artillery base, attack and perhaps overrun and kill the soldiers there. This may be a hypothetical example, but it also hypothetical to project that women could do this job.

It is not desirable or practical to put women in foxholes, or in artillery pits. And according to the Center for Military Readiness, a survey of uniformed women shows that only 7.5% of 30,000 respondents indicated they would be willing to "take a combat arms position, such as the infantry."

This has not kept the social engineers from demanding that the armed forces implement programs which would lower standards to attract, and to allow, more women to participate in activities beyond the average female recruit's physical abilities. Military officers, their careers on the line, have found *ways* to make the demands reality. Some demands have been met by introducing *gender-neutral standards*, a euphemism for double standards based on "the physiological differences between genders." Despite standards and *gender diversity metrics*, women are experiencing a significantly higher rate of debilitating injuries in training than men, particularly to feet, knees and hips. Said another way, it is working on paper but not in the field. That does not bode well for combat operations.

Another worrisome aspect of this push for "equality" revolves around Selective Service laws. As mentioned, currently woman can volunteer for, but cannot be forced into, direct ground combat roles. That is a woman's choice. The exemption of women from Selective Service registration, and from the draft should it ever be reinstatement, rests upon this voluntary status. Should that status finally be legislated off the books, or eviscerated by executive order, the legal exemption will end. Women will not have a choice. As anyone who has ever served knows, your body is not yours; it is the property of Uncle Sam. Women will be assigned to (ordered into) whatever units need replacements. Is that what we, as a people, want? Do we want our daughters to be drafted into frontline units?

As these policies are proceeding other social engineering projects are keeping pace. Pentagon policies toward gay men, lesbians and bisexuals are also evolving. When I was an officer in the Air Force, gay men were not allowed in the military. Years later the policy changed to "Don't ask; Don't tell." That is, if one was gay and was in the military, he was required to keep his sexual preference to himself, and those with whom he served, no matter what they might suspect, were restricted from inquiring into the man's personal life. Under the current administration open displays of homosexuality are not only acceptable, they are celebrated. In February of 2015 Petty Officer 2d Class Thomas Sawicki won the first kiss lottery on return to port of the fast attack submarine USS San Francisco. Not to chagrin but to official approval, he was photographed kissing his boyfriend on the pier at the Point Loma Naval Base in San Diego.

The problem is not what most might presume. As mentioned at the beginning of this section, I do not wish to see a blanket exemption from service for any group. In a 2014 interview Secretary of Defense Chuck Hagel expressed similar sentiments. "Every qualified American who wants to serve our country should have an opportunity *if they fit the qualifications and can do it.*" (my emphasis.) I agree with him. Gay men are still men. Many are highly qualified. I have worked with gay men without difficulty, and I think that some would excel in various military occupational specialties. As I said, I don't believe that is the real problem.

But I do have two objections. First, I do not like seeing the military used for social engineering experiments at the detriment to mission. The military can lead social change—just as it did racial integration decades before the civil rights movement of the 1960s; but it did not then and it should not now degrade its primary mission of national defense in the name of diversity—gender, religious, ethnic or otherwise.

The second problem goes hand-in-hand with the first. Our military culture has always been strong, but the Culture War is tearing it apart. On the news a few years ago there was a video of an American wounded in Afghanistan. He had been loaded into a medical evacuation helicopter. His shirt was torn away. A medic held him and an IV bottle. On his chest one could read a tattoo which read, "For Those I Love, I Will Sacrifice." Last year Greta Van Susteren filmed a special on healing the marriages of veterans suffering from PCSD (post-combat stress disorder). One quote stood out: "What men fear the most is shame and dishonor." Both stories said to me, "That's who we are, that's who we have always been."

But that is changing. William Kilpatrick noted in a July 2014 column:

The administration and the Pentagon may deny it, but the feminization and gaying of the military, together with the blurring of the Army's mission, is bound to have an effect on the attractiveness of the military for young men. It's not a question of whether gays can fight or whether women make good warriors, it's a question of what kind of culture is being created. Right now the U.S. military is in the process of creating the kind of culture that is a guaranteed turn-off for many potential enlistees.

Kilpatrick lays out a convincing argument, explaining first how boys and young men are attracted to military service, or to gangs, because of the sense of bonding and the proof of masculinity that either may confer. He tells us that fatherless boys are most apt "to feel insecure in their masculinity" and most apt to seek out "the ultra-masculine activities of gangs." He then describes a growing pattern amongst fatherless males who first join gangs, then get in trouble, are convicted and incarcerated, and finally find faith while in prison with "...roughly 80 percent... choos[ing] Islam."

Right now Islam is seen as the most powerful gang in the world, one which offers the greatest adventure, plus male bonding and booty. The American military by contrast, along with its problems of culture, has no staying power. The perception is: we may engage with a flourish but soon the nanny state will tell us to abandon the fight. Our politicians not only waste lives—blood and treasure—but they are wasting the heart and soul of a generation, destroying the will of guys to protect and defend, and wasting the will of those who have the fortitude to pull the trigger. A nation that destroys the will of its young men to protect and defend is a nation that is about to be destroyed. Why should our very best risk their lives; why should they endure the hardships; why should they be heroic, if it is all going to be thrown away? ISIS is different, gung-ho. For a young man, what's not to like? It doesn't have a recruitment problem, but the American military does!

Better than two thirds of American youth don't qualify for military service due to obesity, tattoos, lack of education, drug use, and/or a criminal record. Think about this, Popeye, if you have an anchor tattoo on your arm, you're rejected; but if you want a transsexual operation that might be okay! This is not your father's Navy.

If you wish it to be, "Sorry Charlie."

Veteran friends tell me that perhaps the greatest disadvantage suffered by communist forces in Vietnam came not at the disparity in firepower against American troops but at their own, party-imposed dual command structure. At virtually every level of their military—from COSVN headquarters down to squad level, every tactical leader was shadowed by a political counterpart. The tactical soldiers were often well-trained, and many had years of combat experience. The political cadre tended to be driven by ideological purity and personal advancement, and they generally had the ability to override the tactical commander simply by claiming him ideologically impure. One of the most common complaints from the more than 200,000 northern soldiers who defected to the south during the war was what American troops might call "bulls**t orders." The dual structure was terrible for morale, and often tactically destructive.

So now we're pursuing the same course! From the Center for Military Readiness article mentioned above:

> Pentagon officials keep insisting that standards will not be lowered if women become eligible for the combat arms. They also pledge to "set women up for success." Neither promise can be true as long as the ultimate objective is to achieve what the Pentagon-endorsed **Military Leadership Diversity Commission (MLDC)** recommends.
>
> > -Instead of being blind to racial and gender differences the MLDC recommends race and gender consciousness, and assigns a higher priority to "equal opportunity," [than] to military readiness. The 2011 MLDC report recommends that a **"Chief Diversity Officer," (CDO)** be appointed, and promotions should be contingent on meeting "gender diversity metrics" (another name for quotas).

We are indeed in a very odd time. The top military man in the nation, the commander-in-chief, is a civilian. The nation has a long tradition of civilian control of the military. Previous commander-in-chiefs, even if at times they wielded the military like their own personal force, recognized that their relationship with the armed forces was symbiotic. That is, the power of the president, particularly in foreign affairs, rests on the might of the military. Like it or not, previous commander-in-chiefs have been practical enough to recognize this *real politic* relationship. This has changed.

From the sacking of General Stanley McChrystal the president seemingly has enjoyed bitch-slapping senior military commanders. McChrystal was relieved for giving an analytical interview that didn't toe the administration's line. Then General David Petraeus was relieved. The circumstances were different. Petraeus ran the highly successful surge campaign in Iraq in 2007, took over operations in Afghanistan, and became head of the Central Intelligence Agency. He was a rising star with a terrific résumé; and a potential opponent of the administration. When a man like the general is singled out, the strike is preemptive and politically motivated. He's attacked for a flaw, the error hyped and spun. The cesspool of corruption that exists must destroy him before he gathers enough strength to expose their reality. From Jonathan Keiler's article titled *Obama's Generals*:

> Petraeus, who also had policy differences with Obama, was not only forced to resign as CIA chief for an ill-advised romantic dalliance, but was aggressively prosecuted by the Justice Department for trumped-up charges of mishandling classified material—almost exactly what we now know Hillary Clinton did during her tenure as secretary of state on a vaster scale.

General Carter Ham, once head of Africa Command, was made the scapegoat of Benghazi and tossed; Lieutenant General Michael Flynn, once head of the Defense Intelligence Agency, ran afoul of the administration for *realistic* assessment of Islamist terror threats--out; and Colonel John Merna "resigned" as commander of the 31st Marine Expeditionary Unit, (a highly distinguished, first-reaction/tip of the spear amphibious fighting force) for, according to Stars and Stripes, "creating a hostile work environment," and using "intemperate behavior" and "language." (Oh Dear! A hard ass Marine Commander swore at a troop! Patton must be rolling over in his grave.)

The list of top commanders relieved by the current administration is pages and pages long. None were canned for tactical or strategic blunders. They were relieved for cussing, for accusations of sexual abuse, for letting troops pray, for any number of infractions reported by politically correct political cadres. Remember, in today's military, the tactical mission is secondary.

Men are expendable: The ultimate and overriding reason women are protected and generally are not warriors is biological. Here I do not mean the physiological gender differences of speed and strength. Here I am talking about the biological design for the continuation of the species. A religious person might call it God's design; a scientist might say every human being is part of a living biological system in which sex and recombination "achiev[e] fidelity of DNA replication" thus reproducing the genome and counteracting extinction. (Shcherbakov)

In this living biological system the genders have distinct roles. The roles may have blurred due to the success of the species—now numbering over seven billion beings—but the continuation of the species is still dependent upon those roles; and the extinction of the species is but a generation away if those roles are not fulfilled.

Imagine back to the time when the human population of earth was numbered in the thousands, when clans were nomadic, and when wooly mammoths were hunted with spears. Continuation as a species was precarious. Genetic selection favored the best hunter-gathers, the best protector, and the best providers. What needed protection? What needed provisions? Not in the short run. Every being in the short run needs food and security. But in biological time the species' sustenance first goes to the developing future, to the womb, to the content of the womb, to the newborn, to the child. Biologically, the role of women in the continuation of the species, compared to the role of men, is rare. A man carries enough seed, enough sperm, to populate a large city. In his lifetime he can father thousands of offspring. But a woman is very limited in the number of babies she can have. This comparative rarity means the value of women is biologically far greater than the value of men. Camille Paglia expresses it thusly: women hold a "superior biological status as magical life-creator(s)."

The reason why militaries and warrior-classes throughout history have been predominately male has nothing to do with the capabilities of women to attack or defend; it is because men, compared to women, are expendable. Viewing current issue from the perspective of continuation of the species exposes the fallacies in modern trends.

The fact that men are biologically expendable, however, is not an excuse for wasting them. Nor does it mean that of their deaths you can defensively cry out, "What difference does it make?!"

Conclusion: Restoration Strategies

I don't know where the culture war or the relationship between men and women is going to end up, but I think the conflicts that have been created and purposefully amplified are not good. Much of it wasn't and isn't necessary. Much of it hasn't and won't achieve the stated objectives or the ideals of the proponents. Social "gains" have come at significant costs to all but an elite, who have put us at each other's throats. The way we are functioning, and the direction in which we're headed, is strangling the nation. We are in decline. Men feel rejected, denied. The best are withdrawing like the character John Galt in Ayn Rand's *Atlas Shrugged*. Relatively small groups, demanding preference and equality (doesn't preference imply inequality?), have raised such a continuous ruckus the majority has responded as if they were the mouse that roared. Our thinking has lost its base. The will to make the country work has been wasted and is being destroyed. Corruption proliferates. Government and quasi-public institutions have injected themselves, in the words of Richard Viguerie and Mark Fitzgibbons, into:

> ...nearly every aspect of private affairs, and has taken an excessive, intrusive and omnipotent view of what are *public* matters. Given the vast and unilateral authority it claims to have over so much of society and property, government has unmatched opportunity for lawbreaking. It makes and *rigs* the rules in its favor. It cloisters and covers up its lawlessness, and makes it almost impossible to challenge its lawbreaking when exposed. Government lawbreaking is bringing down the greatest and fairest engine of prosperity in history—the American economy. Political establishment lawbreaking is economically and morally rotting America from within.

Pockets of sanity and resistance exist, even flourish. I talk to individuals every day who recognize that major problems persist, yet who have found ways to avoid or counter the fray in their personal lives. Often, when they hear about the writing of *Life Of Men* they offer encouragement.

There are also communities like Roseto, Pennsylvania where traditional values thrive, and health, happiness and longevity are well above the national average. The reason I mention that small town is because it has been studied for more than half a century. Despite high rates of smoking, the liberal consumption of wine, diets which favor meatballs and sausages over lite fare and fast food, and chemically toxic work environments, the death rate from heart attack or stroke in men 55 to 64 is half that of the rest of the country. In Roseto public assistance is minimal. Crime is low. Matching for scores of genetic and societal variables, researchers concluded the positive health consequences had been derived from living in a cohesive, close-knit community. In Roseto elders are incorporated into community activities, not shuffled off to the senior center or nursing homes; housewives, motherhood and the nurturing of children from infancy through adolescence hold greater esteem than working outside the home; fathers are present and are strong role models; neighbors are not obsessed with outdoing each other; and civic and church organizations are a regular part of almost everyone's life.

Do you recall my soft-spoken Italian-American friend—the one who got into it with the P.E.T. instructor? The boyhood he described is reminiscent of that in Roseto, but his family was located in "a neighborhood" of a medium-sized city. The effect on the individual of a close-knit family, within an extended clan, within a greater social network contributes to the establishment of values, virtues and identity; and that seems to be more causative of longevity and happiness than modern nutrition, exercise or life-style. Doctors now call this the Roseto Effect.

But that's been lost. Roseto no longer exists. The town is still there but the magic has dissipated, lost like a morning mist to the encroaching sunlight of today's voracious culture. We've covered numerous aspects of the culture war—the results of skewed facts and lopsided perceptions caused by oxymoronic advocacy journalism, activist academia, and predisposed research, plus publishing prejudices, niche marketing, partisan politics, and Hollywood bias.

What's required to reset America? No amount of tweaking tweets is going to accomplish it. How do we get it back; how do we restore what was once good without also returning to what was once bad? How do we return to a time when neighbor cherished neighbor, when crime was low, when the roles of husband and wife or male and female were complimentary, when individuals and families were self-sustaining and independent, and when respect for self, country, mankind and mother nature were unified and consistently part of our ambient cultural story?

This has not been a war of conflicting ideal between the center left and the center right. I have generally found that the motivation of both centers is to do good; and that most Americans hold similar core. One side is not trying to keep people dependent; the other side is not trying to exploit them or cheat them of their last dime. I am thrilled most people have wonderful ideals. It is incredibly important because that gives us a starting point for recovery.

The culture war that has been raging for decades has waged by radical elements of the far left. Often those leaders and elites have couching their rhetoric in the verbiage of the center or center left. More recently the leaders of the right have launched counter attacks against the exposed left instead of the hidden extremists. When I say we are at each other's throats, this is what I mean. What is necessary from citizens in the first standard deviations to the left and the right, that is from the majority in the center, is to judge rhetoric and policies against results and ramifications using our common ideals as criteria. Having wonderful ideal does not automatically equate with doing good things. If the ramifications of policy are different than what was anticipated, or the outcome of laws and regulations is negative, one must review not ideals but the policies, laws and regulations which caused the detrimental results. If things didn't turn out right, ideals likely do not need to be altered or denied; but the application of those ideals certainly needs to be changed in such a way as to bring the ideal to fruition.

The problems are basic but solutions will not be found in the instantaneous world of mile-wide-by-half-inch-deep communications. For over fifty years progressive elements have worked effectively to change, to reform, and to redefine our national narrative. With each passing decade they've consolidated their advances and pressed forward. Where once we believed in "…ask not what your country can do for you, but what you can do for your country," we now have, at best, a disengaged populace that shirks from civic duties and seeming thinks it supports the military by sticking magnetic ribbons on cars bumpers.

What is required is a campaign no less than the equivalent of Mao's "take the countryside and the cities will fall." In this case we are not talking about physical landmass but about the moral high ground which activists and radicals have assumed and usurped, and which they've defended at all cost. Ancillary to the moral high ground are all the institutions and bureaucracies which propagate cultural story—the news media, entertainment, academia and education. The political establishment and its allies in the radical community are openly contemptuous of anyone who challenges not just their authority but even their opinions. Over and over we've seen masculinity be a main target, and individual men be crushed, chewed up and spit out.

As said before, story creates self-mage, and behavior tends to be consistent with self-image. Control the story and you control self-image and behavior. All socialist, fascist, communist, and autocratic regimes have recognized this process, and all have used it to benefit the few at the expense of the many. Political correctness and all adjunct policies and procedures are designed to impact the national narrative. Much of that impact is false. Fallacious, misleading and/or ambiguous concepts skew the narrative into the land of fiction. Behavior based upon fiction seldom achieves desired long-term goals but frequently produces unintended consequences.

The strategy: A restoration campaign requires motivation and mass. Enough people need to want to modify the present to achieve any success. But wanting is not enough. They must have the will to correct not just the distortions of story but to follow through by reversing laws, policies and procedures created under the spell of fantasy.

Having the will may mean putting up or shutting up; putting their money where their mouth is. Not long ago I was speaking to a young, independent film maker. He said to me, "Hollywood is not liberal because most writers, actors and directors are liberal. Hollywood is liberal because most of the money that backs film is liberal. The money attracts the talent. Liberal money attracts liberal writers, casts and crews which then reflect left-leaning philosophies."

The progression has been different in academia. A film project may last several years from conception through script, production and distribution. Professorships, once tenured, last a lifetime. Many of today's top professors and department chairs, especially in the social sciences and liberal arts, began their careers in the 1960s and 1970s as activists opposing the American involvement in the war in Southeast

Asia. As they became more established they sought to add like-minded colleagues to their departments. Historians and social scientists with opposing views (revisionist views—horrors!) were shunned, not hired. When pundits label academia being heavily liberal, progressive, or socialist then have countless surveys to back the claim. Asked their party affiliation, 100% of the history and political science professors of many top universities answered Democrat. They may demand diversity in skin color and gender-identity, but no diversity in philosophy is allowed. That is a weakness and a flaw which students, parents, restorers and revisionist should not only expose, but should challenge with legal suits. Left unchecked, as it pretty much has been for decades, education—we've said this before—becomes indoctrination.

In every institution, at every level, even in personal exchange, honest men and women must learn to contest the extremes of political correctness. Do you recall my dear family friend, the executive who was angry about the innate prejudice her male cohorts displayed by seemingly expecting her to bring in the coffee? I've finally convinced her there is another explanation. Men are naturally competitive. They will treat any and every new person as a competitor to be mastered until that competitor is accepted as part of the team—or in more primal terms, part of the pact. Biology is basic. Corporate boardrooms are full of Alpha males whose nature is to treat outsiders as subservient. But once a person—male of female—is accepted as part of the pack, the men will defend that person in a way women never will. If your goal is equality, that is to be part of the pack, prove your worth. The return on the effort will enhance your career a hundred fold. Bitching will get you nowhere—except possibly with the help of the state—and victory via the state will never gain you acceptance into the pack.

We cannot take back the country without correcting the national narrative and the ambient cultural story. It seems to me more and more people are applying pressure by the power of the purse. This is a natural process in a free, capitalistic economy. Bias newspapers lose circulation. People get tired of reading what they believe is bills**t. Slanted TV news shows lose viewership. It's the same process. Liberal politicians demand that the pubic (tax dollars) support the media that support their views. They sponsor legislation, and the case they make sounds reasonable, until you realize that most of the programming has a covert, if not overt, slant.

Free market capitalism—not to be confused with vulture capitalism which is not capitalism at all, and also not to be misconstrued as completely without regulation—has given the most people the power to be self-sufficient, socially-mobile, autonomous and free. Restricting commerce, subsidizing an industry or portion of an industry to the detriment of competitors, mandating specific products be purchased, are all antithetic to free market capitalism and antithetic to choice. Yet today even the word capitalism evokes negative stereotypes. The cultural story implanted begins with cartoons watched by three-year olds where the evil businessman chops down the tree of the adorable little squirrel family. Imagine if cartoons instead told stories with morals like Aesop's fables. Would little minds then be better able to handle the onslaught of gibberish they're about to encounter starting in first grade?

Where is our indignation? How, in this time of niche marketing and niche programming, does one reach the others in differing social, religious or political nooks and crannies?

Our open and democratic culture cannot exist without a high degree of individual autonomy. A free society requires that its members are treated, as per Sommers and Satel, as though they are "ethically responsible and personally accountable." For some time I have been saying, "We're Americans. We're better than this." Sommers and Satel identify the elements of *The American Creed* as "self-reliance, stoicism, courage in the face of adversity, and the valorization of excellence." That's the goal, the target of restoration and revitalization. The solution is to restore that creed to the ambient cultural story; to allow individuals to exploit the story in a free, open and competitive economy; and to let social and market forces make spontaneous adjustments.

Without challenge and correction I fear the confluence of the ideologies of the progressives, radicals, communists and fascists, along with government and gender *mafias* will coerce us into worse times. Perhaps much worse times. In my most horrible nightmare, I see the world—my children, grandchildren, and future generations—descending into a 500-year, or a 1000-year, Dark Age.

Then I awake. I think of men like my soft-spoken Italian-American friend. Five years after he attended the P.E.T. class he built his own home. All the bedrooms, including the master, were on the second floor, and all open to a small foyer. When his kids were small he insisted the bedroom doors stay open at night. He's convinced that a feeling of security was imparted by that set-up. His kids, male and female, all now successful in their own right, seem well-adjusted, secure in their own identities and willing to take on the challenges the future holds.

Rereading this chapter I fear I may have come across as an old curmudgeon. I don't really care for that term. Nor do I like the terms senior citizen or elder. The experiences of a life well lived hopefully impart wisdom. At this point of life I prefer to think of my generation as Sages.

Dr. Jeffrey Rabuffo

PART VIII: Sages—Resilience and Legacies

Men get old and die. It is basic biology; part of the life cycle of our species. The fact of death is neither sin nor tragedy. Without death new growth would be stunted. What we do between birth and death we call life. The fourth quarter of life holds wonders and opportunities beyond the wildest dreams of young men; plus hopes and aspirations for a future—for the new growth—beyond one's personal existence. It also holds decline, possibly depression, sometimes heart-wrenching pain. Resilience is imperative until it is impossible.

Ana: The other day I bought an old guy a Coke. I had been sitting in the cafeteria at the cancer center of a local university hospital. Fifteen years earlier in that very room I had learned that my three-month-old granddaughter, Ana, had been diagnosed with leukemia. I had not been back to the center since that time. Memories flooded back.

As happens with these things, everyone had a very positive outlook; everyone was saying things like, "We're going to beat this." But I knew better. I was the grandfather, the father of Anna's father, but also a physician. As a urologist I didn't know much about leukemia, but I knew how to find out. What I discovered was devastating.

I talked to the pediatric oncologist. She told me Anna had an 18% chance of having a two-year event-free survival. That's doctor talk for there's little hope. I felt I needed to help, but being a urologist to in this situation was useless. So I undertook my other roles: grandfather, father, cook, aide.

My son and his wife were basically camped out at the hospital twenty-four hours a day. A group of neighbors had gotten together to look after their home. Some cleaned the house, one cut the lawn, another brought them their mail, and still others paid some of the bills and generally kept things tidy. My role was to provide some meals. Every weekend I would cook up whatever my creative mind could conjure up. When I'm upset I can be very creative. I made traditional meals—spaghetti and meatballs, pot roast, baked chicken—but also chicken stew with baked beans, pork chops with cloves and artichoke hearts, and my all-time favorite, chicken and sauerkraut. I would put it all together in cast iron pots and freeze it; then bring it to their house and put the food in their freezer or fridge so all they need to do was heat it. I would make sure there was always enough food for several days.

That was my way of being the father and the grandfather. I knew what the statistics were saying but there was no way I was going to tell it to my kids. They needed to think the way they were thinking in order to have the strength necessary to deal with what was happening.

Besides cooking I tried to provide what emotional support I could. I bought them an overnight stay at a hotel in a nearby city so they could take a break—spend a night, get a massage, whatever—yet be close enough to return quickly if something disastrous happened. I made sure they had pocket money because I knew they had no time to get to the bank. I checked on their house, checked with the neighbors.

Many pages ago we talked about how men deal with crisis; and we said men tend to internalize their emotions, to bury them as things are unfolding so they can take care of others. My son, Mark, was the perfect example. He told me it was his job to take care of his wife and his daughter. While it was going on he was Mr. Calm providing and protecting. It took a toll on him. My role, as I saw it, was to take care of him so he could fulfill his role. In retrospect it was a generational dynamic—the father taking care of the nuclear family and the grandfather taking care of the extended family.

Being a physician I was also their medical interpreter. I think that was the hardest part. I was pretty certain what was going to happen, but telling them the awful truth would have made things worse. So Mark stayed busy, and I stayed busy, and we were able to tunnel our emotions into some deep, dark part of our brains and lock them in there.

Using that emotional mechanism, or having it as it is not completely voluntary, enabled me to meet my responsibilities as a provider. Over the years I've seen other men and other physicians do the same. Doctors are trained to stay in control. Sometimes patients think that their physician doesn't care because he doesn't share his emotions, but most, I believe, care deeply but hide or bury what they are feeling.

When one has grandchildren, at a stunningly base level, he looks into the future. Many friends, on becoming a grandfather for the first time, have mentioned an unexpected wave of emotions that overwhelmed them. I was no different. A certain pride and a certain new level of protectiveness erupt. Some people talk about grandma and grandpa not having to discipline and not having to deal with day-to-day problems, saying all you have to do is love and guide them. That's part of it. And having hung around for as long as some of us have provides us with a level of experience, insight and judgment that we believe we must pass on. But that's shallow compared to the new insights into life. Suddenly we are looking back to when we were born, to when our fathers were born, and to our grandfathers' and great grandfathers' time. And we are projecting to when our grandchildren will be fifty, then one hundred, and when their grandchildren will be one hundred. We wonder what life will be like for them; we hold aspirations we never knew we held; we feel responsible to the future in a way we never anticipated; and we feel the life cycle of which we are but a link. We've said it before: thinking of one's future implies hope. Thinking of a future beyond one's self is mystical, spiritual. I believe the feelings are buried deep within our DNA. This brings a whole new meaning to the phrase, Biology is Basic.

I remember when they were working on Ana, and all her numbers came back—the chemotherapy results—better than expected, and everybody was happy. That was on a Monday. Then on Tuesday my son called me and said, "You need to come down." This was 10 o'clock at night.

I drove down, got to the hospital, and of course I couldn't get in. I went to the emergency room. Fortunately I was a doctor. I told myself I had to do this. They led me through to the elevators, but I didn't have a card (for the swipe system). I'm going like, "How the hell am I going to get upstairs?" Some way I was going to get up there. My job was to get there and be there. A nurse came down because of shift change. She got off the elevator. I said, "Please, could you swipe your card. I have to get up to pediatrics," and she said, "Okay."

Anna had had a CAT scan. The results were dreadful. The disease had ravaged her brain. As I watched this little child fade from life, at some level the future too faded. I felt helpless and hollow. I barely spoke. My role was to hold my son. His role was to protect his wife.

Later, after it was over, he got angry. Very angry. That was good. He had held his emotions in check through the entire torment. He had shown no weakness. Perhaps that is part of the male code that says, "It is my job to protect. I must be strong." Perhaps it was a matter that to show anger in the midst of crisis defies our natural, corporal make up. But later the pent up hurt erupted. He may have been his own primary target.

One thing about feelings, they don't go away. They reside in the nooks and crannies of our consciousness and sub-consciousness and reassert themselves unexpectedly. When my granddaughter died my role had been to oversee the family and make sure that everyone was as okay as they could be. I lived that role. I shut down my feelings. I kept them in check as my son's rage ran its course. Somehow I knew that my father, long gone, would have approved.

That brings me back to the cafeteria, the old guy and the Coke. Before him he was pushing a walker; behind him he pulled an oxygen tank on little wheels. Affixed to the walker was a small tray on which he'd placed his hamburger, fries and a salad. After he sat down he realized he'd forgotten to get something to drink, and he asked me where the Cokes were. It was a lot easier for me to get up, then for him to twist his body into the walker and grab the oxygen tank. The physician in me assessed him. He appeared to be a long time smoker. His skin was pale, bluish; he had an oxygen nasal cannula in place; and he was unshaven and wheezing audibly.

We chatted for a minute or so, and then I left. I went back to the parking garage. I sat in the car and I started to cry. Not for the old guy, of course, but for me and for my granddaughter. She would have been turning sixteen. I would never get to know her. The tears were long overdue. When you are busy taking care of others, you don't allow yourself the luxury of exposing your humanity. I have had friends, veterans, tell me that in much the same way they've relive the deaths of comrades killed forty-five or fifty years before.

Being in that hospital, helping that old geezer kind of freed me up, kind of allowed me to experience the feelings I had subdued in the moments of crisis. I wasn't a physician or father or grandfather… I was just a man who was very sad because his granddaughter had died.

The Older Man

Life has made us who we are. The loves, the rigors, the tragedies… By the time a man reaches 60 or 70 or 80, he's been beaten and bruised—physically and mentally. Most of us would not trade our scars. They're symbols of our tempering, of how we've been heated and hammered on the anvil of life and forged into steel.

That's not the general perception. At 65 you're supposed to be old. Society almost demands it. I recall one patient brought into the office by his daughter and son-in-law. The two younger people were upset. "Doctor Rabuffo, pleeeeeze tell him to stop." "Stop? Stop what?" It was mid-summer. "He's sixty seven, he shouldn't be doing it." My patient, disheartened, shrugged and said, "I'm fine." I look at the daughter. She was desperate. "He insists on mowing the lawn!" "Oh," I said. Her concern was based strictly on the number of years he'd been alive. He was in great shape. I pointed a finger at him, shook it in his face and said, "You watch… you watch what those Red Sox do. This is the year!"

To some people gray hair is enough to judge a man old, teetering, and probably incompetent. Not long ago I went to see my son's band play at a local dive. I had come from the gym so I had on a sweatshirt. The hood was crumpled up behind my neck. I sat down next to his wife. She leaned over, kissed me on the forehead, then reached back and smoothed out the hood. I pulled back and gave her a "what are you doing?" look. She said, "I didn't want you looking like an old man." I'm thinking, *Am I looking like an old man? I just came from the gym. I just leg-pressed 400 pounds.*

Actually, one of the recurrent themes with the guys at the gym… these guys are all retired, in their 60s or 70s, extremely fit and healthy …is the resentment of the fact that since they have gray hair people think they're feeble and incompetent. I had a conversation with one who coaches wrestling—a part time job with his 13-year-old grandson's team. He was trying to talk to his students about some strategies or holds. One kid began to sass him because he thought the coach was too old to coach wrestling. Now this guy was as fit as anybody you might see; but he had a whole head of hair, and it was gray. He had also been a state champion wrestler. He said, "I talked to this kid about being polite and not saying things like that, but he just wouldn't stop. So I said, "Okay. Let's wrestle." I asked, "What happened?" He said, "I beat the shit out of him. I felt he really needed to learn that just because you're a particular age, things don't stop." I asked, "Did he get it?" He said, "Yeah. He got it… the third time."

With some people it takes more than three times. I was trail running, well trail jogging, and my shoe caught a protruding root. As I stumbled I felt a twinge in my right hamstring. The next day I was having lunch with a younger friend. I limped into the restaurant. He said, "Ah, yer having problems with yer back." I said, "Hamstring," and told him what had happened. He said, "Yer a good example of the active elderly."

If I had enough hair it would have bristled. My first thought was, "Up Yours!" but instead I said, "Excuse me?" He backed off. I told him a story of one of my patients. "He was this wiry little guy; 90 years old. He exercised every morning. He had a 16-pound maul. He'd hold it in one hand and raise and lower it 50 times. Then he'd do it in the other hand. He'd do that every day. He told me, 'One day some guy said to me, 'Wow! Isn't that great that you're so active at your age!' So I said to him, 'Bring me your wife, drop her off and she can tell you tomorrow how active I am.'"

Men are fighters. We don't accept our frailties, our set-backs, our diseases. It's built in to our biological role, and those tags—active elderly, old man, old fart, codger, geezer, senior citizen—are prejudices against the WISE (Wisdom, Intuition, Sagaciousness, Experience), or the term I prefer, The Sage. As with any prejudice, the characteristics bestowed upon the entire class are often based upon a small sampling.

The Sage: Bad Habits, Self-image and Testosterone

We all know the symptoms guys are supposed to exhibit as they get older. Those that smoke, that don't exercise, that have poor diets and familial tendencies toward diabetes, and that have testosterone deficiencies are the ones most apt to meet the stereotype. But if they exercise, eat better, check their testosterone, and eliminate the cigarettes, they live longer, more productive lives.

Testosterone is part of it. For years we've been told that starting at about 35, serum levels of testosterone decrease about 1% per year. That means that by the time a guy is 70 it should be 35% lower. Low testosterone, as noted earlier, can cause a host of physical findings: less muscle mass, more body fat, osteoporosis, increased incidents of depression, less ability to concentrate, and the diminished ability to manage blood sugar. If you think about it, those are the things that describebing *an old man*. He's stooped. He has a withered look. He has a pot-belly and fatty breasts. Those conditions bring on high blood pressure and cardiovascular disease. Because of the increased body fat and less muscle mass, the ability (and often the desire) to exercise dwindles. He's looked on as useless, and sometimes feels that way.

That's the conventional story, but the time line is *not* fated. No one flips a switch at 60 or 70 or 80. And, recent studies challenge the long held belief about testosterone's declines. What we're finding is those physiologic changes, including Low-T, are not due to time, but to the accumulative effect of behavioral and environmental factors: not exercising (for too many this is constant sitting while at work or barely moving while watching TV), poor diet, smoking, decreased social involvement, and perhaps toxin in the food or water supply. Correct those elements and aging slows. This happens in both genders. Have you seen the photo of the Rockette who looks great and is still dancing at 75?! *Va-va-va-vooooom!*

Her routine is pretty intense, but even walking makes a difference. One study concluded that walking 2000 steps per day (that's about one mile) reduces the chance of stroke by 8.1%. I'm not sure who spends all the time on this minutia, but it makes sense. The data suggests that there are physiological changes that occur with time, but many, if not most of the changes are due to bad health habits.

Societal excuses and acceptance of infirmities increase destructive effects. One hurts his back or the flu lingers and saps him of his strength. He interacts with others. They blame it on age—despite bad the health habits. During the summer I was out walking and I linked up with another walker. This was shortly after I'd pulled that hamstring. I mentioned to her that it was bothering me and said, "Don't let me hold you up." She looked at me and said, "It's hell getting old, isn't it?!" I'm thinking *I've been out here or on the trail walking three to five miles a day. I didn't get old in the last month!*

But that is the social mentality. "Ah! Yer just getting' old!" It is said in a way to offer support, not to be nasty or dismissive. "At yer age, you gotta expect these things." It presents one with a ready-made justification, and it becomes validation of age as the reason for the severity of the difficulty. When one accepts the justification it becomes part of his self-image. You might just as well feed him arsenic.

When my mother was 85 I took her to an orthopedic specialist because one of her knees was bothering her. He examined her and said, "Well Mrs. Rabuffo, what do you expect. You're 85." She looked at him and in her stern voice said, "What about my other knee. It doesn't hurt, and it's the same age?"

I'm glad I wasn't her physician. I have had patients say similar things to me, and I've said some of those things to my physician. With my sage patients, whatever their condition, I learned to say, "I'm not going to attribute this to aging. I don't really even know what that is. Let's look at factors we can control."

Some docs haven't learned that. I'm in my doctor's office for a routine physical. I'd had a pretty tough morning, and I'd had three cups of Starbuck's strongest. His PA walks in. She is a drop dead gorgeous blue-eyed blonde. She says, "Your blood pressure is high." I'm thinking, *Honey, you'd raise the blood pressure of a dead man.* [I know, what a sexist jerk!] Then I'm talking to my doctor afterwards and he says, "You have high blood pressure; I don't like that." I told him I know my blood pressure. I take it at home. It's always normal. I couldn't convince him. He wanted to put me on BP medication.

That's one of the prejudices to which my generation is being subjected. Most patients are obedient. "My doctor said I had to do da-dah-da-dah." That's not necessarily a good thing. More and more evidence is mounting to show that what we call physical aging is really a manifestation of bad habits. Some of this—beyond smoking and lack of exercise—is very complex. For example, the more we learn about our internal biome—the microbes that inhabit our intestines, their impact on our immune system, the health consequences of their imbalance or destruction—the less emphasis we place on the passage of time.

As to testosterone, until recently few population-based studies tracked and compared the changing hormone level of the individual subject over time. An Australian study of more than 1500 men, mean age of 54, did just that. Study co-author Garry Wittert, MD, surmised that "Declining testosterone levels are not an inevitable part of the aging process..." and that matched to the individual "...testosterone levels did not decline significantly over five years." He did note that certain factors other than the passage of time "...were linked to lower testosterone levels." These included obesity and depression.

On Retirement

So why 65? Where did that come from? It has been part of the ambient cultural story for a long time. Laws have been designed around the number. Organizations have risen to advocate for the over-65. And at some fast-food joints the cost of a McJunko Burger to a senior citizen is about two bucks less than it is for his adult son. But why not 59 or 71? Or 93?

The convention was established by Fredrick The Great of Prussia (Fredrick II, 1712-1786) at about the same moment Paul Revere was racing toward Lexington, tearing up the countryside on his trusty steed, and warning colonists that regiments of the overbearing regime, demanding gun control, were about to descend upon them and confiscate their firearms. (Hmmmm... that kind of just snuck itself in there.) As an element of Fredrick's *Enlightened Absolutism* (the progressivism of the day), he introduced a social pension which began at 65. Having absolute power he was able to institute the pension by executive decree. Of course, at the time, the average life expectancy at birth in Prussia was only 32.6 years. To be fair the average life expectancy for one who reached 20 in a similar populations (this figure is not available for Prussia) was +34 years. By extrapolation one might estimate that adjusted for infant mortality, life expectancy in Prussia in 1775 was 66.6 years.

At any rate, 240 years later we still have the convention that when one turns 65 some change magically occurs and he is no longer capable of doing his job. His wisdom, judgement and experience may be disregarded or discarded.

The biggest emotional problem for the sage *is* retirement. There are two categories of men entering retirement, and they are not based upon how much money one saved or didn't save, nor upon if one remains local or relocates. They are distinguished by whether one loved his job and didn't want to retire, or if one hated his job and couldn't wait to leave. Sometimes the determinate factor between loving and hating the job was the guy himself, as I had patients who worked for the same company doing the same job who had diametrically opposed attitudes. But that was rare.

More commonly what I saw was the unhappiness of the line workers at the big, local defense plant, or the state workers from various bureaus and commission with offices in our area. The structure of the job, the punching of the clock, the meeting criteria they either didn't understand or thought were ridiculous, made many of these guys say to me, "I'm outa there. I'm goina to take early retirement," or "I wish I'd taken the severance deal when they'd offered it." Many of these guys hated their bosses or their unit managers. Some would leave work, go to the bar, have a couple of beers, then they go home. Everybody dealt with it in their own way. Some shrugged and said dismissively, "It's a job." Others would be angry, seething inside, feeling they'd betrayed themselves by not having done something else with their lives.

On the other hand there were the guys who really loved their jobs. Some of these guys worked in the same plants, did the same jobs, built the same aircraft engines. But more often it was the engineers or industrial designers. As guys got up into management there generally seemed to be more job satisfaction. They tended to be the guys who traveled the world developing new divisions or upgrading foreign departments. I had one patient whose job it was to go all over the world to find tungsten which was needed for the blades. He never wanted to leave. There were also local, independent businessmen who would tell me about their latest innovations, or about new practices or new lines; and local tradesmen who would talk with pride about the house or shopping center they'd just built.

Then they retired. They had been the lead man, the foreman, the sales manager, the senior member of the faculty, or the head of the design department. By the age of 65 they had advanced pretty far in their respective fields. They had clout, vast amounts of knowledge and experience; they went to work—loving it or not—with a purpose. They had problems to think about, to work on, to solve. They had customers or staff. They had value. And suddenly that was gone.

Depression often accompanies retirement. The thing about a job—love it or hate it—is it becomes a large part of one's identity. I am a doctor, lawyer, Indian chief. Men do compartmentalize their self-image—I am a doctor, father, grandfather, gym rat, sailor, lover—but *the job*, that thing he does, or did, for eight or ten hours a day for years, that thing he got ready to go to when he wasn't there, that he bought his car for so he could get there and back, that he bought clothes for because the job demanded specific clothes… that was a big part of who he was. And the people there, the people he saw, the people he spent more waking hours with than his wife, they too were a big part of his self-image.

It is a major adjustment going from whom you thought you were based on your job, to being… being what? I didn't want to end my practice of medicine. I had trepidations. As I approached retirement I came across a study published in the American College of Surgeons Journal. The subject was the cognitive behavior of senior surgeons—those over 60. To the surprise of the researchers the findings showed that senior surgeons were more capable than anticipated. The assumption (hypothesis) had been that the over-60 guy would not be as good as they used to be. But they were. Even at 70 a quarter were still practicing and still deemed to be highly capable.

When I left practice I was lost. Like others, my whole life had been structured. I went to high school with the goal was to get into college; where the goal was to get into medical school; where the goal was to get an internship; where the goal was to get a residency. When I was in college there were no electives. I got a Bachelor of Science degree in biology because that's what you had to do. In medical school there were few choices in the classes; same in internship. Everything was fixed. When I got into practice I went to an office, had "hours," saw patients. I really didn't know anything else. That was the way it was supposed to be. And my patients always took precedence. That's why I'd drag my ass out in the middle of the night or in bad weather or when I really wanted to go to one of my kid's games or meets. When I retired I realized how much of the *other* life I had missed. I literally felt as if I was coming out from being submerged, from being underwater my entire life. The water cleared my eyes. I was now above the sea seeing this massive world around me… but I was a fish out of water.

As I started to let my patients know that I was retiring, all had the same advice: It's going to take you a couple of years, but you better come up with something to get you out of the house because if you don't it'll drive you crazy. Some suggested volunteering. Others warned against that. What the go-volunteer people meant was work for the church or the synagogue or the YMCA or Greenpeace. A few of my patients who were golfers made arrangements to work on the local course in return for free rounds. The don't-volunteer people warned, "If they find out that you're free, everybody will ask you to volunteer. Then you'll never have any free time. It'll be worse than working." Old colleagues advise: "Keep busy. That's how to deal with the void." All said, take some time to figure out who you are and what you want to do.

Some men aim for a second career which is affiliated with what they did. Some men just curl up, stay home and watch TV all day—the unhealthiest thing one could do. You're depressed. You don't exercise. You get in the habit of checking the refrigerator and you gain weight. Depression deepens. More weight, less lean muscle tissue. Your body thinks you've thrown in the towel.

A friend told me this story: At his niece's graduation party from college he had a conversation with her, and he asked her about her plans. She seemed vague. He said to her, "Going through school, and then through college, is like walking up the main path that goes up a steep hill. There are lots of minor paths that branch off your trail and go into the woods, but you stayed on the path. The point you graduated was as if you'd come to an old stone wall that separated the woods below from the meadow above, and you've just come through the gate in the wall. On the other side there is a fan of paths going in all different directions. You can choose any path you wish. Why not...?" He made a few suggestions from traveling the world to working at a resort in the Caribbean. She answered, "Oh, my father would never let me do that." That bothered him. He began to say, but stopped himself, "You've just graduated college. You don't need your father to make your decisions." But she was rigid. In her mind she could only follow the main path. Then he said, "Retirement is another stone wall with a gate."

That made sense—at least to me. I had stayed on the path we chose years ago; had arrived at the second stone wall, the second gate, and before me was the second fan of paths splaying out in a thousand directions.

I retired. I had no clue which path to follow. And did taking one in retirement preclude taking others which looked interesting? I knew I had choices, but I had no inkling. People would say, "What do you want to do?" I'd shrug. Then I knew. It was like a revelation, like the heavens opened and said, "Hey! Jeff! Wake up! You *do* know what you want... what you must do."

Some guys don't. It can be devastating. If one does not handle it well, retirement can lead to depression; depression can lead to various unhealthy coping mechanisms like drinking and being sedentary; and those will lead to obesity, high blood pressure, heart attacks, strokes, and an entire array of ailments. When NASA stopped the Apollo Program, thousands of engineers and technicians were laid-off or forced into early retirement. Nearly a quarter of them had heart attacks the first year out. That is a huge percentage of myocardial infractions in a specific group in a short time. They had lost their identity. Or it had been stripped from them virtually overnight.

If you don't plan your retirement, someone else will plan it for you. If you don't scrutinize your attitude toward your retirement, our culture will guide you into being an old geezer before your time.

Planning for the fourth quarter of life is important to living in the best health possible during what is inevitably a downward spiral. It is not just a matter of planning your finances. It is a matter of planning interests, adventures, achievements, and contributes to family, friends and society. Whatever the activity, it doesn't need to be meaningful to anyone else, but it must be something that is meaningful to you. It could be writing the great American novel or it could be collecting used soda cans for the deposit money; or it could even be working with your 12-year old grandson to rebuild that decrepit 1948 Ford your neighbor's mother had garaged for fifty years—with the plan of giving it to him when he gets his license.

While planning, don't forget to include plans for your sex life—you sexy dog, you!

Sex and The Sage

Here's a research report on sexual activity increasing after fifty years of marriage. Here's an article saying that one third of baby boomers have sexual thoughts (usually intercourse with someone younger) at least once each day. That immediately makes one ask, what's the problem with the other two thirds? Here's a great phrase: "a springboard back into sexual activity." Many researchers are basing their careers on proving men and women can be still sexually active well into the twilight years. We aren't surprised. We know that the human need for intimacy doesn't fade; and we know that men express their emotions via physical contact; we know that sex is the ultimate expression of intimacy; and we know that men at 60 or 80 or 100 are still men.

Twenty-five or thirty years ago when guys in their 60s or 70s came to the office they usually let me know that sexual relations with "the wife" had pretty much disappeared. That was the way they referred to her—*the wife*. Seldom did they use her name. They would say, "The wife is not interested. She's only interested in the grandchildren." For many their sex life had diminished 100%. Some would say, "Well, she's not interested, so, I guess I'm not interested. She's a good companion." That companion term came up a lot. There was a marked decrease in sex, but there were exceptions.

I had maybe ten guys in their 80s who were sexually active. The question in my mind back then was, "Are these guys that healthy because they're sexually active?" or "Are they sexually active because they're exceptionally healthy?" It was kind of a chicken or egg question. I didn't find the answer back then, but I think we're closing in on it now.

I also had older female patients who were sexually active. These are people I knew for years and years so I could have these conversations with them. One gal was 68 when she came in with a bladder infection. She said, "My husband and I..." maybe it was, "My boyfriend and I... were having sex." I asked, "Do you have frequent sex?" She said, "Yes. Two or three times a week." I asked if we could talk about it. She said, "Sure." I said, "You are obviously the exception." She said, "I know that." She had talked to a lot of her friends, and most told her that her sex life was very different than theirs. I asked what makes the difference. She said, "I don't know. I like sex. I've always liked sex. And we have a good relationship. When he wants to have sex it's something we both want to do."

The other side of this: sometimes when I would talk to guys about having surgery and perhaps losing their ability to have an erection because of the surgery, *the wife* would say, "Thank God I don't have to do that anymore." To some it was as if sex were a duty.

Then Viagra came out; and then testosterone became more readily available. A lot of guys came in and ask me about Viagra or testosterone. Numerous incidents happened. The roommate relationship that existed because the woman's sex drive had dropped off, as did the man's, now changed. With Viagra and TRT he was both more able and more willing. Women didn't have an equivalent drug. Conflicts developed. There was a differential level in sex drives within the relationship. He wanted more; she wouldn't or couldn't. Women will tell you that vaginal dryness causes pain during sex, and that the pain keeps them from being sexy or feeling sensual. The pharmaceutical industry rose to the challenge. It's taken years but you've likely seen the commercials for Aspina or one of the other medications. There's a beautiful woman, about 60; the voice over is saying, "You know, sex after menopause doesn't have to hurt. Talk to your doctor." These medications are not hormones. They are the first drugs approved to relieve vaginal symptoms.

What's interesting… this is starting a whole new demand from older women; and from their husbands. The husbands will say, "Go see your doctor, and get this stuff," just as women told men to see their doctor and get a prescription for Viagra.

Getting back to Viagra, guys used to come in and say, "I have to find out why I can't get an erection because my wife thinks I don't love her anymore." The wife was equating his lack of erection with his lack of love for her. I thought it was interesting that women were equating erections with love. It was, and still is not, the kind of thing you hear in politically correct circles. Erections, in those circles, mean perversion or a display of brute force. We don't usually hear that erections are seen by women as an expression of love. But of course, if you consider biology basic you immediately understand. From the guy's side, too, if the wife didn't want to have sex with him, or couldn't, he felt unloved. It works both ways. The whole idea that guys are sex maniacs, and women use sex for love just is not true. Again, biology is basic.

The need for intimacy does not dissipate with age; and older men still express their emotions via physical contact. Sex between a loving couple is an expression of love. That's the ideal for a man and for a woman at any age.

A few years back I did a lecture series with an OB nurse where we went around to nursing homes and talked about sexuality. What we found was that there is sexuality in nursing homes; that it is very normal; and that it's about the human need for intimacy. Generally, there are more women in these homes than men, so there is a lot of female-to-female sexuality that goes on. This is not homosexuality or lesbianism, but is physical contact based on the need for physical intimacy. There is, as you would imagine, also male-female intimacy.

We started going to nursing homes and talking about this, but we were not well received. As a lecture concept it was almost taboo. Sometimes it was the attitude of the families, the adult children of the resident; often the taboo was with the staff or administrators. If a man was found… let's say he is my father and he is a widower and he is found in bed with an unrelated woman… maybe she's a widow… this is voluntary, we are not talking about force or assault, this is still most apt to be interpreted as he's a pervert. In many homes, if this liaison was discovered, he would be restrained and medicated. Actions like that deny the human need, and the male need, for physical intimacy.

The above example is extreme, but there are two points here. One, the sexuality of men and women does not automatically evaporate as they age. It might cease if they are humiliated, or told it is wrong, sinful, or illegal, but attraction remains. The ability to perform, particularly amongst those who take care of their health, also continues.

Medicine and the man of years: We've talked about this before but in a different context. You know that in medicine there are rules or cutoffs that say, "After *this* age, you don't do *this*." A controversy rests upon the arbitrary nature of the rules. Yes, some people who have not lived a healthy life, or who, for whatever reason, are not in good health should not be tested because there is no benefit in finding underlying diseases. Okay. I'll accept that. But what about the people who have taken care of themselves and who, by luck or by skill, have avoided physical deteriorations and potential health disasters? Should the cutoffs for these guys be based only upon age?

Very early in my practice I had a patient who was 90. He showed up at the office in a tie and coat, typical of his generation. He had minimal muscle wasting and looked healthy, but he had cancer of the penis. The standard treatment at the time was to do a partial penectomy; essentially cut off the part of the penis that had the cancer. Even then the discussion was, "This guy is too old to have the procedure. We should do as little as possible because he's going to die soon." I was young and inexperienced. I sent the guy for radiation because that treatment would be easier on him and it would do less harm than surgery. The treatment wasn't effective; the cancer came back.

As my experience grew I came to believe that no matter what the age of the patient, if he has a disease, it is going to progress—so it *should be* treated. Isn't that more cost effective route for society? It's that better for the individual than letting the disease run its course, and then turning around and saying, "See, he's dying from cancer of the penis, or cancer of the kidneys, or cancer of the lungs."? I'd have these conversations with my patients; tell them my experience with similar conditions to theirs, then say, "It's not my job to tell you what disease you should die from. That's not fair to you. You're a healthy guy. You'll likely out live the statistic. I think you should be treated." Just because one is 65, or 70, or 80, I don't think this is a good reason for a cutoff.

I had an incident recently myself. At my physical my physician asked if I wanted a PSA. I said, "Of course." He then began to hem and haw. "Now Jeff, you know…"

The prejudice of arbitrary age cutoffs for medical treatments, and the problems that creates, are getting worse as the medical bureaucracy expands. You should be aware of it, and act to protect yourself and your loved ones.

Resilience and the Bucket Lists: How does one stay resilient during the fourth quarter of life, during a period of inevitable decline which will ultimately end in death? What are the secrets? What does that even mean?

I believe, and more and more research and anecdotal reports backs this up, that the final decline does not need to be a long, painful and fruitless descent that ends too early and with a whimper to boot. The fourth quarter can be robust. The physical slide can be countered via a healthy life styles coupled with preventative measures and proper medical care. Cognitive abilities don't necessarily morph into befuddlement, withdrawal and depression. Indeed there was a recent report out of Stamford University saying that less than 10% of the sage generation fits the stereotypical, irritable old grouch image.

One's sense of well-being may actually rise, and one's relationships may become more intimate and more intense—all contrary to the ambient cultural story and to many earlier scientific studies. Recall the Real War on Science. Many of the older studies on aging had been designed to isolate and eliminate variables based upon life experiences. Eliminating memories and knowledge gained from experience biased the results. But the results were reported over and over and over again so "everyone" thought they were accurate. One might just as well take a group of athletes, *control for* their superior muscle tone by chemically blocking the ability of their muscles to contract, and then *conclude* that they are no better at sprinting than the sedentary. That is just how lopsided many of the studies have been.

More recent brain experimentation builds upon the recognition some sixty or seventy years ago of what came to be called plastic recovery. At that time it was believed that one's brain was set by childhood, that the number of cells remained constant until they began dying off as part of the aging process. The belief paralleled the later thought on testosterone's decline and many other assumptions about aging. It was said that if a person incurred a brain injury, that part of the brain was lost forever. But it was then noted that people did recover both abilities and memories. This was thought to be other healthy areas of the brain taking over the functions of the diseased or damaged section. This explained the partial recovery of stroke victims. Then it was discovered that the damaged areas to some extent healed and regained their functionality. Then came findings that the brain is not a static organ but is full of growing and ever-changing tissue. That was first thought to be only in the ganglia support tissues, but then found also to be true of the neurons. Finally it was found that the process never stops. Sages have amazing brains when they haven't been convinced that they are fading curmudgeons. The have vast amounts of data stored which may create retrieval lag times. The data may also need to be correlated to the current situation—and where youth may react faster that may be because they are choosing between only a few options where the sage fine tunes his response from hundreds of potentials. Isn't that what wisdom is—the contemplation of an array of data and an array of known forms, then the creative combining elements and forms to produce spot-on results? Cognitive decline and memory loss will eventually happen. It is not part of the aging process, it is part of the dying process.

The saddest aspect of the old age stereotypes is that when a man believes them, when he accepts them as true and internalizes them, he then behaves in a manner consistent with these beliefs—that is he expects to decline and allows his physical and mental performance to drop.

So, what are the secrets to halting the decline of our mental capacities, to remaining robust, and to having an amazing fourth quarter?

They are not secrets. We've already talked about diet, exercise, and interests. One tactic I like is the bucket list. I've always been a "To Do" list maker. That helps prioritize items and assists in scheduling time. Bucket lists aren't so different. They are a method of focusing interests during a specific period. I think every guy should have one. Or two. Or three. Why not?

A bucket list doesn't mean you have to say you're going to go climb Mt. Kilimanjaro, but it might say, "I want to read War and Peace," or I want to have the best organic vegetable garden in town." Actually, I kind of like the idea of climbing Kilimanjaro, but that might be out of the reach of most people. How about Mt. Adams in Washington State, or Mt. Washington in New Hampshire? You'll have to train for any of those climbs. What could be better? Well, maybe include significant others: "I want to take my grandkids to Yosemite and climb the Mist Trail to Vernal Falls."

The point is, have something you're looking forward to doing, something you want to produce, something you want to accomplish, something you want to give to someone else. That is what makes one resilient. That focus on the future equates with hope. And being hopeful is the opposite of being angry or depressed or slothful or stuck in a rut. Hope lowers stress which lowers the production of cortisol which lowers inflammation. Hope makes you healthier. Better health means a better retirement, a better life. And a better life means you've got more things you can do with the grandkids, the kids, the wife, and your fishing buddies.

Older guys used to come into the office to get checked out for one problem or another. We'd talk. They had all these plans. I used to think that some were in denial. Guy comes in; me, "How you doing?" Him, "Well, my blood pressure is good. Doc says my blood sugar is good. I'm good to go." Lots of these guys had other problems but they weren't going to let those problems stop them from bringing the grandkids to Disneyland. They wanted to deal with the problems so they could do the things that they wanted to do, but if the problem wasn't solvable, they wanted to ignore it for as long as possible. Why not? We men may feel vulnerable. We may keep the problem to ourselves—part of provide and protect—even if our bodies are telling us we're not as young as we used to be. In the deep crevasses of our minds we may be wondering if this symptom or that is the beginning of the end. We worry, but we often hide our most intimate fears from others and from ourselves. Colleagues used to say, "Oh, that guy is in denial." Me: I'm thinking, so what? If you can't effect a situation what's the problem with putting it aside and concentrating on the situations you can effect? This is kind of like benign neglect, or constructive neglect, in child rearing; this is benign or constructive denial. That doesn't mean we actually don't recognize what's going on, it means we have the courage to act, to go forward, to live despite that knowledge.

Grandkids, Extended Families, Tribes: Grandkids—I know I've mention them often, but I don't feel that's an over emphasis. In an AARP article by Suzanne Braun Levine titled Better Than Sex? She writes:

> Friends experience ecstatic bonding with grandchildren. ("When I'm, expecting a call from my granddaughter, my heart beats as if I were awaiting a call from a lover," one told me.)

I concur. I think it is built into us, into our DNA, and if it isn't felt it is because of an imbalance on one's thoughts, or an indoctrination which tells one that the child belongs not to the parents and the family but to the village or the community. I have five grandchildren, and my darling Ana. When my first granddaughter was born I went up to FAO Schwartz and bought the biggest friggin teddy bear you ever saw. It was gigantic. But it was like—when you were a young parent and you didn't have the ability to do that for your kids, but now... maybe grandchildren become surrogates for what we wished we could have given our children. But it is much more than that. I remember walking through that mall with this big bear. And I remember all the older guys that were about my age, as they passed by me they smiled. They knew.

The connection between generations is first biological, then cultural. From our grandparents, through our parents, to us, to our kids and grandkids and maybe great grandchildren, we see, feel and sense the continuity and wonder of life. Not just the life of an individual but the life of the species as demonstrated in our extended families. When we recognize it—it is so much more, so much deeper that recognition—we are in awe. There is no hope greater that this hope.

Sociologists and social workers tell us that elders, to remain healthy, must remain social. Amongst the more politically correct the term family is considered to be a bit outdated, old fashioned, even *exclusive* or limiting. We are a very mobile society and grandma and grandpa not only no longer live in the same house with the grandkids, they no longer live in the same state, or even the same region of the country. So instead of saying families, sociologists like to talk in terms of tribes, or *moias*—groups of lifelong alliances as per Dan Buettner. Some of us might instead say extended circle of friends or intimate circle of friends.

However you wish to describe it, your social group and your ties to those in the group, in Buettner's words "trumps just about everything else when it comes to your health." We've explored this when we reviewed the Roseto Effect. It isn't new. But some elements of the interactions may be.

This is a small sample, but in my experience when men retired their social life picked up. They went to more parties, went out to dinner more often... until they got to the age where they could no longer drive at night. That tended to happen in their 80s. We are a mobile society and most of that mobility depends upon automobiles. When the ability to drive is lost, social life becomes limited. In this time of disparate living arrangements, that has greater consequences than it did when three generations live *at home*.

To compensate, most of the patients I had who matured into their late 70s or 80s got rid of their house because it is "Too big." That's the term they'd use. "There used to be six of us living there, now there's only two." And they'd say they couldn't keep up with it, with the maintenance and care. So they were going to downsize.

Here in Middletown, and where I grew up in Brooklyn, there were a lot of three story homes. That's where the family was. That was the family dwelling. As time went by people moved up or down. The oldest people lived on the first floor; the youngest people lived on the third floor. But there were people around to help and to talk to. The grandparents were there to teach the young people their favorite recipes, and the kids would take grandpa to the doctor while the middle aged people went to work. That's disappearing if it hasn't already. That was a big social issue for many patients.

They were often unhappy about leaving the home where they raised their children; and sometimes would say, "No matter where we go, it is not going to be as nice as where we are." So they didn't want to leave, but aging, maybe a drop in income, coerced them to abandon what had been the root of their lives.

Like a job, a house... *my house*... is part of one's identity. When I wasn't working I was mowing the lawn, planting the garden, doing repairs. The wife made most of the decisions about how the place was decorated, I moved the furniture. This is where Uncle Joe used to sit when he came from Easter dinner. When the kids were little and when dad came over he used to like to lay on the couch and they'd take their nap resting on his chest. Here's where we buried the kids guinea pigs when they died. On Super Bowl Sunday there'd be a dozen of us in there around the TV. This is the stove in which I concocted those meals when Anna was in the hospital. If one is not prepared for it, if one cannot change focus, leaving the family home can be devastating.

A lot of my patients went into adult communities. These were condos or homes or apartments where the association or the owner provides the services. Some of these homes were very nice. I have a good friend who used to be the chaplain at the hospital. His wife is a research scientist. She's still working, consulting; he volunteers at the hospital. They have one of these homes. It's smaller than what they had, but it's not confining. Downsizing is common; it is not always traumatic.

An alternative to the adult living community is the assisted living facility. The latter is sometimes attached to the former. These are transition communities, and they have become a huge business. One pays a premium when they buy into these communities with all their services.

Typically the next phase in the social life of the sage in modern America seems to be the medical merry-go-round. It begins when one of the two, husband or wife, gets sick. This usually starts in their late 70s or 80s. Now someone is always seeing a doctor and the couple's social life revolves around medical care. Transportation becomes a greater problem. They move to assisted care. The problem with assisted care is that it can be very good, very efficient, very nice—too nice. The apartment of the sage is cleaned by the staff. Someone monitors the medications he takes. Downstairs, the dining hall looks more like a four-star restaurant and at every meal he is handed a menu—even if the choices are limited. His clothes are washed, his hair is combed, his pajamas are laid out, and if need be his ass is wiped. What's the problem?! The problem is that the meaning of life is devalued, the pride in living, in being as self-sufficient as possible, is removed. One becomes a unit to be maintained. Assisted living can be the nicest ultimate denial of ones humanity every conceived.

One of the things I would see in these patients was anger. It wasn't crankiness. It was anger, and often they themselves didn't recognize the reasons why they were angry. I would see these people. They would come in either hanging on to an arm, shuffling, or in a wheelchair. They were often impatience with their caregivers about their clothes not being put back on right, or, "God Damn it. Watch out. You're hurting me." There is a lot of unhappiness. As soon as they did something for themselves, or by themselves, the anger dissolved. You could see their feeling of satisfaction.

Toward the very end, when they would feel that their bodies had betrayed them—that is a phrase I heard many times—there was resentment coupled with acceptance mixed the pride of who they had been and what the legacy they were leaving all clustered in with a million emotions or none at all.

Sometime men talk about exit strategies. One friend, an old paratrooper, would cheerfully say he planned his last act to be skydiving without a chute; another liked the idea of taking his sea kayak out from the shore and paddling until he could paddle no further; and a third, a hiker, wanted his last hike to be deep into the back country where he would coat his clothing with honey and lay up against an old sugar pine. I don't think the last sounds at all appealing, but the concept of returning the atoms and molecules of one's body back to the natural cycle isn't the least bit repulsive. Part of me will become the wings of a butterfly; part of me the eyes of a hawk.

The Sage

Men get old and die. It is basic biology. Resilience is imperative until it is impossible.

Sage is the age of wisdom, the age of judgment; if the individual does not see this, does not feel this, he will not make it part of his self-image, and he will not act wisely. But if he internalizes the image, he will be a counselor, a sage; and he will be an asset to the community and the world—while he is here, and after he is gone.

Men want to leave a legacy. It is their final act of providing and protecting. They want to leave the next generation not just economic or physical aid, but to leave the wisdom acquired during their life. Call this Life Lessons, Lessons Learned, or the Wisdom of the Ages. The importance of this final act can be seen throughout the recorded history of the human race… indeed, it is the history of the human race.

#   #   #

SOURCES

Books

Brizendine, Louann, M.D.; The Male Brain; Broadway Books; New York; 2010.

Dalrymple, Theodore; Anything Goes: The Death of Honesty; Monday Books, United Kingdom, 2011.

Einstein, Albert, and Infeld, Leopold; The Evolution of Physics: From Early Concepts to Relativity and Quanta; A Touchstone Book; Simon & Schuster; New York; 1938.

Friendenberg, Edgar Z.; The Vanishing Adolescent; Dell Books; New York; 1959.

Good, Mary-Jo DelVecchio; American Medicine: The Quest For Competence; University of California Press; Berkeley and Los Angeles, CA; 1995.

Gordon, Thomas; P.E.T.: Parent Effectiveness Training: The Tested New Way To Raise Responsible Children; A Plume Book, New American Library; New York; 1975.

Hendon, Herbert, and Haas, Ann Pollinger; Wounds Of War: The Psychological Aftermath of Combat in Vietnam; Basic Books; New York; 1984.

Lane, Carl; A Nation Wholly Free: The Elimination of the National Debt in the Age of Jackson; Westholme Publishing, LLC; Yardley, Pennsylvania; 2014.

Peck, M. Scott, M.D.; The Road Less Traveled: A New Psychology of Love, Traditional Values and Spiritual Growth; Simon & Schuster; New York; 1978.

Shilts, Randy; <u>And The Band Played On: Politics, People and the AIDS Epidemic</u>; St Martin's Press, New York, NY; 1987.

Smith, Helen, PhD; <u>Men on Strike: Why Men Are Boycotting Marriage, Fatherhood, and the American Dream—and Why It Matters</u>; Encounter Books; New York; 2013.

Sommers, Christina Hoff; <u>The War Against Boys</u>; Simon & Schuster; New York; 2013.

Venker, Suzanne; <u>The War on Men</u>; WND Books; Washington, D.C.; 2013.

Articles

Azerrad, Jacob, PhD; *The Real Biederman Scandal*; Alliance for Human Research Protection; July 22, 2011.

Bathinay, S, Claussen, M, et.al; *Combined biogeophysical and biogeochemical effects of large-scale forest cover changes in the MPI earth system model*; Biogeosciences; http://www.researchgate.net/publication/230258408_Assessing_climate_model_sensitivity_to_prescribed_deforested_landscapes; May 4, 2010.

Bean, Matt; *8 Steps to Prevent Prostate Cancer; Men's Health*; Rodale, Inc.; www.menshealth.com/mhlists/prevent_prostate_cancer/printer.php2010.

Bernstein, Elizabeth; *How Often Should Married Couples Have Sex?*; The Wall Street Journal; online.wsj.com/news/articles/SB; April 22, 2013.

Bernstein, Elizabeth; *Counselors Say Men Are More Willing to Try Couples When It Focuses on Results;* The Wall Street Journal; online.wsj.com/; August 15, 2014.

Bloom, Trystan; *Nebraska School Tells Teachers To Avoid 'Gendered Expressions'*; The Daily Caller;

http://dailycaller.com/2014/10/07/nebraska-school-tells-teachers-to-avoid-gendered-expressions/; October 7, 2014.

Braithwaite, R. Scott, MD, MS; *EMB's Six Dangerous Words*; JAMA; November 2013.

Brogan, Jacob; *Lies, Damned Lies, and Medical Science*; The Atlantic; November, 2010.

Burke, Jennifer; *Teachers to Students: 'The competitive "urge to Win" will be Kept to a Minimum'*; Tea Party Network News; May 22, 2014.

Burke, Matthew M; *Firing the Fighting Generals*; Stars and Stripes; May 21, 2014.

Carroll, Conn; *White House Rape Data "Not Supported By The Scientific Evidence"*; Tipsheet, Townhall.com; December 31, 2014.

Chlebowski, Rowan T., et.al.; *Breast Cancer after Use of Estrogen plus Progestin in Postmenopausal Women;* The New England Journal of Medicine; http://www.nejm.org/doi/full/10.1056/NEJMoa0807684; February 5, 2009.

Classics In Oncology: *Charles Brenton Huggins*; CA: A Cancer Journal for Clinicians, Volume 22, Issue 4; The American Cancer Society; Wiley Online Library; http://onlinelibrary.wiley.com/doi/10.3322/canjclin.22.4.230/pdf; Article first published online: 30 December 2008.

Clifton, Jim (Chairman and CEO at Gallup); *The Big Lie: 5.6% Unemployment;* Feb 3, 2015.

Cohen, Patricia; *Genetic Basis for Crime: A New Look*; The New York Times; www.nytims.com/2011/06/20/arts/genetics-and-crime-at-isstitute-of-justice-conference; June 19, 2011.

Comorbid ADHD With Depression Increases Bipolar Conversion Risk; Comorbid ADHD With Depression Increases Bipolar Conversion Risk; October 17, 2014.

Conner, Steve; *The hardwired difference between male and female brains could explain why men are 'better at map reading'; and why women are 'better at remembering a conversation'*; The Independent; www.independent.co.uk/life-style/the-hardwired-difference-between-male-and-female-brains; December 13, 2013.

Craviotto, Daniel F., Jr; *A Doctor's Declaration of Independence: It's time to defy health-care mandates issued by bureaucrats not in the healing profession*; The Wall Street Journal; April 28, 2014.

Del Vecchio, John M.; *The Importance of Story: Individual and Cultural Effects of Skewing the Realities of American Involvement in Southeast Asia for Social, Political and/or Economic Ends*; Delivered in conference: The Vietnam Center, Texas Tech University; 1997.

Derr, Erik; *"Adam and Eve" Genes Suddenly Split About 200 Million Years Ago;* www.latinpost.com; April 24, 2014.

Evidence Mounting For Exercise As an ADHD Treatment; PsychiatryAdvisor; http://www.psychiatryadvisor.com/evidence-mounting-for-exercise-as-an-adhd-treatment/article/375213/?DCMP=EMC-PA_Update&CPN=&spMailingID=9613745&spUserID=NzYyNzY0MzE3OTgS1&spJobID=400485068&spReportId=NDAwNDg1MDY4S0; October 03, 2014.

Finley, Gordon E., Ph.D.; *Sex: The New War On Men*; NewsWithViews.com; May 4, 2014.

Flowers, Lynda; Noel-Miller, Claire [AARP Public Policy Institute], Okrent, Deanna [Alliance for Health Reform]; Colonoscopy Screening after the Affordable Care Act: Cost Barriers Persist for Medicare Beneficiaries; Insight on the Issues 87, AARP Public Policy Institute, http://nccrt.org/wp-content/uploads/colonoscopy-screening-after-aca-insight-AARP-ppi-health.pdf; December, 2013.

Freedman, Dan; *Senators reintroduce bill on campus sexual assault*; The News-Times; Danbury, CT; February 27, 2015.

Freeman ER, Bloom DA, McGuire EJ; *A Brief History of Testosterone*; US National Library of Medicine, National Institute of Health; http://www.ncbi.nlm.nih.gov/pubmed/11176375; Journal of Urology; February 2001.

Friedman, Richard A,; *Why Teenages Act Crazy*; Sunday Review, Opinion; New York Times Now; June 28, 2014.

Fung, Brian; Infographic: *The Average Person Gets 9,672 Minor Injuries in a Lifetime*; The Atlantic; http://www.theatlantic.com/health/archive/2012/05/infographic-the-average-person-gets-9-672-minor-injuries-in-a-lifetime/257777/; May 29, 2012.

Galston, William A.; *The Secret to Taming Health-Care Costs: Oregon's innovative approach shows that states may lead the way*; The Wall Street Journal, January 31, 2015.

Groening, Chad; *Transgender In The Military: President wants transgender in military says defense analyst*; http://onenewsnow.com/national-security/2014/05/13/president-wants-transgenders-in-military-says-national-defense-analyst#.VRSqGY10zIU; OneNewsNow.com; May 13, 2014

Gottlieb, Lori; *The Sexless Marriage*; The New York Times Magazine; February 9, 2014.

Gordon, Serna; *1 in 13 U.S. Schoolkids Takes Psych Meds*; HealthDay News; April 24, 2014.

Grohol, John M., Psy.D.; *Women Taking Antidepressants: Improve Sexuality with Exercise*; World of Psychology;

http://psychcentral.com/blog/archives/2014/04/29/women-taking-antidepressants-improve-sexuality-with-exercise/

Hall, Wynton; *Economic Death Spiral: More American Businesses Dying That Starting*; Breitbart News; http://www.breitbart.com/big-government/2015.01/14/economic-death-spiral-more-american-businesses-dying-than-starting/; January 14, 2015.

Hanson, David J, Ph.D.; *History of Alcohol and Drinking around the World*; http://www2.potsdam.edu/alcohol/Controversies/1114796842.html#.VNvJ5o10zIU; Alcohol: Problems and Solutions; Adapted from Hanson, David J.; Preventing Alcohol Abuse: Alcohol, Culture and Control; Wesport, CT; Praeger, 1995.

Harden, Nathan; *Man, Sex, God, and Yale*; Imprimis, A Publication of Hillsdale College; January 2013.

Haverluck, Michael F.; *Wesleyan Univ. pulls men-only frats, pushes housing for 15 'sexualities'*; OneNewsNow.com; Fresh Ink; http://www.gopusa.com/freshink/2015/02/27/wesleyan-univ-pulls-men-only-frats-pushes-housing-for-15-sexualities/?subscriber=1; February 27, 2015.

Hunt, April; *Concern over High Medication Rate among Foster Kids*; Atlanta Journal-Constitution; 25 February 2011.

Jacobson, William A; *Is Dartmouth now a due process danger zone for men?*; Legal Insurrection; February 15, 2014.

JAMA Advisory.com; JAMA: Nearly 25% of colonoscopies may be 'inappropriate'; http://www.advisory.com/daily-briefing/2013/03/13/jama-nearly-of-colonoscopies-may-be-inappropriate; March 13, 2013.

Keiler, Jonathan; *Obama's Generals*; The American Thinker; http://www.americanthinker.com/articles/2015/03/obamas_generals.html; March 13, 2015.

Kilpatrick, William; *The Gender Confusion Challenge to Army Recruitment*; http://www.crisismagazine.com/2014/mission-impossible-armys-recruitment-problem; Crisis Magazine; July 17, 2014.

Koslow, Sally; *Generation SEX: They couldn't get enough during the sexual revolution. Are boomers still turned on?;* AARP, The Magazine; August/September 2014.

Loeb, Stacy and Catalona, William J.; *The Prostate Health Index: a new test for the detection of prostate cancer;* US National Library of Medicine ; National Institutes of Health; Therapeutic Advances in Urology; http://www.ncbi.nlm.nih.gov/pmc/articles/PMC3943368/; April 2014.

Martosko, David; *Obamacare program costs $50,000 in taxpayer money for every American who gets health insurance, says bombshell budget report*; The Daily Mail; http://www.dailymail.co.uk/news/article-2927348/Obamacare-program-costs-50-000-American-gets-health-insurance-says-bombshell-budget-report.html; January 26, 2015.

McSwain, Dan; *Obamacare deals blow to one-doctor medicine*; UTSanDiego.com; April 26, 2014.

Medved, Michael; *The Utopian Left and Its War On Science*; TruthRevolt.org; http://www.michaelmedved.com/column/utopian-left-war-science/; March 20, 2014.

Mercola, Joseph M., MD; *Eight Amazing Health Benefits Of Kissing Your Loved Ones;* Mercola.com; January 30, 2014.

McEvoy, Victoria, MD; *Why 'Metrics' Overload Is Bad Medicine: Doctors must focus on lists and box-checking rather than patients*; The Wall Street Journal, February 12, 2014.

Meyer, Ali; *62.8%: Labor Force Participation Has Hovered Near 37-Year-Low for 11 Months;* CNS News; http://www.cnsnews.com/news/article/ali-meyer/628-labor-force-participation-has-hovered-near-37-year-low-11-months; March 6, 2015.

Morris, Dick; Lunch Alert: Obama's War on Doctors; Dick Morris TV; http://www.dickmorris.com/obamas-war-doctors-dick-morris-tv-lunch-alert/?utm_source=dmreports&utm_medium=dmreports&utm_campaign=dmreports; December 11, 2014.

Mukherji, Deborah; Temraz, Sally; Wehbe, David; Shamseddine, Ali; *Angiogenesis and anti-angiogenic therapy in prostate cancer;* Critical Reviews in Oncology/Hematology, Volume 87, Issue 2; ***http://www.sciencedirect.com/science/article/pii/S1040842813000048;***August 2013;

Nazworth, Napp; *LGBTTQQFAGPBDSM? Housing for 15 Alternative Sexualities Is OK, but Men-Only Fraternities Are Not, Wesleyan University Says*; http://www.christianpost.com/news/lgbttqqfagpbdsm-housing-for-15-alternative-sexualities-is-ok-but-men-only-fraternities-are-not-wesleyan-university-says-134684/; Christian Post; February 24, 2015.

Nef, Serge, and Paradal, Luis F.; *Hormones in male sexual development*; Genes and Development; Cold Spring Harbor Laboratory Press; http://genesdev.cshlp.org/content/14/24/3075.full; 10-11-2001.

Northrup, Christiane, M.D.; *It's Time to Learn the Difference*; http://www.drnorthrup.com/its-time-to-learn-difference/; accessed May 2015.

Owens, Brian; *Harvard Scientists Disciplined for Not Disclosing Ties to Drug Companies*; Nature.com; July 4, 2011.

Paglia, Camille; Camille Paglia: The Modern Campus Cannot Comprehend Evil; **IDEAS CULTURE**, Time; http://time.com/author/camille-paglia/; Sept. 29, 2014.

Passary, Sumit ; *Al Gore Proposes To 'Punish Climate Change Deniers'*; Tech Times; http://www.techtimes.com/articles/40270/20150317/al-gore-proposes-to-punish-climate-change-deniers.htm; March 17, 2015.

Pear, Robert; As Medicaid Rolls Swell, Cuts in Payments to Doctors Threaten Access to Care; http://www.nytimes.com/2014/12/28/us/obamacare-medicaid-fee-increases-expiring-.html?_r=0; The New York Times; December 27, 2014.

Perry, Mark J., and Briggs, Andrew G.; *The '77 Cents on the Dollar' Myth About Women's Pay*; Opinion: The Wall Street Journal; http://www.wsj.com/articles/SB10001424052702303532704579483752909957472; April 7, 2014.

Persaud, Natasha ; Digital Content Editor; *Complete Family History May Improve Prostate Cancer (PCa) Screening; Renal & Urology News*; http://www.renalandurologynews.com/prostate-cancer-family-history/article/386224/; December 02, 2014.

Prelutsky, Burt; *War & Peace*; The Patriot Post: Voice of Essential Liberty: Right Opinion; September 9, 2014.

Rabin, Roni Caryn; *A Glut of Antidepressants*; The New York Times; August 12, 2013
Raisanen, Ulla; *Men and Eating Disorders*; University of Oxford; Open: British Medical Journal, April 8, 2014 **(the title of this article needs to be verified)

Reynolds, Gretchen; *Put the Physical in Education*; New York Times, Phys Ed, http://well.blogs.nytimes.com/2014/09/04/adhd-children-excercise-pe/?_php=true&_type=blogs&_r=0; September 4, 2014.

Rabinowitz, Dorothy; *A Dishonest Rewrite of the Duke Lacrosse Case*; The Wall Street Journal; May 18, 2014.

Rosin, Hanna; *The End of Men*; The Atlantic; www.theatlantic.com/magazine/pring/2010/07/the-end-of-men/308135/; July 2010.

Scafidi, Benjamin; *The School Staffing Surge: Decades of Employment Growth in America's Public Schools;* Friedman Foundation For Educational Choice; *http://www.edchoice.org/Research/Reports/The-School-Staffing-Surge--Decades-of-Employment-Growth-in-Americas-Public-Schools--Part-2.aspx;* February, 28. 2013.

Sharav, Vera Hassner; *America's Children Under Stress*; Alliance For Human Research Protection; March 30, 2011.

Shcherbakov, Victor P; *Biological species is the only possible form of existence for higher organisms: the evolutionary meaning of sexual reproduction*; US National Library of Medicine,
National Institutes of Health;
http://www.ncbi.nlm.nih.gov/pmc/articles/PMC2847548/; March 22, 2010.

Sherr, Lynn; *Leading By Example: How three of the most influential women in America are empowering young girls*; Parade Magazine; March 9, 2014.

Sommers, Christina Hoff; *No, Women Don't Make Less Money Than Men*; U.S. News; http://www.thedailybeast.com/articles/2014/02/01/no-women-don-t-make-less-money-than-men.html; February 1, 2014.

Sommers, Christina Hoff ; *5 Feminist Myths That Will Not Die*; Time, OPINION FEMINISM;
http://time.com/3222543/5-feminist-myths-that-will-not-die/; September 2, 2014.

Sowell, Thomas; *The Inequality Bogeyman*; Creators.com; January 28,

2014.

Sowell, Thomas; *The "war on women" political slogan is in fact a war against common sense*; (various) Creators.com, National Review Online,

Real Clear Politics; http://www.creators.com/opinion/thomas-sowell/statistical-frauds.html; April 23, 2014.

Statistic Brain; *High School Dropout Statistics*; http://www.statisticbrain.com/high-school-dropout-statistics/; accessed Sptember 2014.

Stossel, John; *War on Women*; JFS Productions, LLC; Creator.com; http://www.creators.com/opinion/john-stossel/war-on-women.html; March 12, 2014.

Swanson, Emily; *Major Survey Finds Record Low Confidence in Government*; Associated Press; March 11, 2015.

Uzzo, Robert G., MD, FACS; *Physicians and the Medical-Industrial Complex*; RENAL & UROLOGY NEWS; http://www.renalandurologynews.com/medical-industrial-complex-physicians-healthcare-system/article/374091/?DCMP=EMC-RENALUROLOGY_TODAYSUPDATE&CPN=&spMailingID=9653541&spUserID=NzYyNzY0MzE3OTgS1&spJobID=400877874&spReportId=NDAwODc3ODc0S0; September 30, 2014.

Viguerie, Richard A., Fitzgibbons, Mark J; *The Law That Governs Government: Reclaiming The Constitution From Usurpers and Society's Biggest Lawbreakers;* ConservativeHQ.com; October 25, 2011.

Von Drehle, David; Feeling Deflated? The low-T industry wants to pump you up; Time; August 15, 2014.

Ward, Brian W, Ph.D.; Dahlhamer, James M, Ph.D.; Galinsky, Adena M, Ph.D.; Joestl, Sarah S, Dr. P.H.; *Sexual Orientation and Health Among U.S. Adults*: National Health Interview Survey, 2013; National Health Statistics Report, Number 77; National Center for Health Statistics , U.S. Department of Health and Human Services, Centers for Disease Control and Prevention; July 15, 2014.

Watson, Paul Joseph; *The War On Men: 10 Ways Masculinity is Under Attack*; InfoWars.com; February 19, 2014.

Westerhoff, Nikolas; *Why Do Men Buy Sex?;* Scientific American; May 1, 2012.

Wikipedia: *Daring Young Man On The Flying Trapeze*; a.k.a. *The Man On The Flying Trapeze*; Original version; 1837.

Wilde, Robert; *Neurologist Claims There Is No Such Thing As ADHD*, Breitbart News; http://www.breitbart.com/Big-Government/2014/03/11/Shocking-Neurologist-Claims; March 11, 2014.

Wommack, Keith; *Health regardless of lifestyle, diet, and genes?* (The Reseto Effect); KeithWommack.com; June 10, 2013.

Others

Center for Military Readiness: Policy Analysis; *Defense Department Deliberately Moving to Implement Policies Known To Harm Military Women*; CRM; March 2014.

Does having a Y chromosome make someone a man?; The Intersex Society of North America (ISNA): http://www.isna.org/faq/y_chromosome; accessed June 2014.

Feminism and Pop Culture Wage War Against Fathers, The Patriot Post: Voice of Essential Liberty; Daily Digest for Tuesday; http://patriotpost.us/digests/28333; August 19, 2014.

NBC News; *Gay Male Couple's 'First Kiss' Makes Navy History*; http://www.nbcnews.com/news/us-news/gay-male-couples-first-kiss-makes-navy-history-n303691; February 10, 2015.

Oppressed by the Ivy League; Review & Outlook, The Wall Street Journal; April 4, 2014.

(Press Release: Carol Fass Publicity & Public Relations; NY, NY); re: Will Courtenay, PhD: Dying To Be Men, Routledge, 2011; and article Esquire Magazine; Nov 2011.
Renal and Urology News; *Testosterone Therapy Does Not Raise Heart Attack Risk;* http://www.renalandurologynews.com/testosterone-therapy-heart-attack-risk-hypogonadism/article/374992/?DCMP=EMC-RENALUROLOGY_TODAYSUPDATE&CPN=&spMailingID=9603568&spUserID=NzYyNzY0MzE3OTgS1&spJobID=400272352&spReportId=NDAwMjcyMzUyS0; October 03, 2014.

Sex and Brains: Vive la difference!; The Economist; www.economist.com/node/21591157; December 7, 2013.

Social and Cultural Aspects of Drinking; Social Issues Research Center, Oxford, UK; www.sirc.org/publik/drinking-origins.html; August 4, 2014.

U.S. Department of Education, National Center for Education Statistics; Digest of Education Statistics; Table 303.10; http://nces.ed.gov/programs/digest/d13/tables/dt13_303.10.asp; 2013; Indicators of Crime and Safety-2013; and http://nces.ed.gov/programs/crimeindicators/crimeindicators2013/ind_22.asp; 2013.

U.S. Department of Health and Human Services; Substance Abuse and Mental Health Services Administration; Administration for Children and Families; National Center on Substance Abuse and Child Welfare; *Substance-Exposed Infants;* https://www.ncsacw.samhsa.gov/resources/substance-exposed-infants.aspx; accessed April 2015.

Wikipedia; *Duke lacrosse case*; http://en.wikipedia.org/wiki/Duke_lacrosse_case; accessed February 27, 2015.

Dr. Jeffrey Rabuffo

CPSIA information can be obtained at www.ICGtesting.com
Printed in the USA
BVOW11*1441161115

426886BV00003B/7/P

9 780692 532010